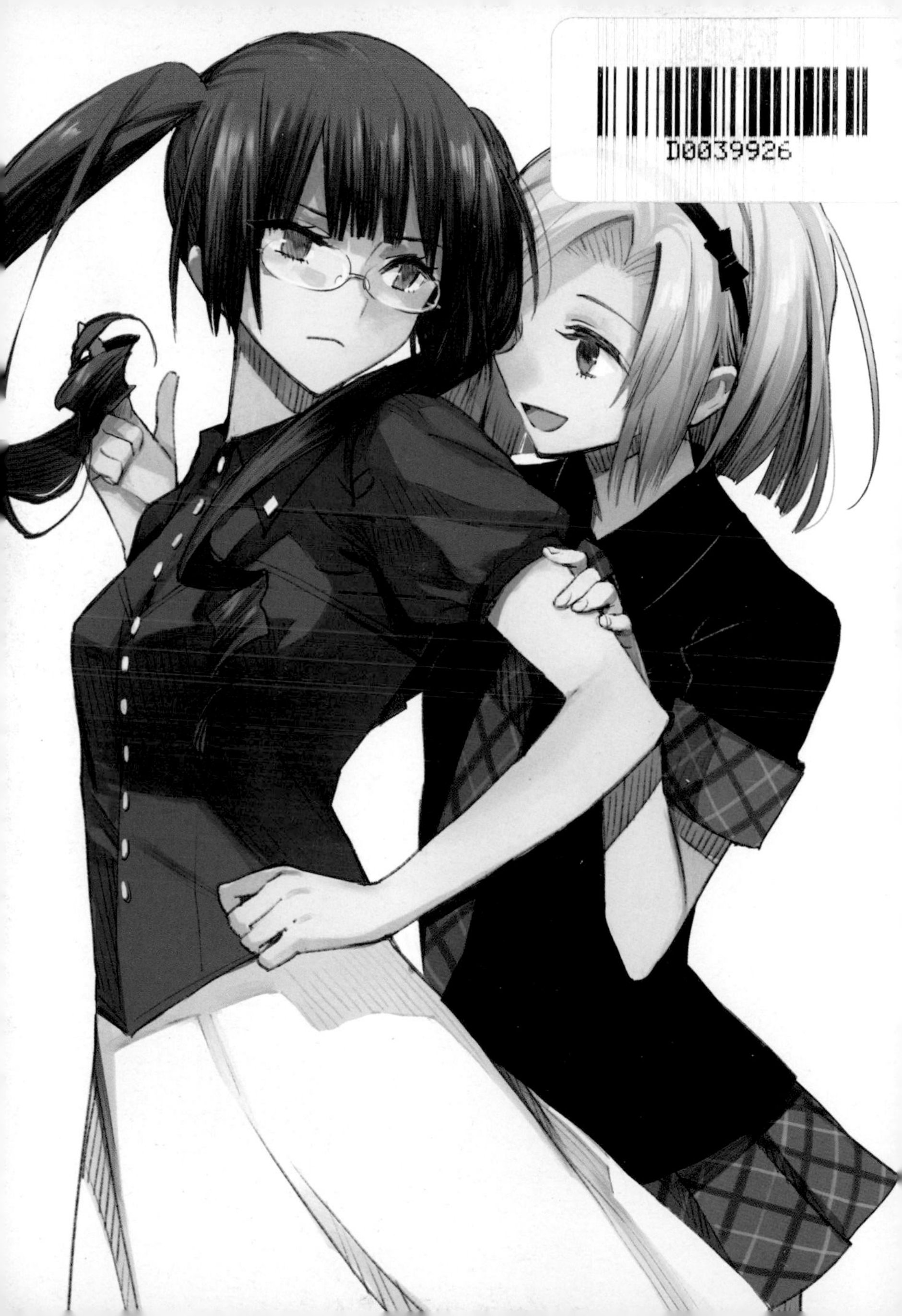

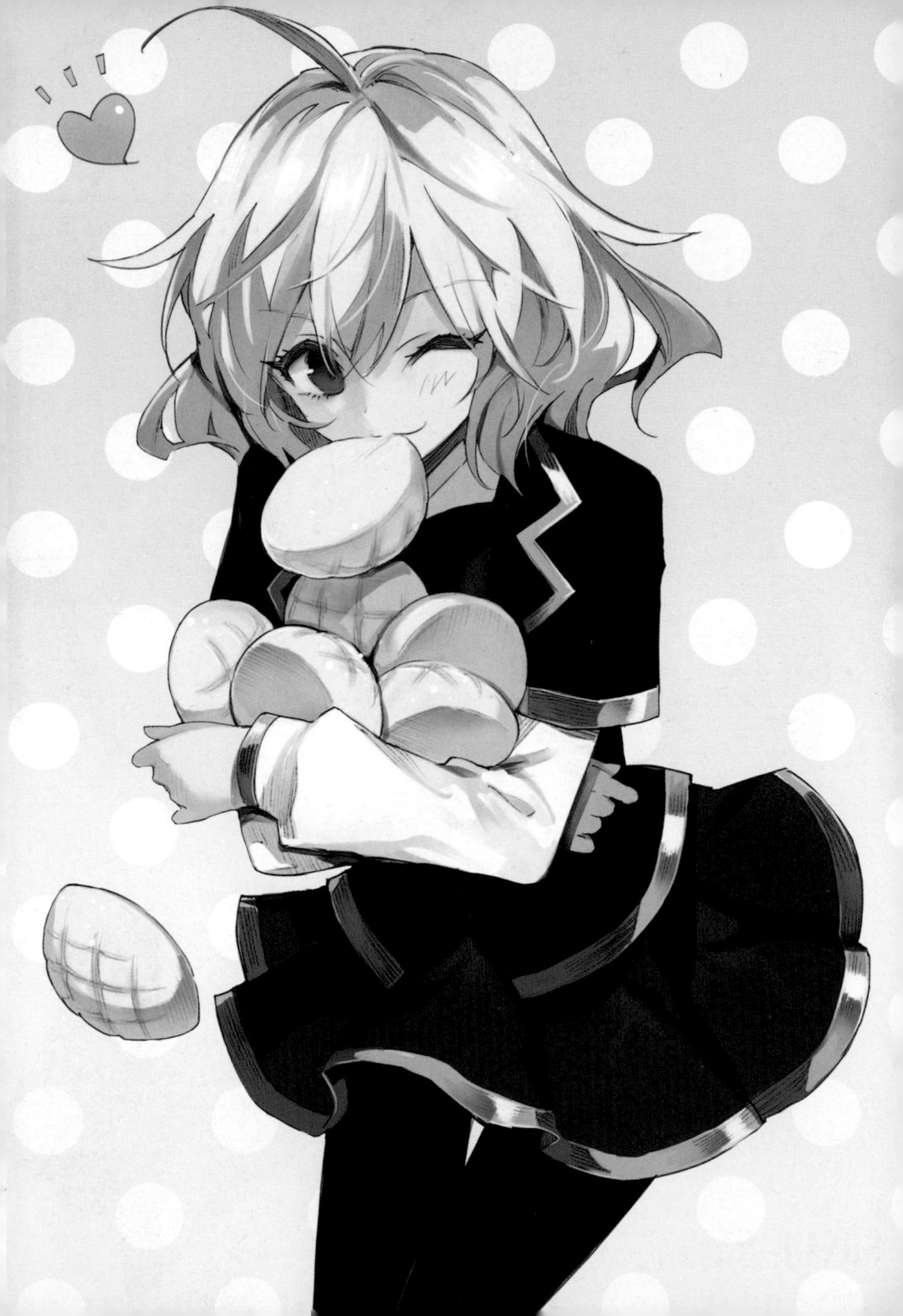

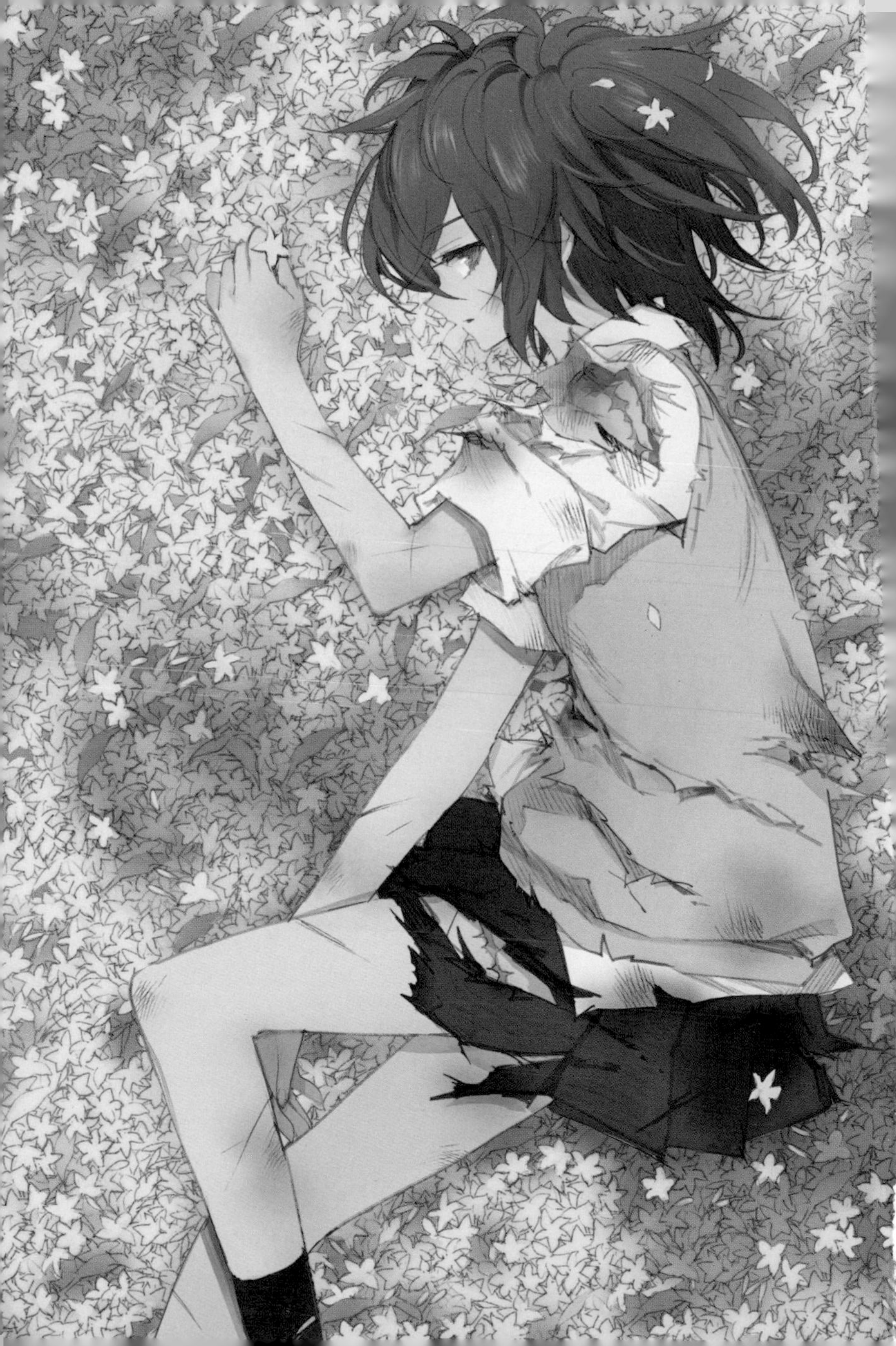

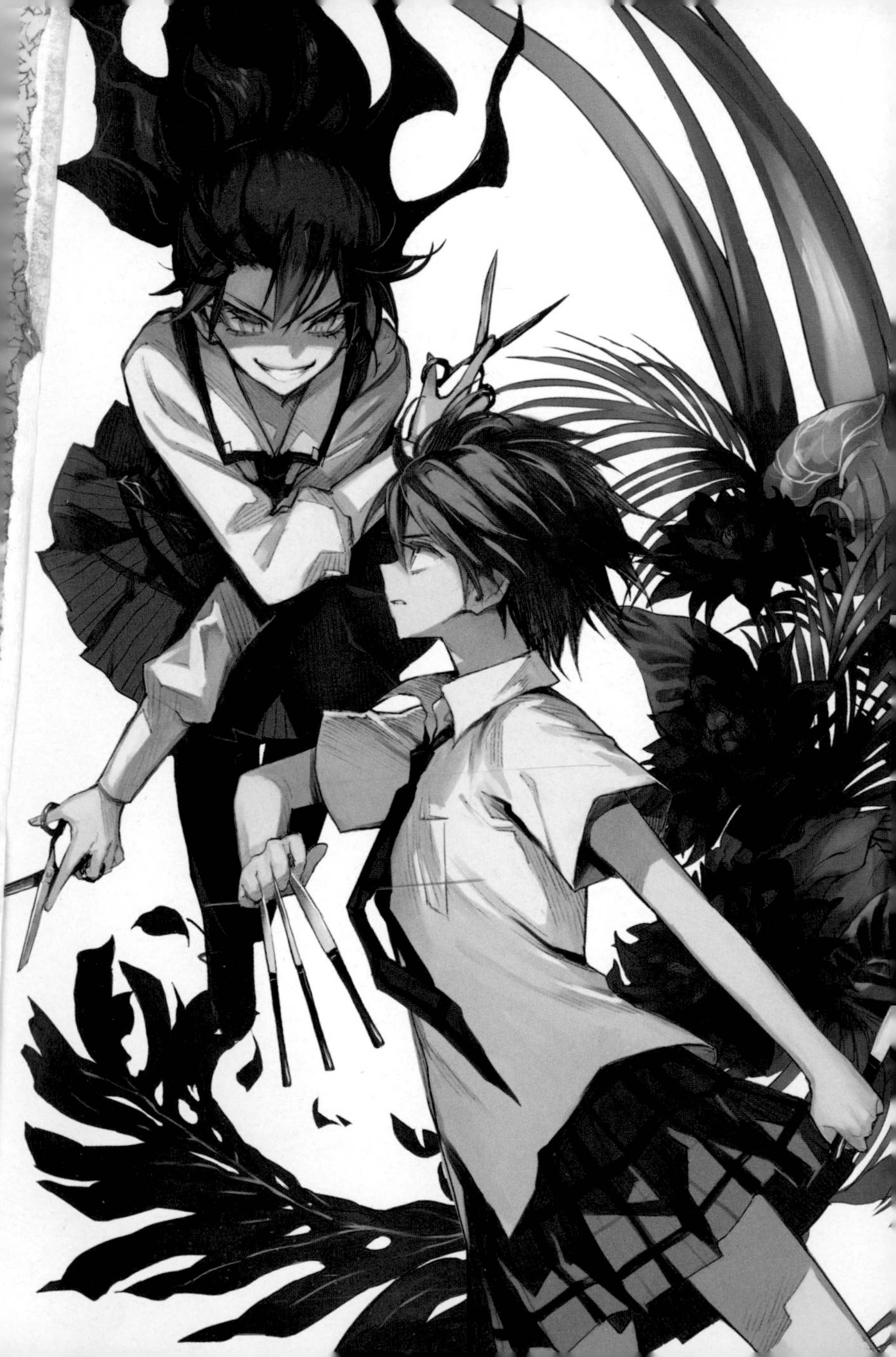

Akuma no Ric

riddle story of a

2

story by
YUN KOUGA

art by
SUNAO MINAKATA

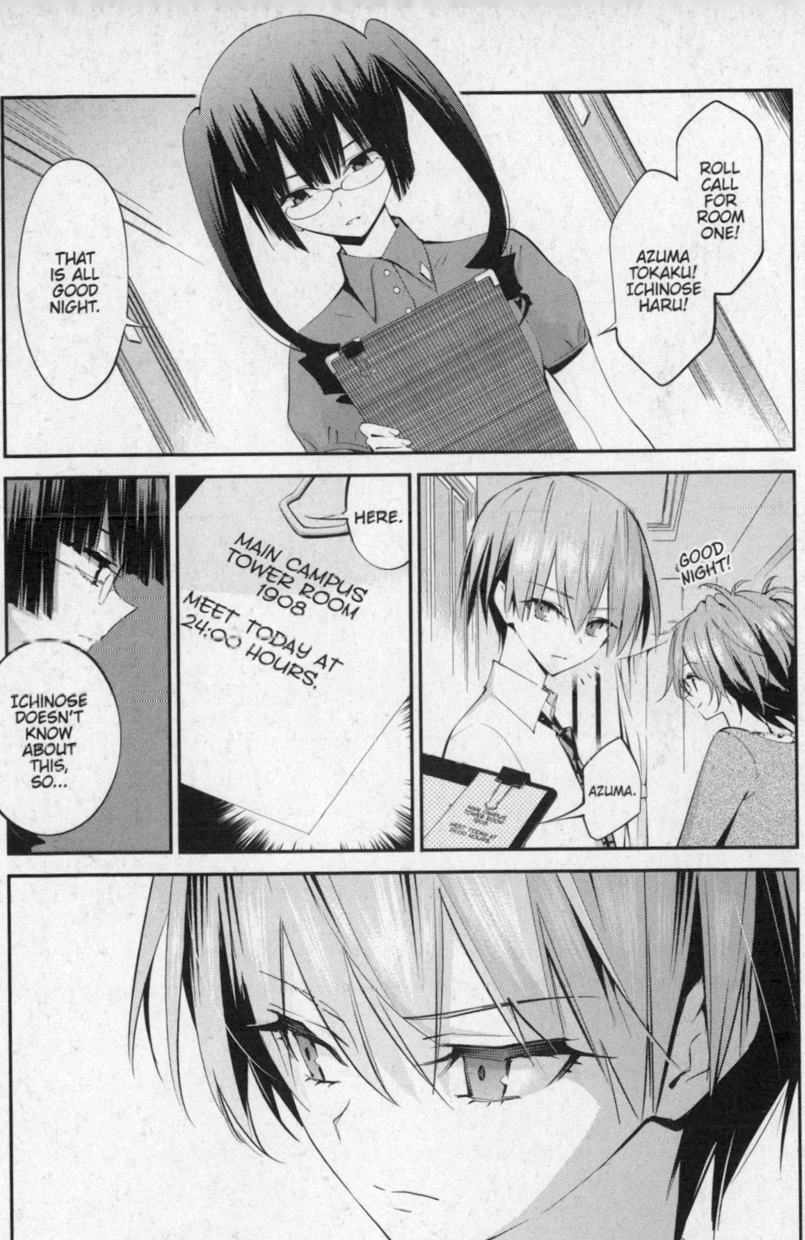
ROLL CALL FOR ROOM ONE!
AZUMA TOKAKU! ICHINOSE HARU!
THAT IS ALL GOOD NIGHT.
GOOD NIGHT!
AZUMA.
HERE.
MAIN CAMPUS TOWER ROOM 1908
MEET TODAY AT 24:00 HOURS.
ICHINOSE DOESN'T KNOW ABOUT THIS, SO...

Chapter 9
Adjudicator

riddle story of devil

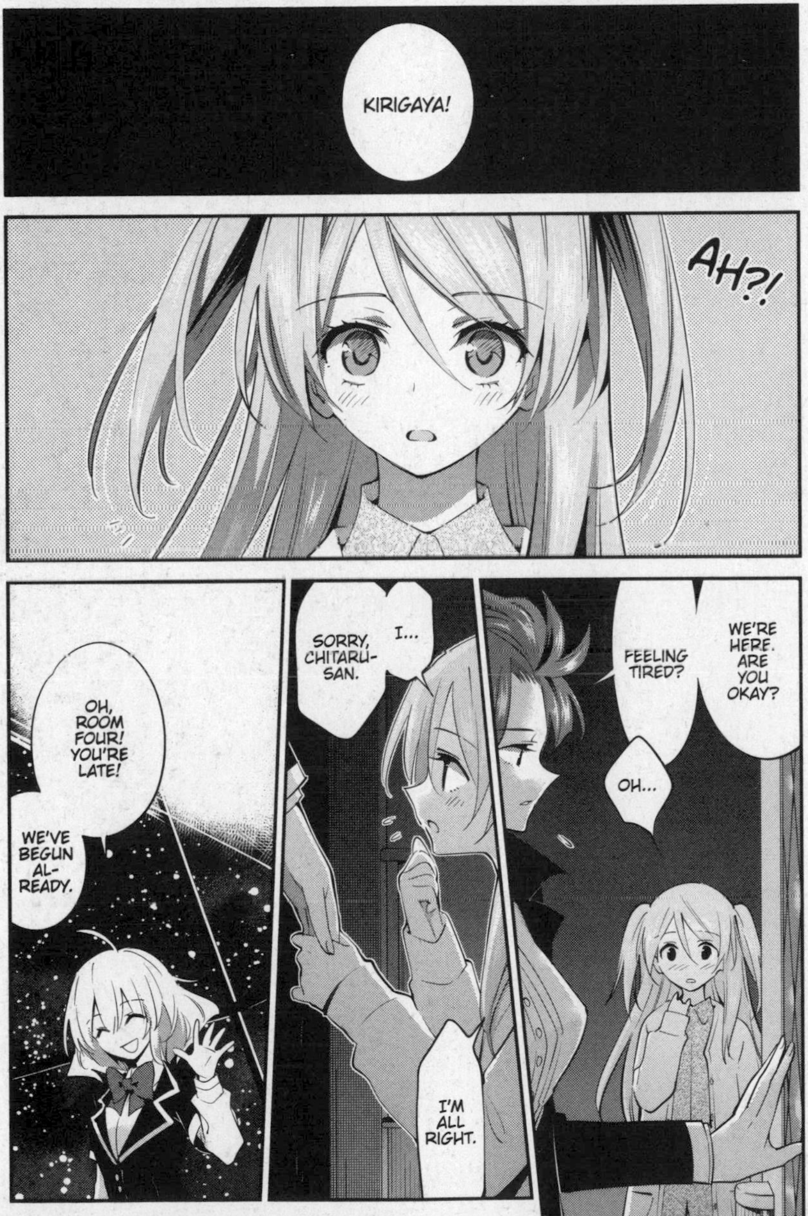
KIRIGAYA!
AH?!
WE'RE HERE. ARE YOU OKAY?
FEELING TIRED?
OH...
I...
SORRY, CHITARU-SAN.
I'M ALL RIGHT.
OH, ROOM FOUR! YOU'RE LATE!
WE'VE BEGUN AL-READY.

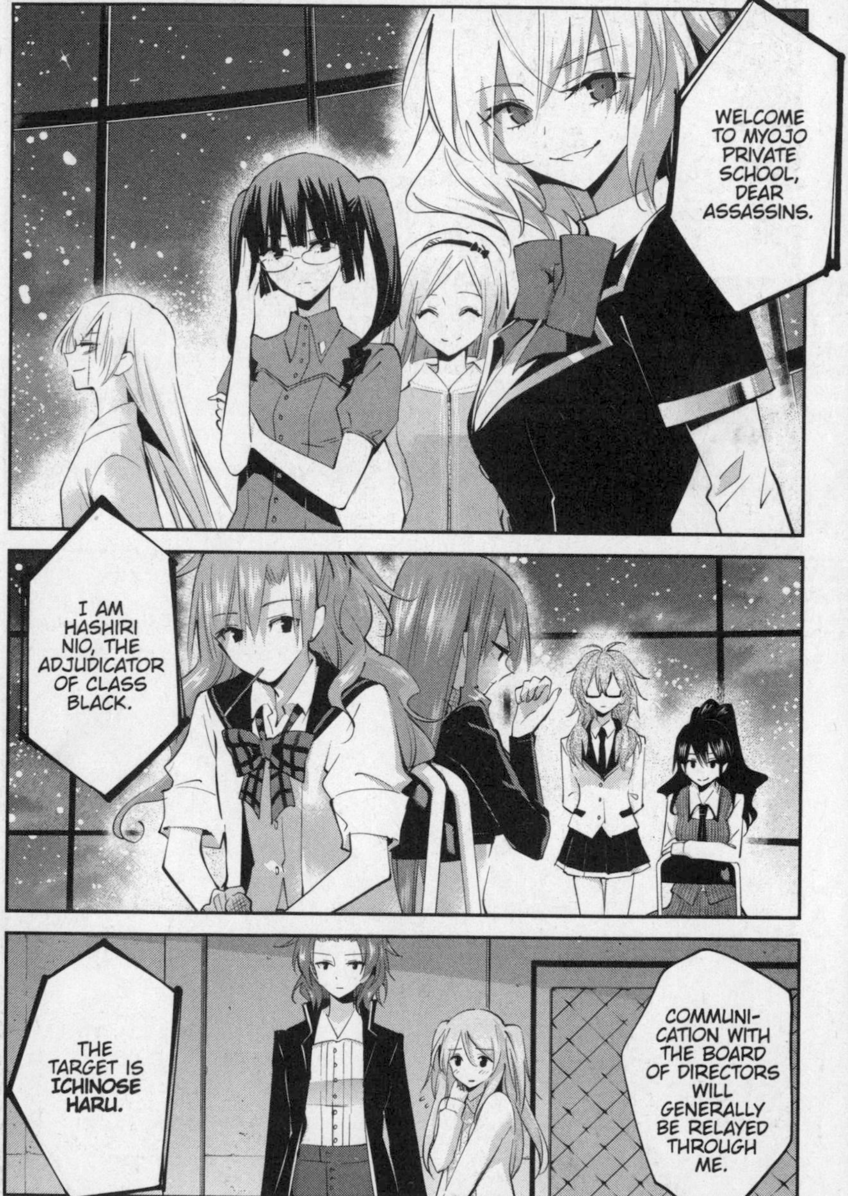
WELCOME TO MYOJO PRIVATE SCHOOL, DEAR ASSASSINS.
I AM HASHIRI NIO, THE ADJUDICATOR OF CLASS BLACK.
COMMUNICATION WITH THE BOARD OF DIRECTORS WILL GENERALLY BE RELAYED THROUGH ME.
THE TARGET IS ICHINOSE HARU.

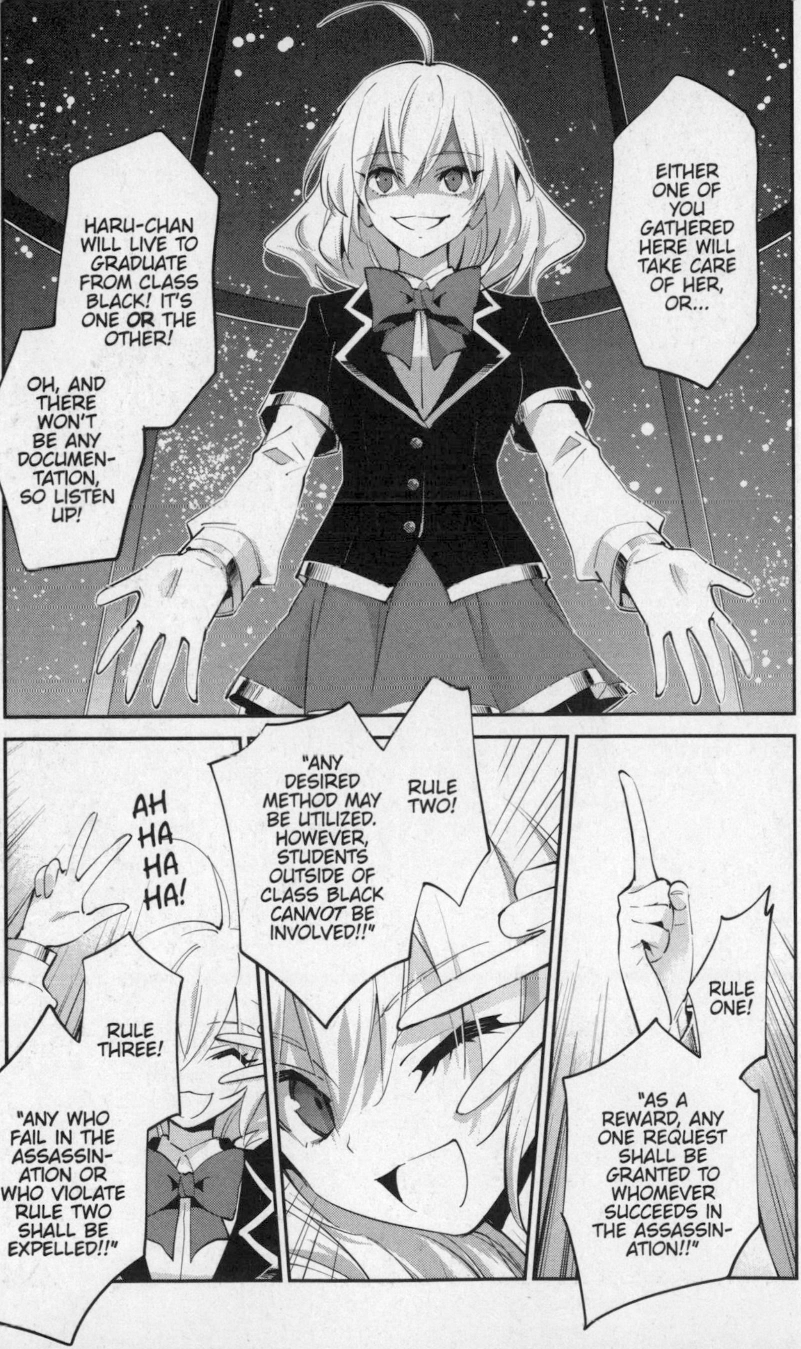
EITHER ONE OF YOU GATHERED HERE WILL TAKE CARE OF HER, OR...
HARU-CHAN WILL LIVE TO GRADUATE FROM CLASS BLACK! IT'S ONE **OR** THE OTHER!
OH, AND THERE WON'T BE ANY DOCUMENTATION, SO LISTEN UP!
RULE ONE!
"AS A REWARD, ANY ONE REQUEST SHALL BE GRANTED TO WHOMEVER SUCCEEDS IN THE ASSASSINATION!!"
RULE TWO!
"ANY DESIRED METHOD MAY BE UTILIZED. HOWEVER, STUDENTS OUTSIDE OF CLASS BLACK *CANNOT* BE INVOLVED!!"
AH HA HA HA!
RULE THREE!
"ANY WHO FAIL IN THE ASSASSINATION OR WHO VIOLATE RULE TWO SHALL BE EXPELLED!!"

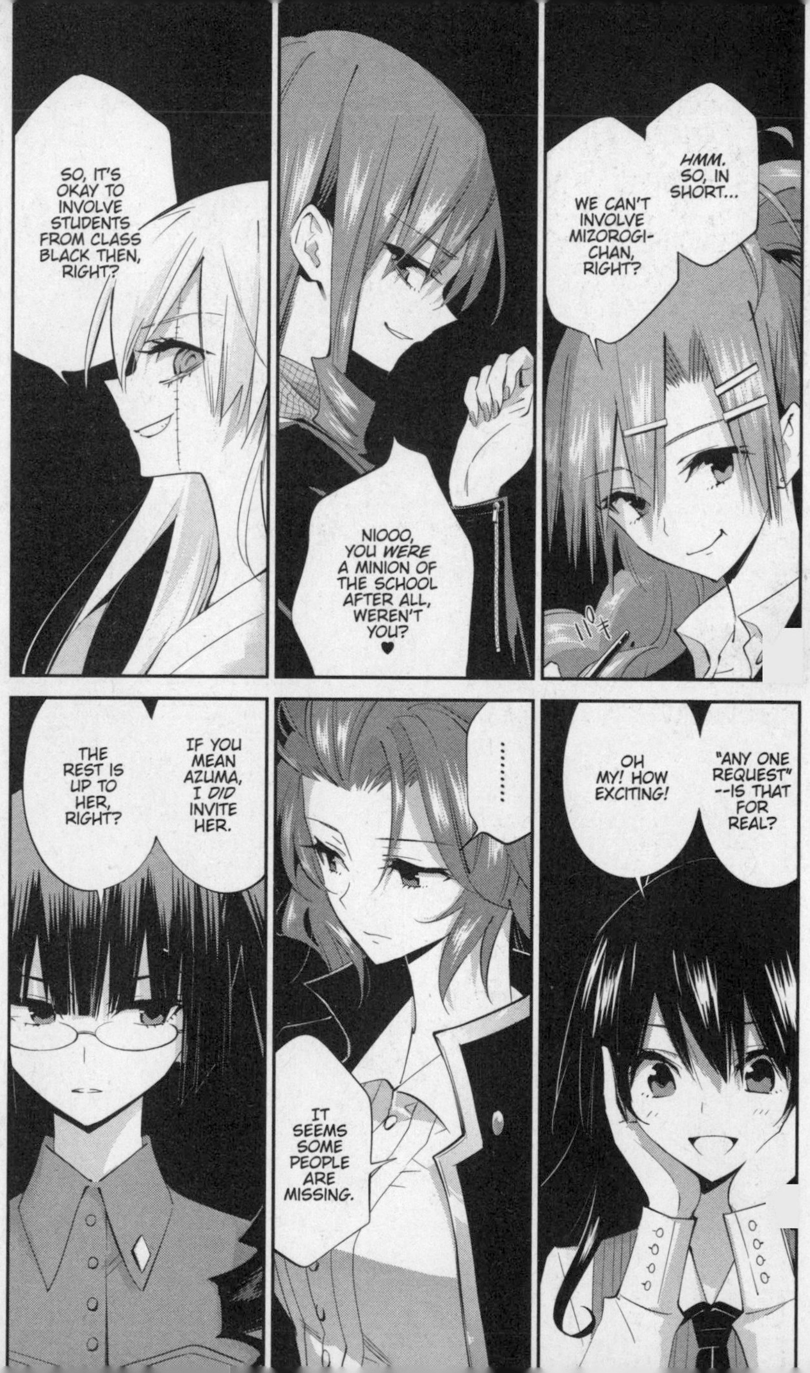
HMM. SO, IN SHORT...
WE CAN'T INVOLVE MIZOROGI-CHAN, RIGHT?
NIOOO, YOU *WERE* A MINION OF THE SCHOOL AFTER ALL, WEREN'T YOU? ♥
SO, IT'S OKAY TO INVOLVE STUDENTS FROM CLASS BLACK THEN, RIGHT?
"ANY ONE REQUEST" --IS THAT FOR REAL?
OH MY! HOW EXCITING!
....
IT SEEMS SOME PEOPLE ARE MISSING.
IF YOU MEAN AZUMA, I *DID* INVITE HER.
THE REST IS UP TO HER, RIGHT?

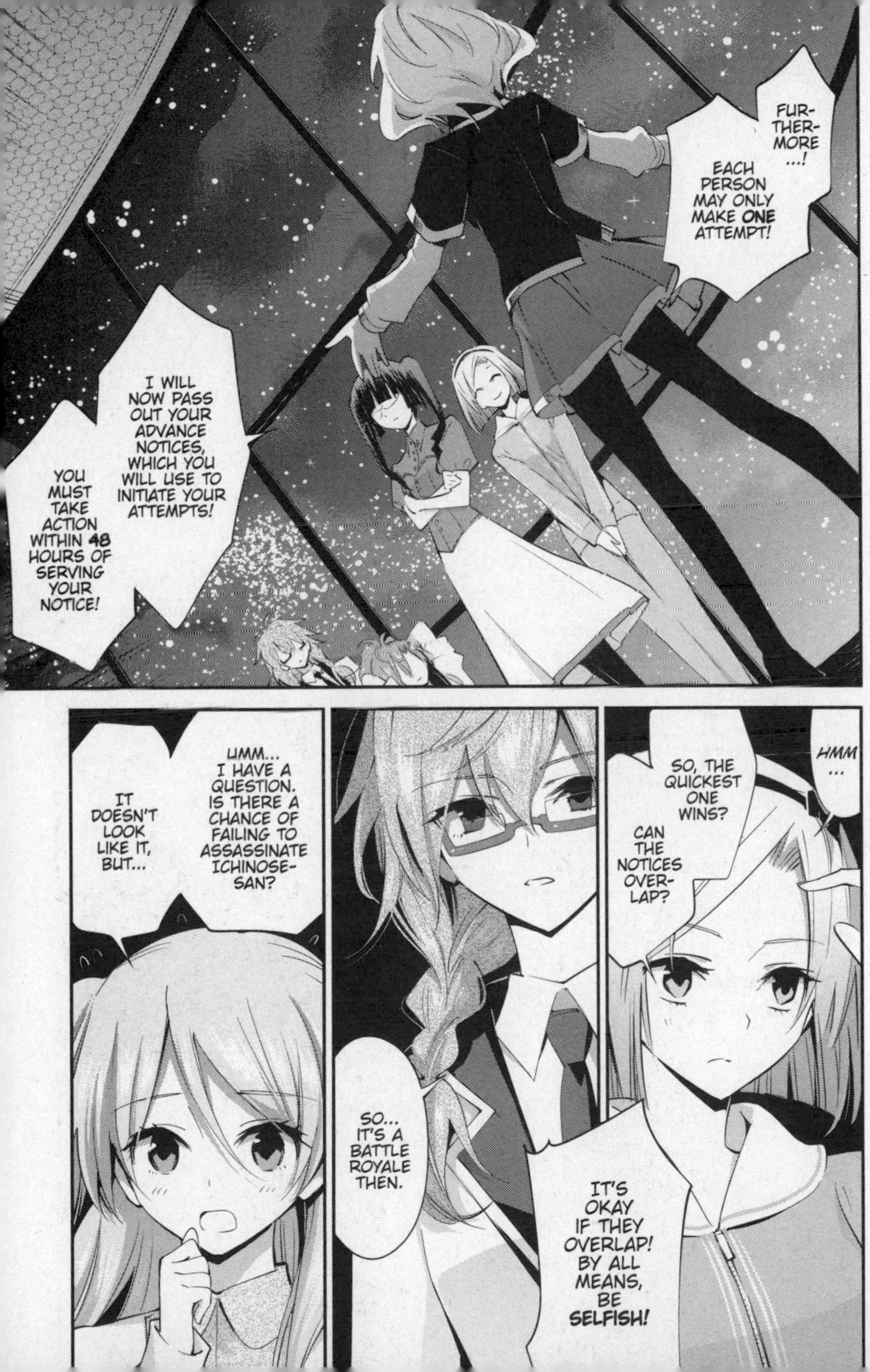
FURTHERMORE...!
EACH PERSON MAY ONLY MAKE ONE ATTEMPT!
I WILL NOW PASS OUT YOUR ADVANCE NOTICES, WHICH YOU WILL USE TO INITIATE YOUR ATTEMPTS!
YOU MUST TAKE ACTION WITHIN 48 HOURS OF SERVING YOUR NOTICE!
HMM...
SO, THE QUICKEST ONE WINS?
CAN THE NOTICES OVERLAP?
IT'S OKAY IF THEY OVERLAP! BY ALL MEANS, BE SELFISH!
SO... IT'S A BATTLE ROYALE THEN.
UMM... I HAVE A QUESTION. IS THERE A CHANCE OF FAILING TO ASSASSINATE ICHINOSE-SAN?
IT DOESN'T LOOK LIKE IT, BUT...

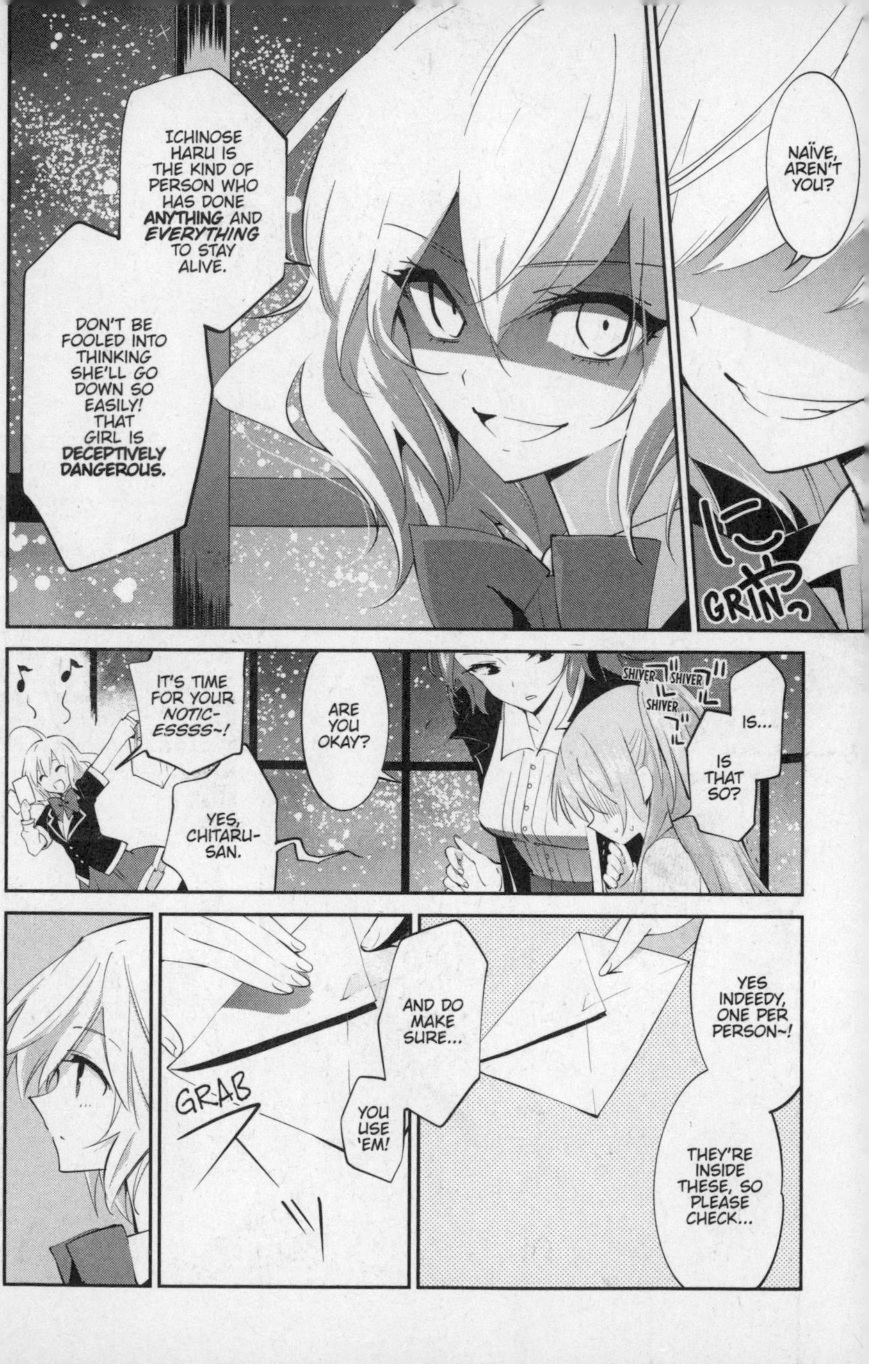
NAÏVE, AREN'T YOU?
GRIN
ICHINOSE HARU IS THE KIND OF PERSON WHO HAS DONE ANYTHING AND EVERYTHING TO STAY ALIVE.
DON'T BE FOOLED INTO THINKING SHE'LL GO DOWN SO EASILY! THAT GIRL IS DECEPTIVELY DANGEROUS.
SHIVER SHIVER
SHIVER
IS...
IS THAT SO?
ARE YOU OKAY?
YES, CHITARU-SAN.
IT'S TIME FOR YOUR NOTIC-ESSSS~!
YES INDEEDY, ONE PER PERSON~!
THEY'RE INSIDE THESE, SO PLEASE CHECK...
AND DO MAKE SURE...
GRAB
YOU USE 'EM!

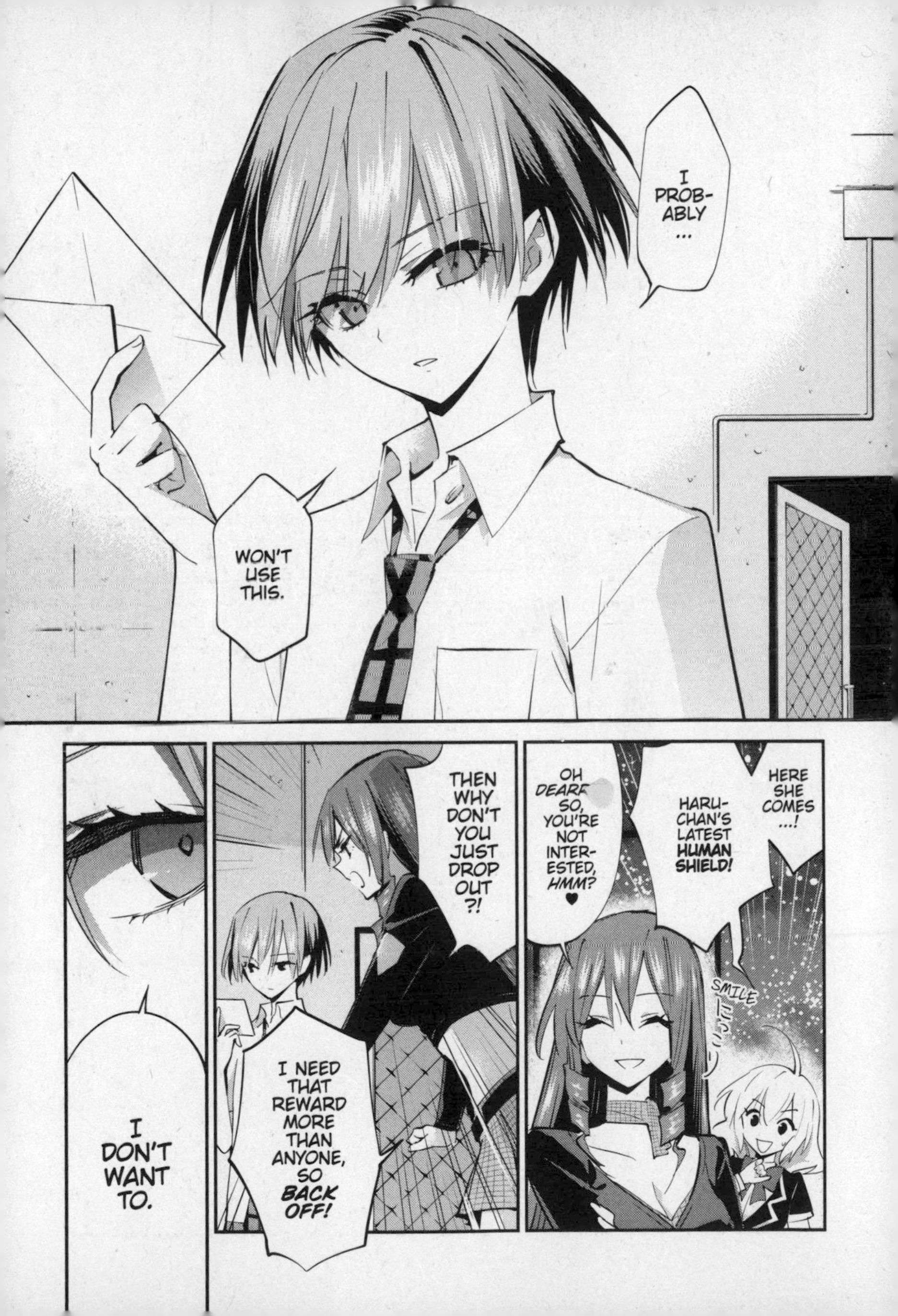
I PROBABLY...
WON'T USE THIS.
HERE SHE COMES...!
HARU-CHAN'S LATEST HUMAN SHIELD!
OH DEAR
SO, YOU'RE NOT INTERESTED, HMM? ♥
SMILE
THEN WHY DON'T YOU JUST DROP OUT?!
I NEED THAT REWARD MORE THAN ANYONE, SO BACK OFF!
I DON'T WANT TO.

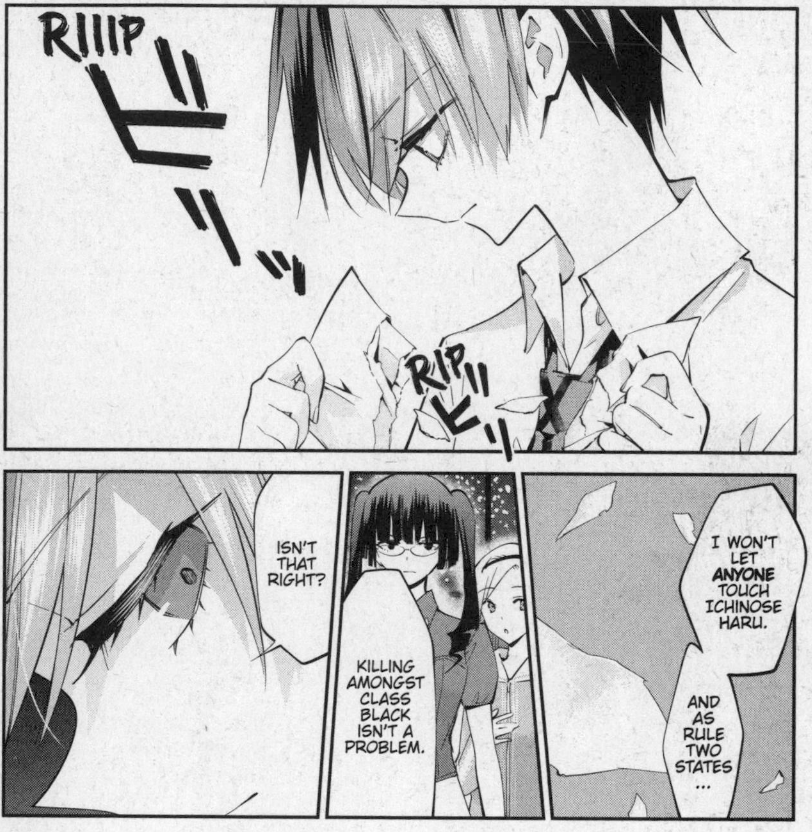
RIIIP
RIP
I WON'T LET **ANYONE** TOUCH ICHINOSE HARU.
AND AS RULE TWO STATES ...
KILLING AMONGST CLASS BLACK ISN'T A PROBLEM.
ISN'T THAT RIGHT?

Backdoor Orientation, Completed.

Chapter 10
First Warning

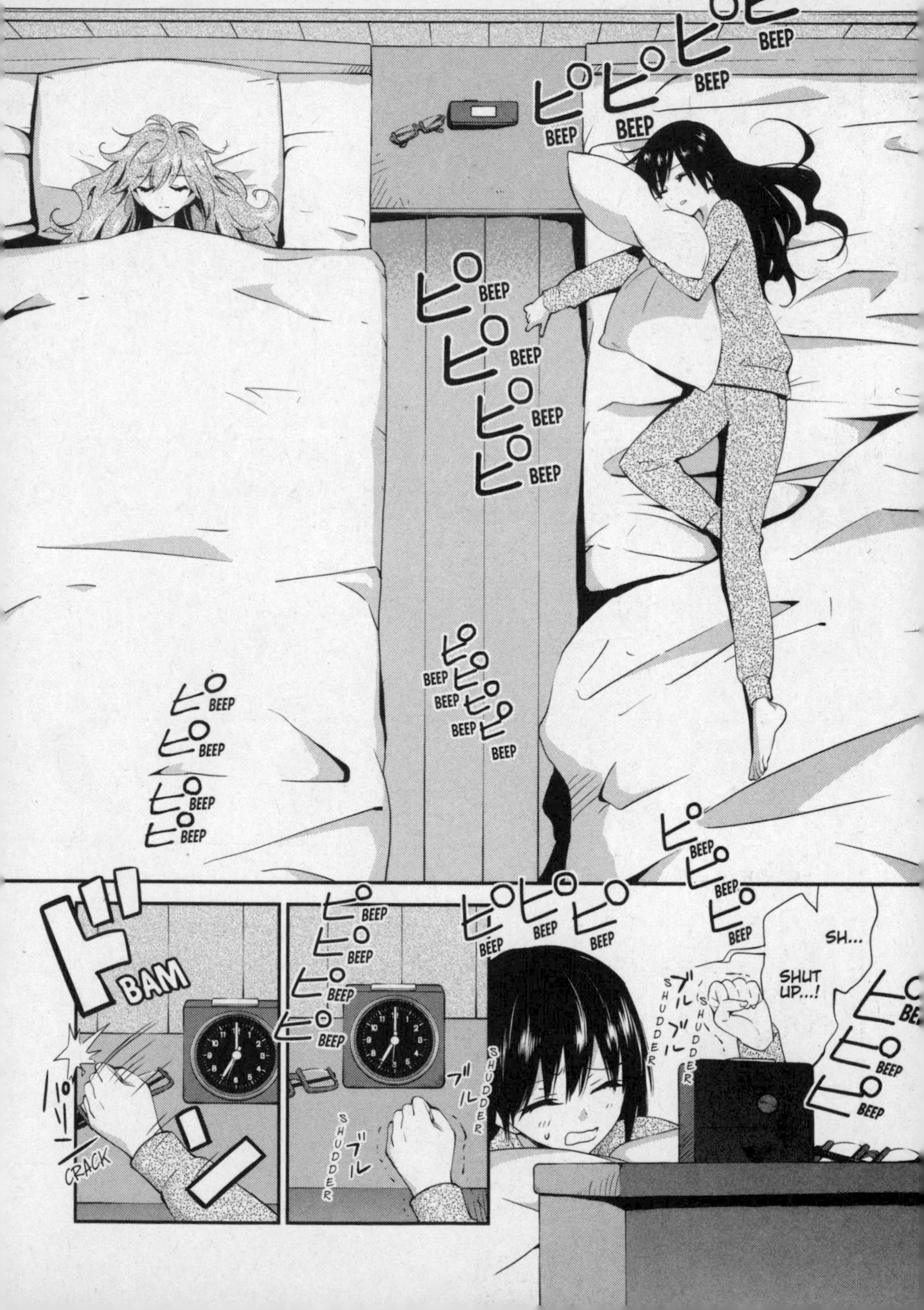

ピ BEEP ピ BEEP ピ BEEP ピ BEEP
ピ BEEP ピ BEEP ピ BEEP ピ BEEP
ピ BEEP ピ BEEP ピ BEEP ピ BEEP
ピ BEEP ピ BEEP ピ BEEP ピ BEEP
ピ BEEP ピ BEEP ピ BEEP
ピ BEEP ピ BEEP ピ BEEP
SH...
SHUT UP...!
ブルブル SHUDDER
ブル SHUDDER
ピ BEEP ピ BEEP ピ BEEP
ピ BEEP ピ BEEP ピ BEEP ピ BEEP
ブル SHUDDER
ブル SHUDDER
ド BAM
CRACK

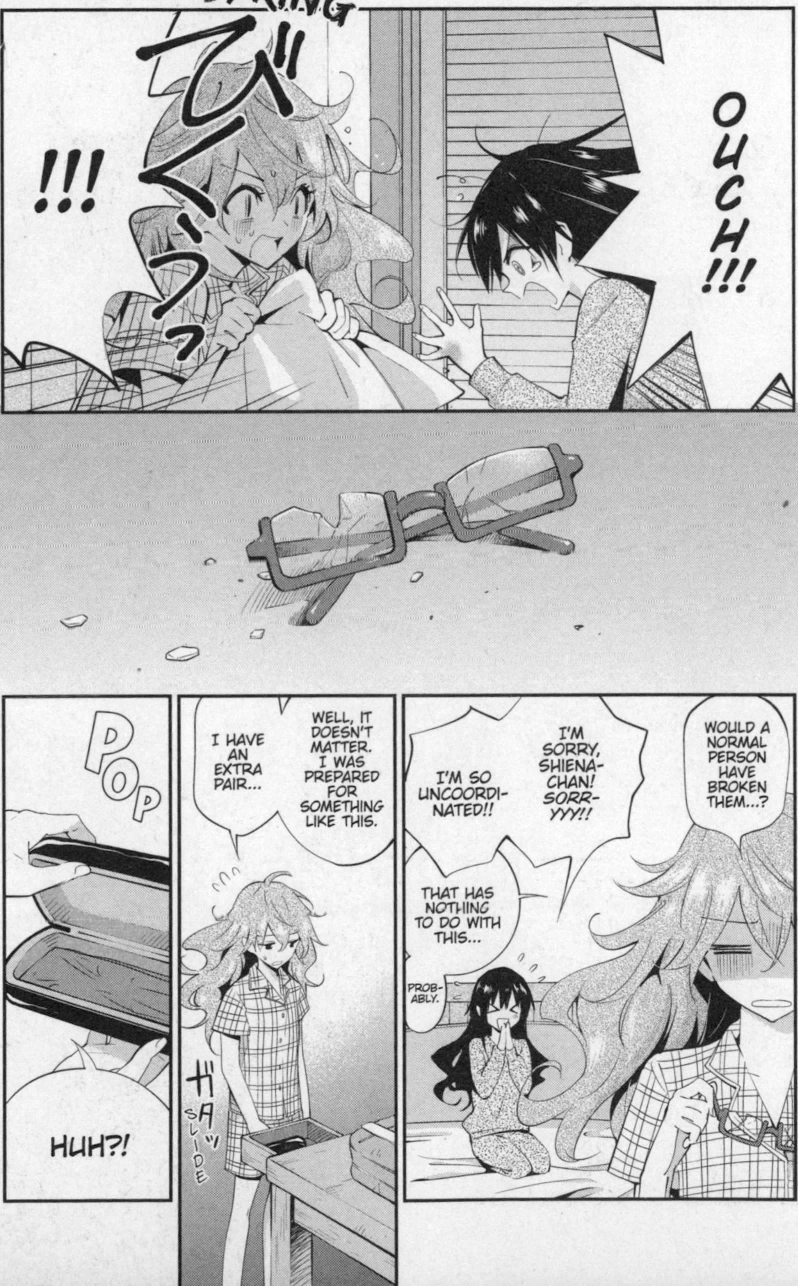
OUCH!!!
SPRING
びくぅっ
!!!
WOULD A NORMAL PERSON HAVE BROKEN THEM...?
I'M SORRY, SHIENA-CHAN! SORR-YYY!!
I'M SO UNCOORDI-NATED!!
THAT HAS NOTHIING TO DO WITH THIS...
PROB-ABLY.
WELL, IT DOESN'T MATTER. I WAS PREPARED FOR SOMETHING LIKE THIS.
I HAVE AN EXTRA PAIR...
ガタッ SLIDE
POP
HUH?!

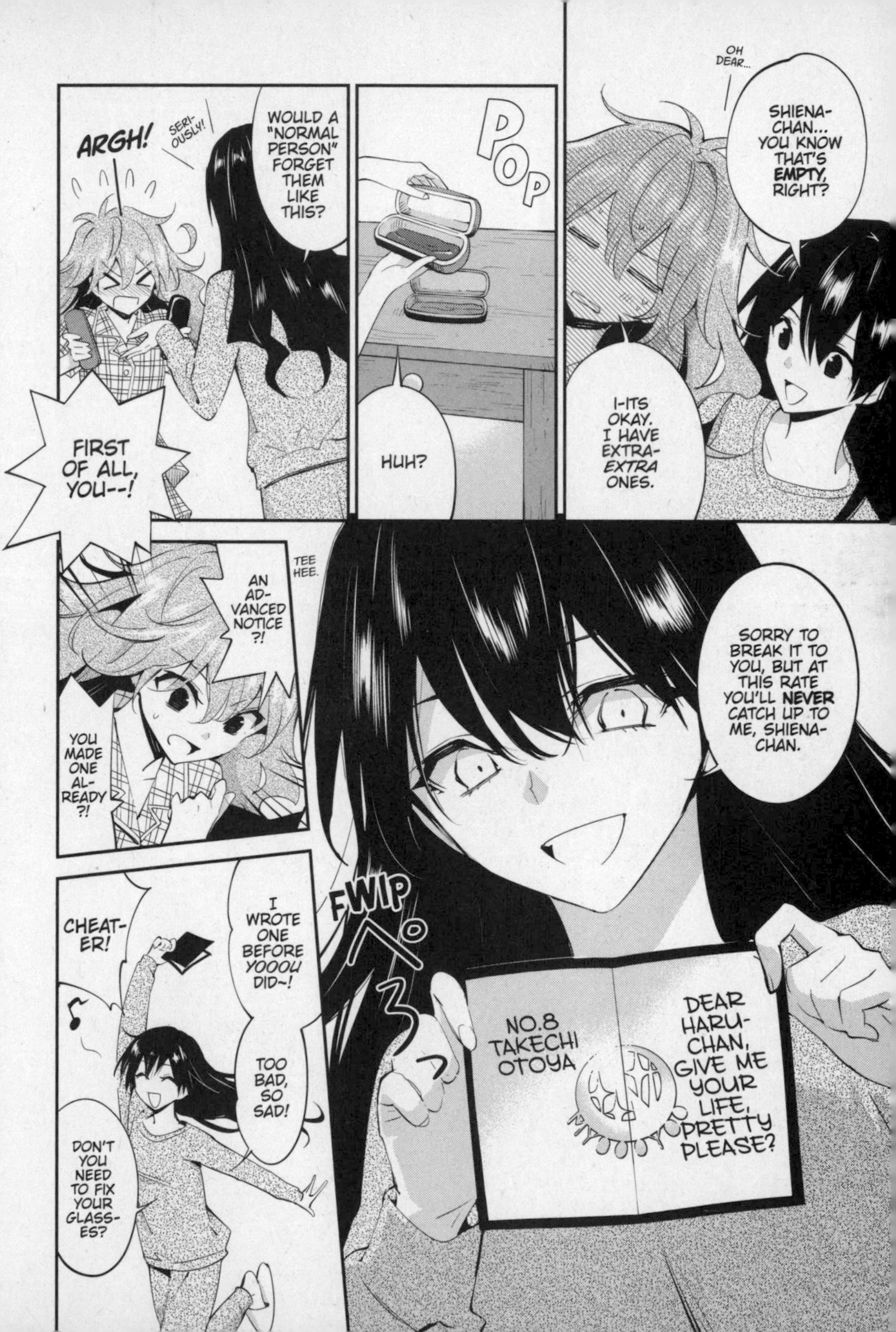
OH DEAR...
SHIENA-CHAN... YOU KNOW THAT'S **EMPTY**, RIGHT?
I-ITS OKAY. I HAVE EXTRA-*EXTRA* ONES.
POP
HUH?
WOULD A "NORMAL PERSON" FORGET THEM LIKE THIS?
SERIOUSLY!
ARGH!
FIRST OF ALL, YOU--!
SORRY TO BREAK IT TO YOU, BUT AT THIS RATE YOU'LL **NEVER** CATCH UP TO ME, SHIENA-CHAN.
FWIP
DEAR HARU-CHAN, GIVE ME YOUR LIFE, PRETTY PLEASE?
NO.8 TAKECHI OTOYA
TEE HEE.
AN ADVANCED NOTICE?!
YOU MADE ONE ALREADY?!
I WROTE ONE BEFORE *YOOOU* DID~!
CHEATER!
TOO BAD, SO SAD!
DON'T YOU NEED TO FIX YOUR GLASSES?

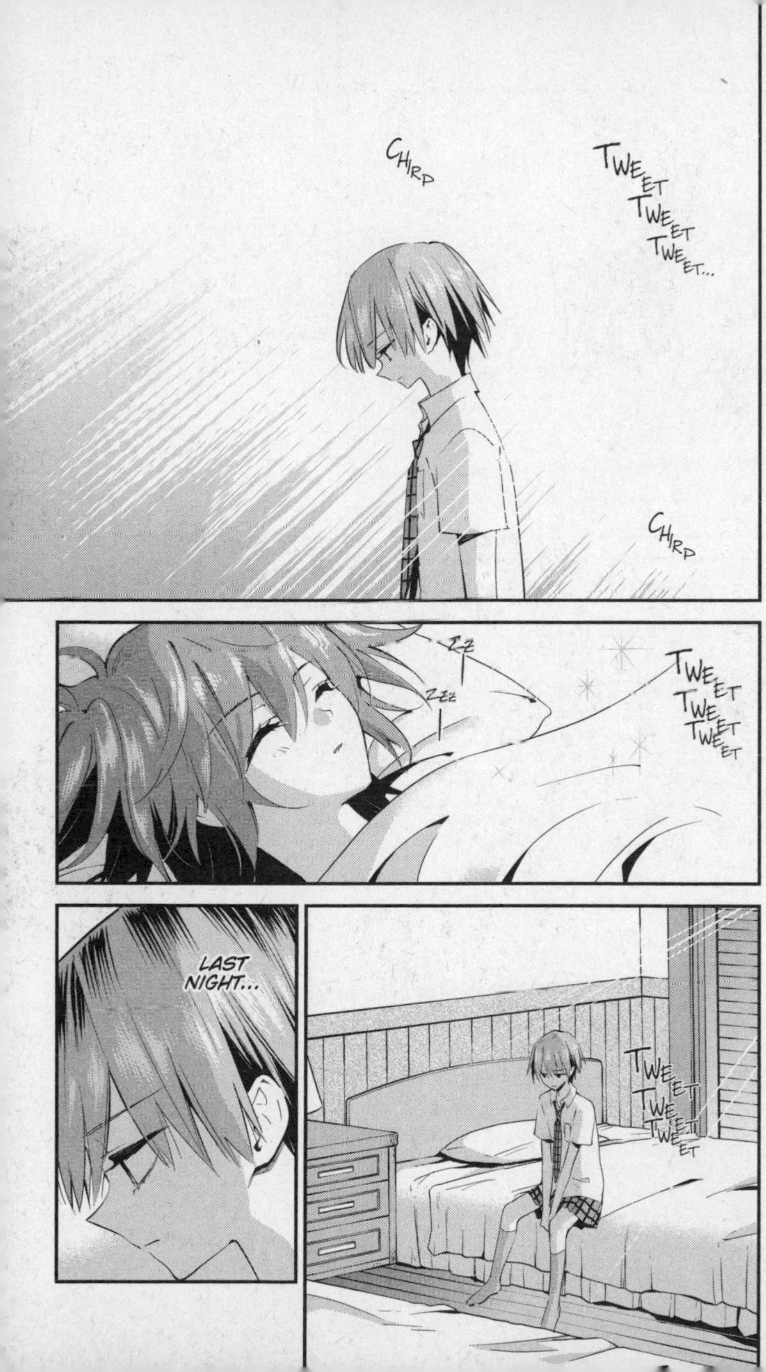
TWEET TWEET TWEET...
CHIRP
CHIRP
TWEET TWEET TWEET
ZZZ
ZZZ
TWEET TWEET TWEET
LAST NIGHT...

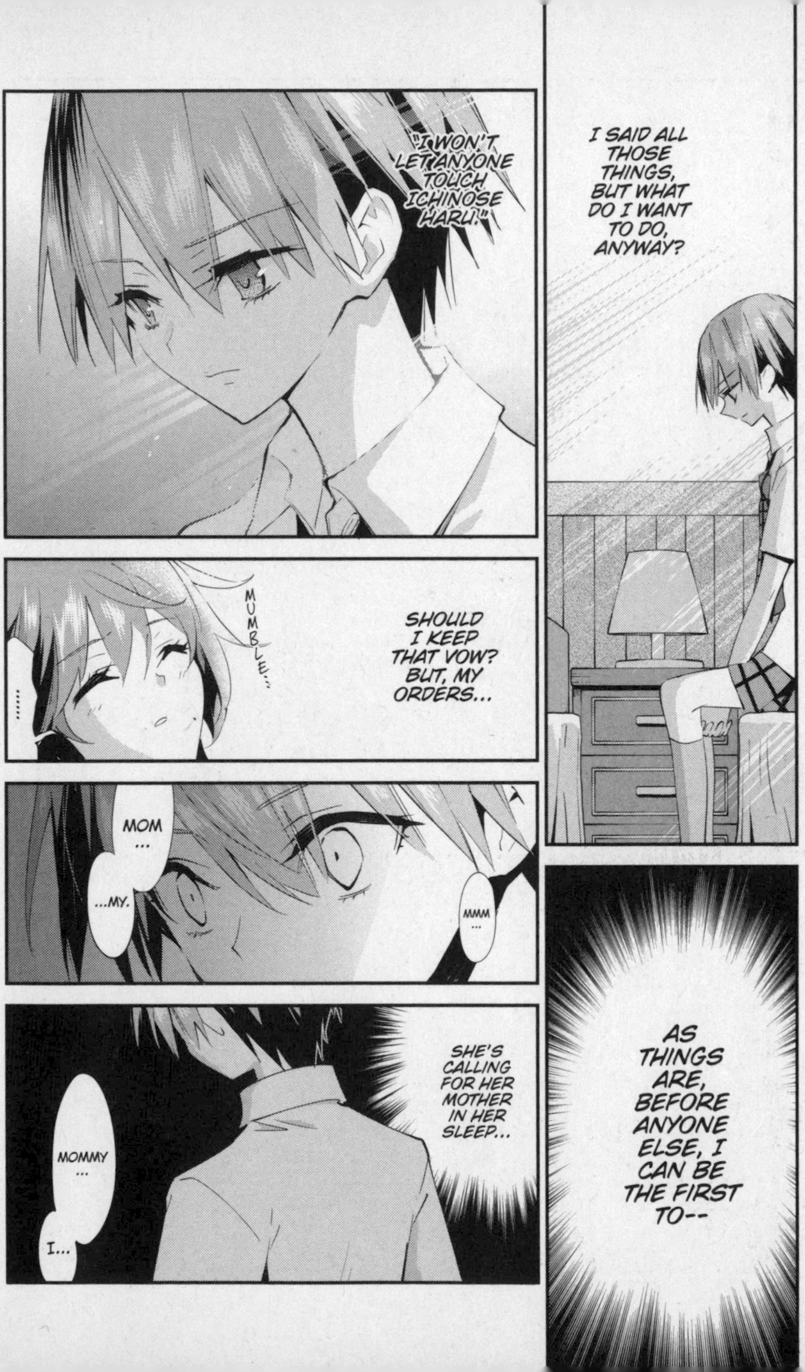
I SAID ALL THOSE THINGS, BUT WHAT DO I WANT TO DO, ANYWAY?
"I WON'T LET ANYONE TOUCH ICHINOSE HARU."
SHOULD I KEEP THAT VOW? BUT, MY ORDERS...
MUMBLE...
......
MOM...
...MY.
MMM...
SHE'S CALLING FOR HER MOTHER IN HER SLEEP...
MOMMY...
I...
AS THINGS ARE, BEFORE ANYONE ELSE, I CAN BE THE FIRST TO--

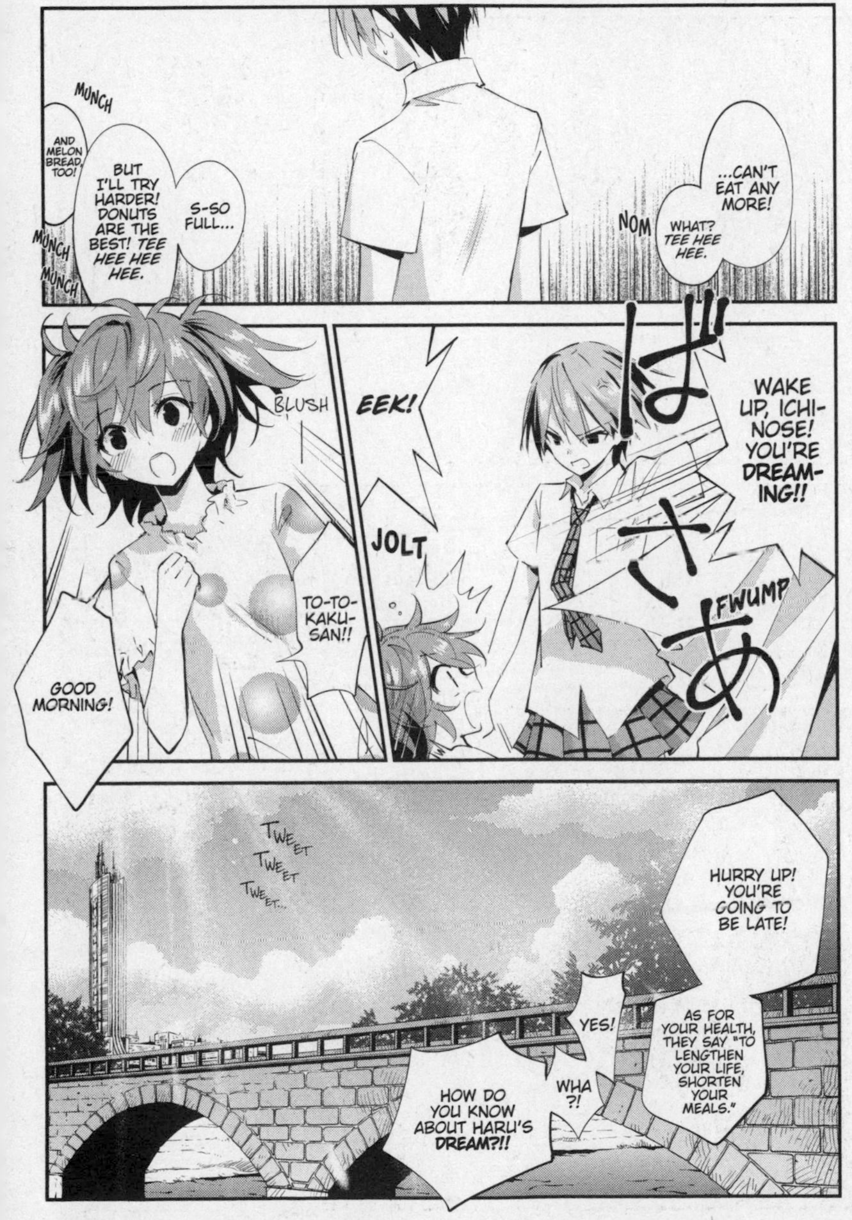
...CAN'T EAT ANY MORE!
WHAT? TEE HEE HEE.
NOM
S-SO FULL...
BUT I'LL TRY HARDER! DONUTS ARE THE BEST! TEE HEE HEE HEE.
AND MELON BREAD, TOO!
MUNCH
MUNCH
MUNCH
ばさぁ
WAKE UP, ICHI-NOSE! YOU'RE DREAM-ING!!
FWUMP
JOLT
EEK!
BLUSH
TO-TO-KAKUSAN!!
GOOD MORNING!
HURRY UP! YOU'RE GOING TO BE LATE!
AS FOR YOUR HEALTH, THEY SAY "TO LENGTHEN YOUR LIFE, SHORTEN YOUR MEALS."
YES!
WHA?!
HOW DO YOU KNOW ABOUT HARU'S DREAM?!!
TWEET
TWEET
TWEET...

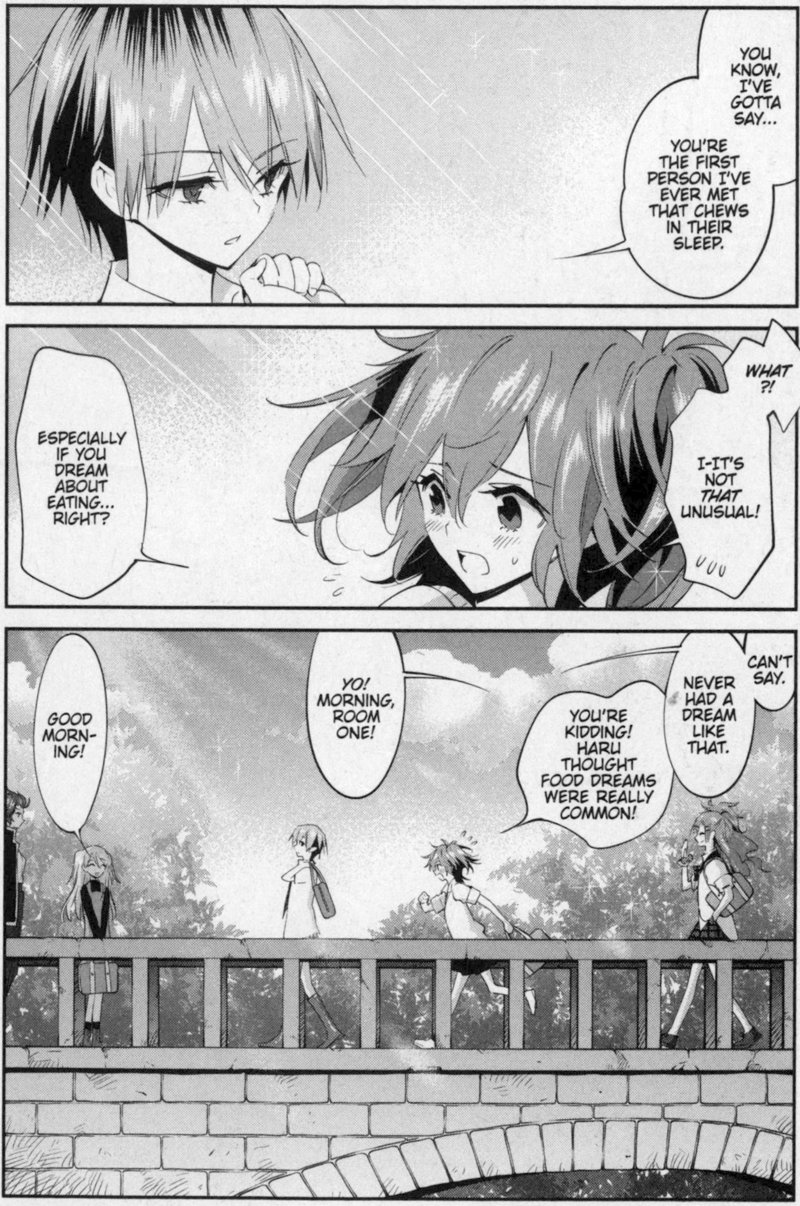
YOU KNOW, I'VE GOTTA SAY...
YOU'RE THE FIRST PERSON I'VE EVER MET THAT CHEWS IN THEIR SLEEP.
WHAT ?!
I-IT'S NOT *THAT* UNUSUAL!
ESPECIALLY IF YOU DREAM ABOUT EATING... RIGHT?
CAN'T SAY.
NEVER HAD A DREAM LIKE THAT.
YOU'RE KIDDING! HARU THOUGHT FOOD DREAMS WERE REALLY COMMON!
YO! MORNING, ROOM ONE!
GOOD MORN-ING!

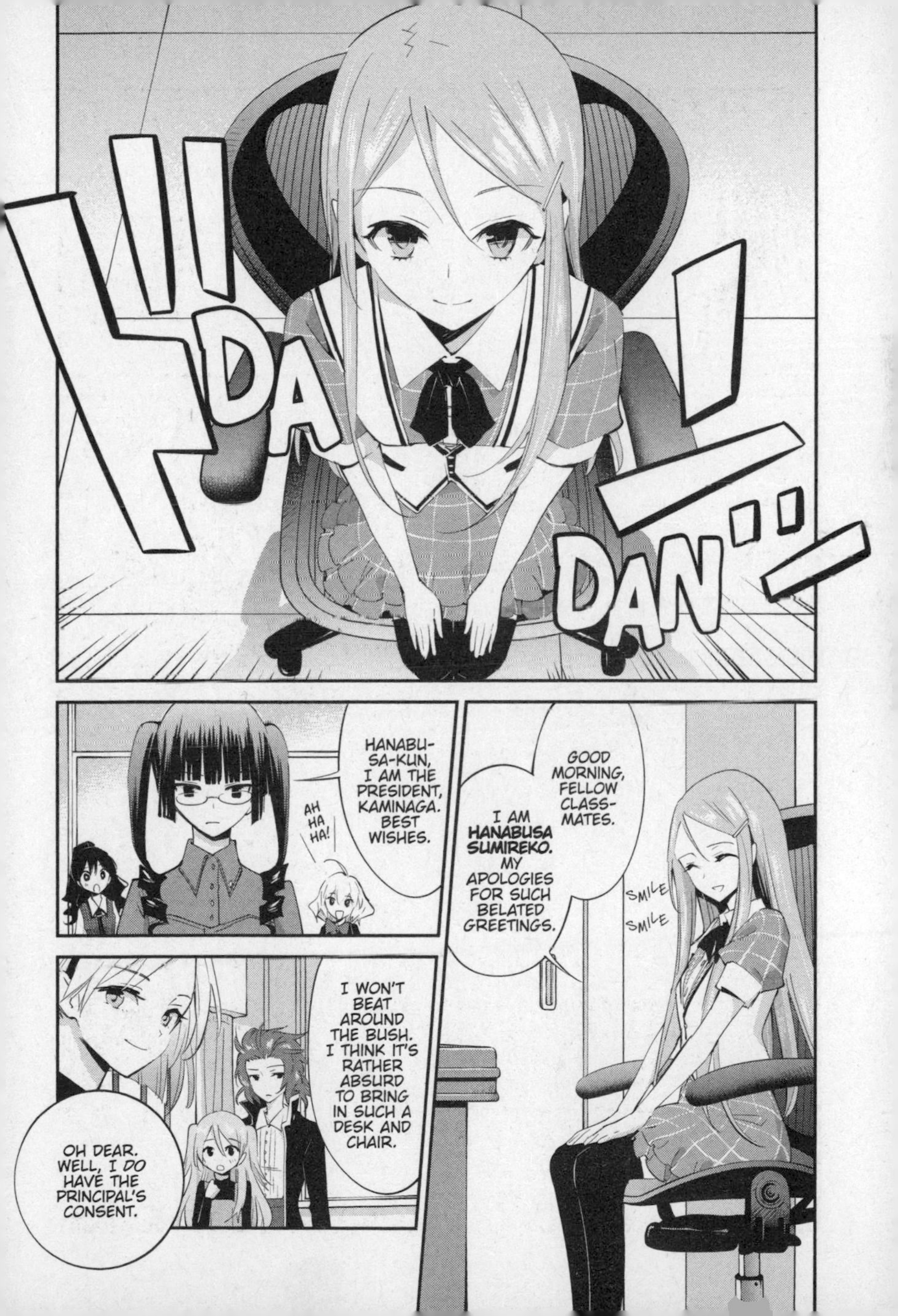
DA
DAN
GOOD MORNING, FELLOW CLASS-MATES.
I AM HANABUSA SUMIREKO. MY APOLOGIES FOR SUCH BELATED GREETINGS.
SMILE
SMILE
HANABU-SA-KUN, I AM THE PRESIDENT, KAMINAGA. BEST WISHES.
AH HA HA!
I WON'T BEAT AROUND THE BUSH. I THINK IT'S RATHER ABSURD TO BRING IN SUCH A DESK AND CHAIR.
OH DEAR. WELL, I DO HAVE THE PRINCIPAL'S CONSENT.

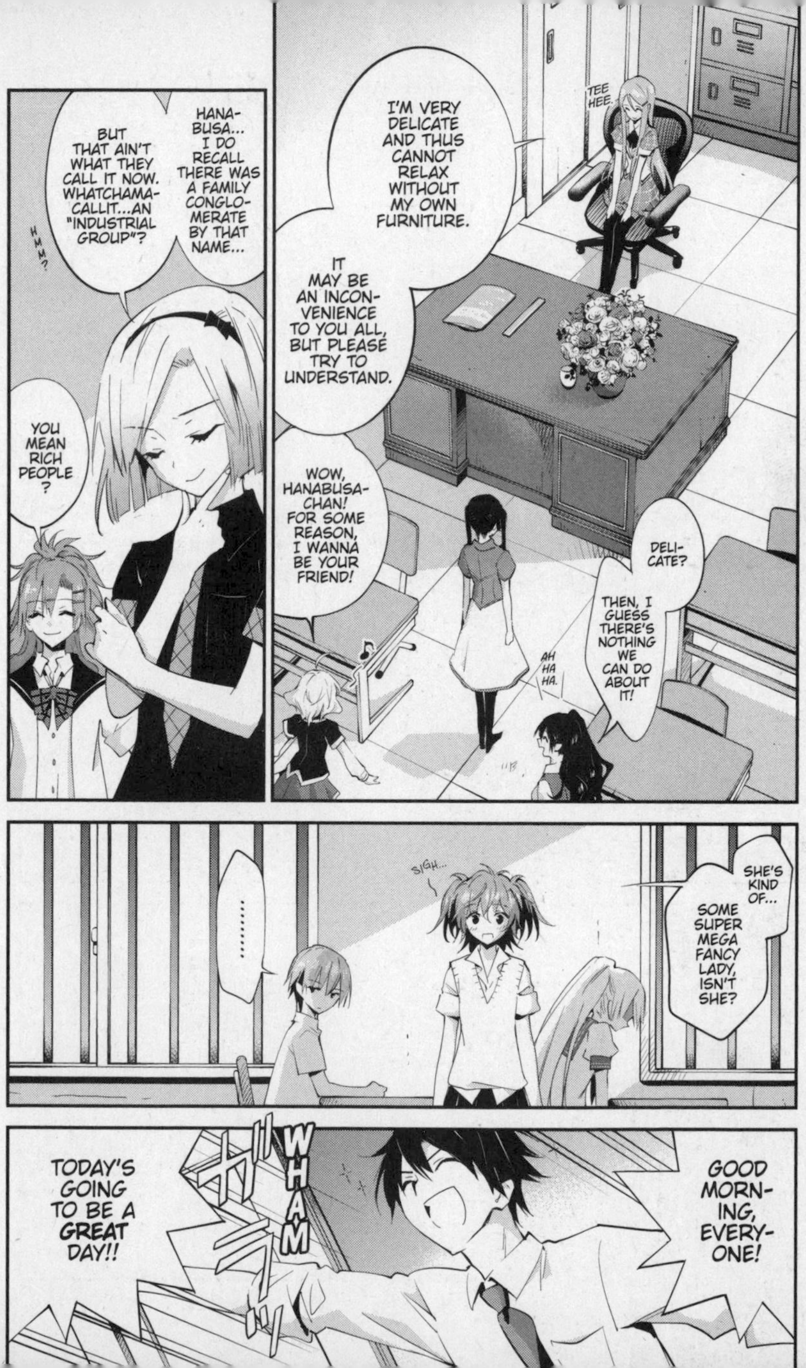
TEE HEE.
I'M VERY DELICATE AND THUS CANNOT RELAX WITHOUT MY OWN FURNITURE.
IT MAY BE AN INCONVENIENCE TO YOU ALL, BUT PLEASE TRY TO UNDERSTAND.
DELICATE?
THEN, I GUESS THERE'S NOTHING WE CAN DO ABOUT IT!
AH HA HA.
WOW, HANABUSA-CHAN! FOR SOME REASON, I WANNA BE YOUR FRIEND!
HANABUSA... I DO RECALL THERE WAS A FAMILY CONGLOMERATE BY THAT NAME...
BUT THAT AIN'T WHAT THEY CALL IT NOW. WHATCHAMACALLIT...AN "INDUSTRIAL GROUP"?
HMM?
YOU MEAN RICH PEOPLE?
SHE'S KIND OF... SOME SUPER MEGA FANCY LADY, ISN'T SHE?
SIGH...
....
GOOD MORNING, EVERYONE!
WHAM
TODAY'S GOING TO BE A GREAT DAY!!

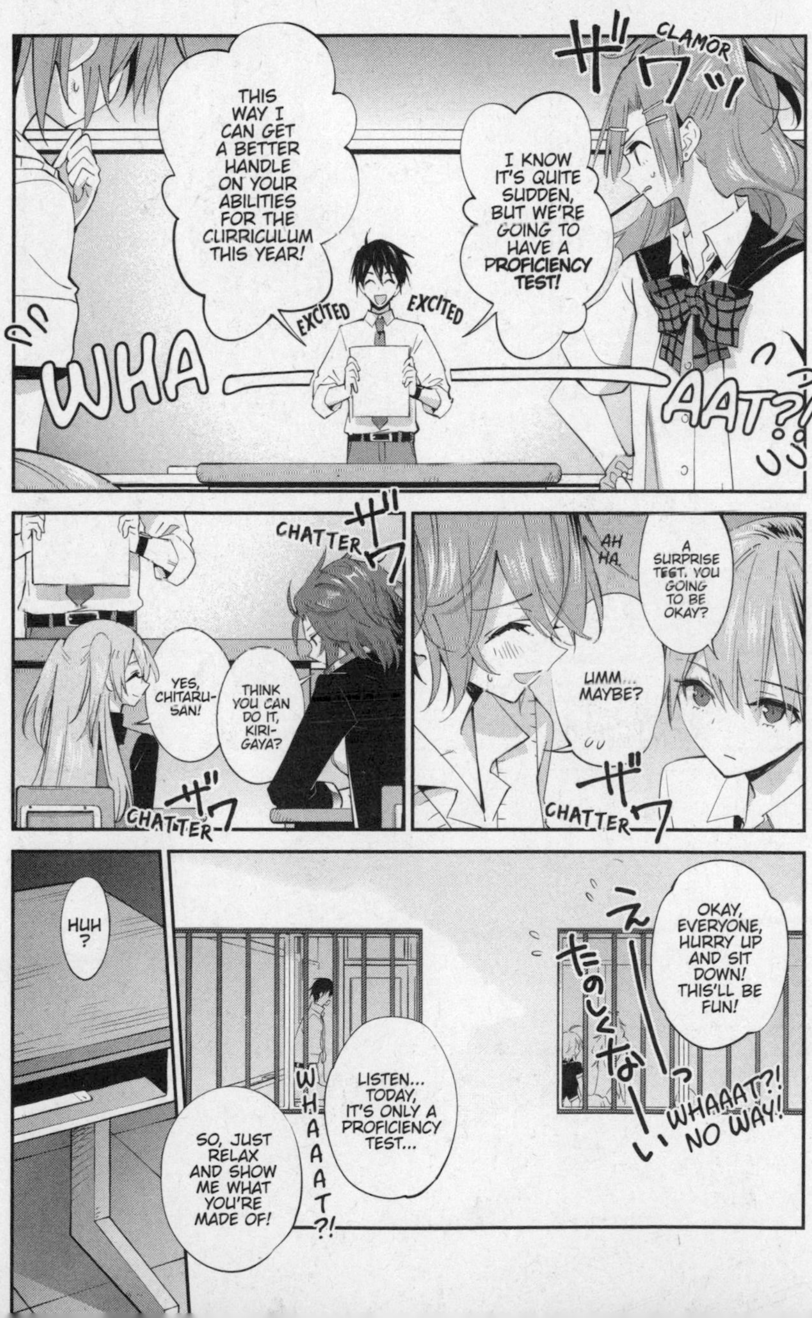
ザワッ
CLAMOR
I KNOW IT'S QUITE SUDDEN, BUT WE'RE GOING TO HAVE A PROFICIENCY TEST!
THIS WAY I CAN GET A BETTER HANDLE ON YOUR ABILITIES FOR THE CURRICULUM THIS YEAR!
EXCITED
EXCITED
WHA— —AAT?!
AH HA.
A SURPRISE TEST. YOU GOING TO BE OKAY?
UMM... MAYBE?
ザワ
CHATTER
ザワ
CHATTER
THINK YOU CAN DO IT, KIRI-GAYA?
YES, CHITARU-SAN!
ザワ
CHATTER
OKAY, EVERYONE, HURRY UP AND SIT DOWN! THIS'LL BE FUN!
えーーっ
たのしくなーーい
WHAAAT?! NO WAY!
LISTEN... TODAY, IT'S ONLY A PROFICIENCY TEST...
WHAAAT?!
SO, JUST RELAX AND SHOW ME WHAT YOU'RE MADE OF!
HUH?

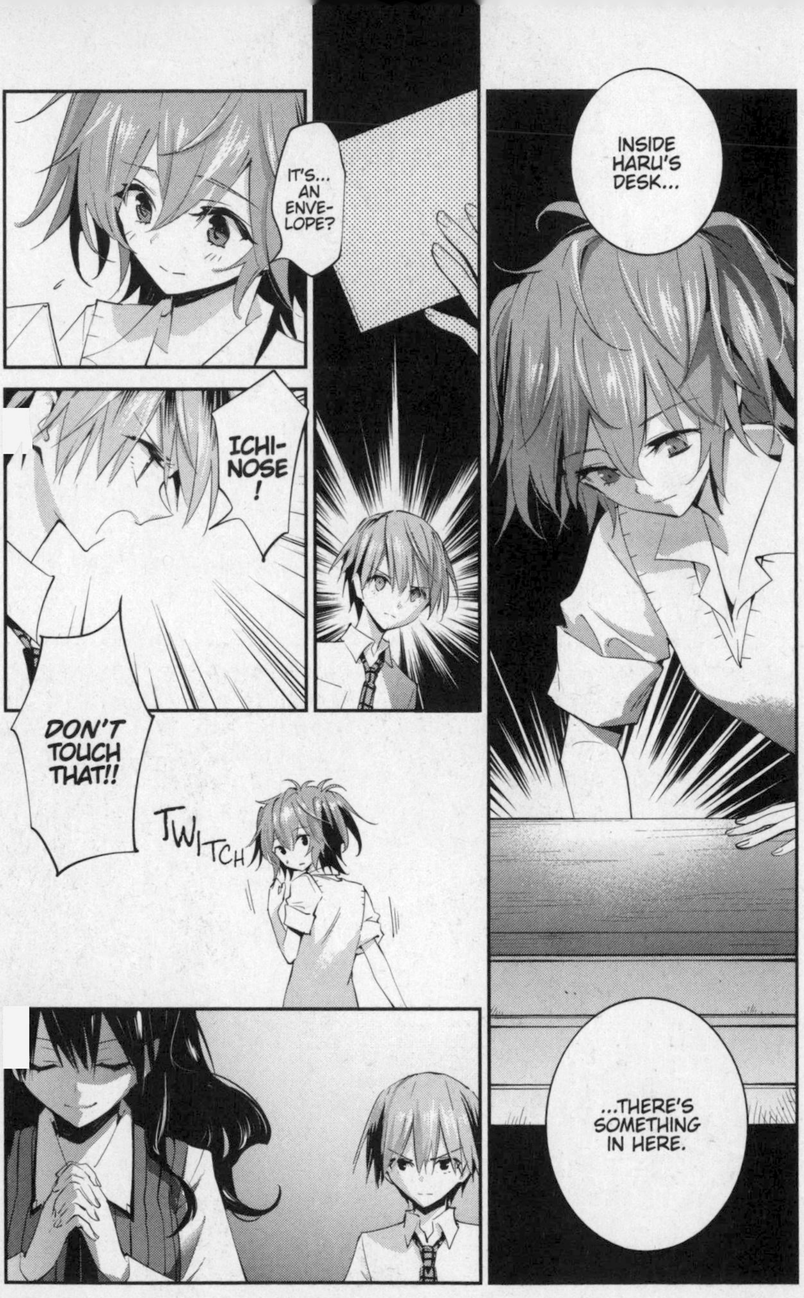
INSIDE HARU'S DESK...
...THERE'S SOMETHING IN HERE.
IT'S... AN ENVE-LOPE?
ICHI-NOSE!
DON'T TOUCH THAT!!
TWITCH

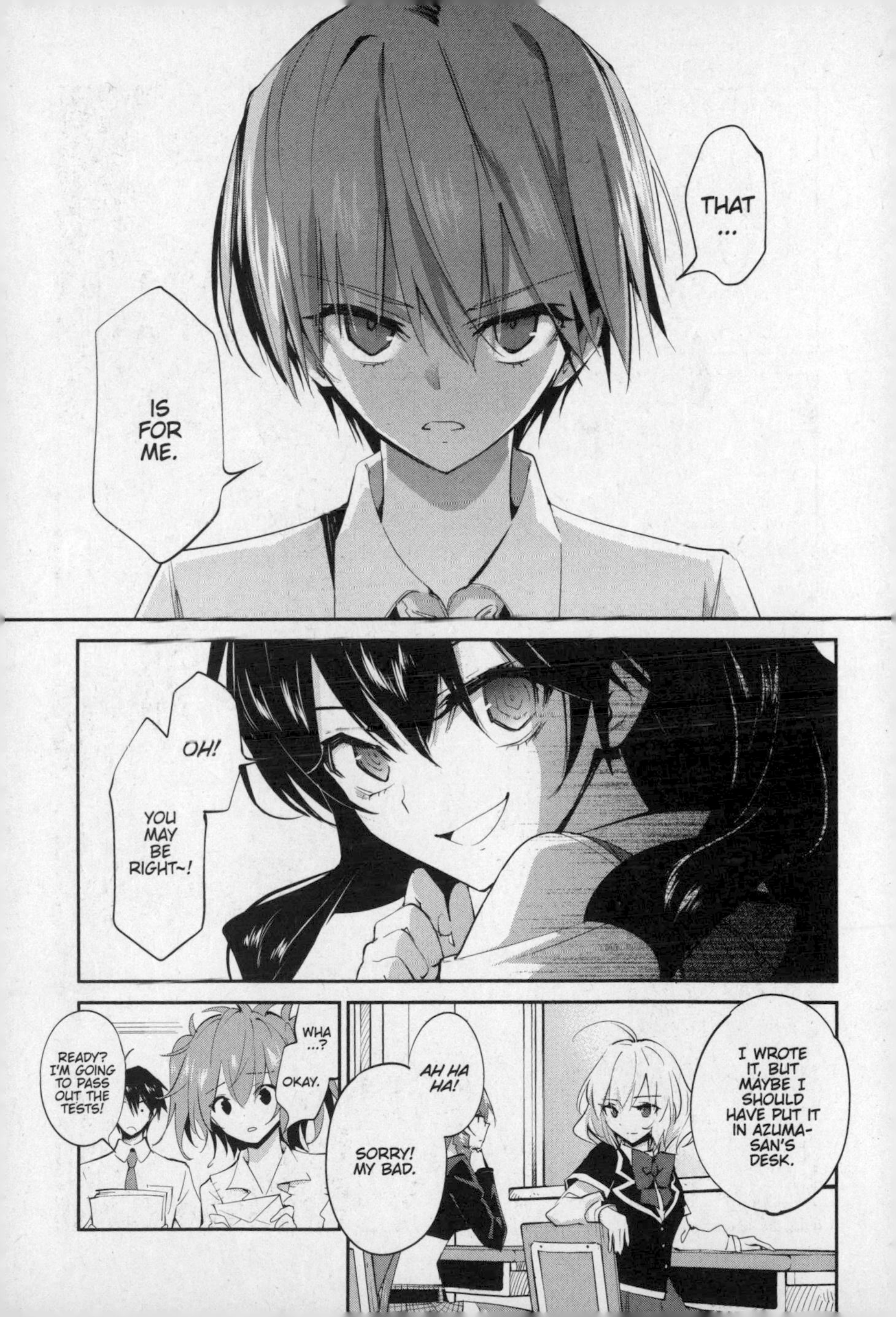
THAT ...
IS FOR ME.
OH!
YOU MAY BE RIGHT~!
I WROTE IT, BUT MAYBE I SHOULD HAVE PUT IT IN AZUMA-SAN'S DESK.
AH HA HA!
SORRY! MY BAD.
WHA ...?
OKAY.
READY? I'M GOING TO PASS OUT THE TESTS!

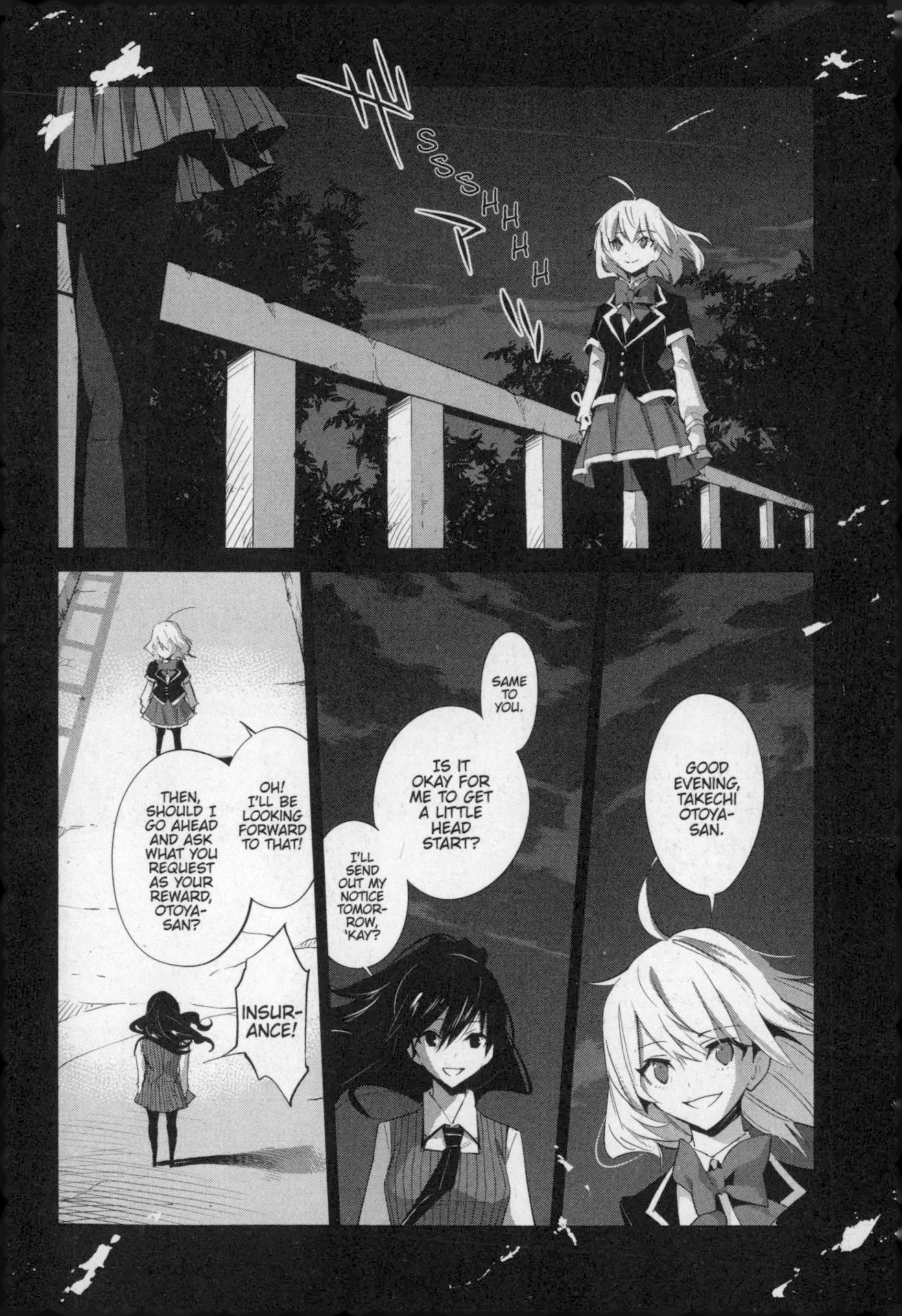
SSSHHHHH
GOOD EVENING, TAKECHI OTOYA-SAN.
SAME TO YOU.
IS IT OKAY FOR ME TO GET A LITTLE HEAD START?
I'LL SEND OUT MY NOTICE TOMOR-ROW, 'KAY?
OH! I'LL BE LOOKING FORWARD TO THAT!
THEN, SHOULD I GO AHEAD AND ASK WHAT YOU REQUEST AS YOUR REWARD, OTOYA-SAN?
INSUR-ANCE!

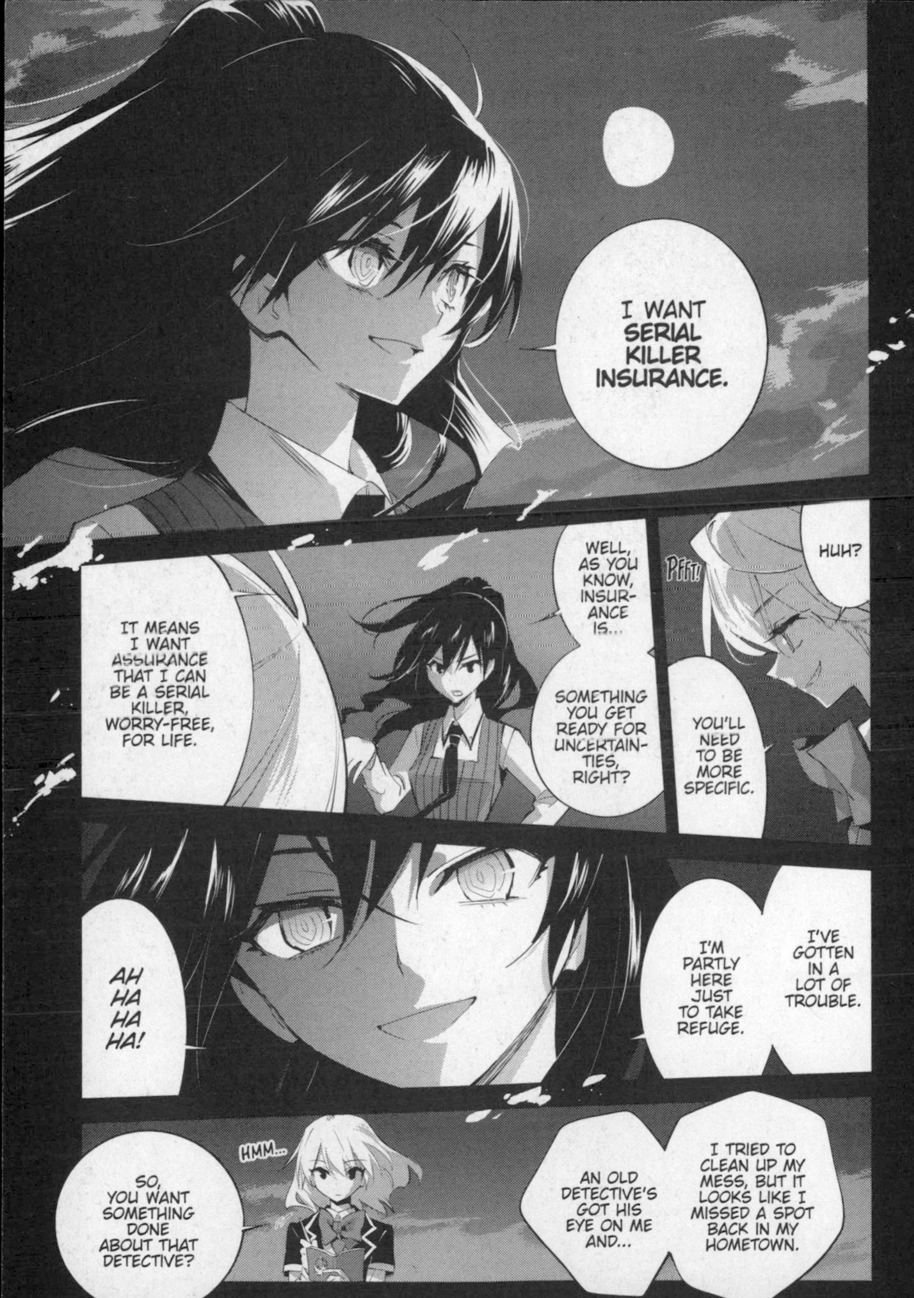
I WANT SERIAL KILLER INSURANCE.
HUH?
PFFT!
YOU'LL NEED TO BE MORE SPECIFIC.
WELL, AS YOU KNOW, INSURANCE IS...
SOMETHING YOU GET READY FOR UNCERTAINTIES, RIGHT?
IT MEANS I WANT ASSURANCE THAT I CAN BE A SERIAL KILLER, WORRY-FREE, FOR LIFE.
I'VE GOTTEN IN A LOT OF TROUBLE.
I'M PARTLY HERE JUST TO TAKE REFUGE.
AH HA HA HA!
I TRIED TO CLEAN UP MY MESS, BUT IT LOOKS LIKE I MISSED A SPOT BACK IN MY HOMETOWN.
AN OLD DETECTIVE'S GOT HIS EYE ON ME AND...
HMM...
SO, YOU WANT SOMETHING DONE ABOUT THAT DETECTIVE?

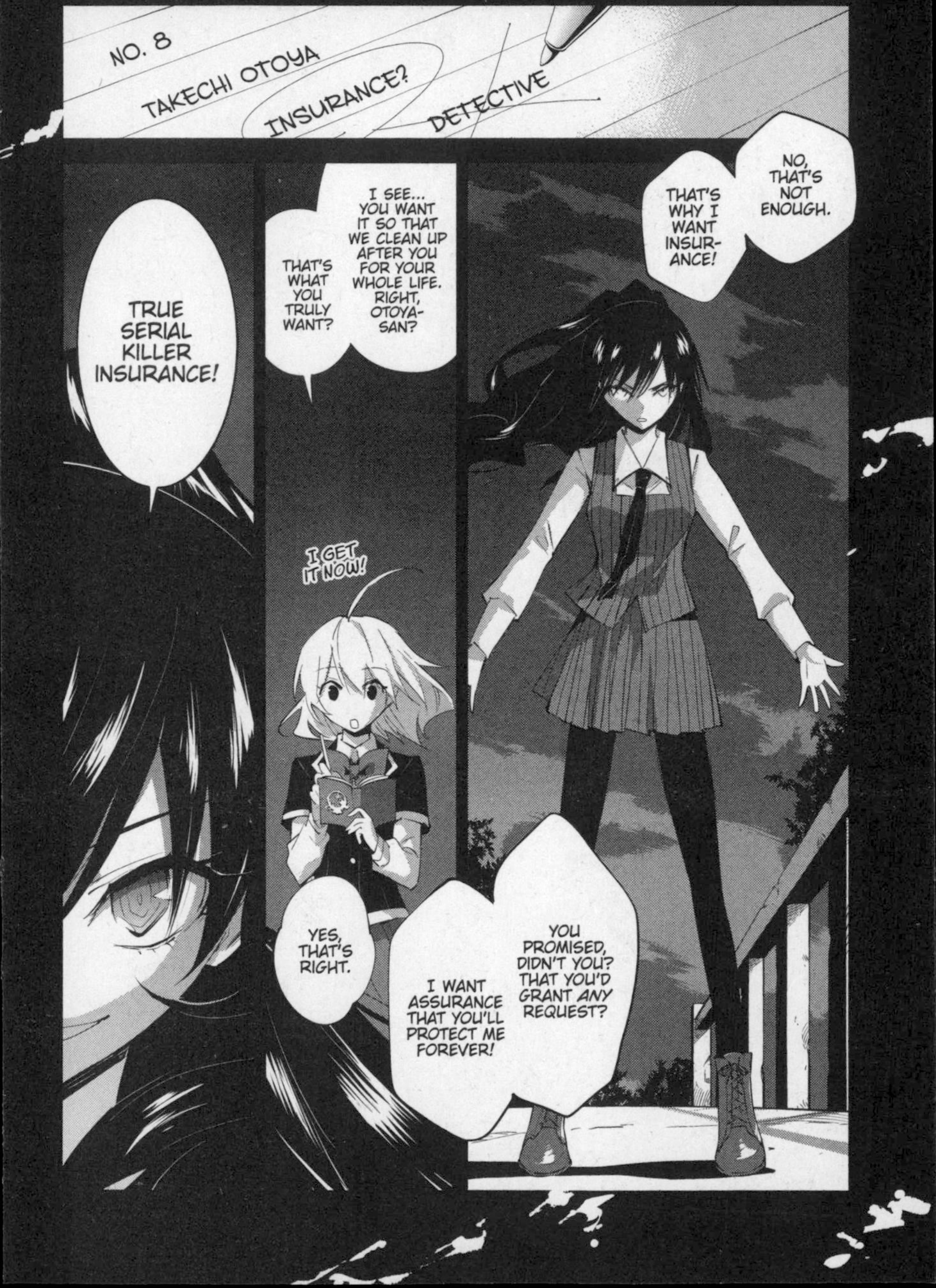
NO. 8
TAKECHI OTOYA
INSURANCE?
DETECTIVE
NO, THAT'S NOT ENOUGH.
THAT'S WHY I WANT INSURANCE!
YOU PROMISED, DIDN'T YOU? THAT YOU'D GRANT ANY REQUEST?
I WANT ASSURANCE THAT YOU'LL PROTECT ME FOREVER!
I SEE... YOU WANT IT SO THAT WE CLEAN UP AFTER YOU FOR YOUR WHOLE LIFE. RIGHT, OTOYA-SAN?
THAT'S WHAT YOU TRULY WANT?
I GET IT NOW!
YES, THAT'S RIGHT.
TRUE SERIAL KILLER INSURANCE!

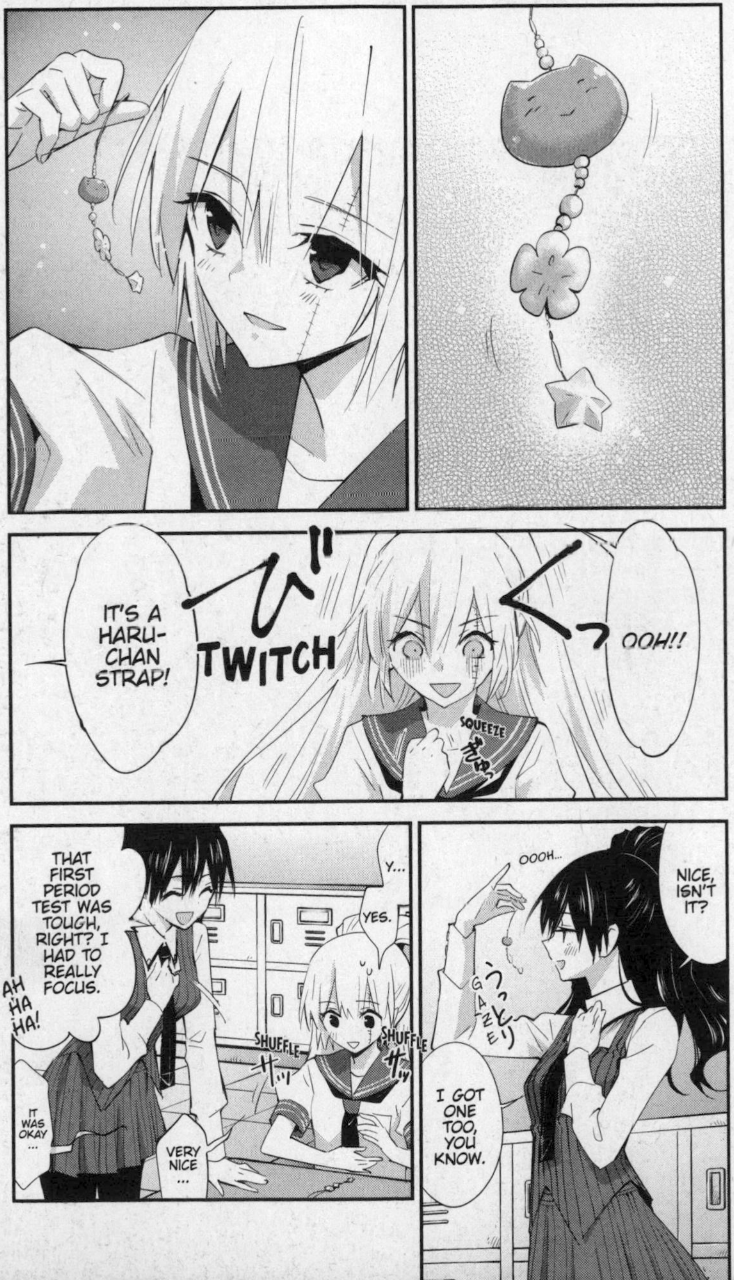
OOH!!
くっ
SQUEEZE
ぎゅっ
び
TWITCH
IT'S A HARU-CHAN STRAP!
NICE, ISN'T IT?
OOOH...
GAZE
うっとり
I GOT ONE TOO, YOU KNOW.
Y... YES.
SHUFFLE
サッ
THAT FIRST PERIOD TEST WAS TOUGH, RIGHT? I HAD TO REALLY FOCUS.
AH HA HA!
SHUFFLE
サッ
VERY NICE ...
IT WAS OKAY ...

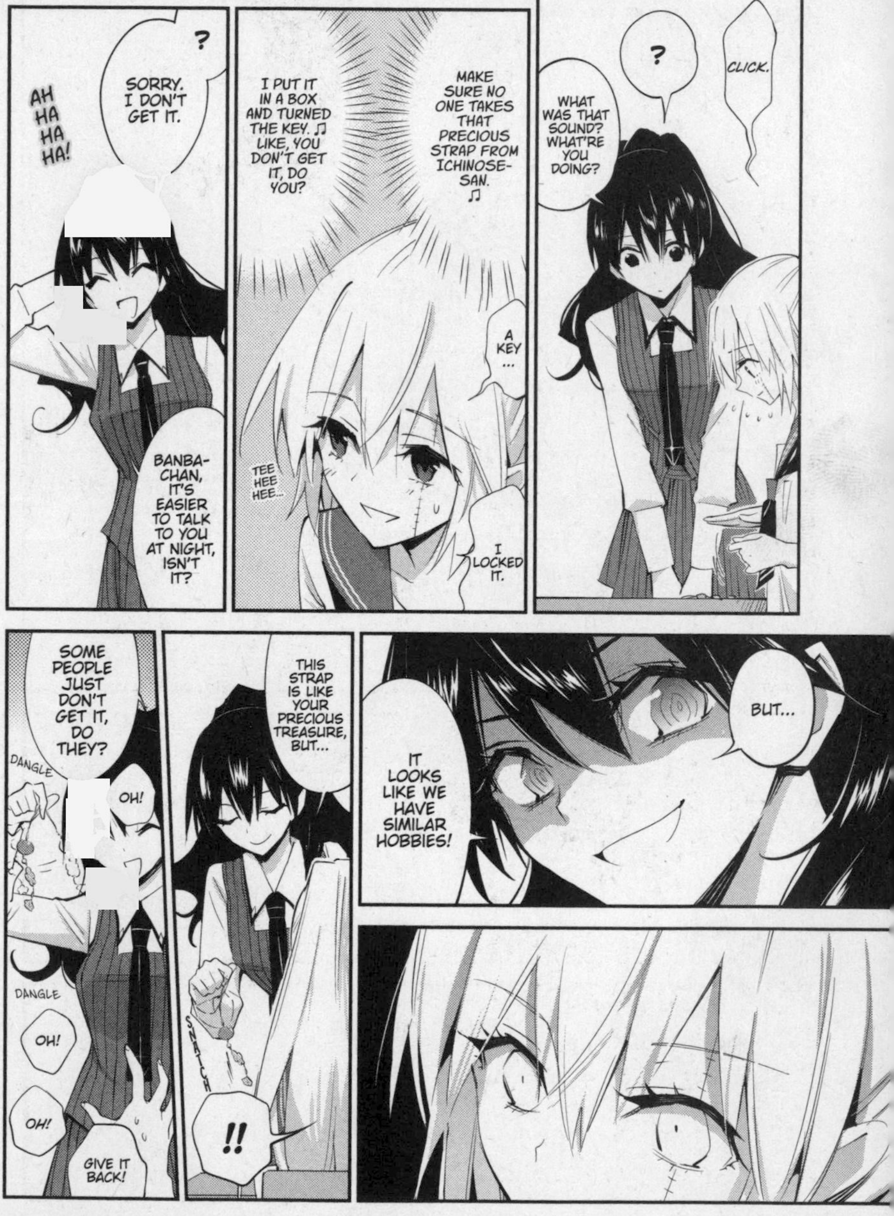
CLICK.
?
WHAT WAS THAT SOUND? WHAT'RE YOU DOING?
MAKE SURE NO ONE TAKES THAT PRECIOUS STRAP FROM ICHINOSE-SAN. ♫
I PUT IT IN A BOX AND TURNED THE KEY. ♫ LIKE, YOU DON'T GET IT, DO YOU?
A KEY...
TEE HEE HEE...
I LOCKED IT.
?
SORRY. I DON'T GET IT.
AH HA HA HA!
BANBA-CHAN, IT'S EASIER TO TALK TO YOU AT NIGHT, ISN'T IT?
BUT...
IT LOOKS LIKE WE HAVE SIMILAR HOBBIES!
THIS STRAP IS LIKE YOUR PRECIOUS TREASURE, BUT...
SNATCH
!!
SOME PEOPLE JUST DON'T GET IT, DO THEY?
DANGLE
OH!
DANGLE
OH!
OH!
GIVE IT BACK!

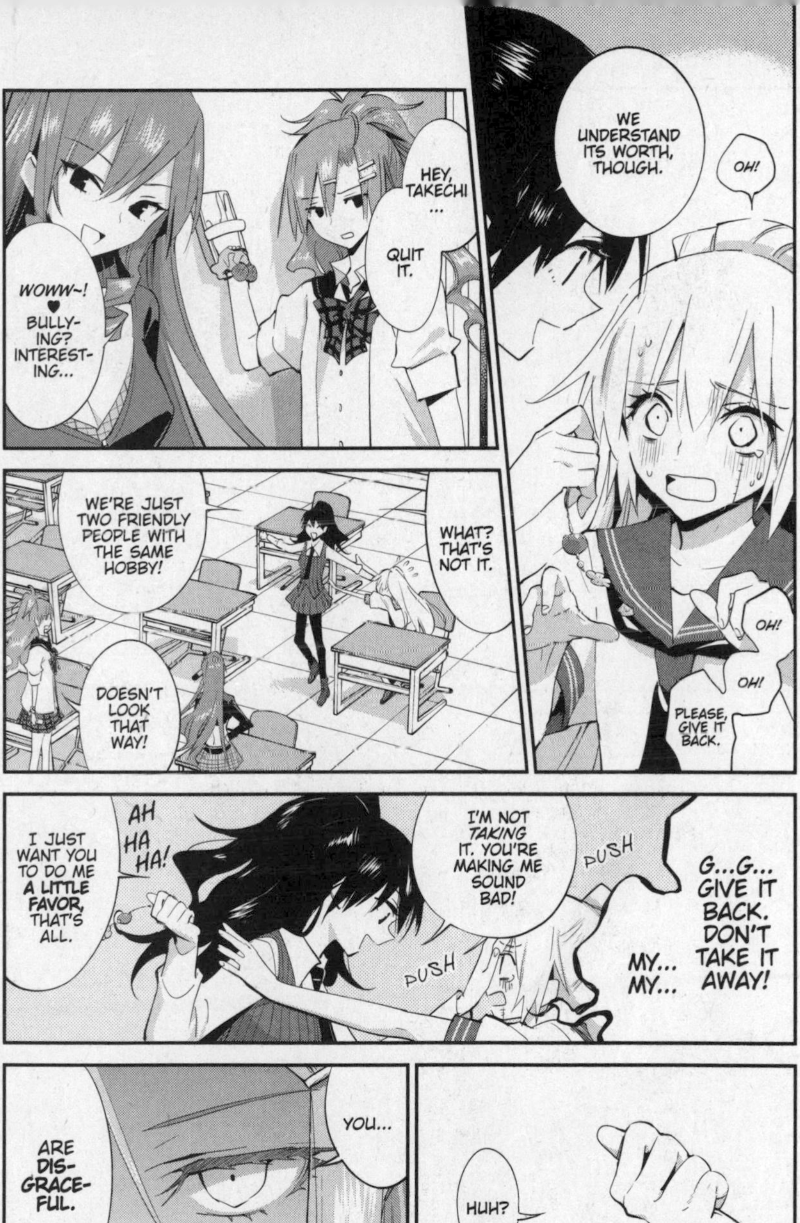
WE UNDERSTAND ITS WORTH, THOUGH.
OH!
OH!
OH!
PLEASE, GIVE IT BACK.
HEY, TAKECHI ...
QUIT IT.
WOWW~! ♥ BULLY-ING? INTEREST-ING...
WHAT? THAT'S NOT IT.
WE'RE JUST TWO FRIENDLY PEOPLE WITH THE SAME HOBBY!
DOESN'T LOOK THAT WAY!
G...G... GIVE IT BACK. DON'T TAKE IT AWAY!
MY... MY...
PUSH
I'M NOT *TAKING* IT. YOU'RE MAKING ME SOUND BAD!
PUSH
AH HA HA!
I JUST WANT YOU TO DO ME **A LITTLE FAVOR,** THAT'S ALL.
HUH?
YOU...
ARE DIS-GRACE-FUL.

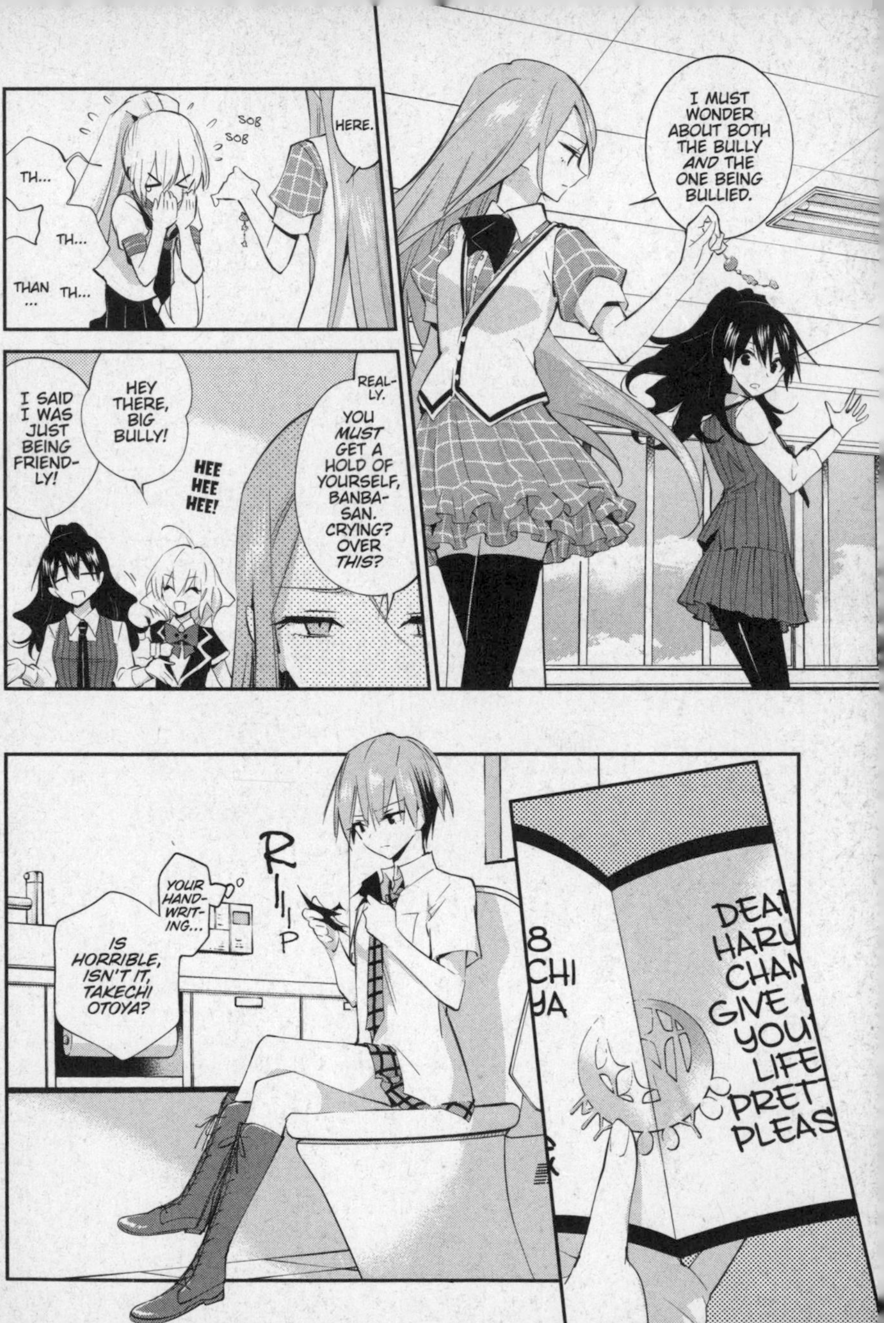
I MUST WONDER ABOUT BOTH THE BULLY AND THE ONE BEING BULLIED.
HERE.
SOB SOB
TH...
TH...
TH...
THAN...
REALLY. YOU MUST GET A HOLD OF YOURSELF, BANBA-SAN. CRYING? OVER THIS?
HEY THERE, BIG BULLY!
HEE HEE HEE!
I SAID I WAS JUST BEING FRIENDLY!
DEA
HARU
CHAN
GIVE
YOU
LIFE
PRETT
PLEAS
RIIIIP
YOUR HANDWRITING...
IS HORRIBLE, ISN'T IT, TAKECHI OTOYA?

riddle story of devil

Chapter 11
Commence Operations

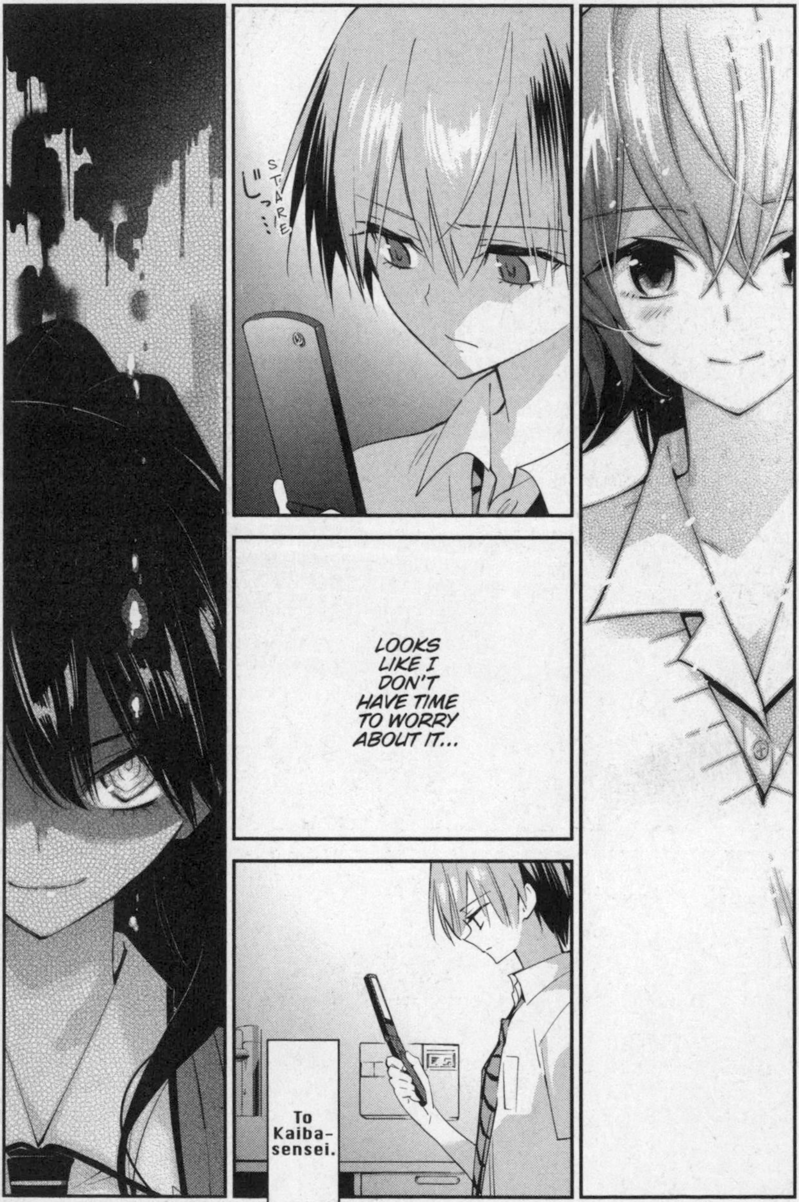
じっ…
STARE
LOOKS LIKE I DON'T HAVE TIME TO WORRY ABOUT IT...
To Kaiba-sensei.

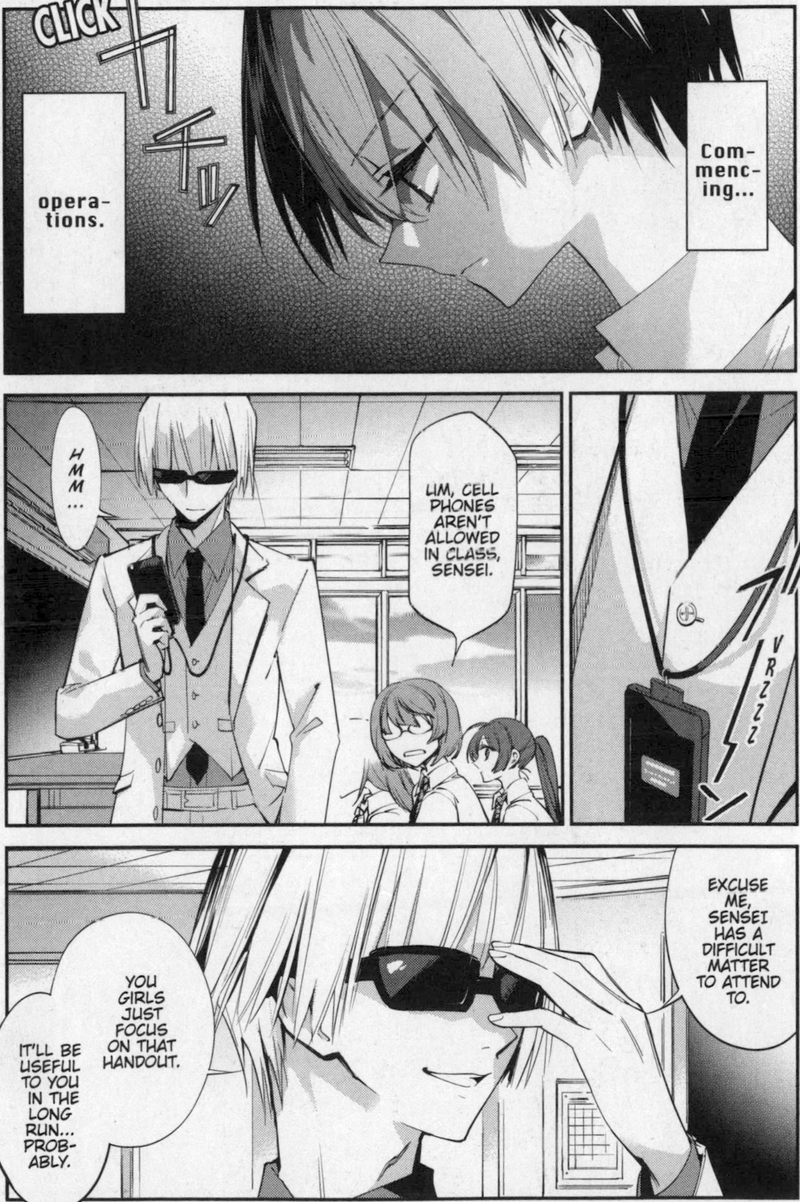
Commencing...
CLICK
operations.
VRZZZ
UM, CELL PHONES AREN'T ALLOWED IN CLASS, SENSEI.
HMM...
EXCUSE ME, SENSEI HAS A DIFFICULT MATTER TO ATTEND TO.
YOU GIRLS JUST FOCUS ON THAT HANDOUT.
IT'LL BE USEFUL TO YOU IN THE LONG RUN... PROBABLY.

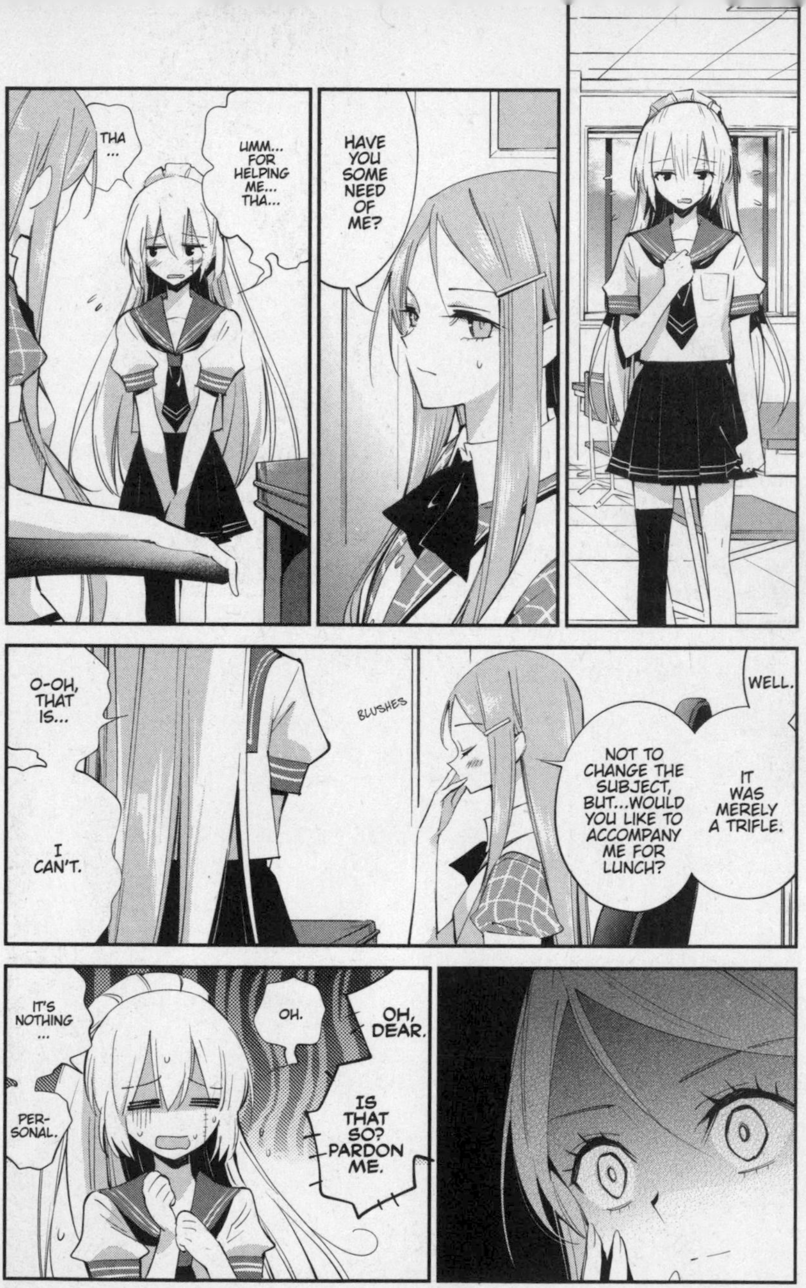
HAVE YOU SOME NEED OF ME?
UMM... FOR HELPING ME... THA...
THA ...
WELL.
IT WAS MERELY A TRIFLE.
NOT TO CHANGE THE SUBJECT, BUT...WOULD YOU LIKE TO ACCOMPANY ME FOR LUNCH?
BLUSHES
O-OH, THAT IS...
I CAN'T.
OH, DEAR.
OH.
IS THAT SO? PARDON ME.
IT'S NOTHING ...
PER-SONAL.

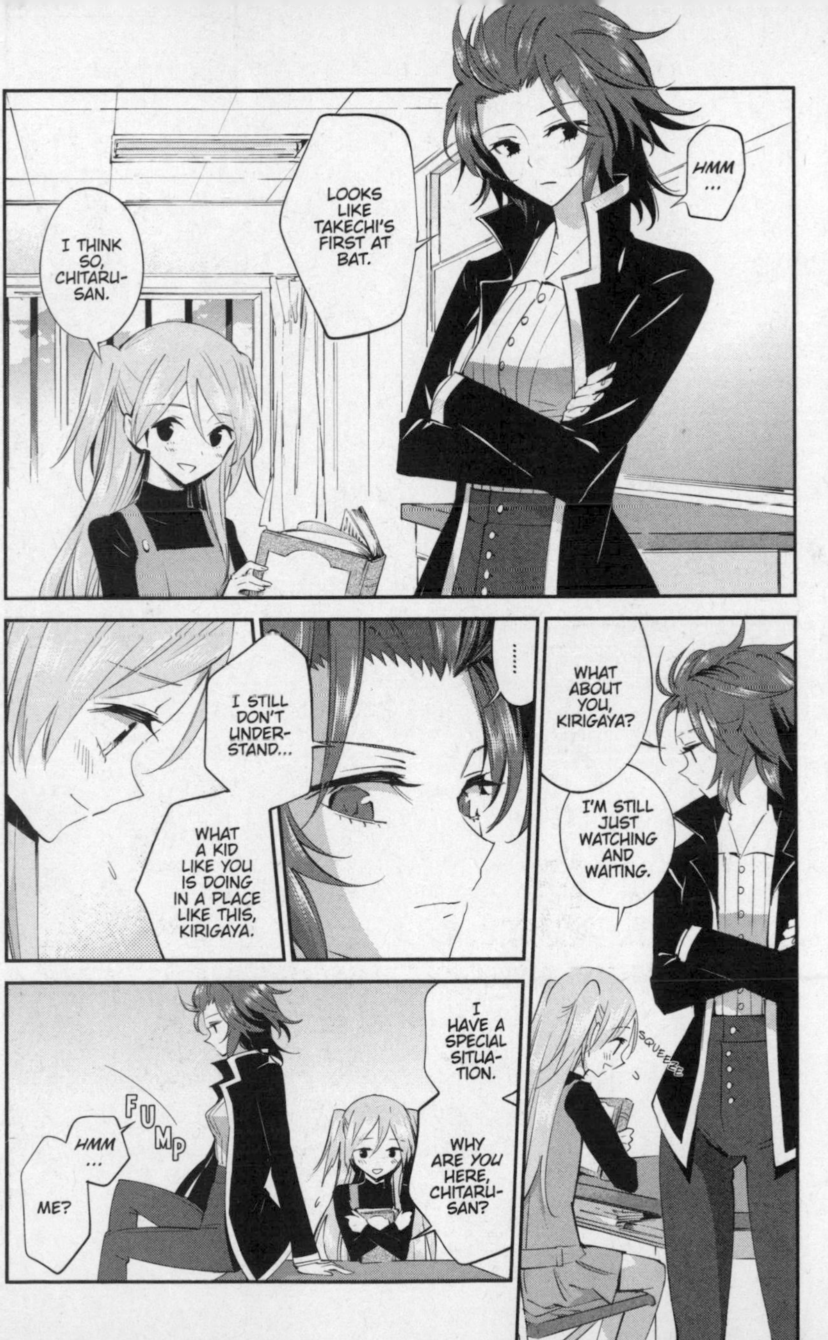
HMM ...
LOOKS LIKE TAKECHI'S FIRST AT BAT.
I THINK SO, CHITARU-SAN.
WHAT ABOUT YOU, KIRIGAYA?
I'M STILL JUST WATCHING AND WAITING.
SQUEEZE
......
I STILL DON'T UNDER-STAND...
WHAT A KID LIKE YOU IS DOING IN A PLACE LIKE THIS, KIRIGAYA.
I HAVE A SPECIAL SITUA-TION.
WHY ARE *YOU* HERE, CHITARU-SAN?
FUMP
HMM ...
ME?

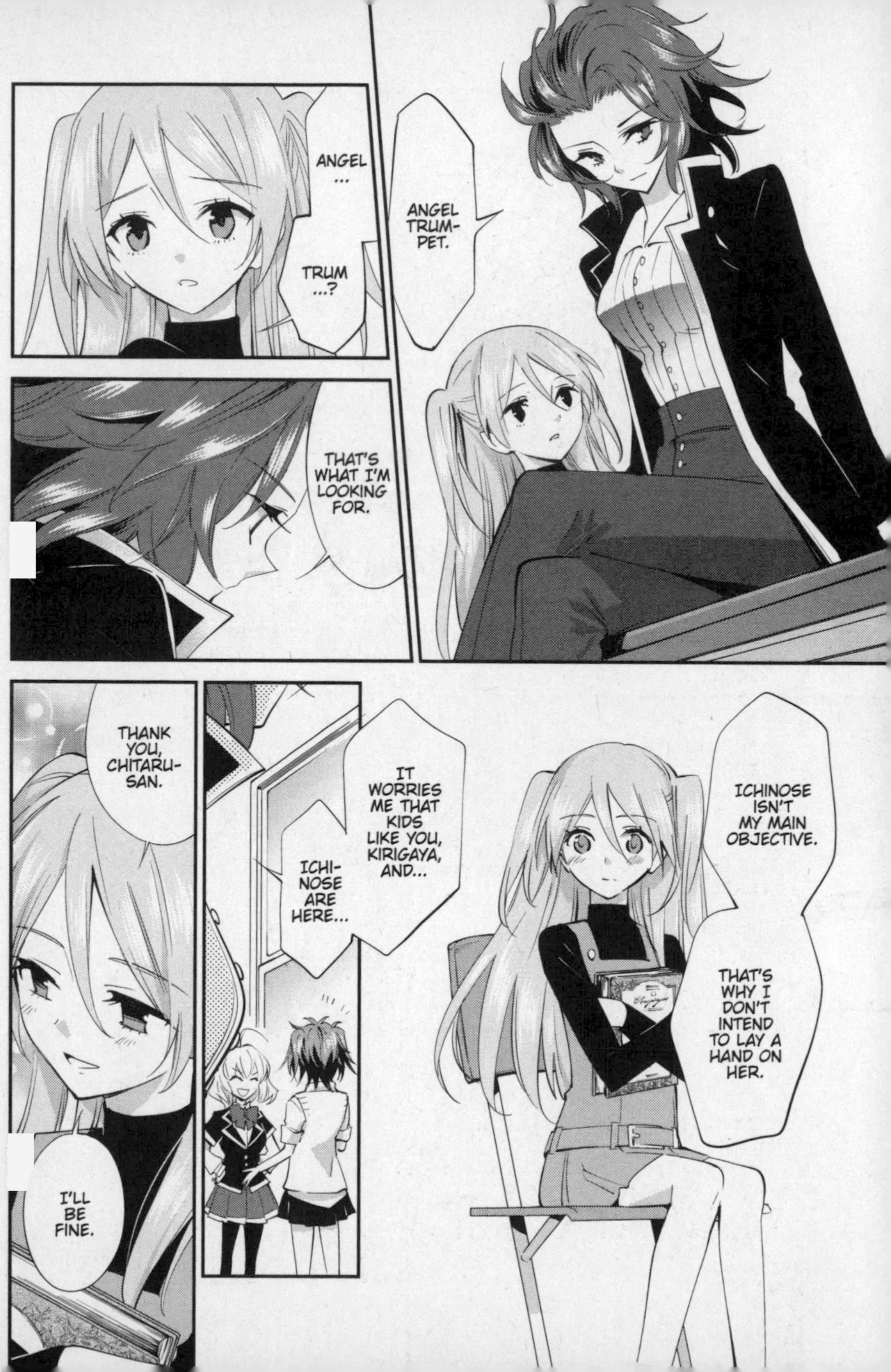
ANGEL TRUM-PET.
ANGEL ...
TRUM ...?
THAT'S WHAT I'M LOOKING FOR.
ICHINOSE ISN'T MY MAIN OBJECTIVE.
THAT'S WHY I DON'T INTEND TO LAY A HAND ON HER.
IT WORRIES ME THAT KIDS LIKE YOU, KIRIGAYA, AND...
ICHI-NOSE ARE HERE...
THANK YOU, CHITARU-SAN.
I'LL BE FINE.

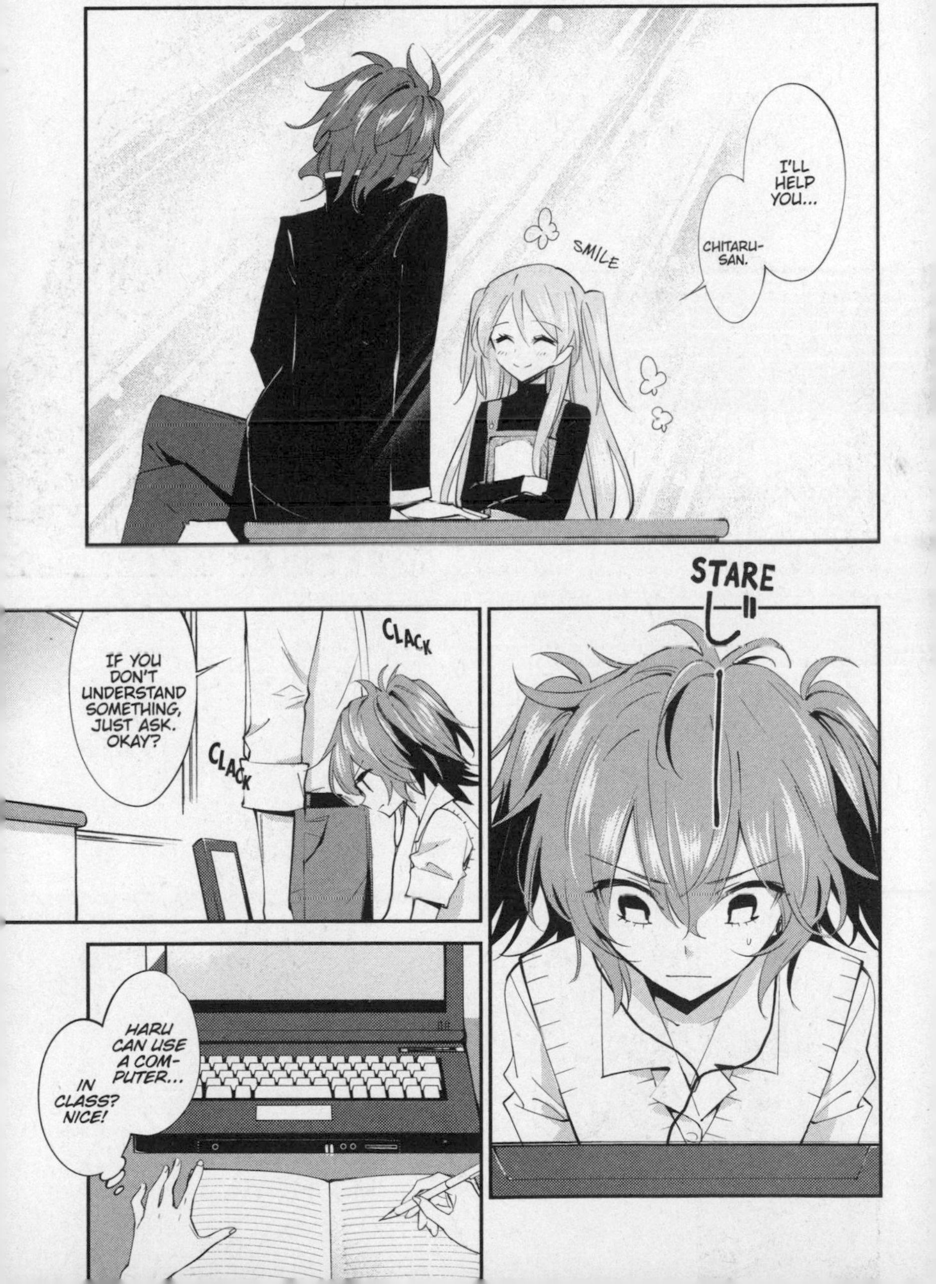
I'LL HELP YOU...
CHITARU-SAN.
SMILE
STARE
CLACK
IF YOU DON'T UNDERSTAND SOMETHING, JUST ASK. OKAY?
CLACK
HARU CAN USE A COMPUTER...
IN CLASS? NICE!

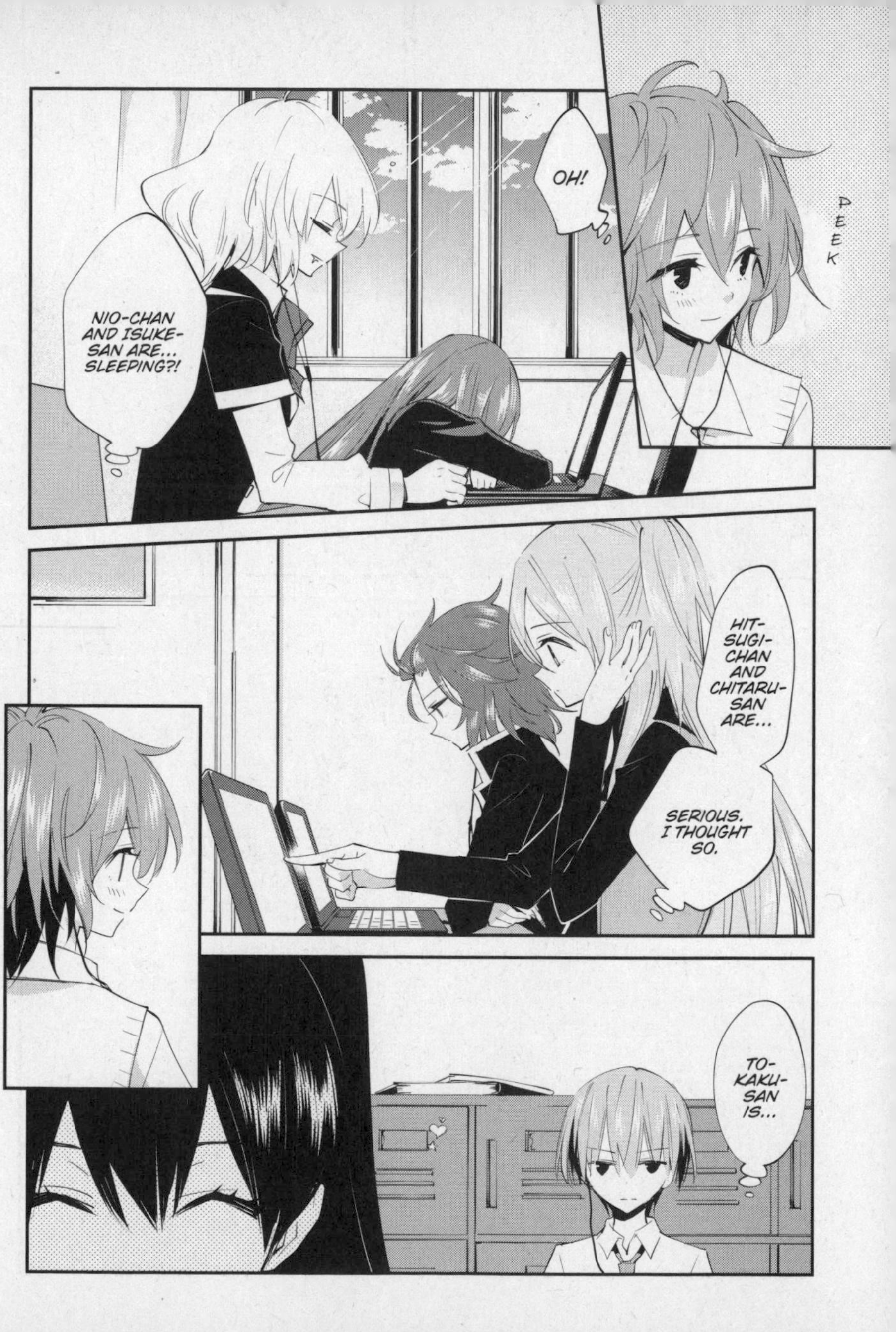
OH!
PEEK
NIO-CHAN AND ISUKE-SAN ARE... SLEEPING?!
HIT-SUGI-CHAN AND CHITARU-SAN ARE...
SERIOUS. I THOUGHT SO.
TO-KAKU-SAN IS...

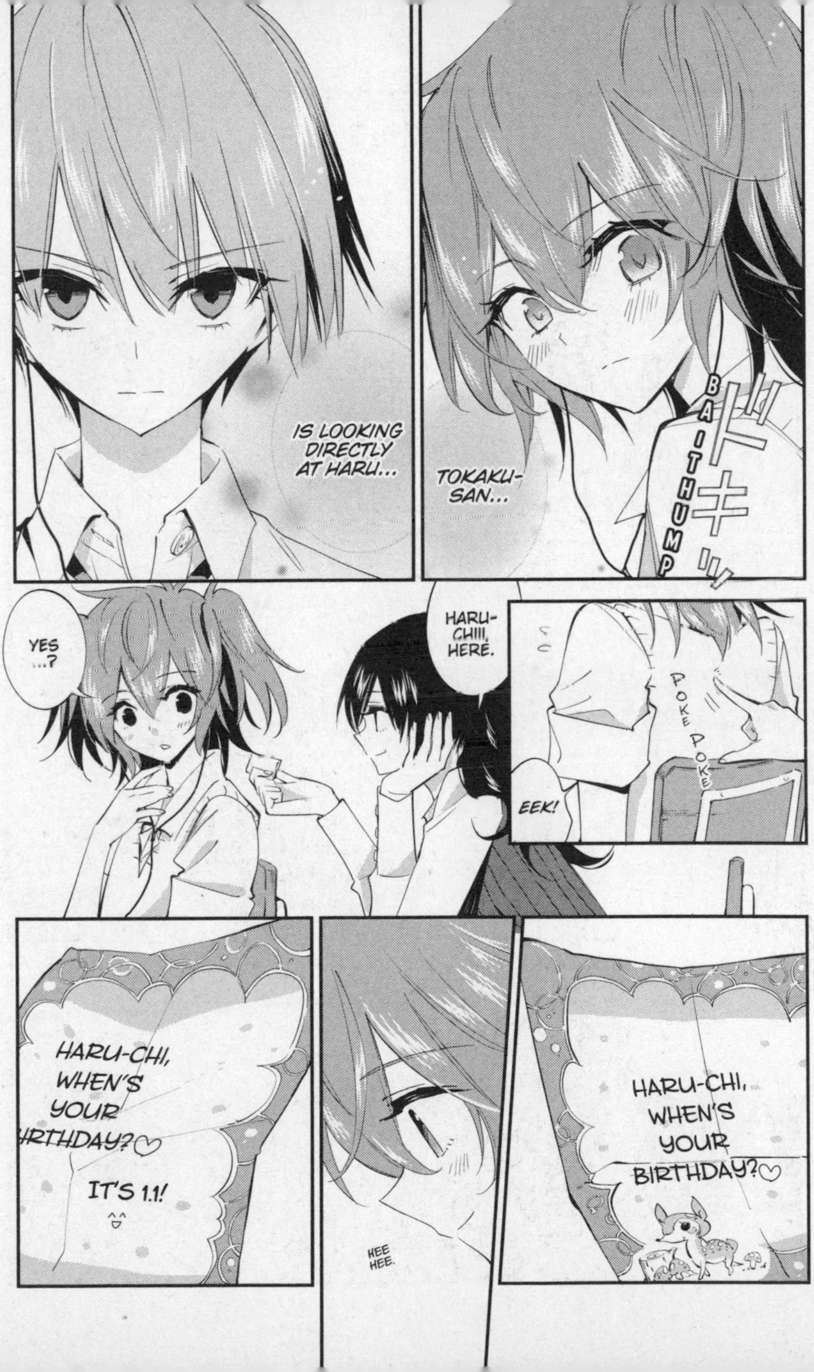
TOKAKU-SAN...
BA-THUMP
IS LOOKING DIRECTLY AT HARU...
POKE POKE
EEK!
HARU-CHIII, HERE.
YES ...?
HARU-CHI, WHEN'S YOUR BIRTHDAY?♡
HEE HEE.
HARU-CHI, WHEN'S YOUR IRTHDAY?♡
IT'S 1.1!
^^

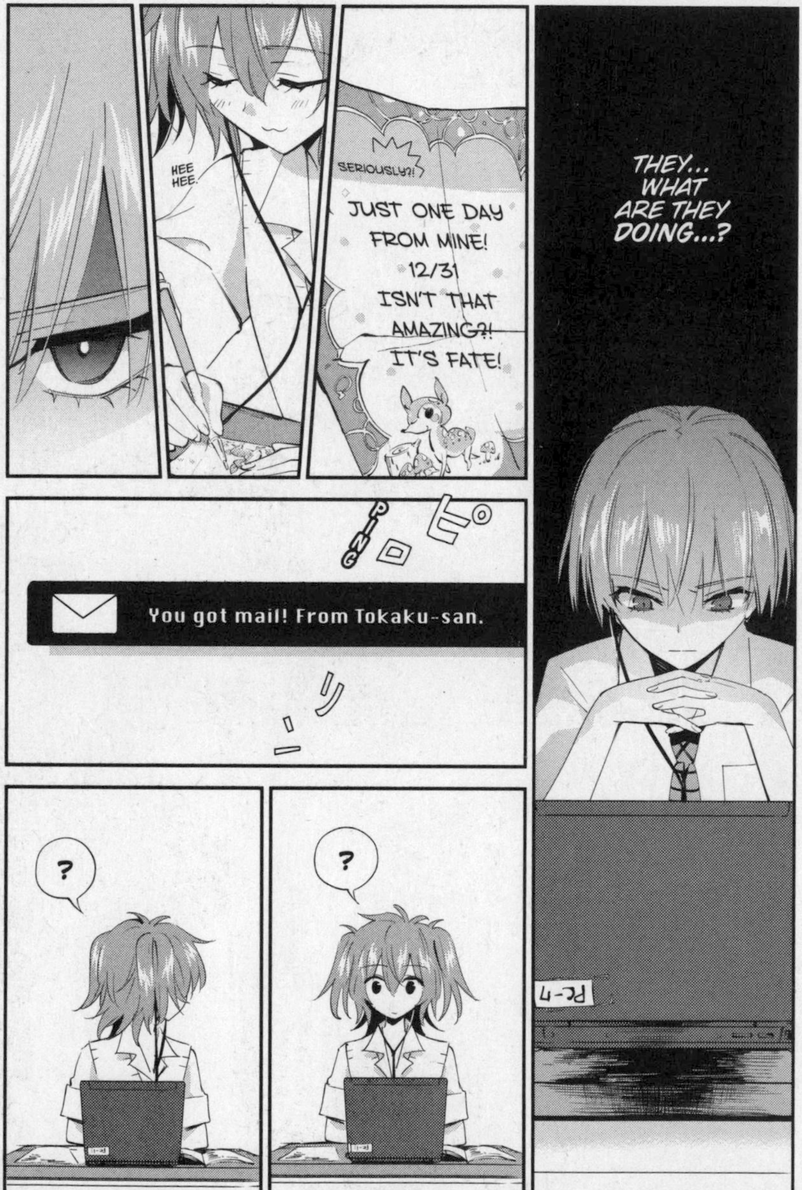
THEY... WHAT ARE THEY DOING...?
SERIOUSLY?!
JUST ONE DAY FROM MINE! 12/31 ISN'T THAT AMAZING?! IT'S FATE!
HEE HEE.
PING
You got mail! From Tokaku-san.
?
?

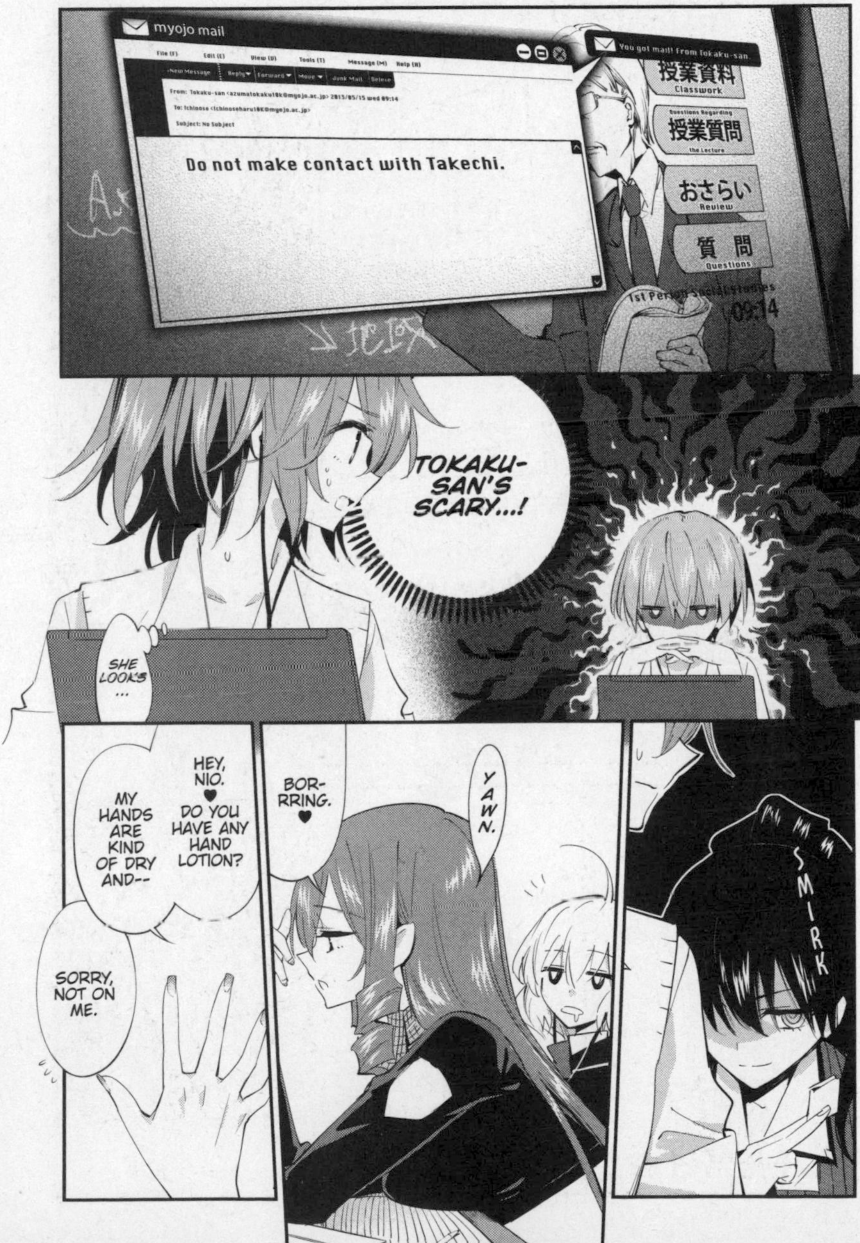
myojo mail
File (F) Edit (E) View (V) Tools (T) Message (M) Help (H)
+New Message Reply Forward Move Junk Mail Delete
From: Tokaku-san <azumatokaku18k@myojo.ac.jp> 2015/05/15 wed 09:14
To: Ichinose <ichinoseharu18K@myojo.ac.jp>
Subject: No Subject
Do not make contact with Takechi.
You got mail! From Tokaku-san.
授業資料 Classwork
Questions Regarding 授業質問 the Lecture
おさらい Review
質問 Questions
09:14
TOKAKU-SAN'S SCARY...!
SHE LOOKS...
SMIRK
YAWN.
BORR-RRING. ♥
HEY, NIO. ♥ DO YOU HAVE ANY HAND LOTION?
MY HANDS ARE KIND OF DRY AND--
SORRY, NOT ON ME.

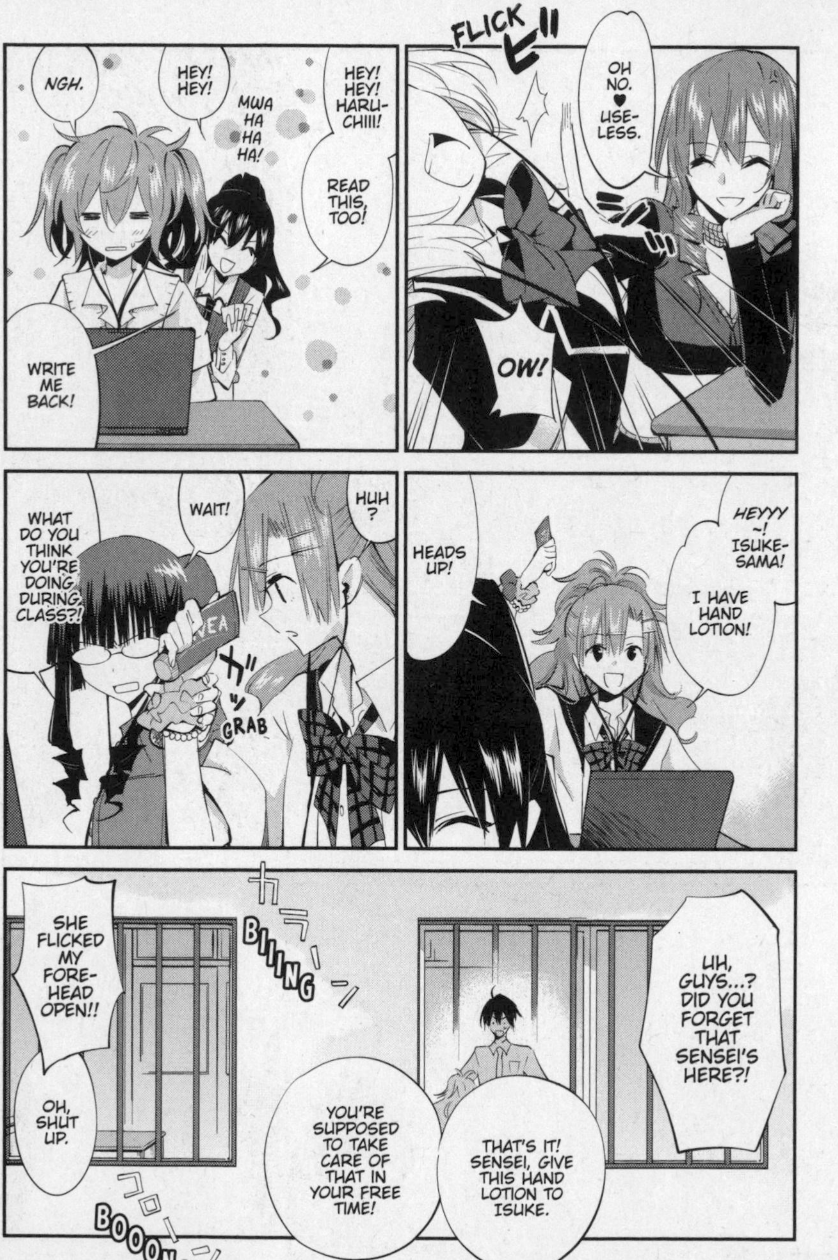
FLICK
OH NO. ♥ USE-LESS.
OW!
HEY! HEY! HARU-CHIII!
READ THIS, TOO!
MWA HA HA HA!
HEY! HEY!
NGH.
WRITE ME BACK!
HEYYY ~! ISUKE-SAMA!
I HAVE HAND LOTION!
HEADS UP!
HUH ?
WAIT!
WHAT DO YOU THINK YOU'RE DOING DURING CLASS?!
GRAB
UH, GUYS...? DID YOU FORGET THAT SENSEI'S HERE?!
THAT'S IT! SENSEI, GIVE THIS HAND LOTION TO ISUKE.
YOU'RE SUPPOSED TO TAKE CARE OF THAT IN YOUR FREE TIME!
BIIING
SHE FLICKED MY FORE-HEAD OPEN!!
OH, SHUT UP.
BOOONG

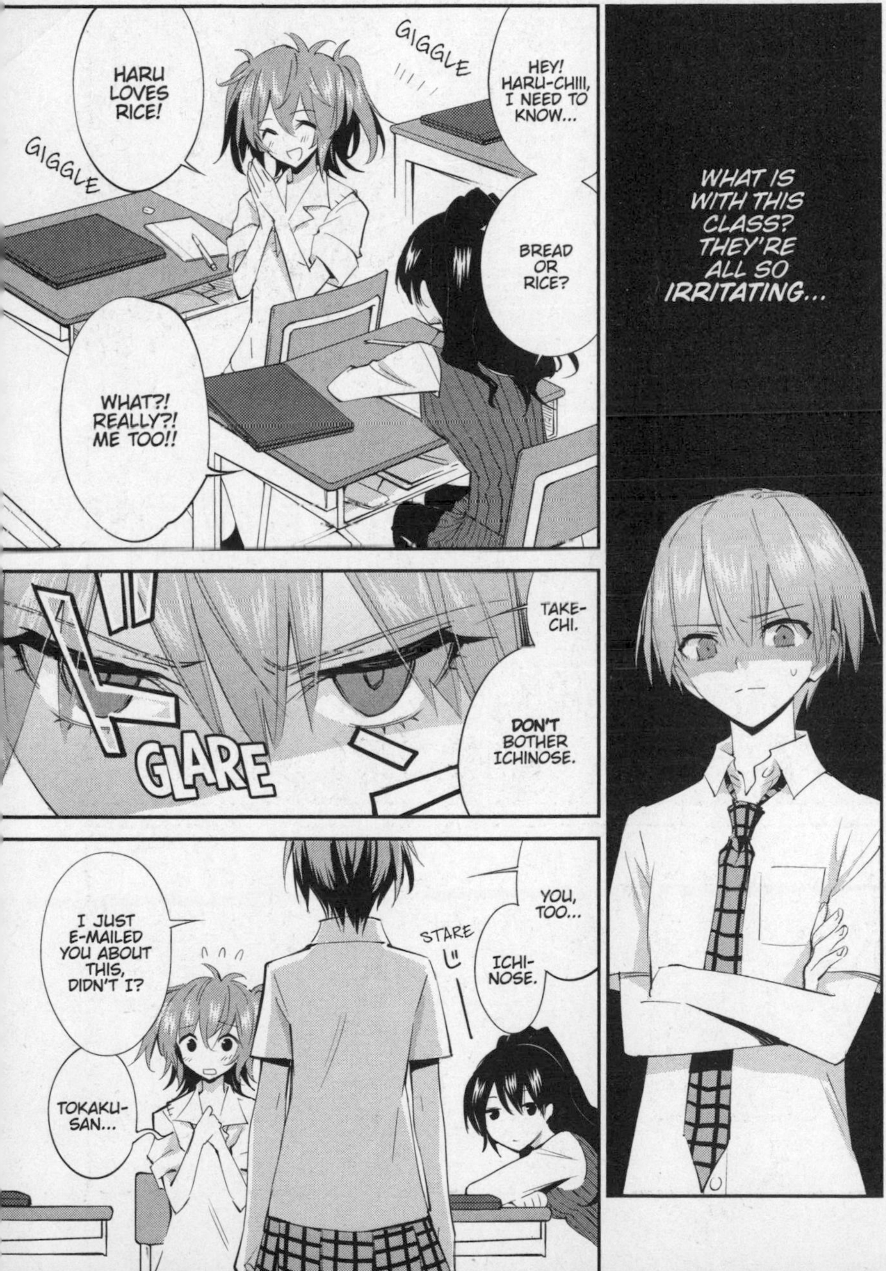
WHAT IS WITH THIS CLASS? THEY'RE ALL SO IRRITATING...
HEY! HARU-CHIII, I NEED TO KNOW...
GIGGLE
BREAD OR RICE?
HARU LOVES RICE!
GIGGLE
WHAT?! REALLY?! ME TOO!!
TAKE-CHI.
DON'T BOTHER ICHINOSE.
GLARE
YOU, TOO...
ICHI-NOSE.
STARE
I JUST E-MAILED YOU ABOUT THIS, DIDN'T I?
TOKAKU-SAN...

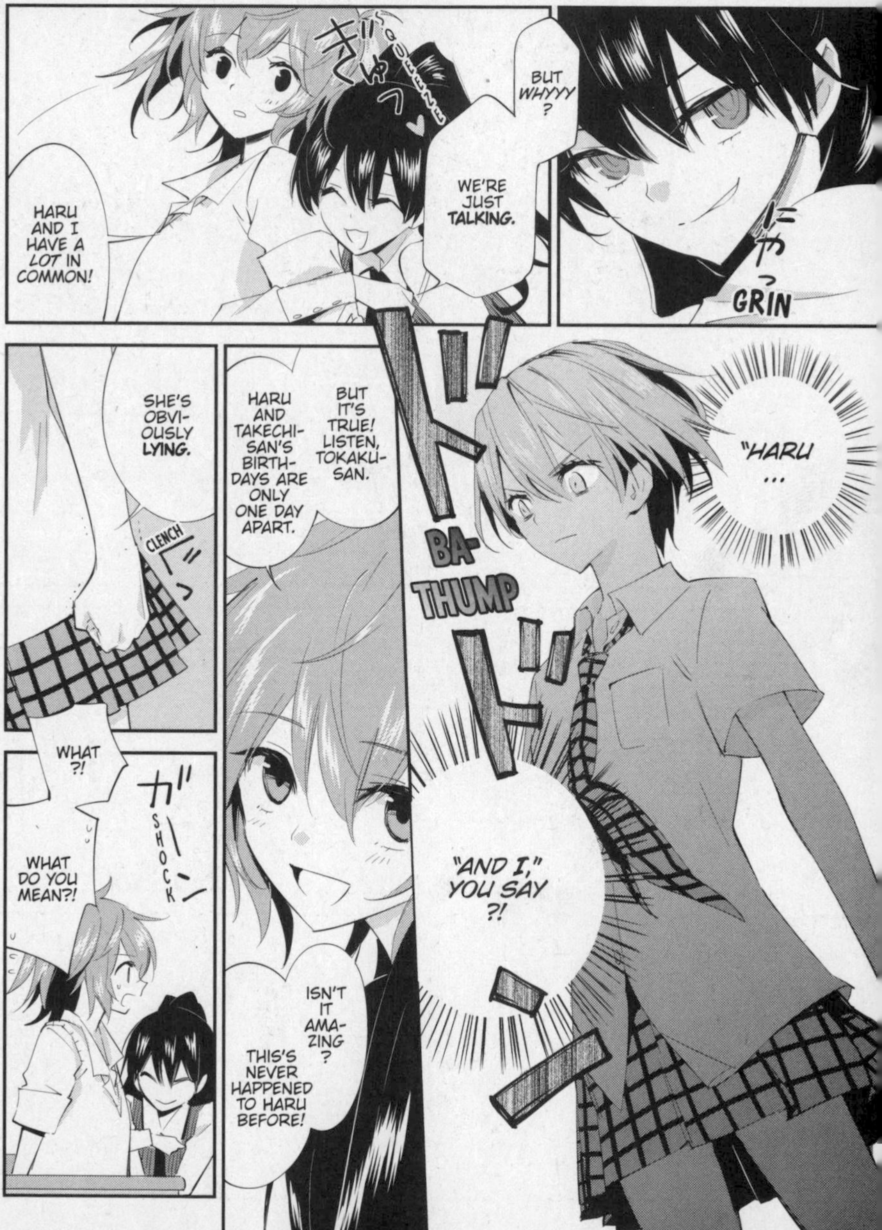
GRIN
BUT WHYYY?
WE'RE JUST TALKING.
SQUEEZE
HARU AND I HAVE A LOT IN COMMON!
"HARU ...
BA-THUMP
"AND I," YOU SAY ?!
BUT IT'S TRUE! LISTEN, TOKAKU-SAN.
HARU AND TAKECHI-SAN'S BIRTHDAYS ARE ONLY ONE DAY APART.
ISN'T IT AMAZING?
THIS'S NEVER HAPPENED TO HARU BEFORE!
SHE'S OBVIOUSLY LYING.
CLENCH
WHAT?!
SHOCK
WHAT DO YOU MEAN?!

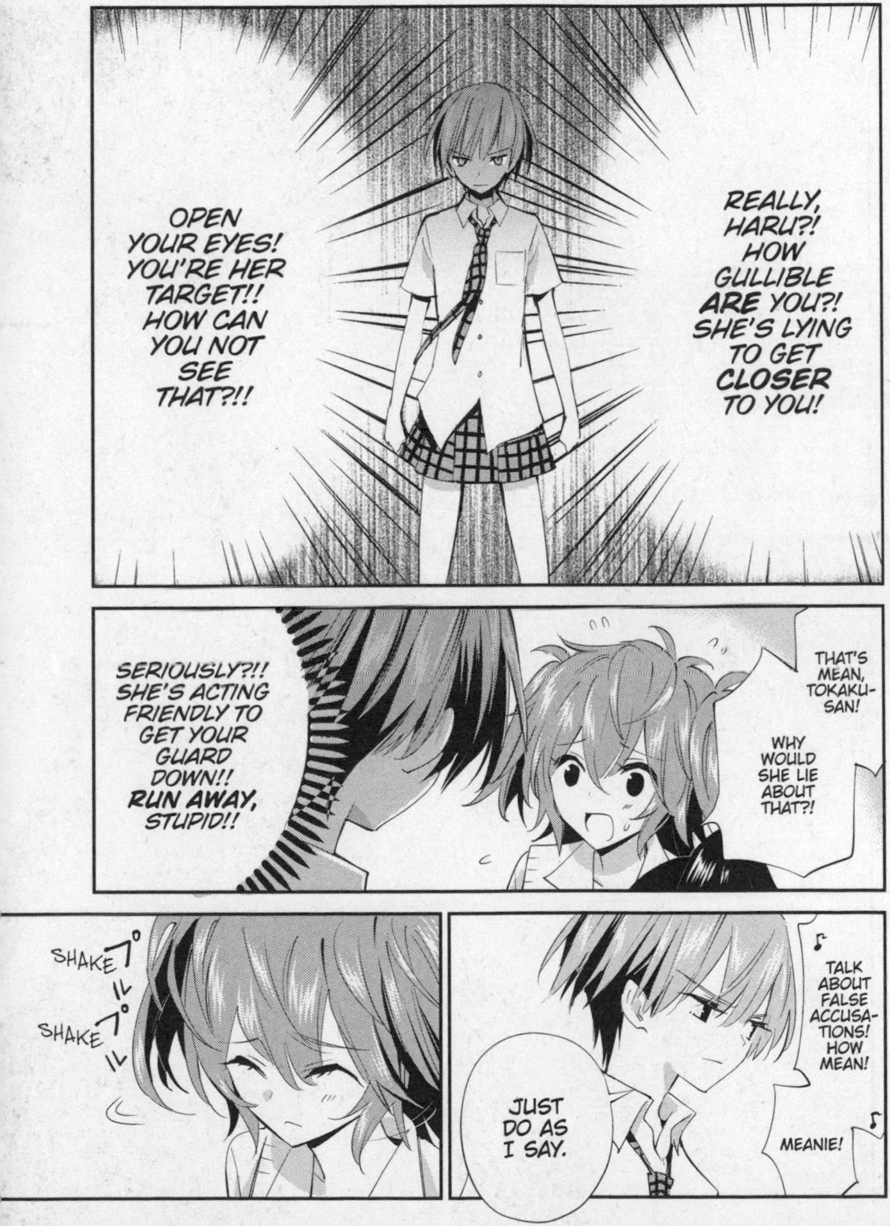
REALLY, HARU?! HOW GULLIBLE ARE YOU?! SHE'S LYING TO GET CLOSER TO YOU!
OPEN YOUR EYES! YOU'RE HER TARGET!! HOW CAN YOU NOT SEE THAT?!!
THAT'S MEAN, TOKAKU-SAN!
WHY WOULD SHE LIE ABOUT THAT?!
SERIOUSLY?!! SHE'S ACTING FRIENDLY TO GET YOUR GUARD DOWN!! RUN AWAY, STUPID!!
TALK ABOUT FALSE ACCUSATIONS! HOW MEAN!
MEANIE!
JUST DO AS I SAY.
SHAKE
SHAKE

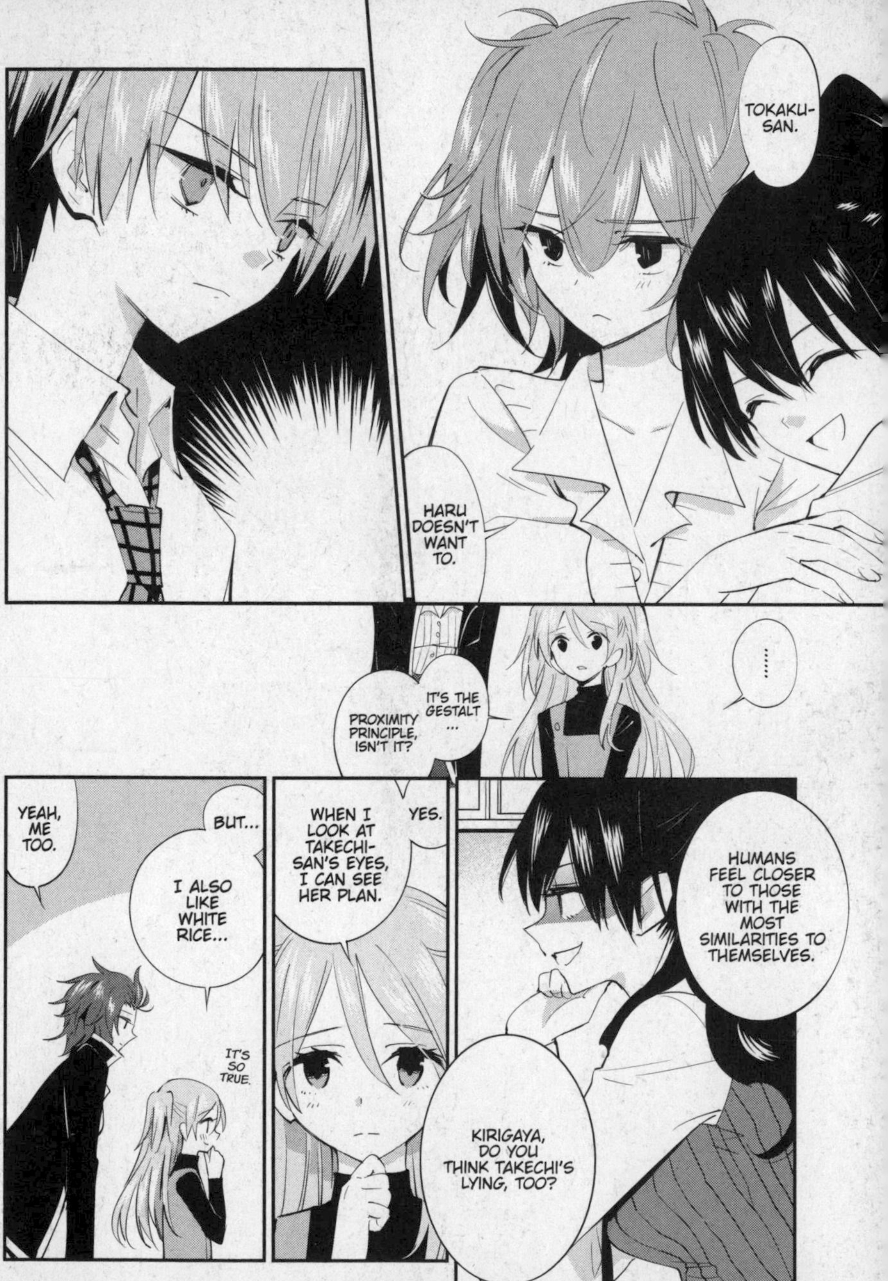
TOKAKU-SAN.
HARU DOESN'T WANT TO.
......
IT'S THE GESTALT ... PROXIMITY PRINCIPLE, ISN'T IT?
HUMANS FEEL CLOSER TO THOSE WITH THE MOST SIMILARITIES TO THEMSELVES.
KIRIGAYA, DO YOU THINK TAKECHI'S LYING, TOO?
YES.
WHEN I LOOK AT TAKECHI-SAN'S EYES, I CAN SEE HER PLAN.
BUT...
I ALSO LIKE WHITE RICE...
YEAH, ME TOO.
IT'S SO TRUE.

Chapter 12
Bullying Isn't Nice, You Know

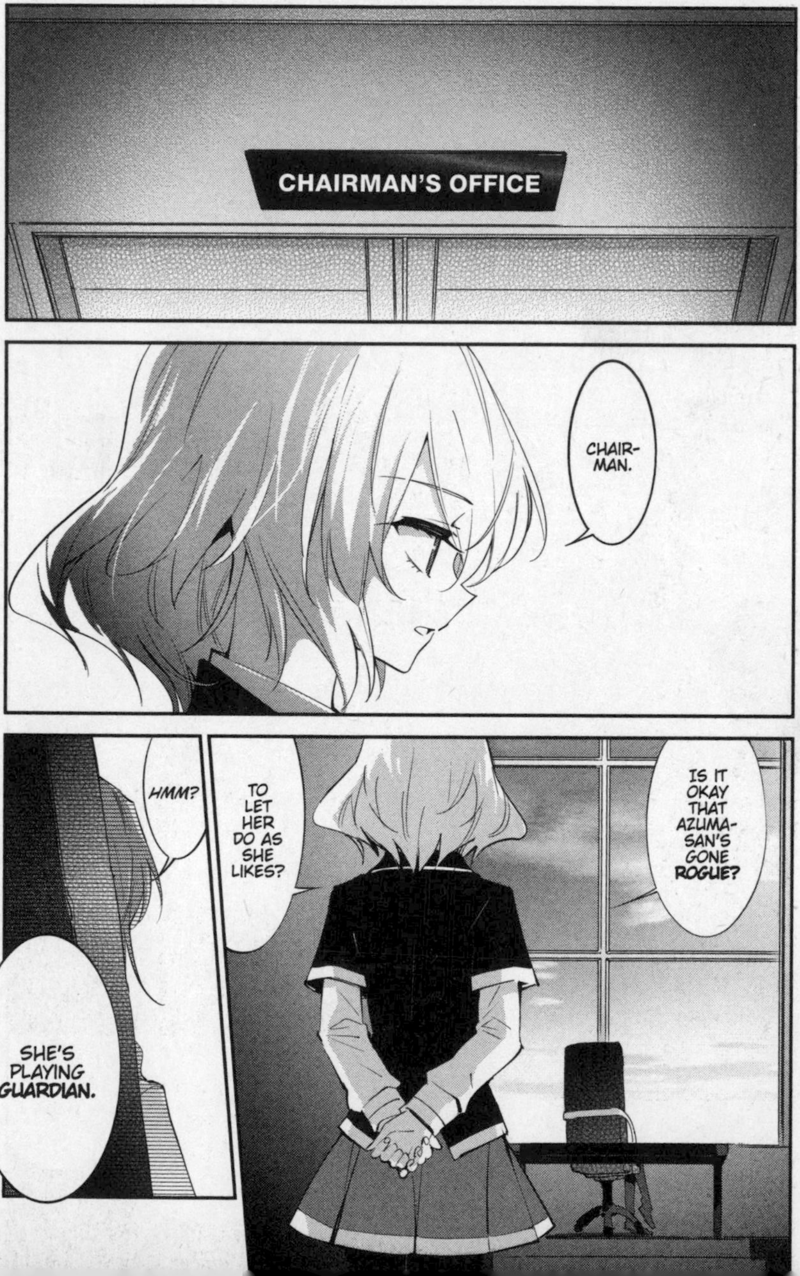
CHAIRMAN'S OFFICE
CHAIR-MAN.
IS IT OKAY THAT AZUMA-SAN'S GONE ROGUE?
TO LET HER DO AS SHE LIKES?
HMM?
SHE'S PLAYING GUARDIAN.

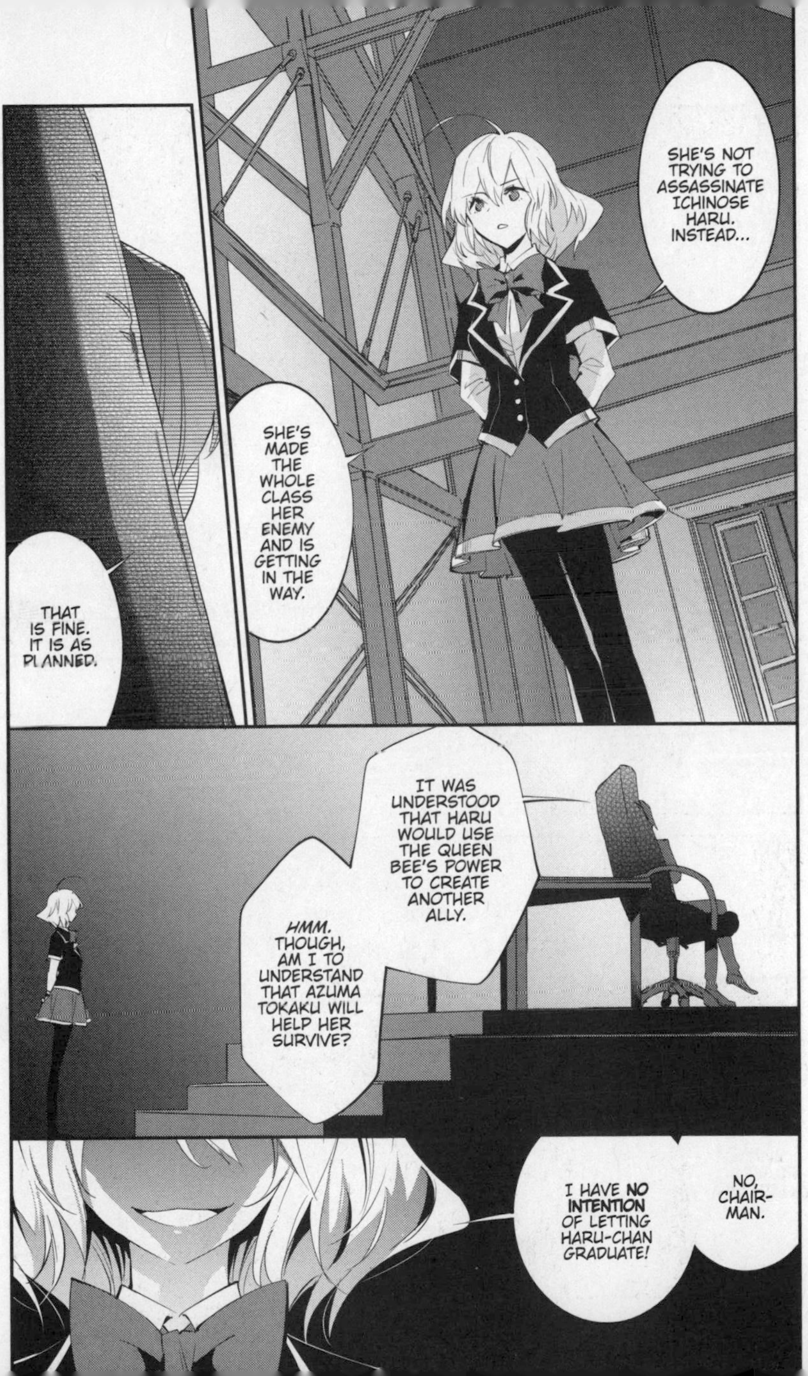
SHE'S NOT TRYING TO ASSASSINATE ICHINOSE HARU. INSTEAD...
SHE'S MADE THE WHOLE CLASS HER ENEMY AND IS GETTING IN THE WAY.
THAT IS FINE. IT IS AS PLANNED.
IT WAS UNDERSTOOD THAT HARU WOULD USE THE QUEEN BEE'S POWER TO CREATE ANOTHER ALLY.
HMM. THOUGH, AM I TO UNDERSTAND THAT AZUMA TOKAKU WILL HELP HER SURVIVE?
NO, CHAIRMAN.
I HAVE NO INTENTION OF LETTING HARU-CHAN GRADUATE!

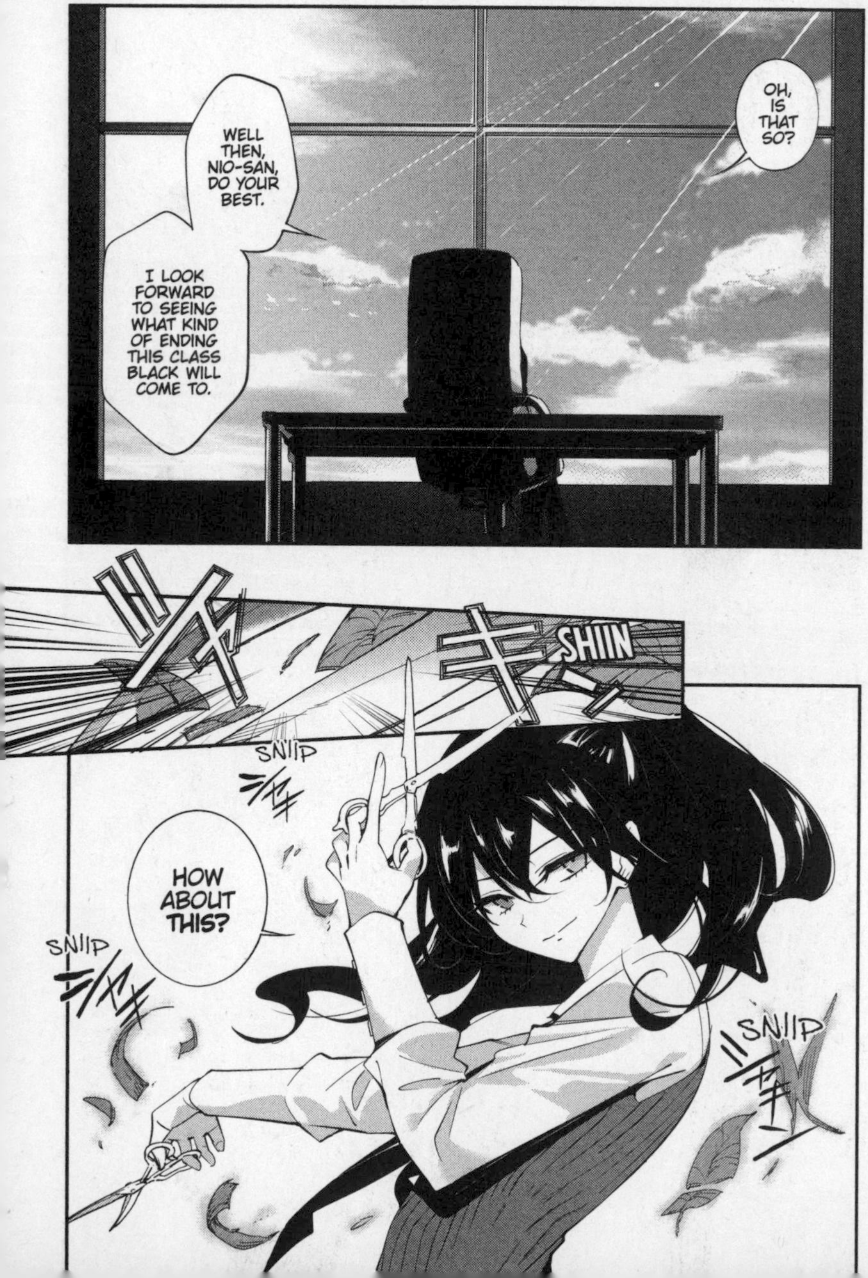
OH, IS THAT SO?
WELL THEN, NIO-SAN, DO YOUR BEST.
I LOOK FORWARD TO SEEING WHAT KIND OF ENDING THIS CLASS BLACK WILL COME TO.
SHIIN
SNIIP
HOW ABOUT THIS?
SNIIP
SNIIP

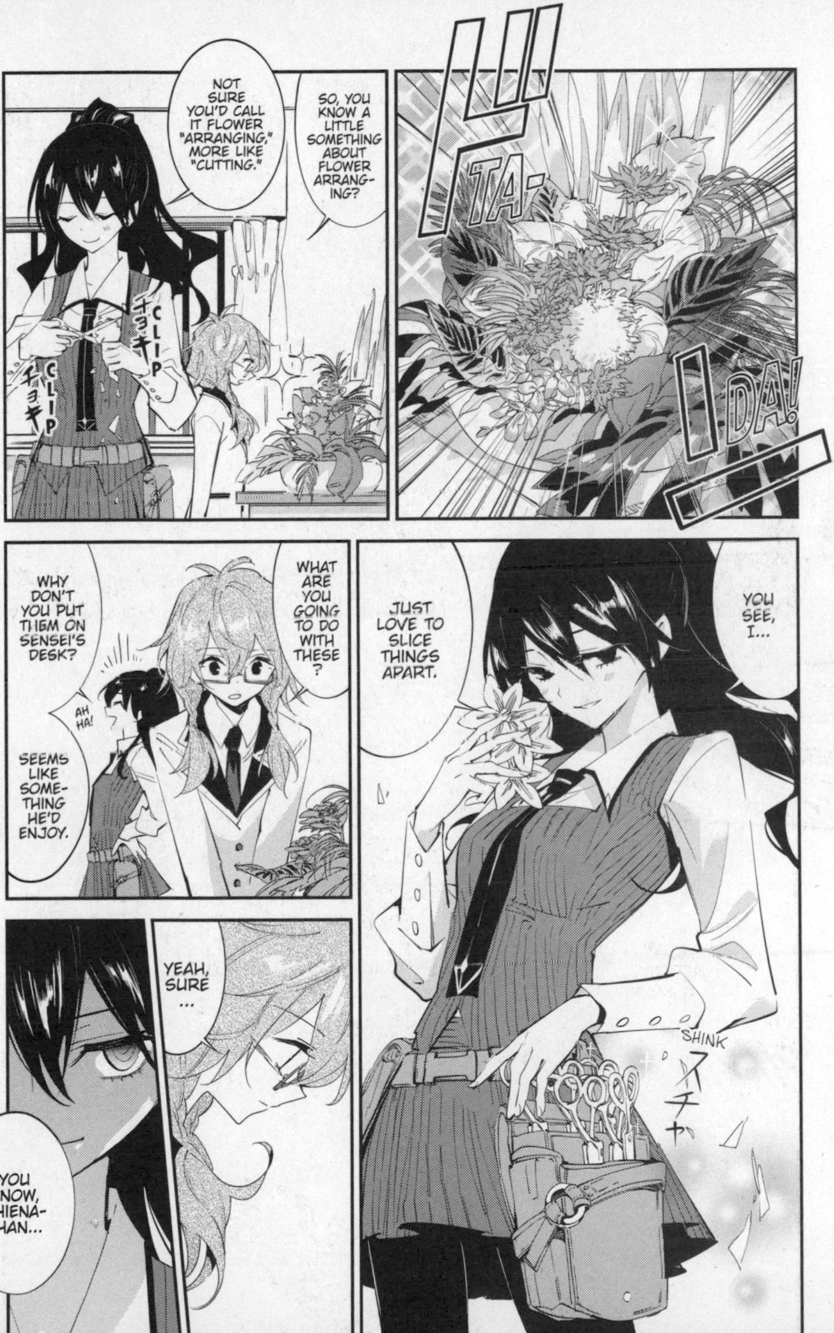
TA-
DA!
SO, YOU KNOW A LITTLE SOMETHING ABOUT FLOWER ARRANGING?
NOT SURE YOU'D CALL IT FLOWER "ARRANGING," MORE LIKE "CUTTING."
チョキ CLIP
チョキ CLIP
YOU SEE, I...
JUST LOVE TO SLICE THINGS APART.
SHINK
スチャ
WHAT ARE YOU GOING TO DO WITH THESE?
WHY DON'T YOU PUT THEM ON SENSEI'S DESK?
AH HA!
SEEMS LIKE SOMETHING HE'D ENJOY.
YEAH, SURE ...
YOU KNOW, SHIENA-CHAN...

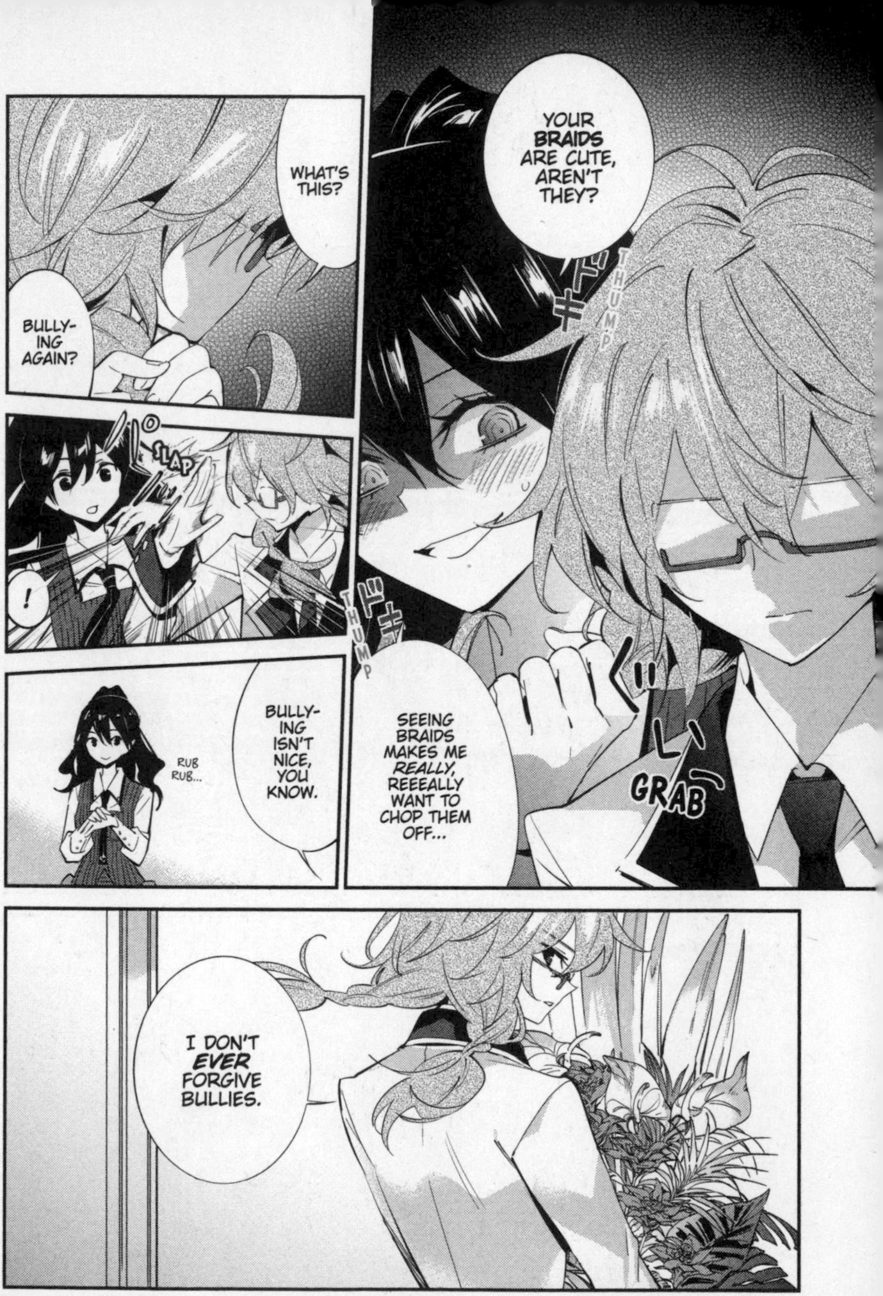
YOUR BRAIDS ARE CUTE, AREN'T THEY?
ドキ THUMP
ドキ THUMP
SEEING BRAIDS MAKES ME *REALLY*, REEEALLY WANT TO CHOP THEM OFF...
GRAB
WHAT'S THIS?
BULLY-ING AGAIN?
SLAP
!
BULLY-ING ISN'T NICE, YOU KNOW.
RUB RUB...
I DON'T *EVER* FORGIVE BULLIES.

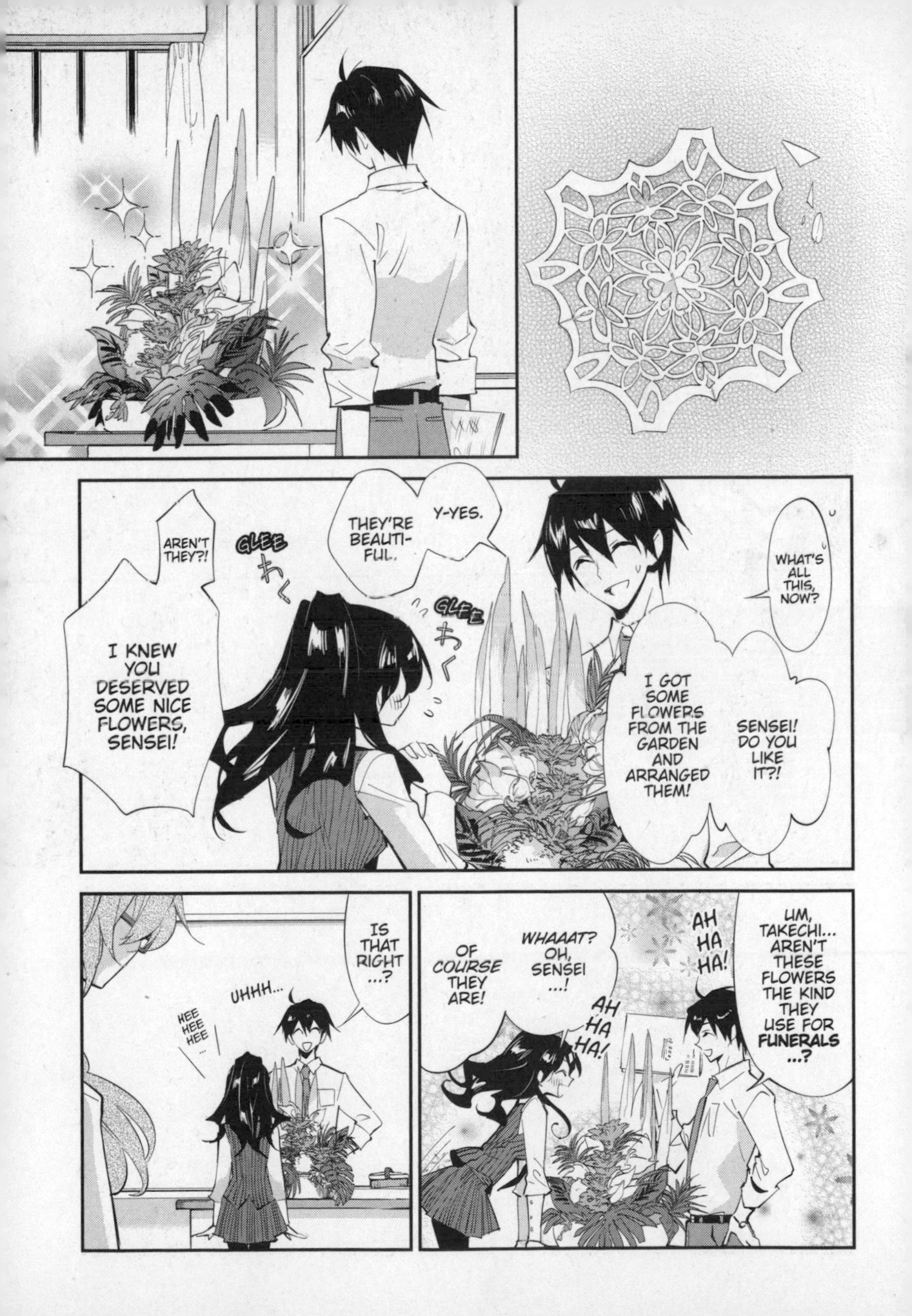
WHAT'S ALL THIS, NOW?
SENSEI! DO YOU LIKE IT?!
I GOT SOME FLOWERS FROM THE GARDEN AND ARRANGED THEM!
Y-YES.
THEY'RE BEAUTI-FUL.
GLEE わく
GLEE わく
AREN'T THEY?!
I KNEW YOU DESERVED SOME NICE FLOWERS, SENSEI!
UM, TAKECHI... AREN'T THESE FLOWERS THE KIND THEY USE FOR FUNERALS...?
AH HA HA!
WHAAAT? OH, SENSEI...!
AH HA HA!
OF COURSE THEY ARE!
IS THAT RIGHT...?
UHHH...
HEE HEE HEE...

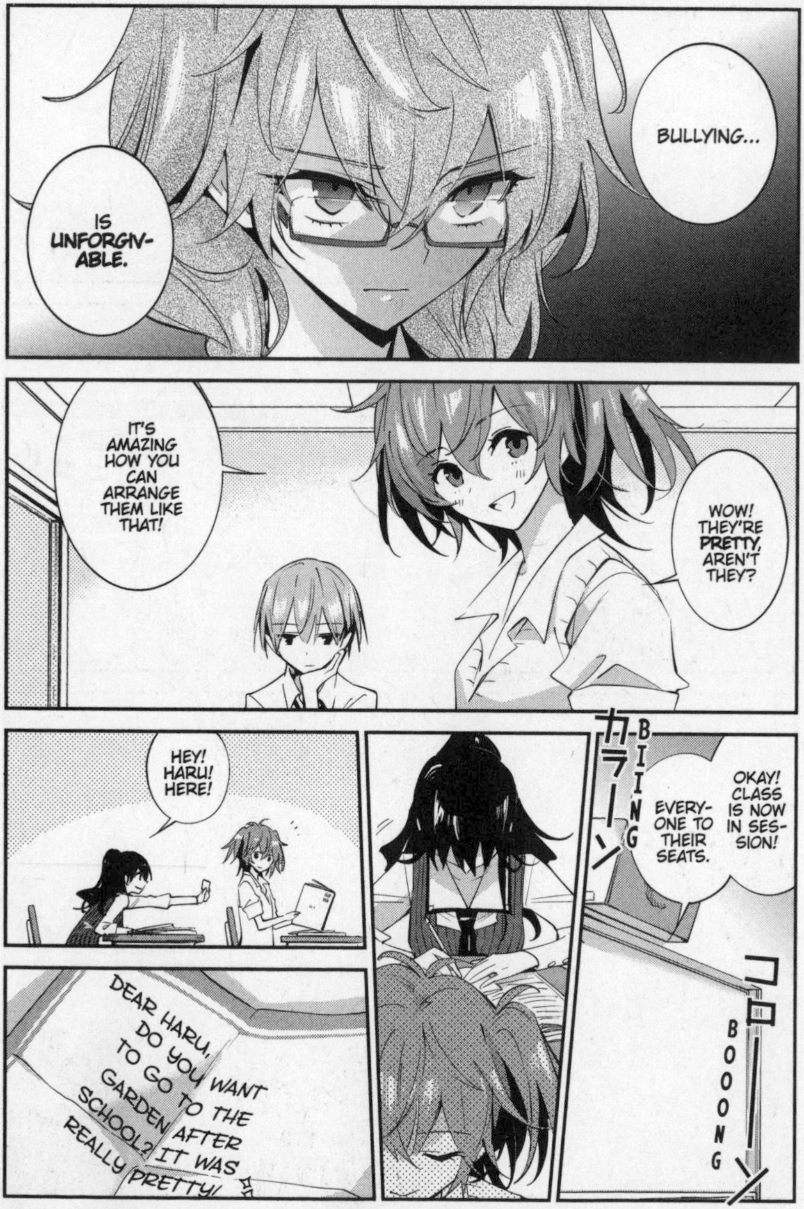
BULLYING...
IS UNFORGIV-ABLE.
WOW! THEY'RE PRETTY, AREN'T THEY?
IT'S AMAZING HOW YOU CAN ARRANGE THEM LIKE THAT!
カラーン
BIING
OKAY! CLASS IS NOW IN SES-SION!
EVERY-ONE TO THEIR SEATS.
コローン
BOOOONG
HEY! HARU! HERE!
DEAR HARU, DO YOU WANT TO GO TO THE GARDEN AFTER SCHOOL? IT WAS REALLY PRETTY!

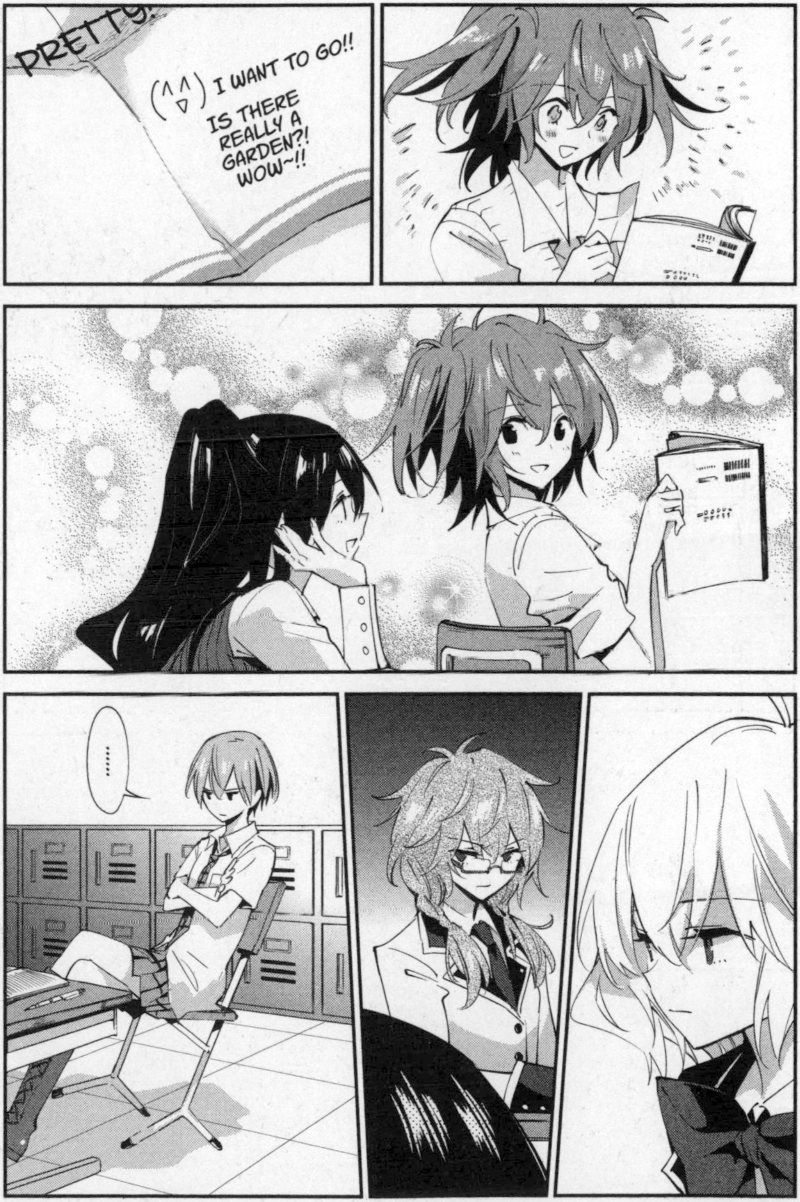
PRETTY!
(^▽^) I WANT TO GO!!
IS THERE REALLY A GARDEN?! WOW~!!
......

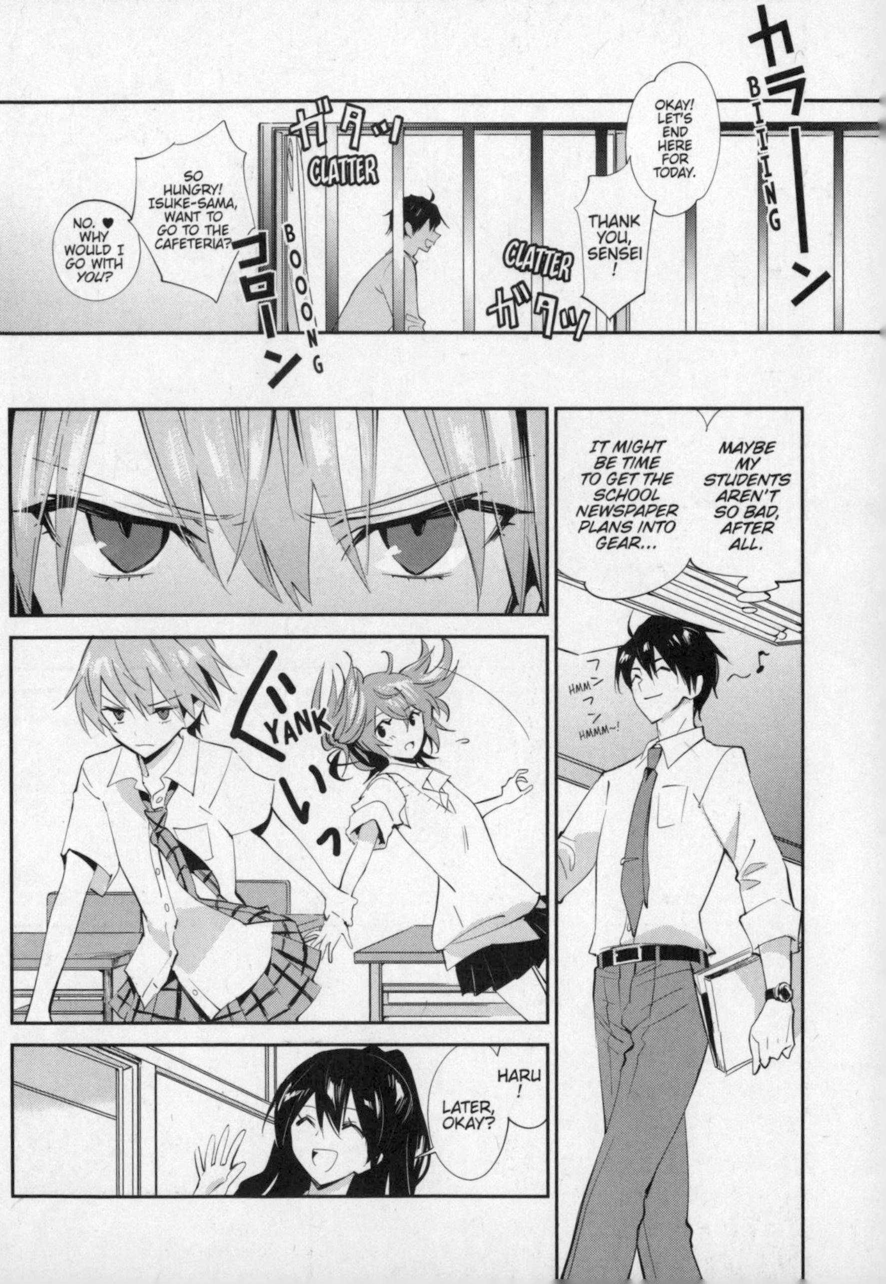
カラーン
BIIIING
OKAY! LET'S END HERE FOR TODAY.
THANK YOU, SENSEI!
ガタッ
CLATTER
ガタッ
CLATTER
コローン
BOOOONG
SO HUNGRY! ISUKE-SAMA, WANT TO GO TO THE CAFETERIA?
NO. ♥ WHY WOULD I GO WITH YOU?
MAYBE MY STUDENTS AREN'T SO BAD, AFTER ALL.
IT MIGHT BE TIME TO GET THE SCHOOL NEWSPAPER PLANS INTO GEAR...
フン フン
HMM HMMM~!
ぐいっ
YANK
HARU!
LATER, OKAY?

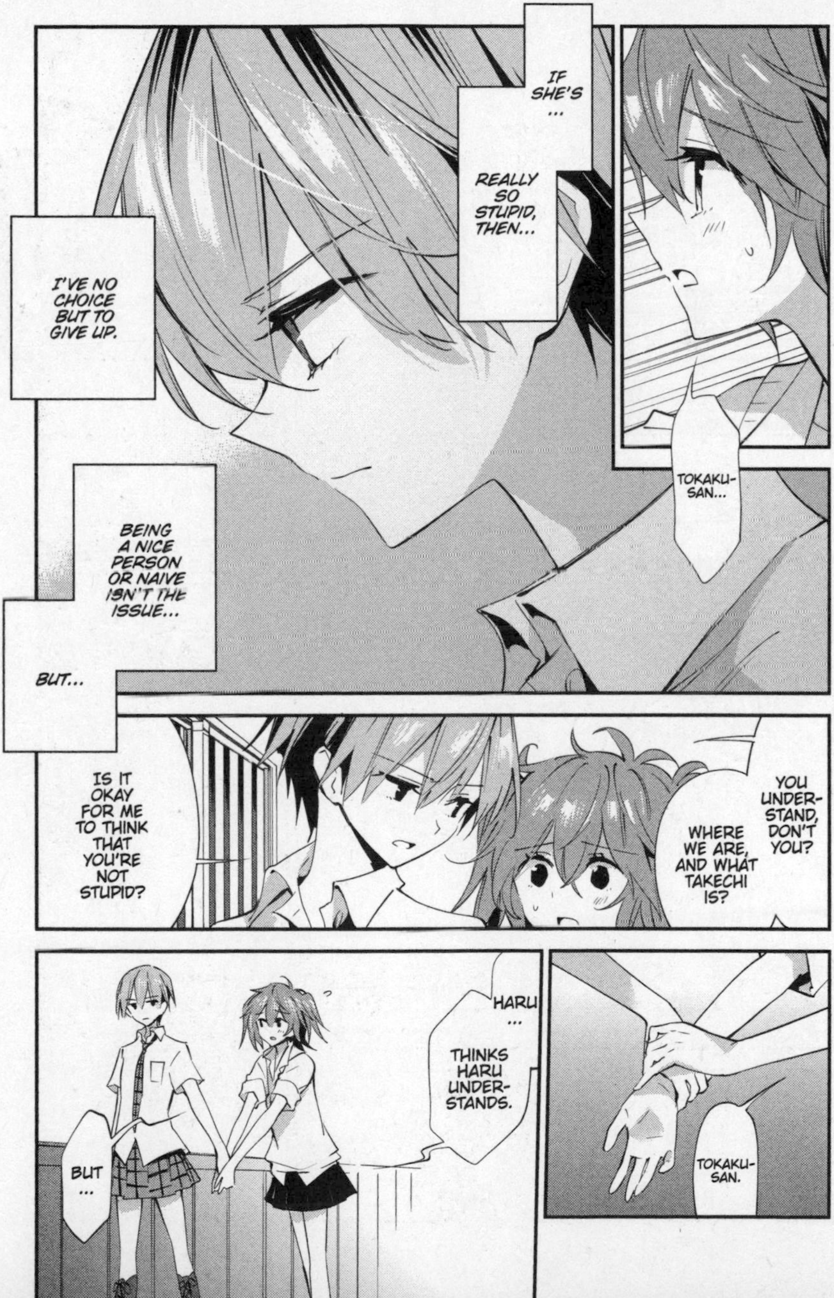
IF SHE'S ...
REALLY SO STUPID, THEN...
I'VE NO CHOICE BUT TO GIVE UP.
TOKAKU-SAN...
BEING A NICE PERSON OR NAIVE ISN'T THE ISSUE...
BUT...
YOU UNDERSTAND, DON'T YOU?
WHERE WE ARE, AND WHAT TAKECHI IS?
IS IT OKAY FOR ME TO THINK THAT YOU'RE NOT STUPID?
TOKAKU-SAN.
HARU ...
THINKS HARU UNDERSTANDS.
BUT ...

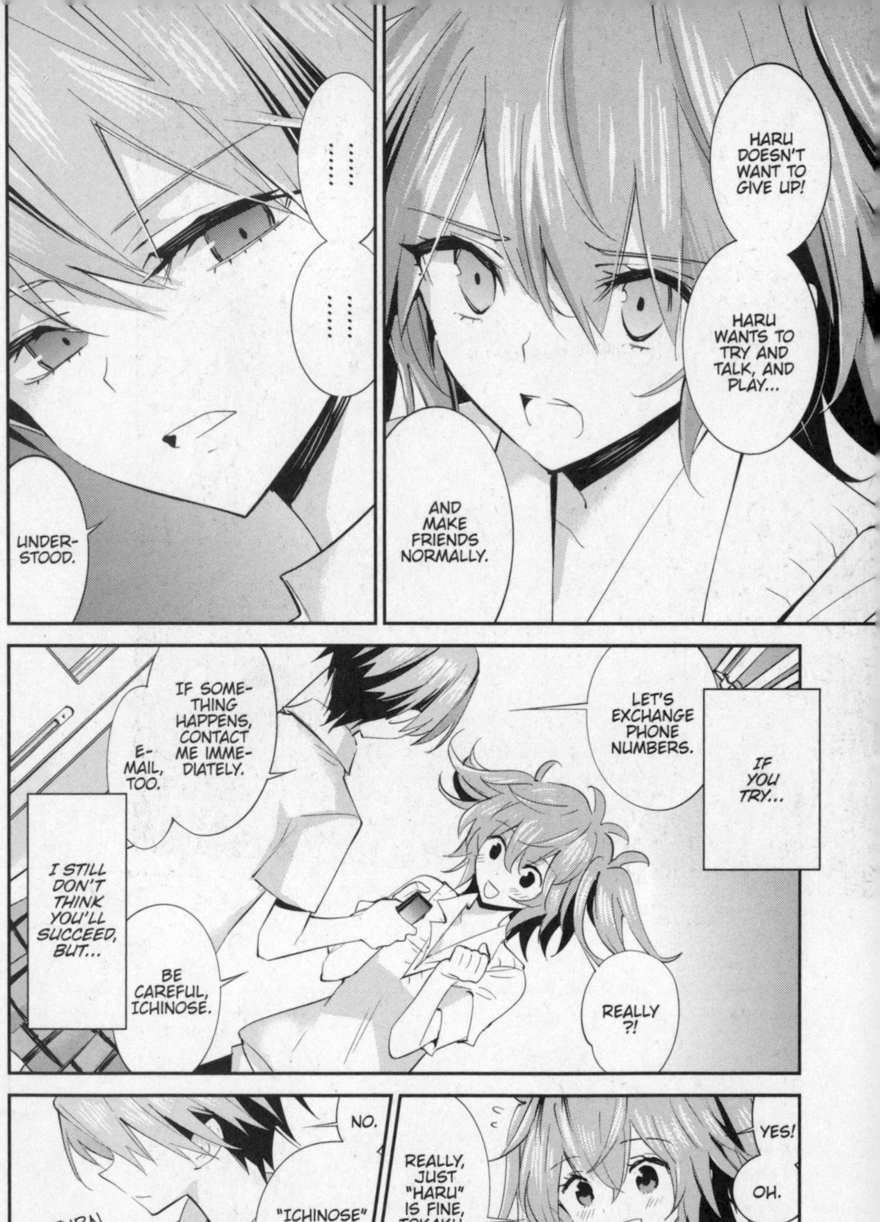
HARU DOESN'T WANT TO GIVE UP!
HARU WANTS TO TRY AND TALK, AND PLAY...
AND MAKE FRIENDS NORMALLY.
......
......
UNDER-STOOD.
IF YOU TRY...
LET'S EXCHANGE PHONE NUMBERS.
IF SOME-THING HAPPENS, CONTACT ME IMME-DIATELY.
E-MAIL, TOO.
REALLY?!
I STILL DON'T THINK YOU'LL SUCCEED, BUT...
BE CAREFUL, ICHINOSE.
YES!
OH.
REALLY, JUST "HARU" IS FINE, TOKAKU-SAN.
NO.
"ICHINOSE" IS FINE.
TURN

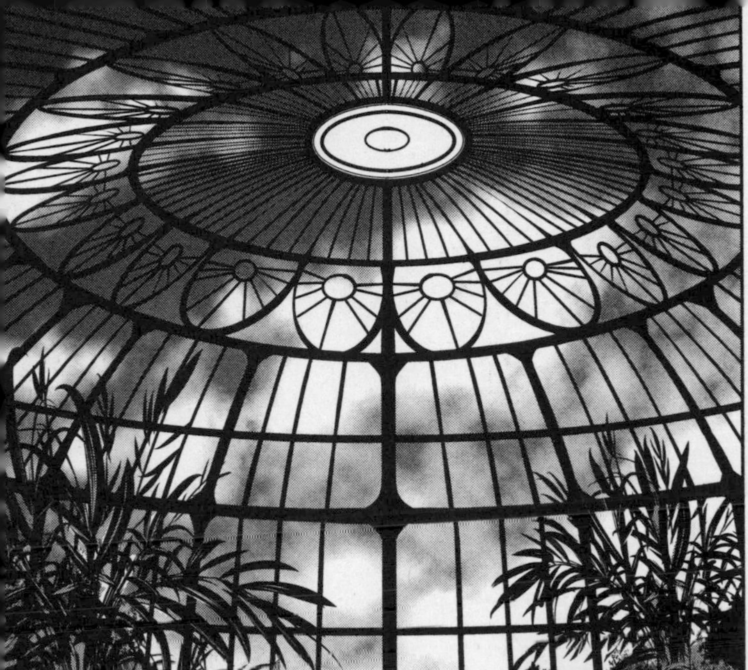

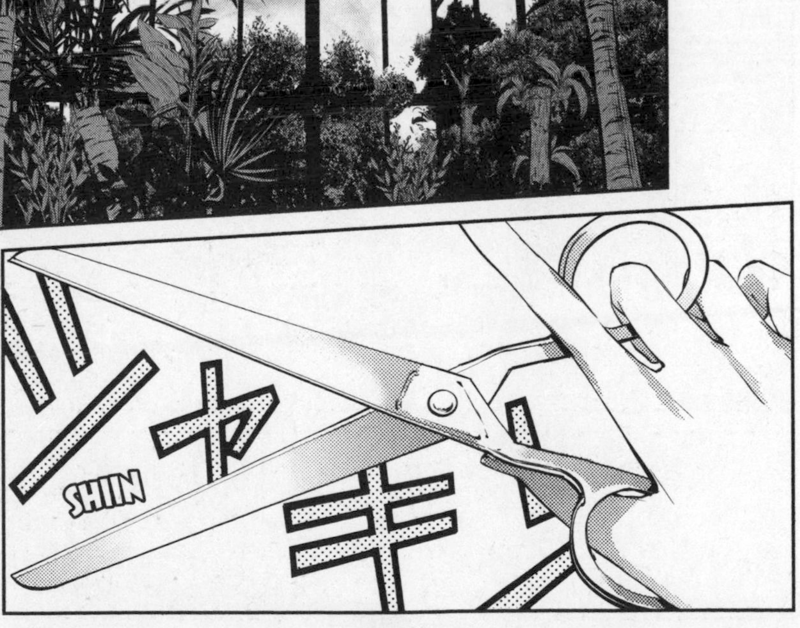
シャキン
SHIIN

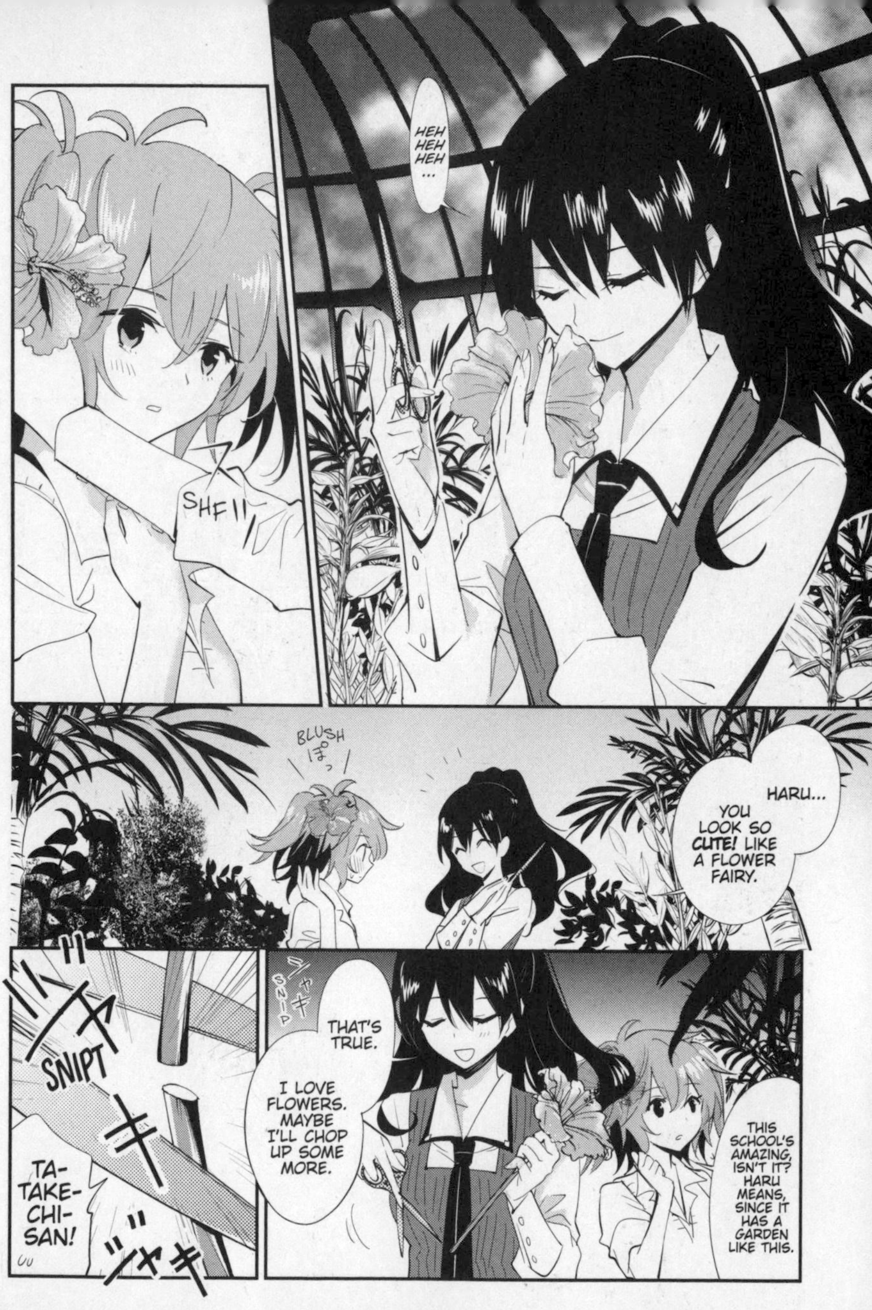
HEH HEH HEH...
SHF!!
HARU... YOU LOOK SO CUTE! LIKE A FLOWER FAIRY.
BLUSH
ぽっ
THIS SCHOOL'S AMAZING, ISN'T IT? HARU MEANS, SINCE IT HAS A GARDEN LIKE THIS.
シャキ
SNIP
THAT'S TRUE.
I LOVE FLOWERS. MAYBE I'LL CHOP UP SOME MORE.
ジャキ
SNIPT
TA-TAKECHI-SAN!
ジャキ

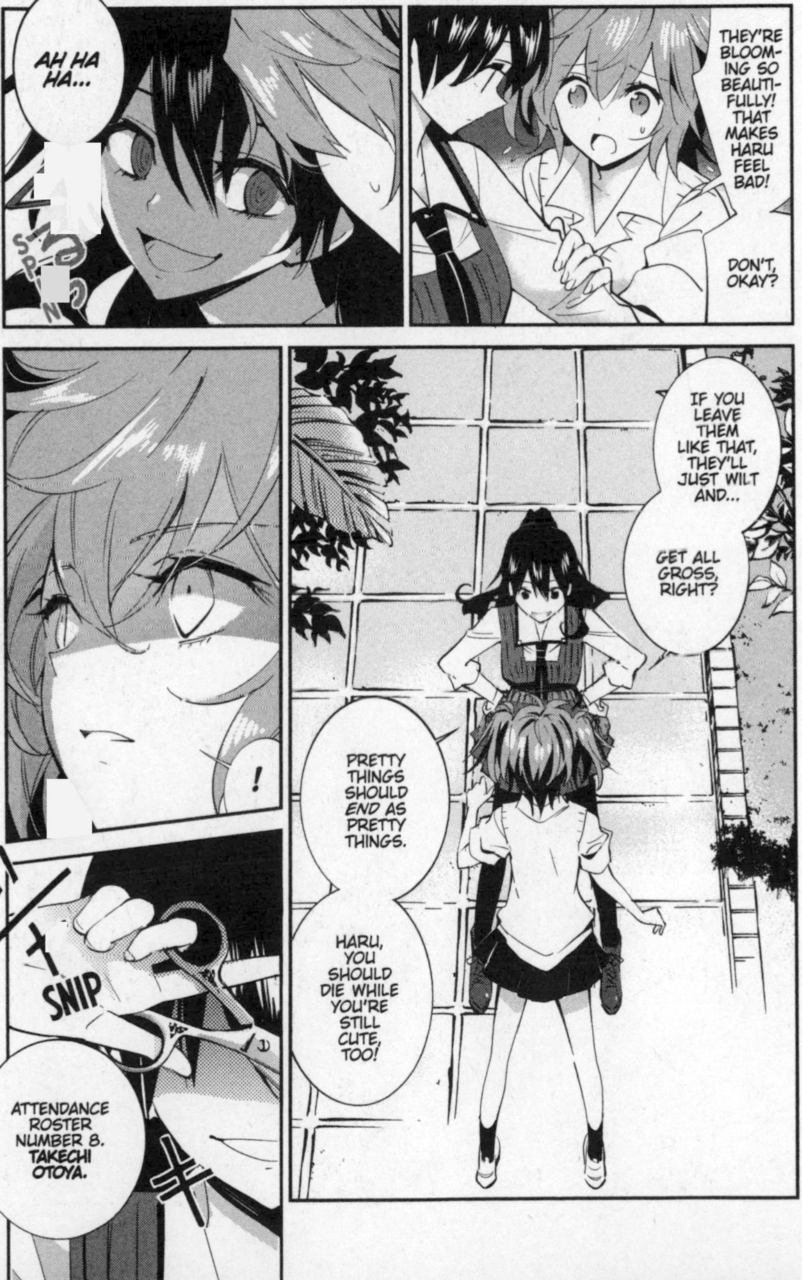
THEY'RE BLOOMING SO BEAUTIFULLY! THAT MAKES HARU FEEL BAD!
DON'T, OKAY?
AH HA HA...
SPIN
IF YOU LEAVE THEM LIKE THAT, THEY'LL JUST WILT AND...
GET ALL GROSS, RIGHT?
PRETTY THINGS SHOULD *END* AS PRETTY THINGS.
HARU, YOU SHOULD DIE WHILE YOU'RE STILL CUTE, TOO!
!
SNIP
ATTENDANCE ROSTER NUMBER 8. **TAKECHI OTOYA.**

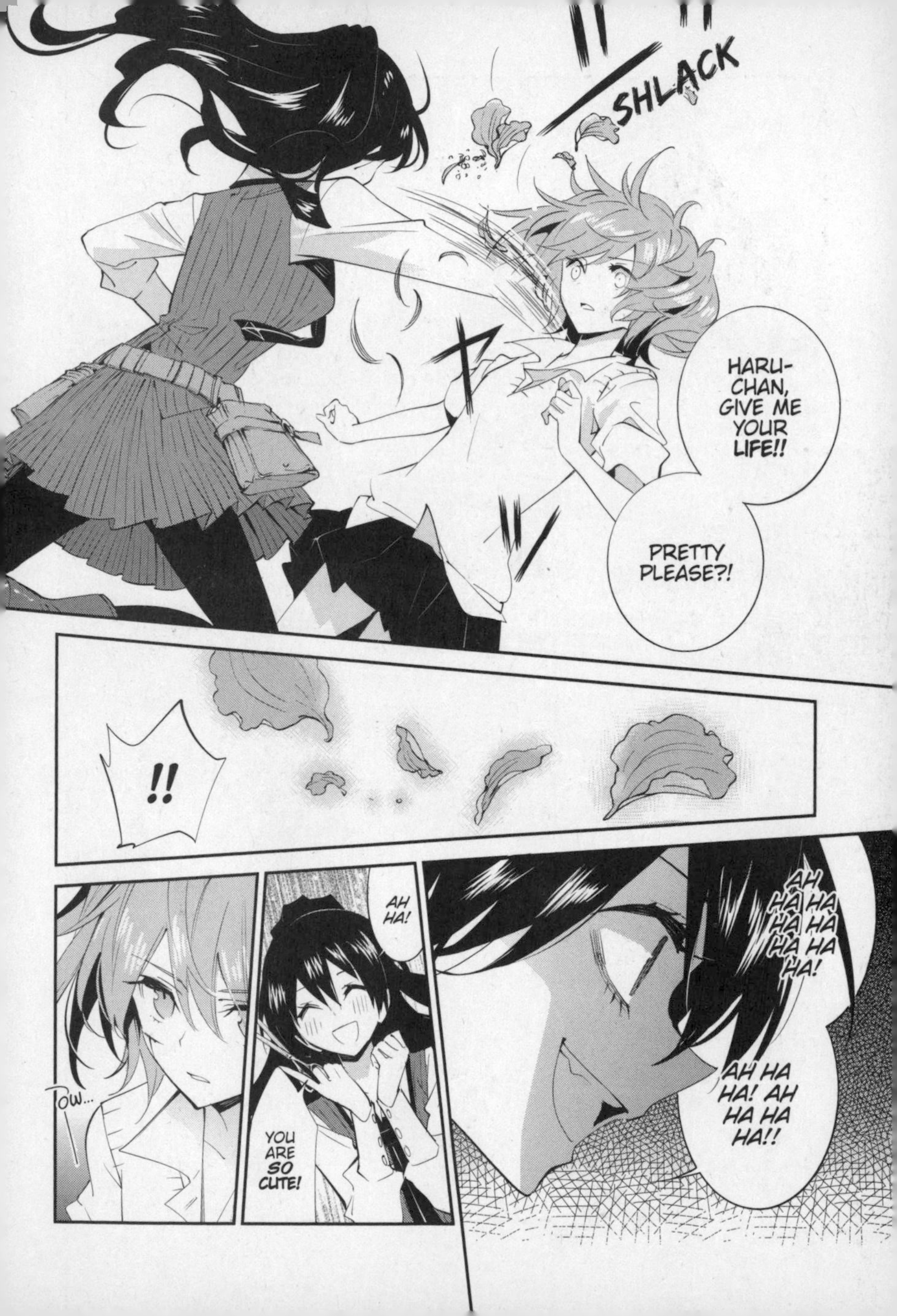
SHLACK
HARU-CHAN, GIVE ME YOUR LIFE!!
PRETTY PLEASE?!
!!
AH HA HA HA HA HA HA HA HA!
AH HA HA! AH HA HA HA!!
AH HA!
YOU ARE SO CUTE!
Tow...

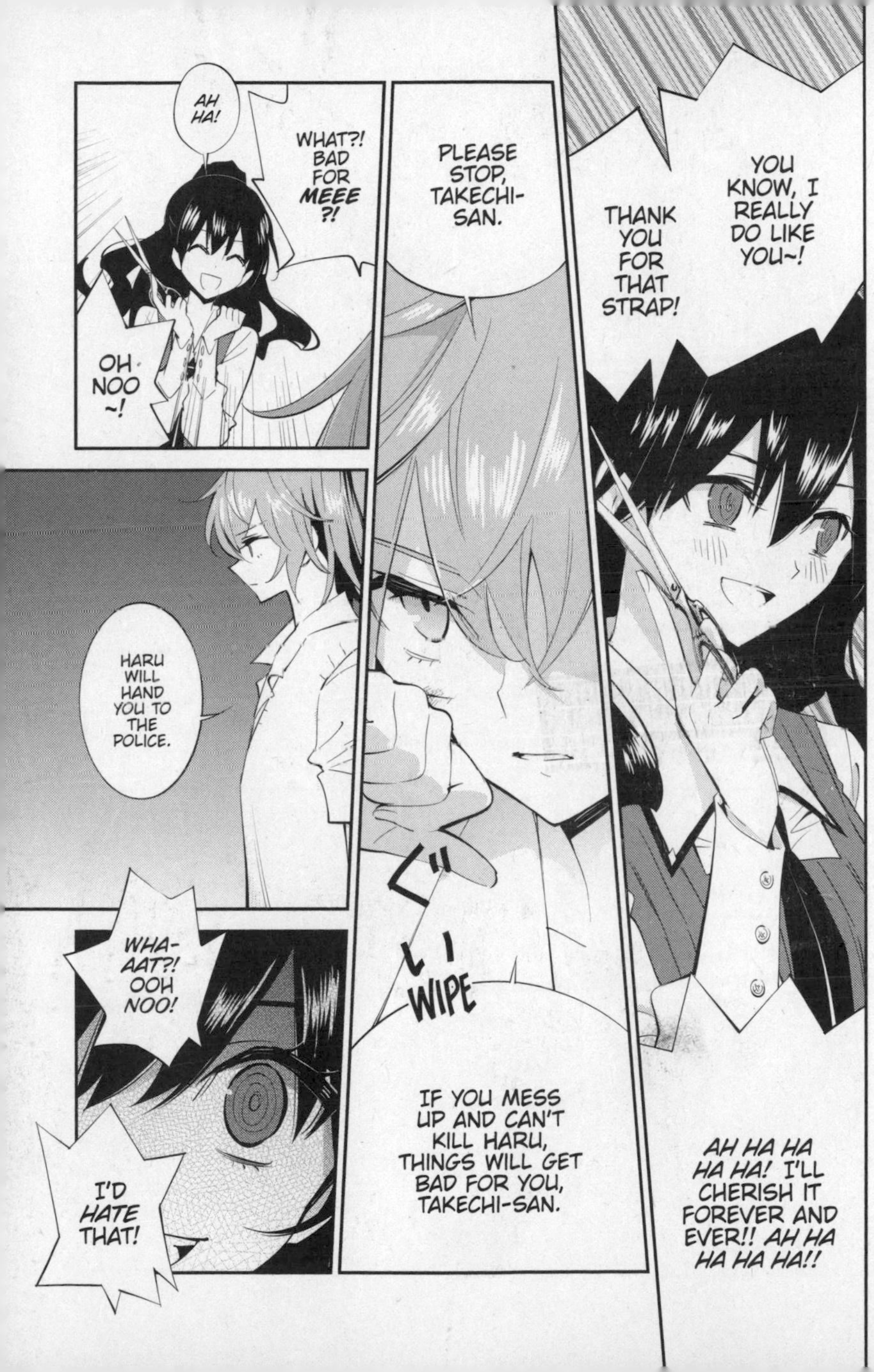
YOU KNOW, I REALLY DO LIKE YOU~!
THANK YOU FOR THAT STRAP!
AH HA HA HA HA! I'LL CHERISH IT FOREVER AND EVER!! AH HA HA HA HA!!
PLEASE STOP, TAKECHI-SAN.
WIPE
IF YOU MESS UP AND CAN'T KILL HARU, THINGS WILL GET BAD FOR YOU, TAKECHI-SAN.
AH HA!
WHAT?! BAD FOR MEEE ?!
OH NOO ~!
HARU WILL HAND YOU TO THE POLICE.
WHA-AAT?! OOH NOO!
I'D HATE THAT!

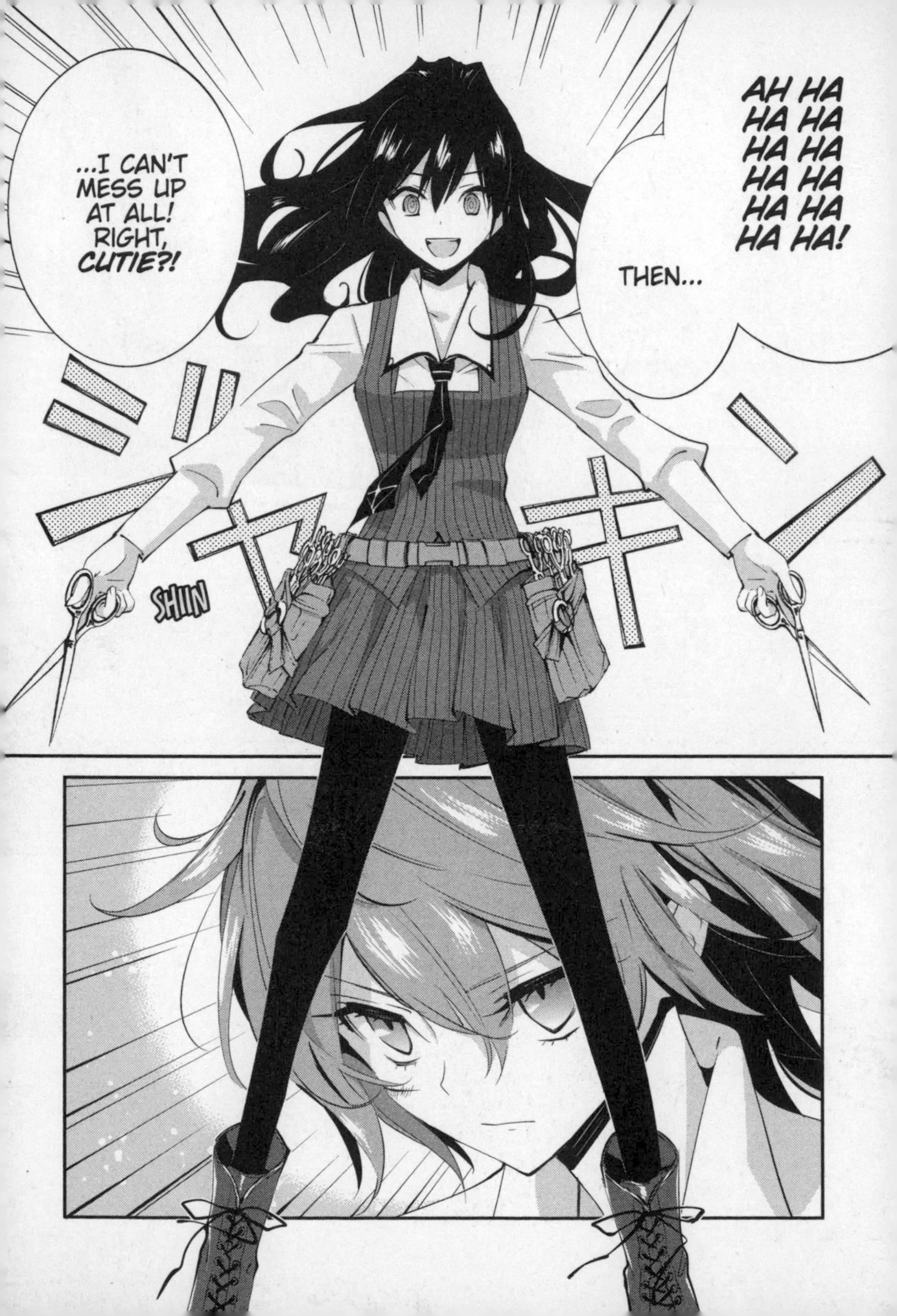
AH HA HA HA HA HA HA HA HA HA HA HA!
THEN...
...I CAN'T MESS UP AT ALL! RIGHT, CUTIE?!
ジャキーン
SHIIN

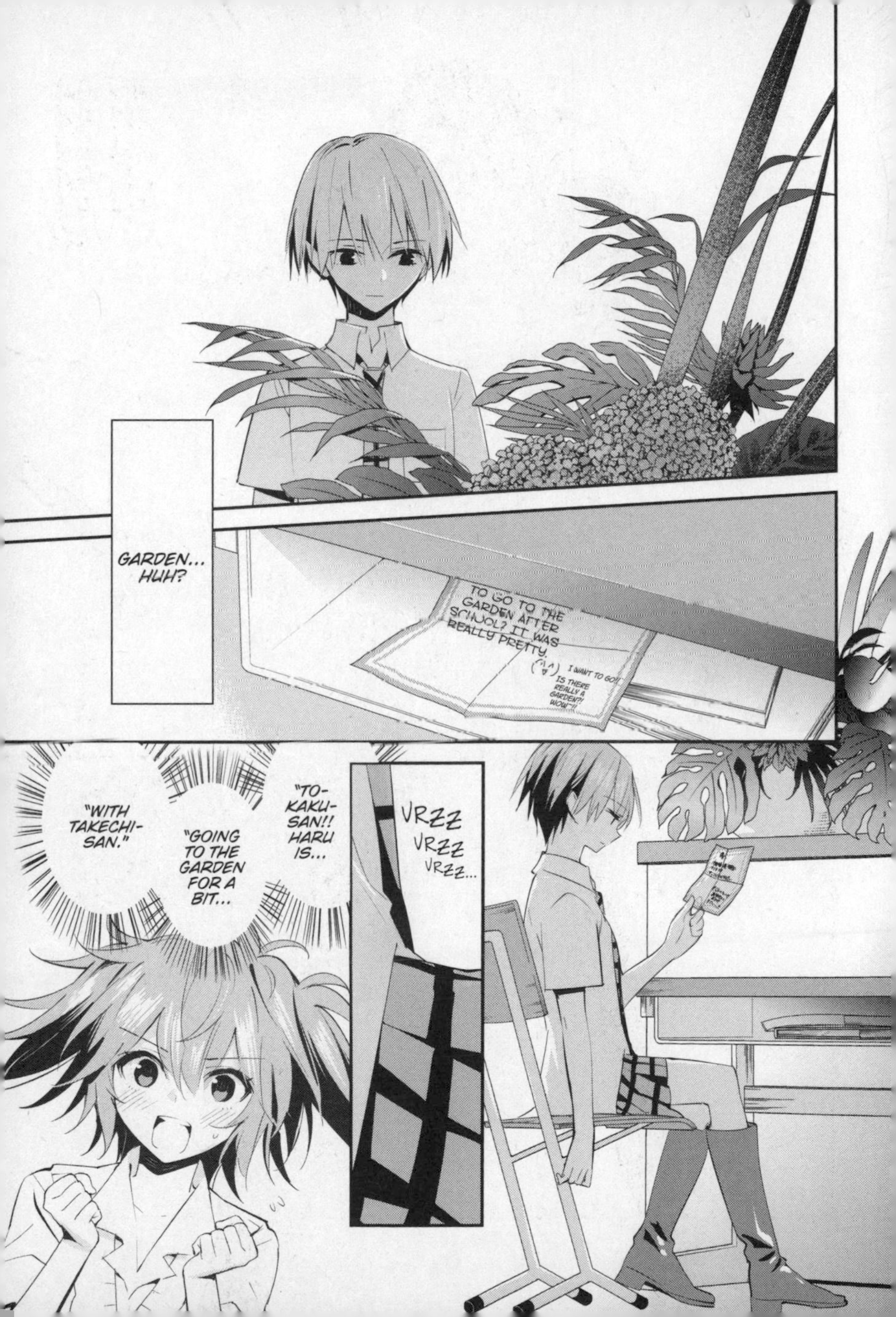
TO GO TO THE GARDEN AFTER SCHOOL? IT WAS REALLY PRETTY.
I WANT TO GO!! IS THERE REALLY A GARDEN?! WOW!!
GARDEN... HUH?
VRZZ VRZZ VRZZ...
"TO-KAKU-SAN!! HARU IS...
"GOING TO THE GARDEN FOR A BIT...
"WITH TAKECHI-SAN."

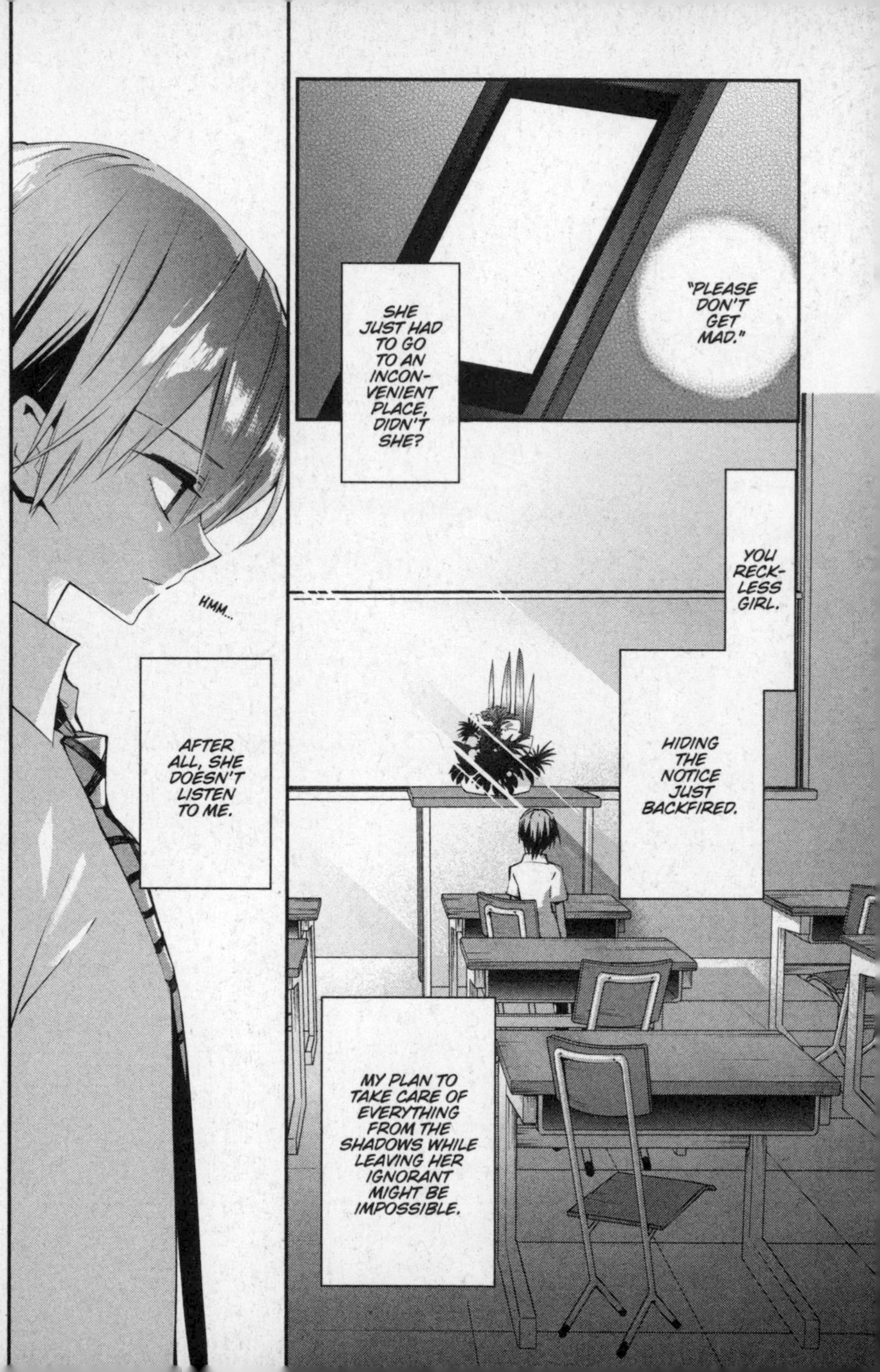
"PLEASE DON'T GET MAD."
SHE JUST HAD TO GO TO AN INCON-VENIENT PLACE, DIDN'T SHE?
YOU RECK-LESS GIRL.
HIDING THE NOTICE JUST BACKFIRED.
MY PLAN TO TAKE CARE OF EVERYTHING FROM THE SHADOWS WHILE LEAVING HER IGNORANT MIGHT BE IMPOSSIBLE.
HMM...
AFTER ALL, SHE DOESN'T LISTEN TO ME.

Chapter 13
Poisonous Flower

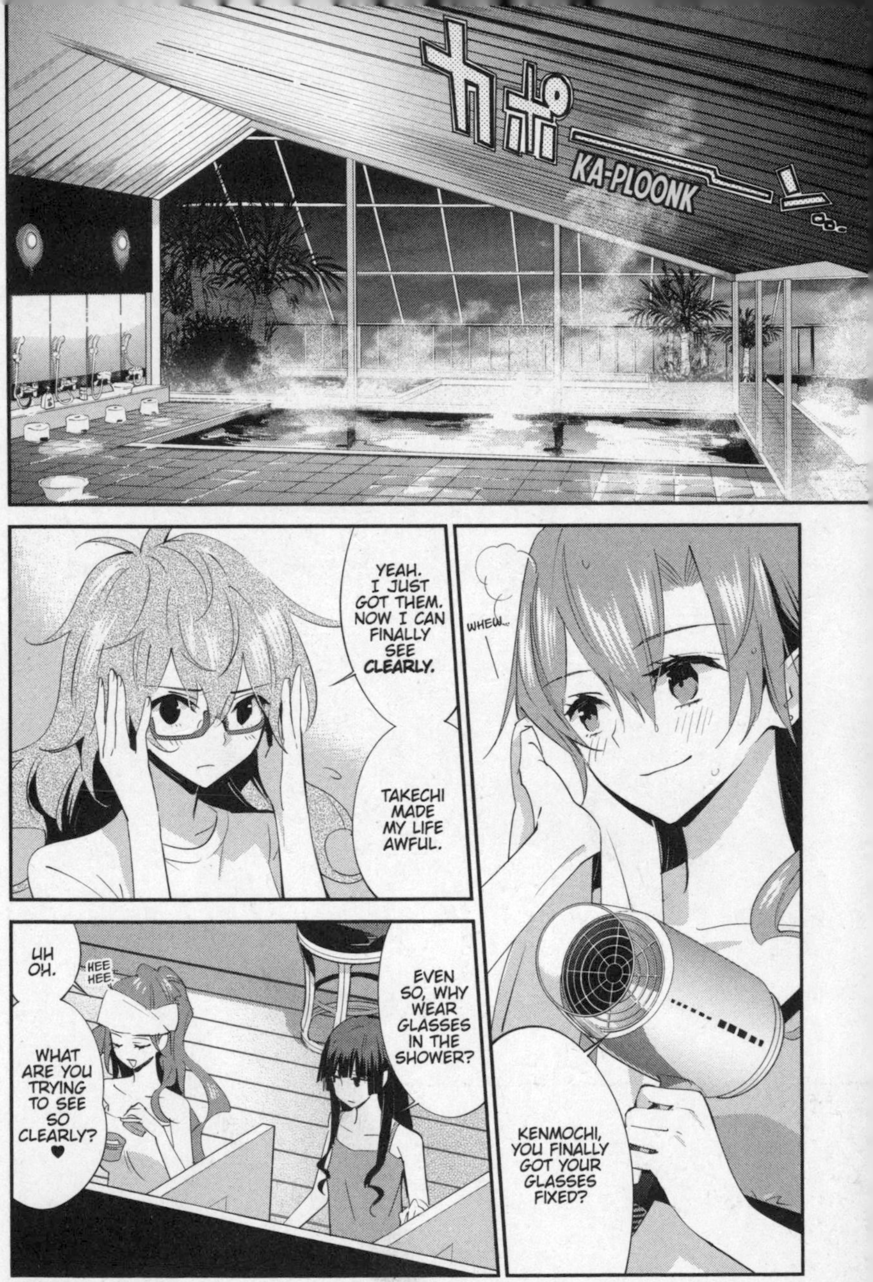
カポ
KA-PLOONK
WHEW...
KENMOCHI, YOU FINALLY GOT YOUR GLASSES FIXED?
YEAH. I JUST GOT THEM. NOW I CAN FINALLY SEE **CLEARLY.**
TAKECHI MADE MY LIFE AWFUL.
EVEN SO, WHY WEAR GLASSES IN THE SHOWER?
UH OH.
HEE HEE.
WHAT ARE YOU TRYING TO SEE SO CLEARLY? ♥

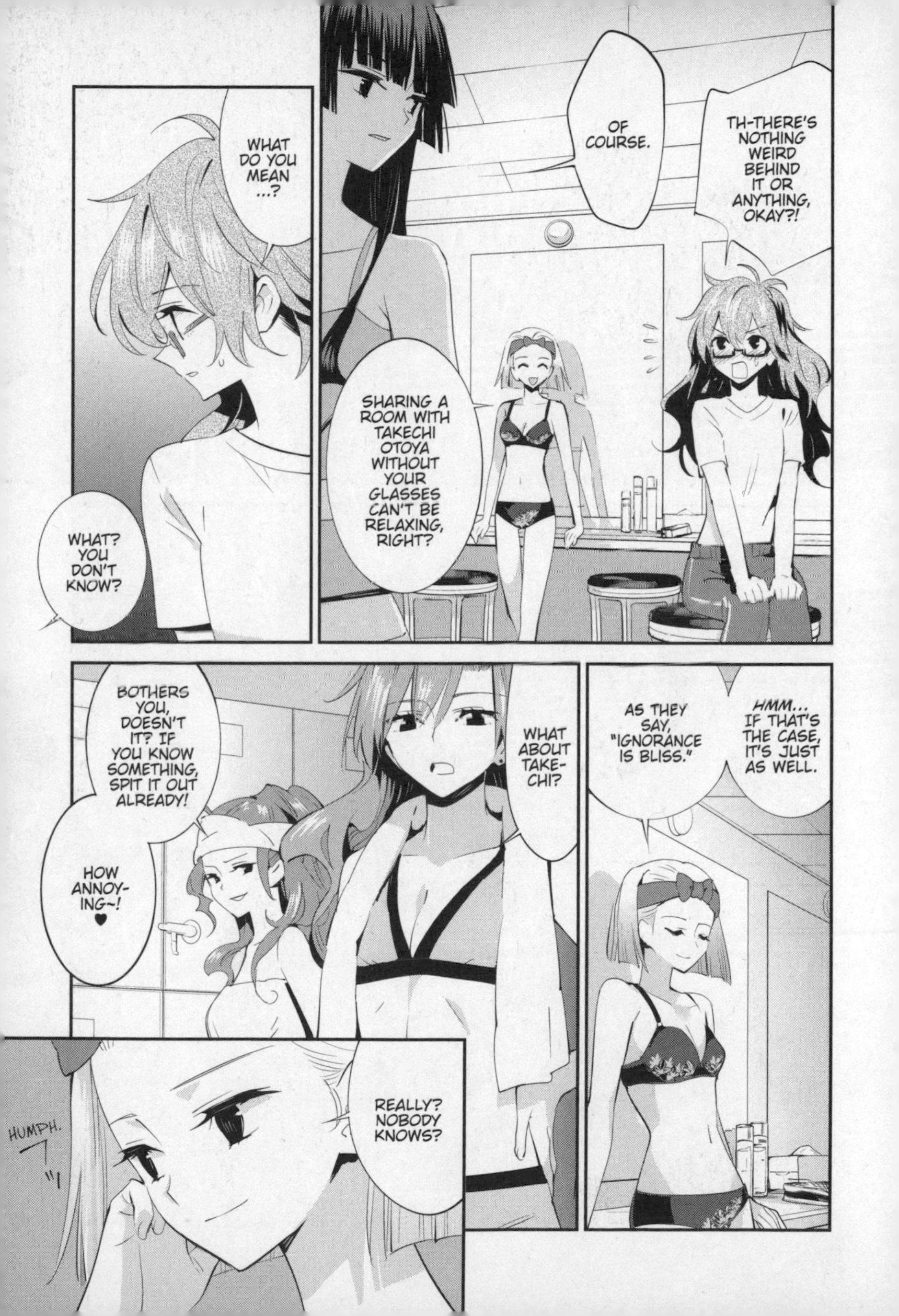
TH-THERE'S NOTHING WEIRD BEHIND IT OR ANYTHING, OKAY?!
OF COURSE.
SHARING A ROOM WITH TAKECHI OTOYA WITHOUT YOUR GLASSES CAN'T BE RELAXING, RIGHT?
WHAT DO YOU MEAN ...?
WHAT? YOU DON'T KNOW?
HMM... IF THAT'S THE CASE, IT'S JUST AS WELL.
AS THEY SAY, "IGNORANCE IS BLISS."
WHAT ABOUT TAKE-CHI?
BOTHERS YOU, DOESN'T IT? IF YOU KNOW SOMETHING, SPIT IT OUT ALREADY!
HOW ANNOY-ING~! ♥
REALLY? NOBODY KNOWS?
HUMPH.

BA-THUMP

THIS IS TAKECHI'S DOING.

WHAT?!

J! Japan Newspaper
2012/12/23 11:...

21st Century Jack the Ripp

The shocking remains of a female resident in an apartment in the Edogawa ward of Tokyo have been uncovered.

The remains were discovered around 7:30 on the 22nd, when a colleague, whose suspicions were aroused by her unexcused absence, visited the residence.

...of cutting wounds across the ...e immediate cause was

...ent complex that became the scene of the crime.

I SEE.

OH MY...

I DIDN'T KNOW. DOES THAT MEAN I WAS SLEEPING IN THE SAME ROOM AS A SERIAL KILLER?

AH HA!

WOW.

SO, WE HAD A PSYCHO IN OUR RANKS? ♥

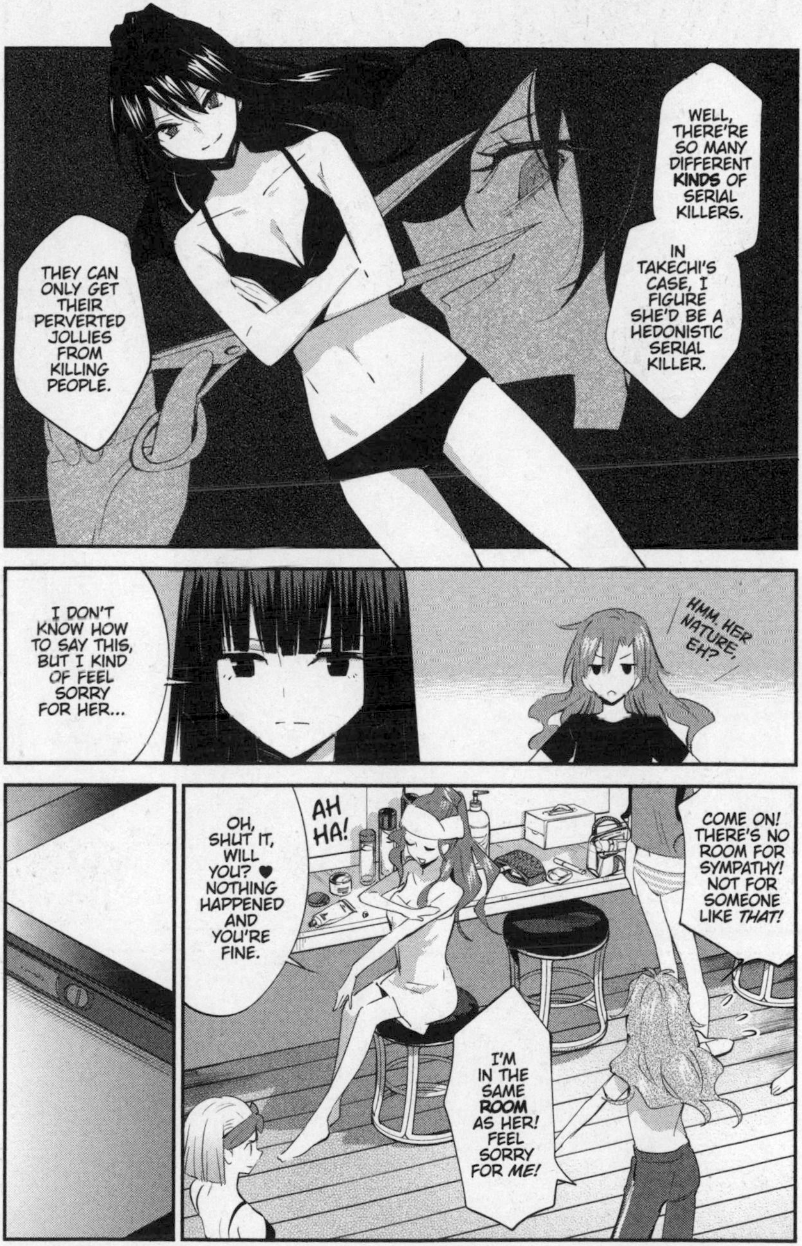
WELL, THERE'RE SO MANY DIFFERENT KINDS OF SERIAL KILLERS.
IN TAKECHI'S CASE, I FIGURE SHE'D BE A HEDONISTIC SERIAL KILLER.
THEY CAN ONLY GET THEIR PERVERTED JOLLIES FROM KILLING PEOPLE.
HMM. HER NATURE, EH?
I DON'T KNOW HOW TO SAY THIS, BUT I KIND OF FEEL SORRY FOR HER...
COME ON! THERE'S NO ROOM FOR SYMPATHY! NOT FOR SOMEONE LIKE THAT!
AH HA!
OH, SHUT IT, WILL YOU? ♥ NOTHING HAPPENED AND YOU'RE FINE.
I'M IN THE SAME ROOM AS HER! FEEL SORRY FOR ME!

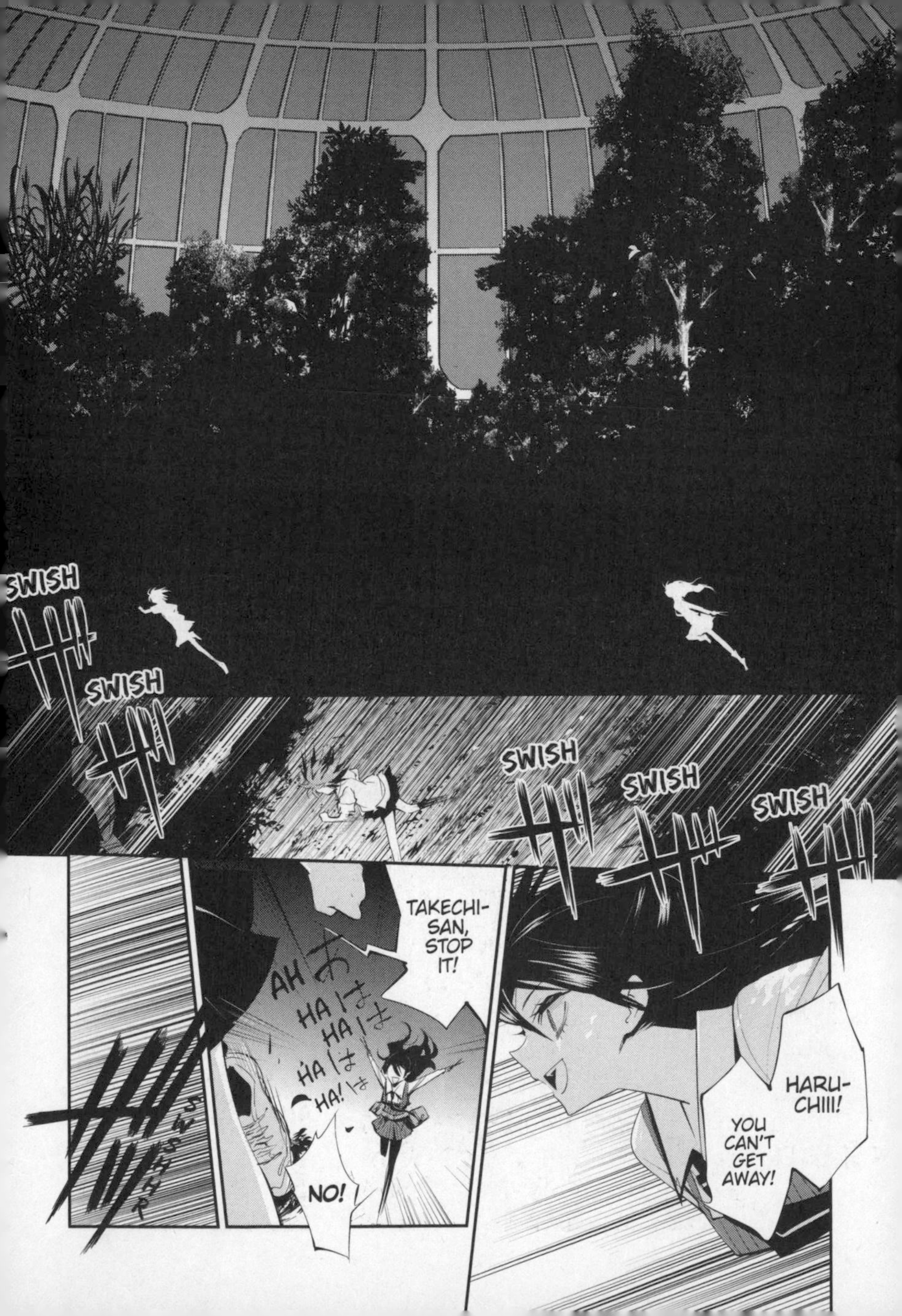
SWISH
SWISH
SWISH
SWISH
SWISH
HARU-CHIIII!
YOU CAN'T GET AWAY!
TAKECHI-SAN, STOP IT!
AH HA HA HA HA!
NO!
SWSHHR

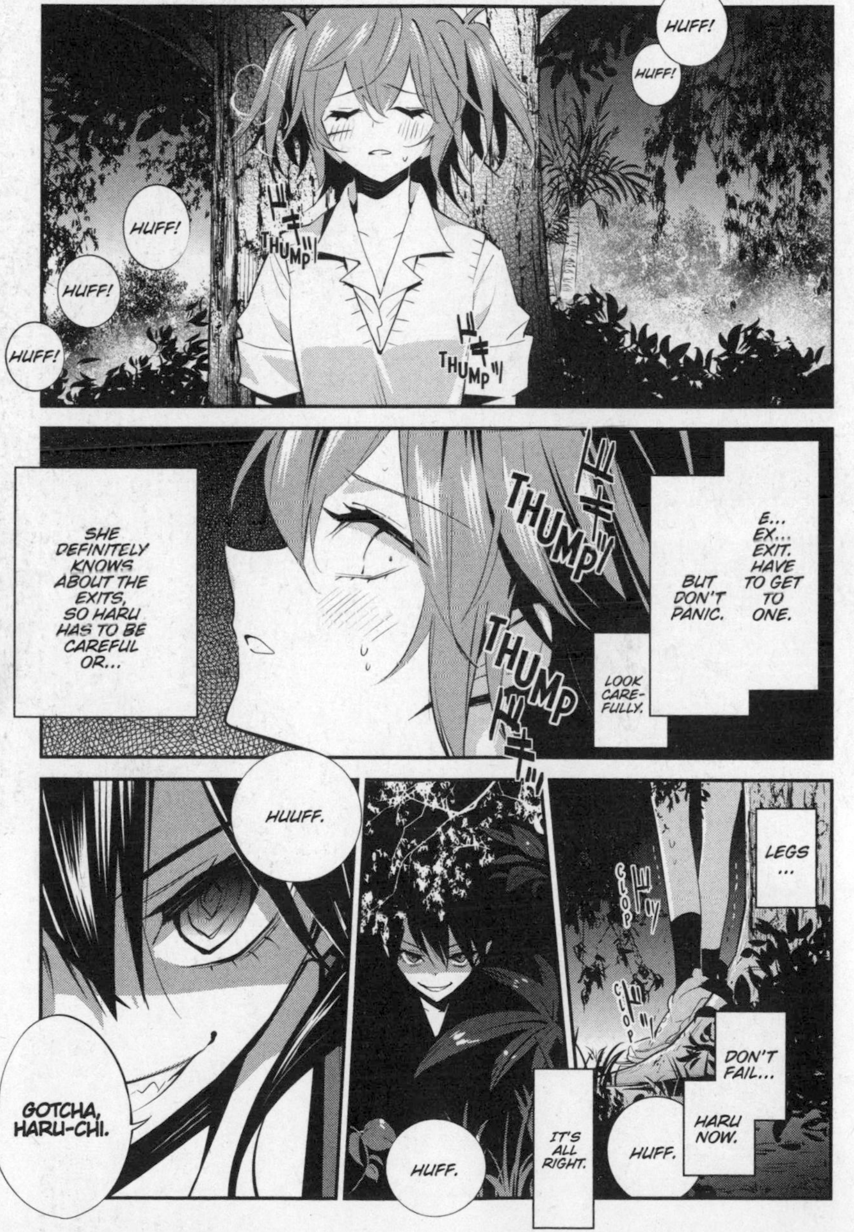
HUFF!
HUFF!
THUMP
HUFF!
HUFF!
HUFF!
THUMP
E... EX... EXIT. HAVE TO GET TO ONE.
BUT DON'T PANIC.
LOOK CAREFULLY.
THUMP
THUMP
SHE DEFINITELY KNOWS ABOUT THE EXITS, SO HARU HAS TO BE CAREFUL OR...
LEGS...
CLOP
CLOP
DON'T FAIL...
HARU NOW.
HUFF.
IT'S ALL RIGHT.
HUFF.
HUUFF.
GOTCHA, HARU-CHI.

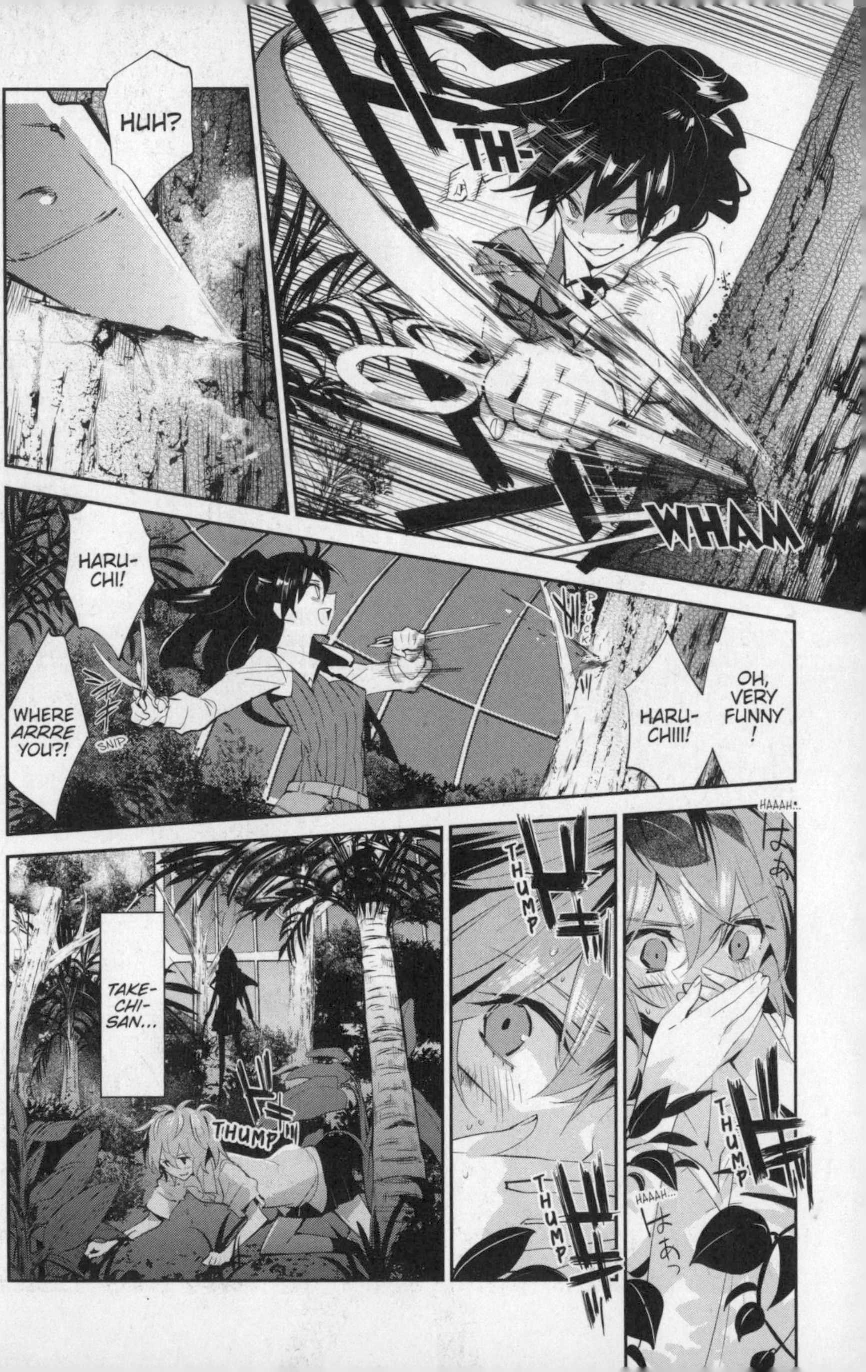
TH-
WHAM
HUH?
OH, VERY FUNNY!
HARU-CHIII!
PLUCK
HARU-CHI!
WHERE ARRRE YOU?!
SNIP
HAAAH...
THUMP
HAAAH...
はあっ
THUMP
THUMP
TAKE-CHI-SAN...
THUMP

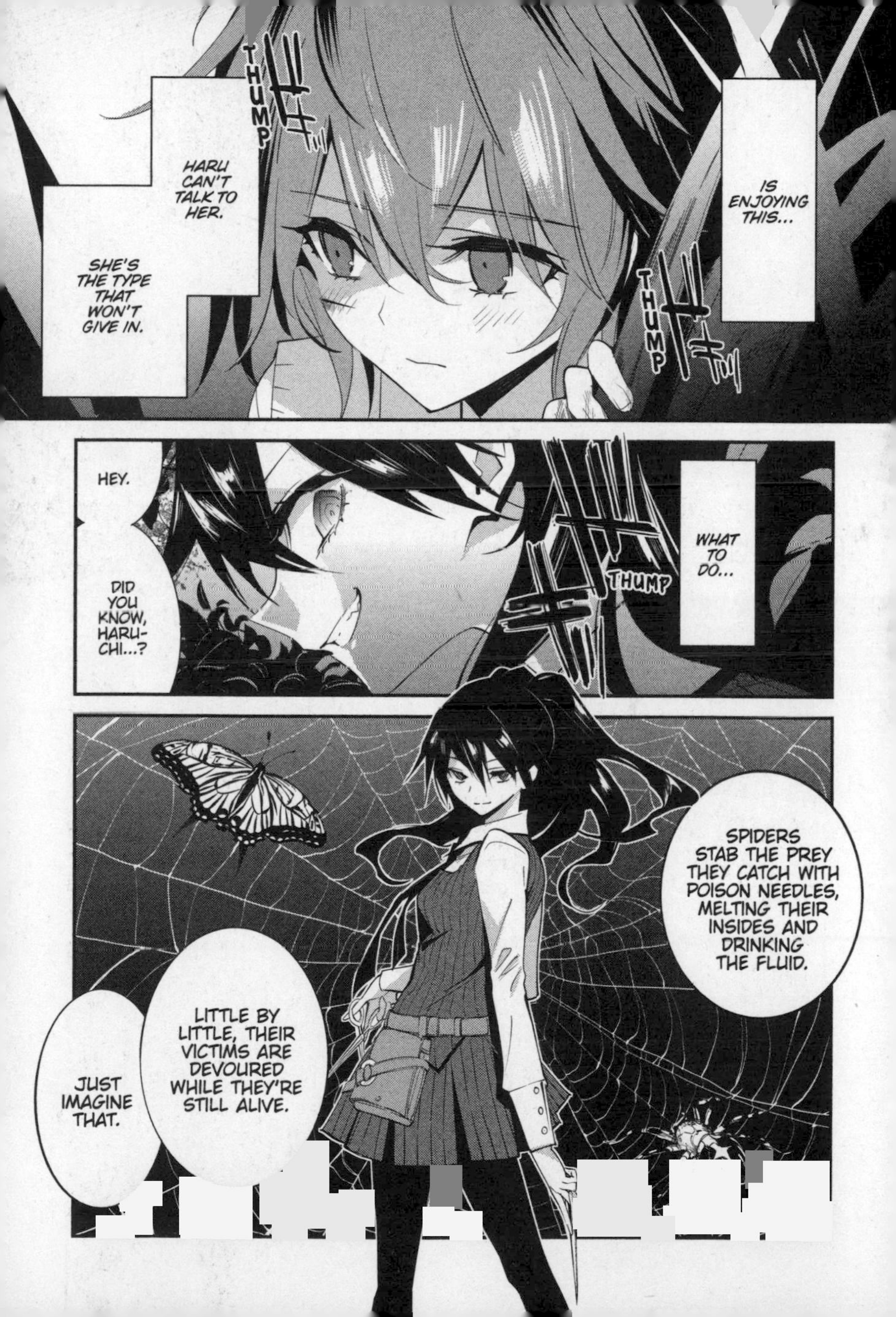
IS ENJOYING THIS...
THUMP
THUMP
HARU CAN'T TALK TO HER.
SHE'S THE TYPE THAT WON'T GIVE IN.
WHAT TO DO...
THUMP
HEY.
DID YOU KNOW, HARU-CHI...?
SPIDERS STAB THE PREY THEY CATCH WITH POISON NEEDLES, MELTING THEIR INSIDES AND DRINKING THE FLUID.
LITTLE BY LITTLE, THEIR VICTIMS ARE DEVOURED WHILE THEY'RE STILL ALIVE.
JUST IMAGINE THAT.

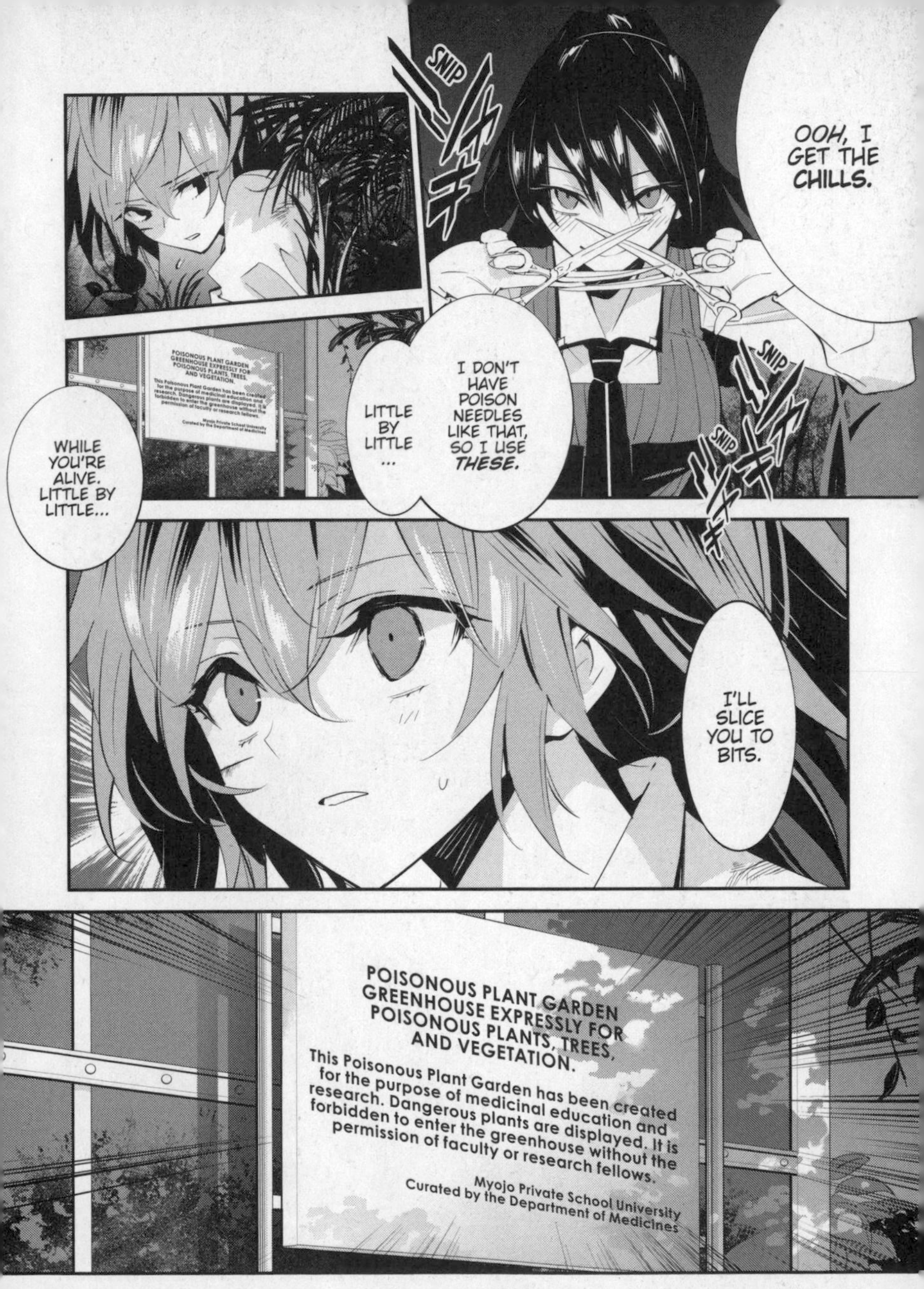
SNIP
OOH, I GET THE CHILLS.
I DON'T HAVE POISON NEEDLES LIKE THAT, SO I USE THESE.
SNIP
SNIP
LITTLE BY LITTLE ...
WHILE YOU'RE ALIVE. LITTLE BY LITTLE...
I'LL SLICE YOU TO BITS.
POISONOUS PLANT GARDEN GREENHOUSE EXPRESSLY FOR POISONOUS PLANTS, TREES, AND VEGETATION.
This Poisonous Plant Garden has been created for the purpose of medicinal education and research. Dangerous plants are displayed. It is forbidden to enter the greenhouse without the permission of faculty or research fellows.
Myojo Private School University
Curated by the Department of Medicines

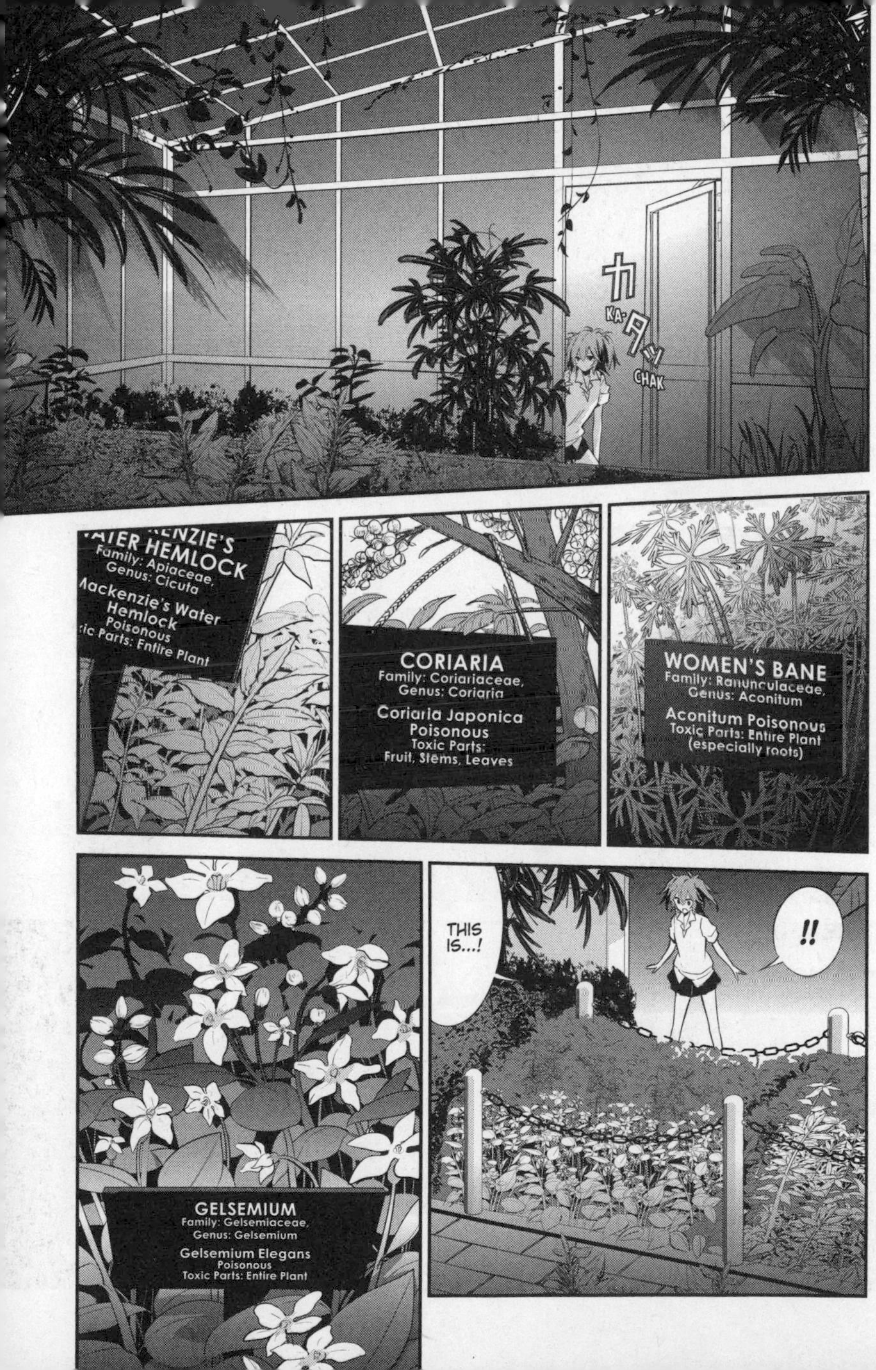

カタッ
KA-CHAK
WOMEN'S BANE
Family: Ranunculaceae,
Genus: Aconitum
Aconitum Poisonous
Toxic Parts: Entire Plant
(especially roots)
CORIARIA
Family: Coriariaceae,
Genus: Coriaria
Coriaria Japonica
Poisonous
Toxic Parts:
Fruit, Stems, Leaves
ENZIE'S
ATER HEMLOCK
Family: Apiaceae,
Genus: Cicuta
ackenzie's Water
Hemlock
Poisonous
ic Parts: Entire Plant
!!
THIS IS...!
GELSEMIUM
Family: Gelsemiaceae,
Genus: Gelsemium
Gelsemium Elegans
Poisonous
Toxic Parts: Entire Plant

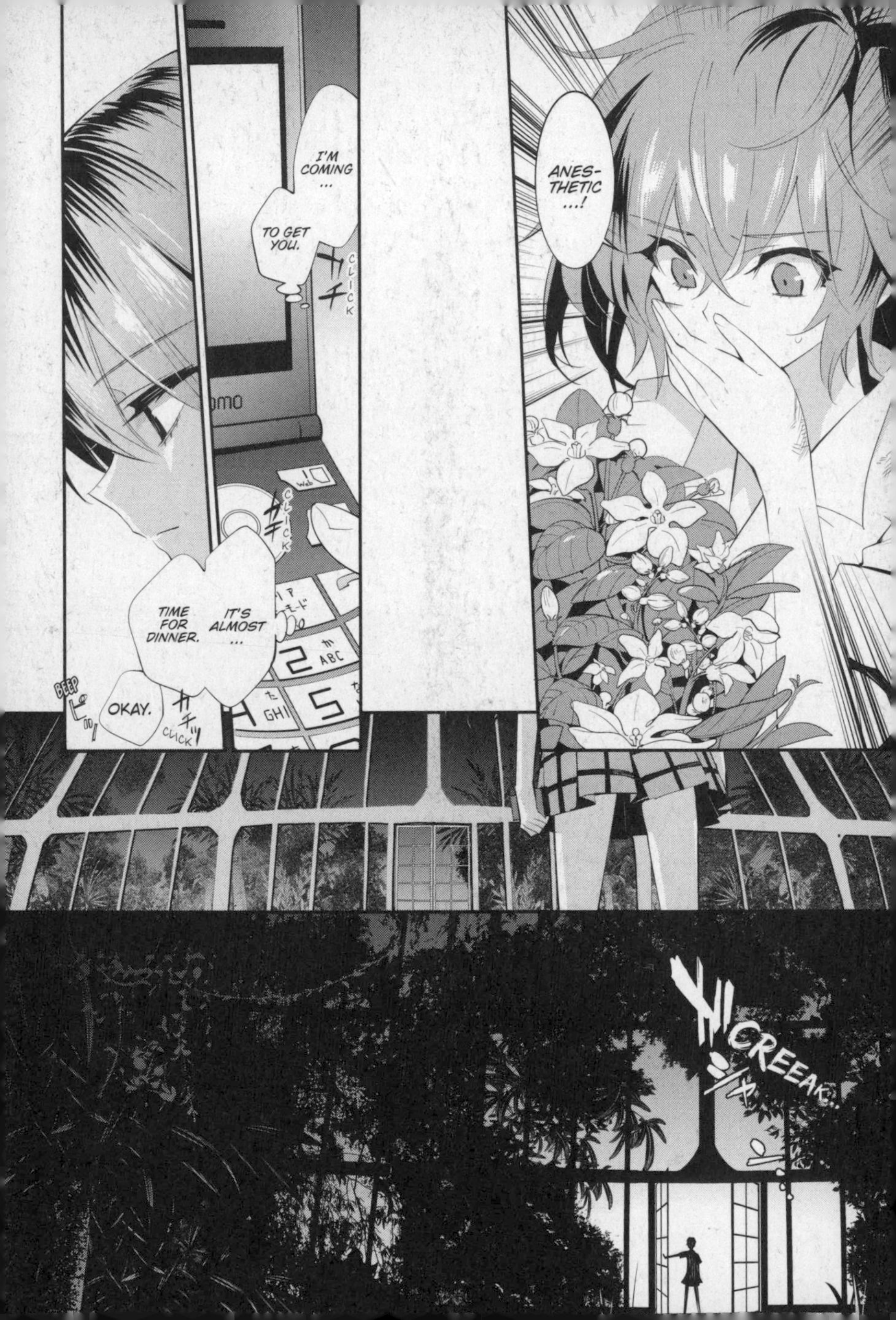
ANES-THETIC ...!
I'M COMING ...
TO GET YOU.
CLICK
CLICK
IT'S ALMOST ...
TIME FOR DINNER.
OKAY.
CLICK
BEEP
CREEAK...

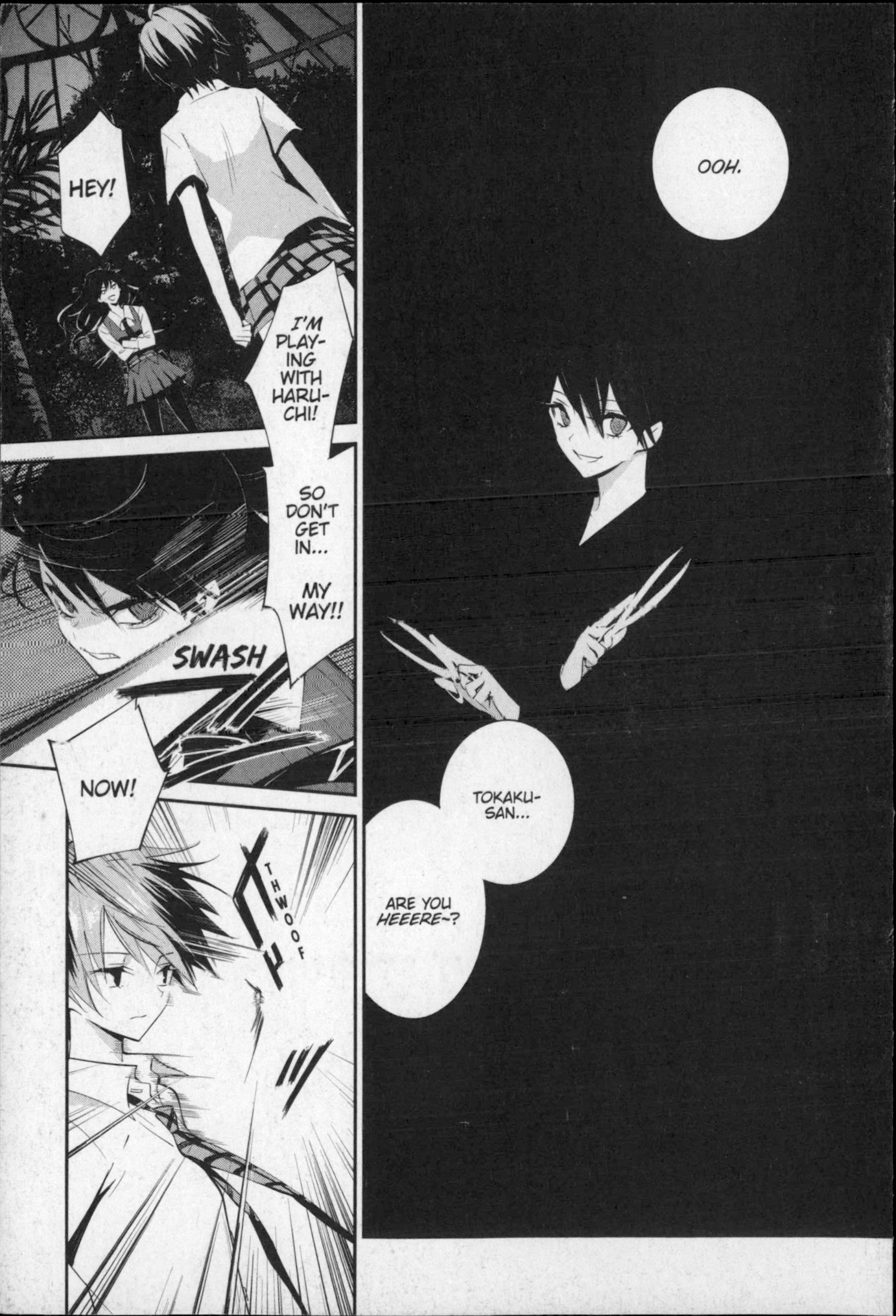
OOH.
TOKAKU-SAN...
ARE YOU HEEERE~?
HEY!
I'M PLAYING WITH HARU-CHI!
SO DON'T GET IN... MY WAY!!
SWASH
NOW!
THWOOF

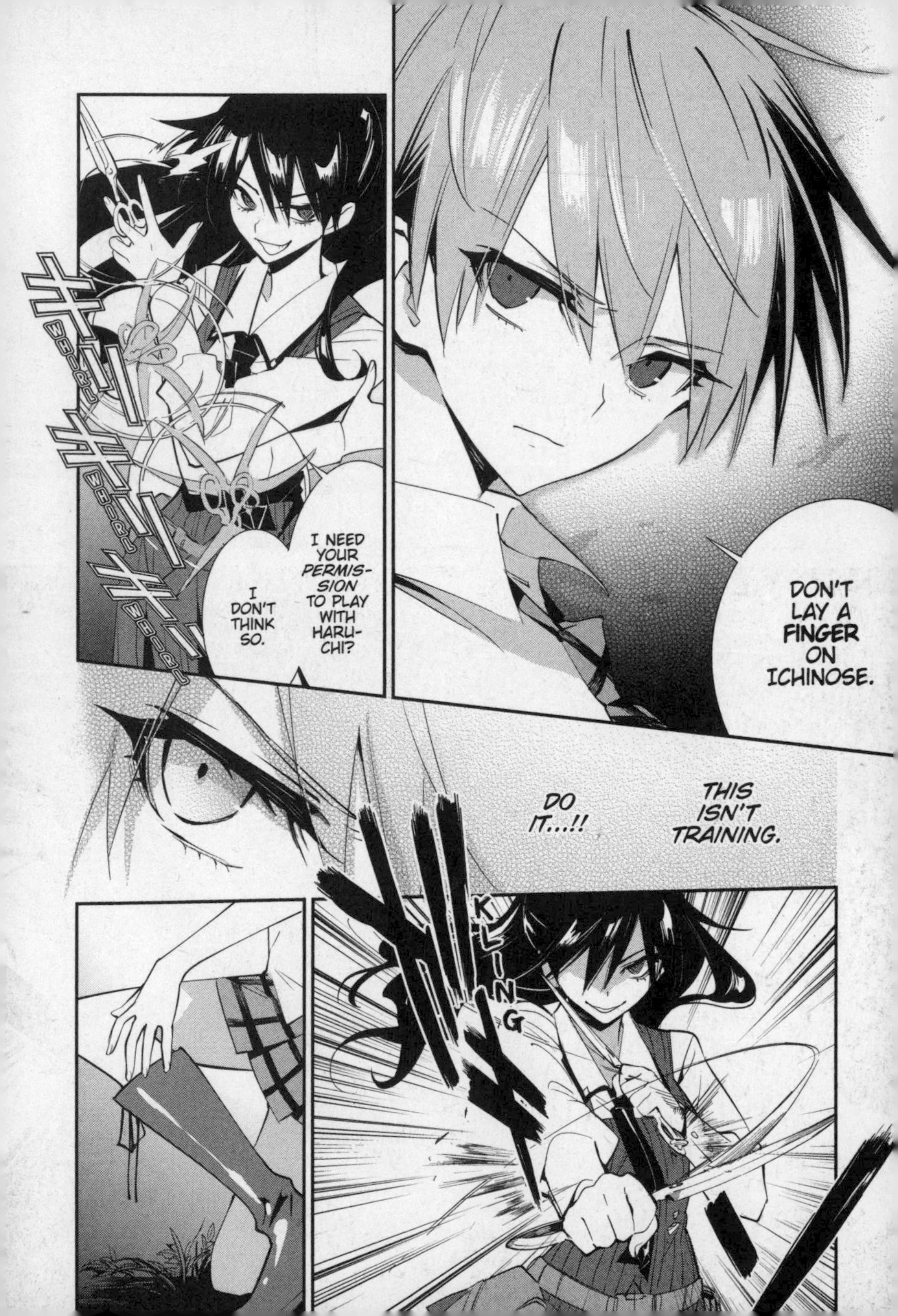
DON'T LAY A FINGER ON ICHINOSE.
I NEED YOUR PERMISSION TO PLAY WITH HARU-CHI?
I DON'T THINK SO.
WHIRL
WHIRL
WHIRL
THIS ISN'T TRAINING.
DO IT...!!
KLING

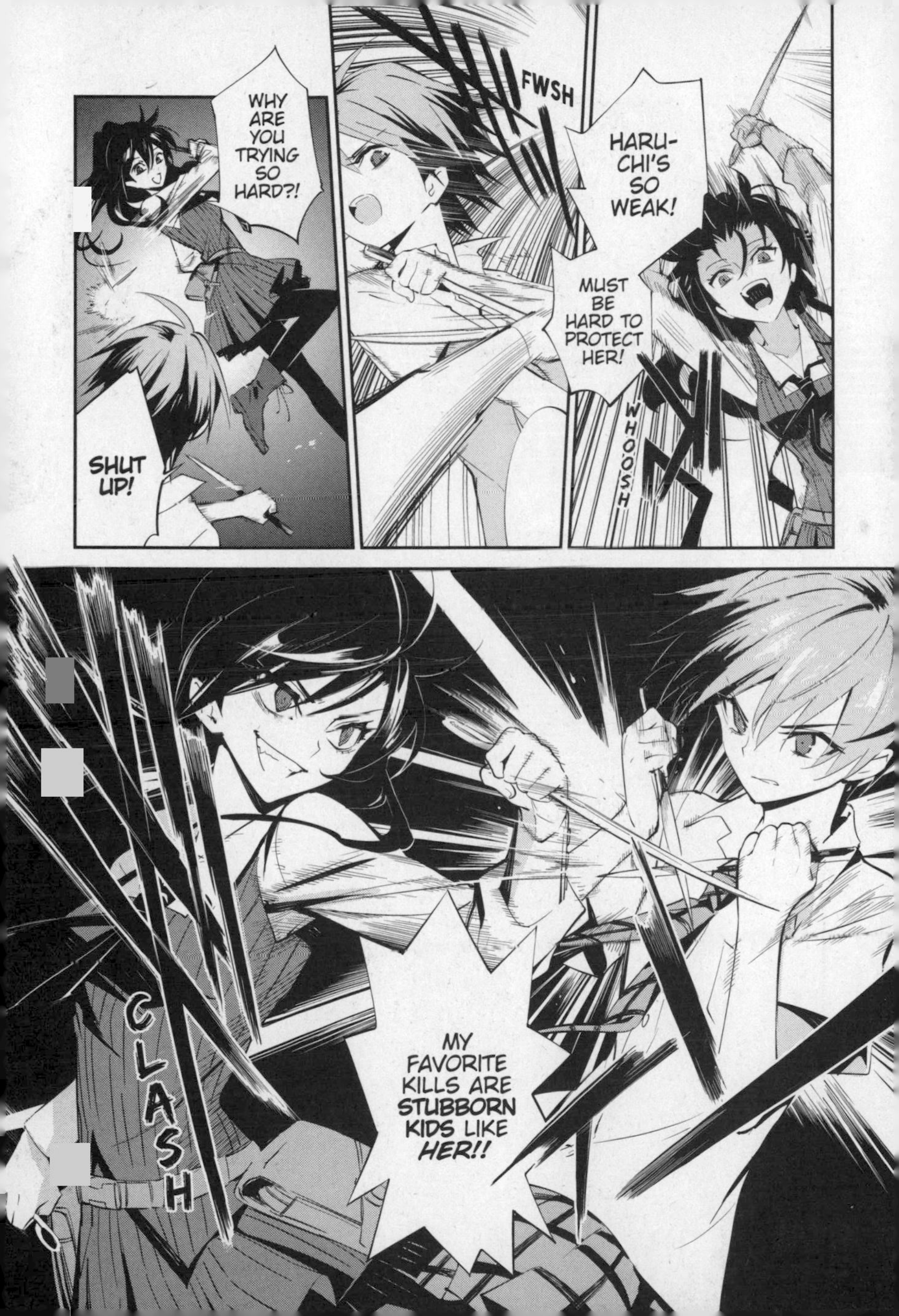
HARU-CHI'S SO WEAK!
MUST BE HARD TO PROTECT HER!
WHOOOSH
FWSH
WHY ARE YOU TRYING SO HARD?!
SHUT UP!
MY FAVORITE KILLS ARE STUBBORN KIDS LIKE HER!!
CLASH

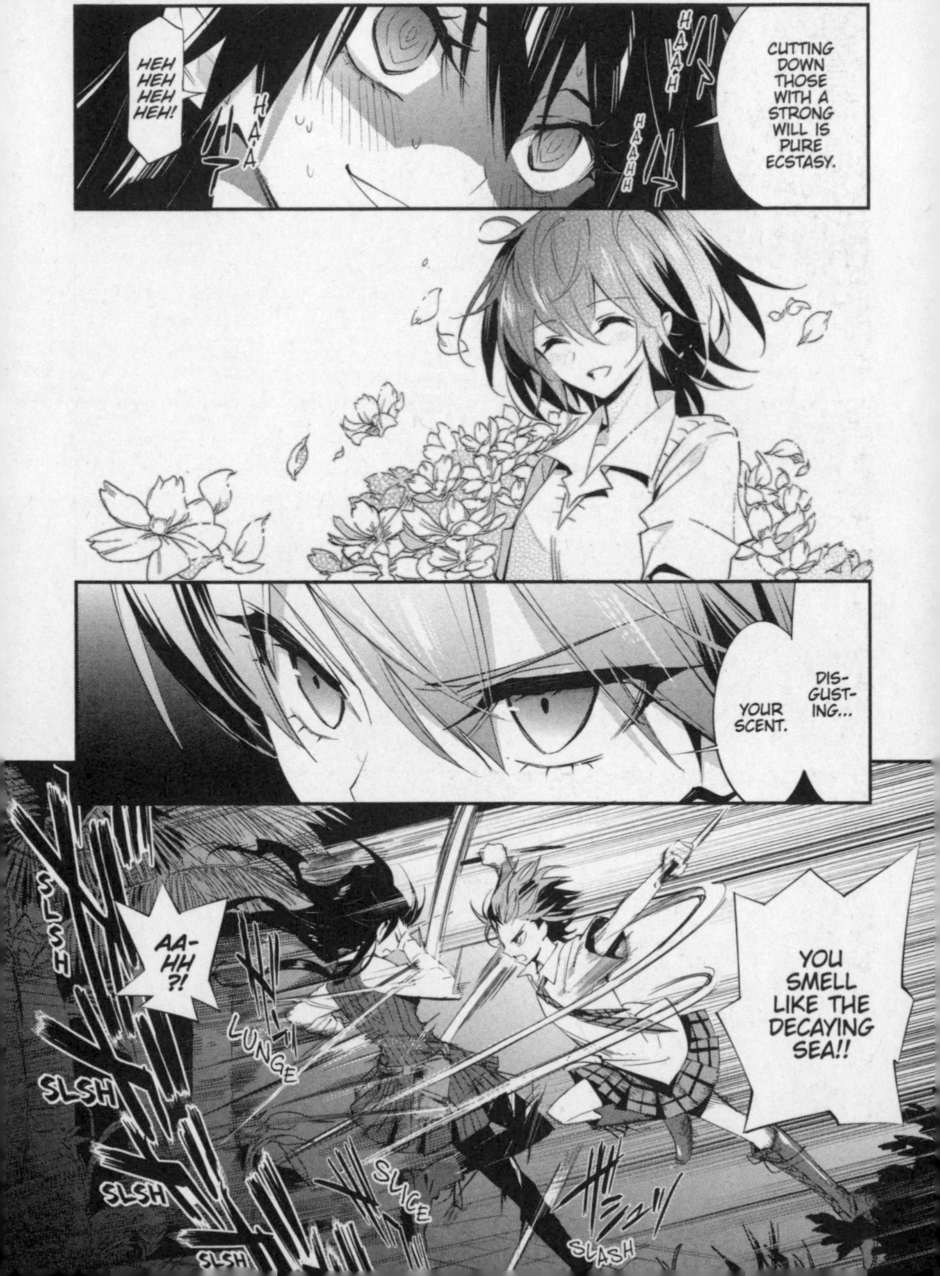
CUTTING DOWN THOSE WITH A STRONG WILL IS PURE ECSTASY.
HAAAH
HAAHH
HAA
HEH HEH HEH HEH!
DIS-GUSTING...
YOUR SCENT.
YOU SMELL LIKE THE DECAYING SEA!!
AA-HH?!
LUNGE
SLICE
SLASH
SLSH
SLSH
SLSH
SLSH

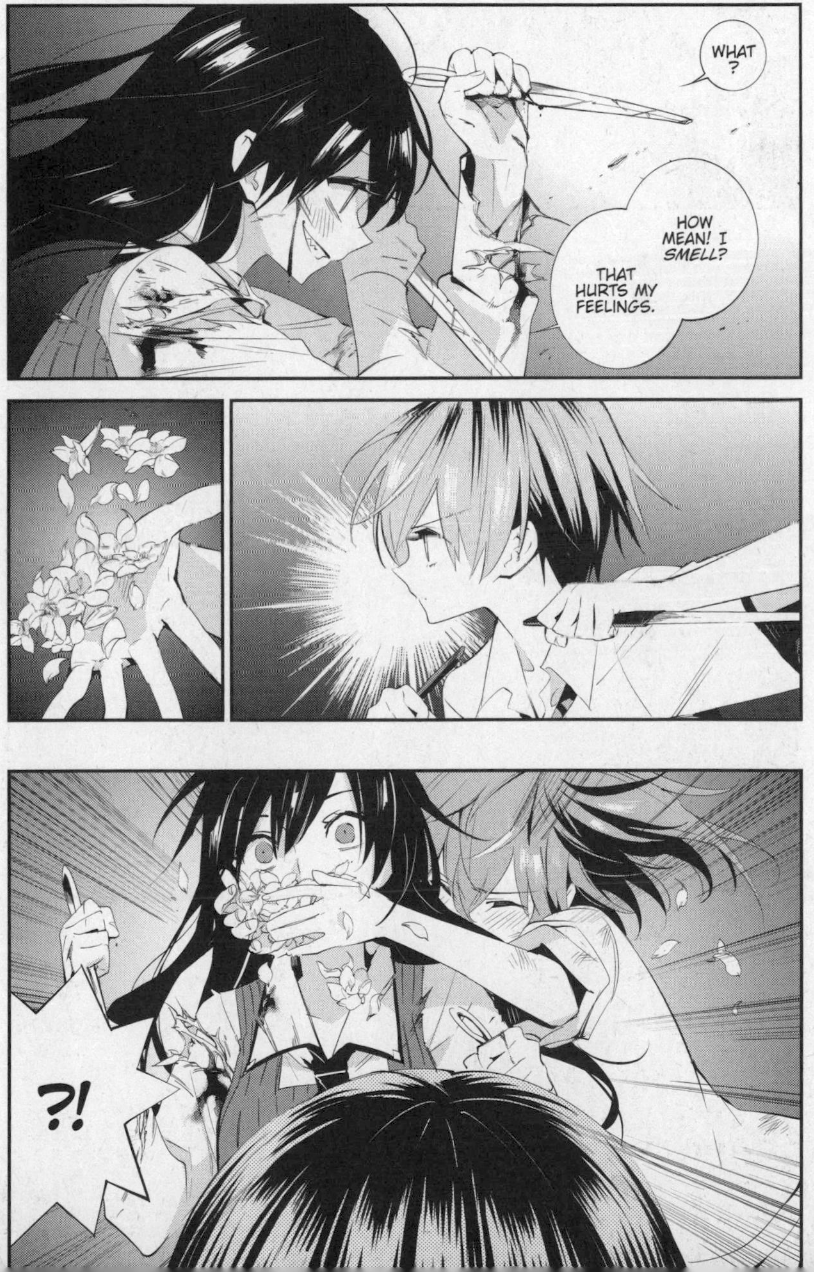
WHAT?
HOW MEAN! I SMELL?
THAT HURTS MY FEELINGS.
?!

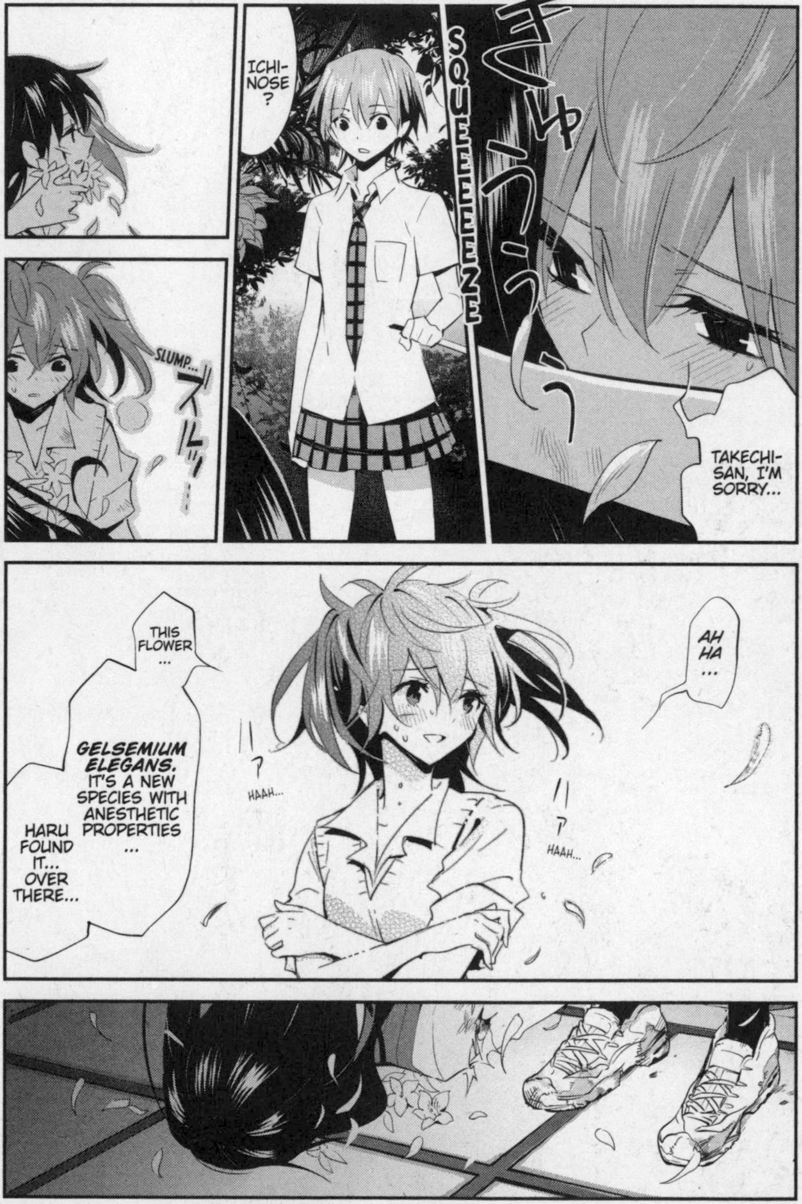
SQUEEEEEZE
TAKECHI-SAN, I'M SORRY...
ICHI-NOSE?
SLUMP...
ズルッ
AH HA ...
ハァ
HAAH...
ハァ
HAAH...
THIS FLOWER ...
GELSEMIUM ELEGANS. IT'S A NEW SPECIES WITH ANESTHETIC PROPERTIES ...
HARU FOUND IT... OVER THERE...

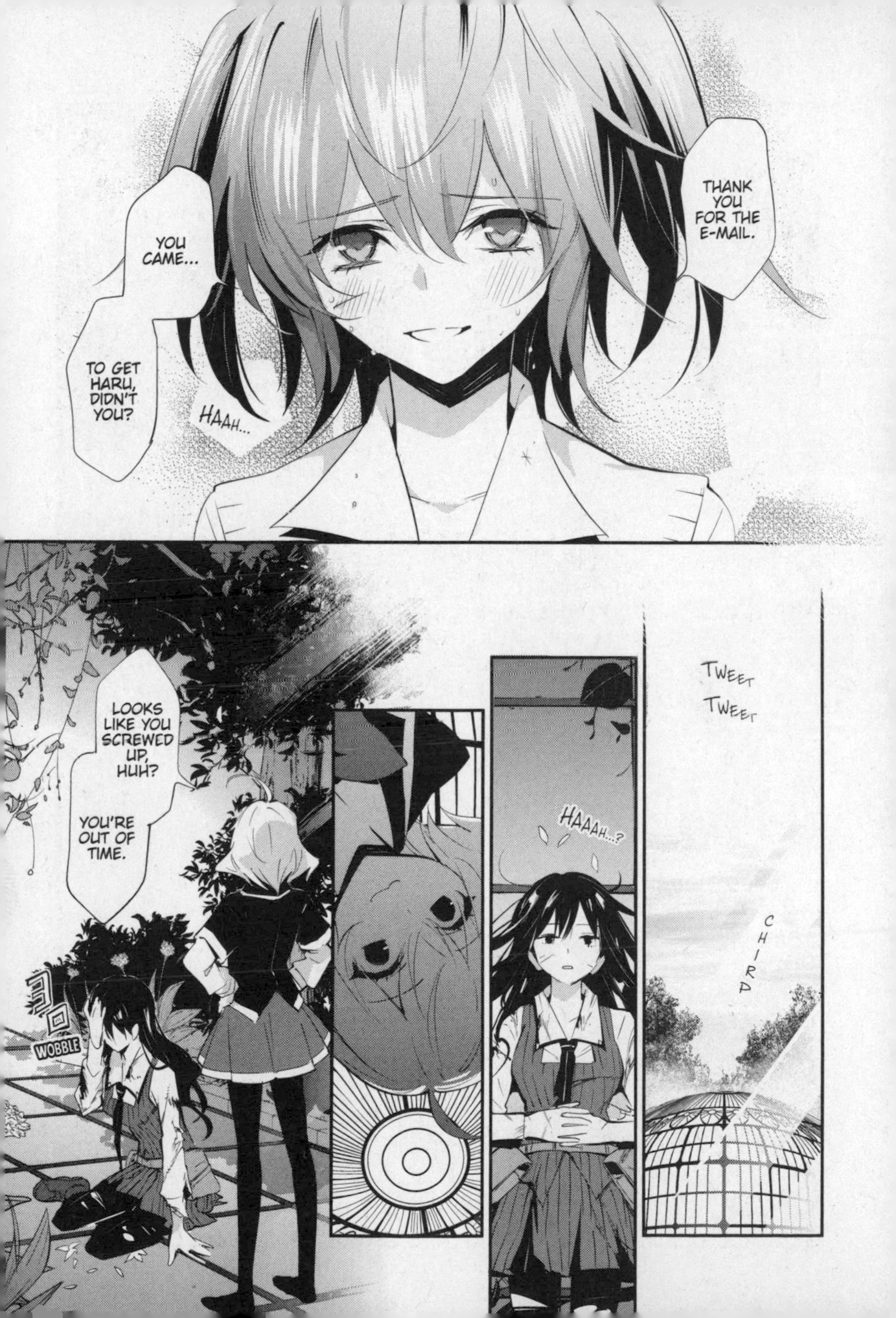
THANK YOU FOR THE E-MAIL.
YOU CAME...
TO GET HARU, DIDN'T YOU?
HAAH...
TWEET TWEET
CHIRP
HAAAH...?
LOOKS LIKE YOU SCREWED UP, HUH?
YOU'RE OUT OF TIME.
WOBBLE

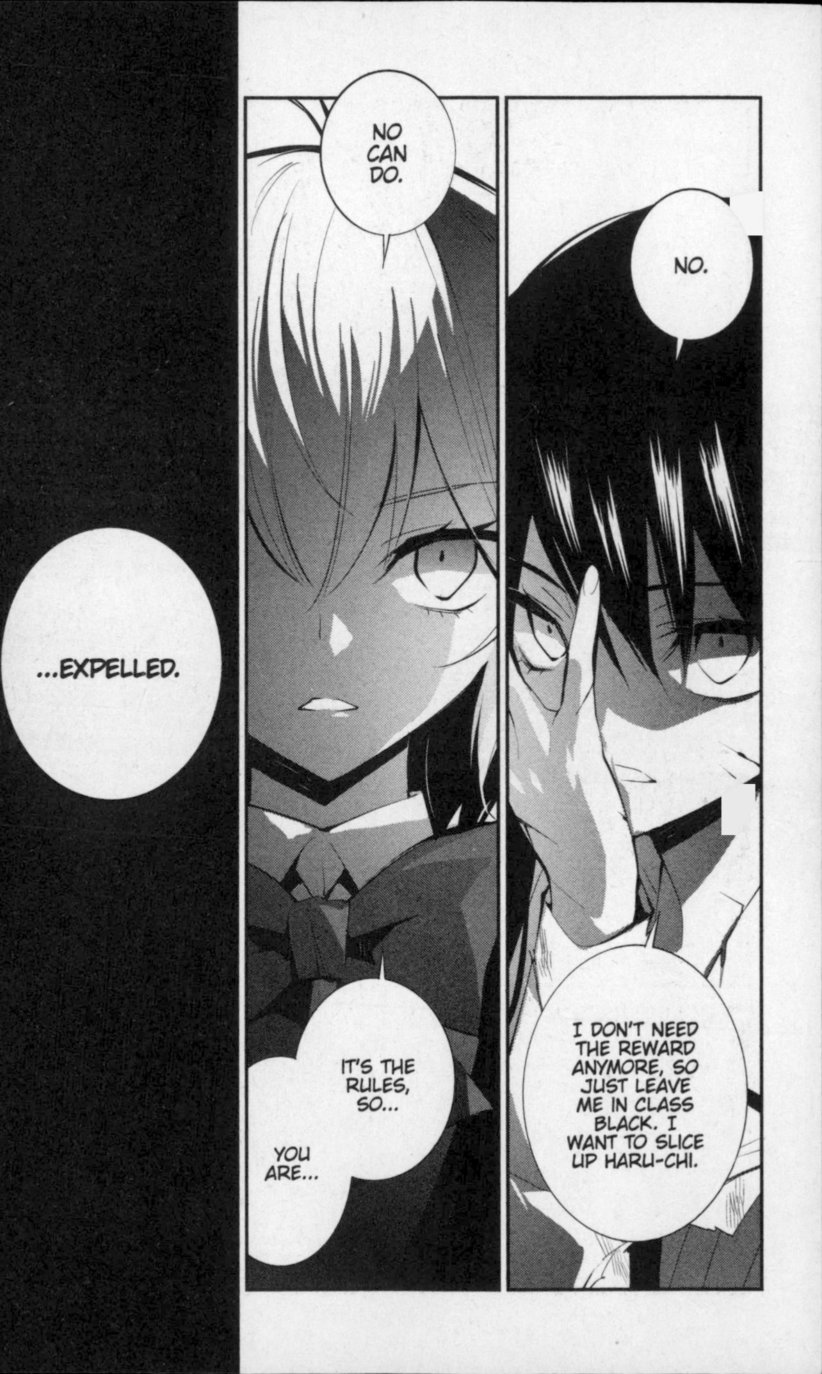
NO.
I DON'T NEED THE REWARD ANYMORE, SO JUST LEAVE ME IN CLASS BLACK. I WANT TO SLICE UP HARU-CHI.
NO CAN DO.
IT'S THE RULES, SO...
YOU ARE...
...EXPELLED.

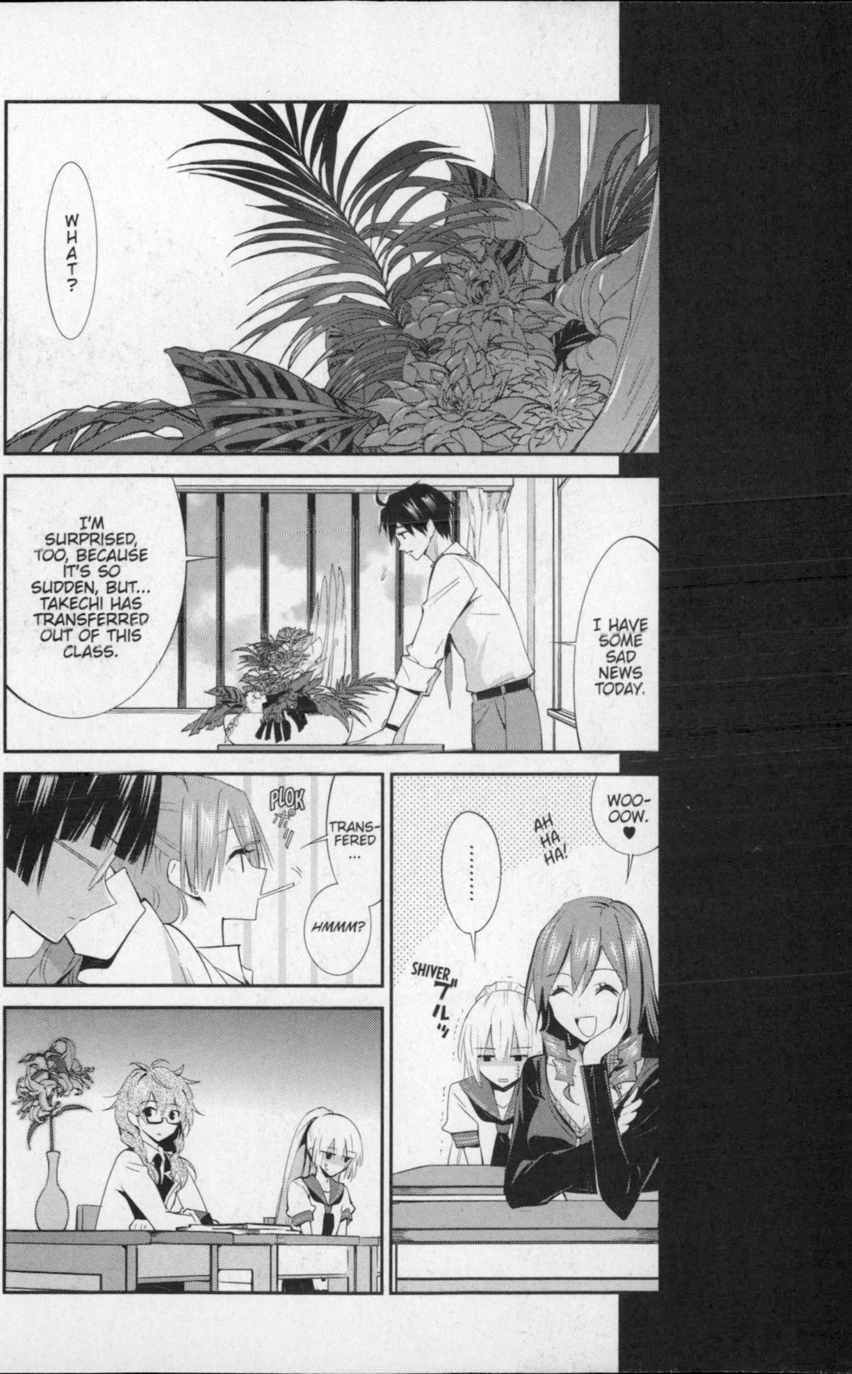
WHAT?
I HAVE SOME SAD NEWS TODAY.
I'M SURPRISED, TOO, BECAUSE IT'S SO SUDDEN, BUT... TAKECHI HAS TRANSFERRED OUT OF THIS CLASS.
WOOO-OOW. ♥
AH HA HA!
......
SHIVER ブルッ
PLOK
TRANS-FERED ...
HMMM?

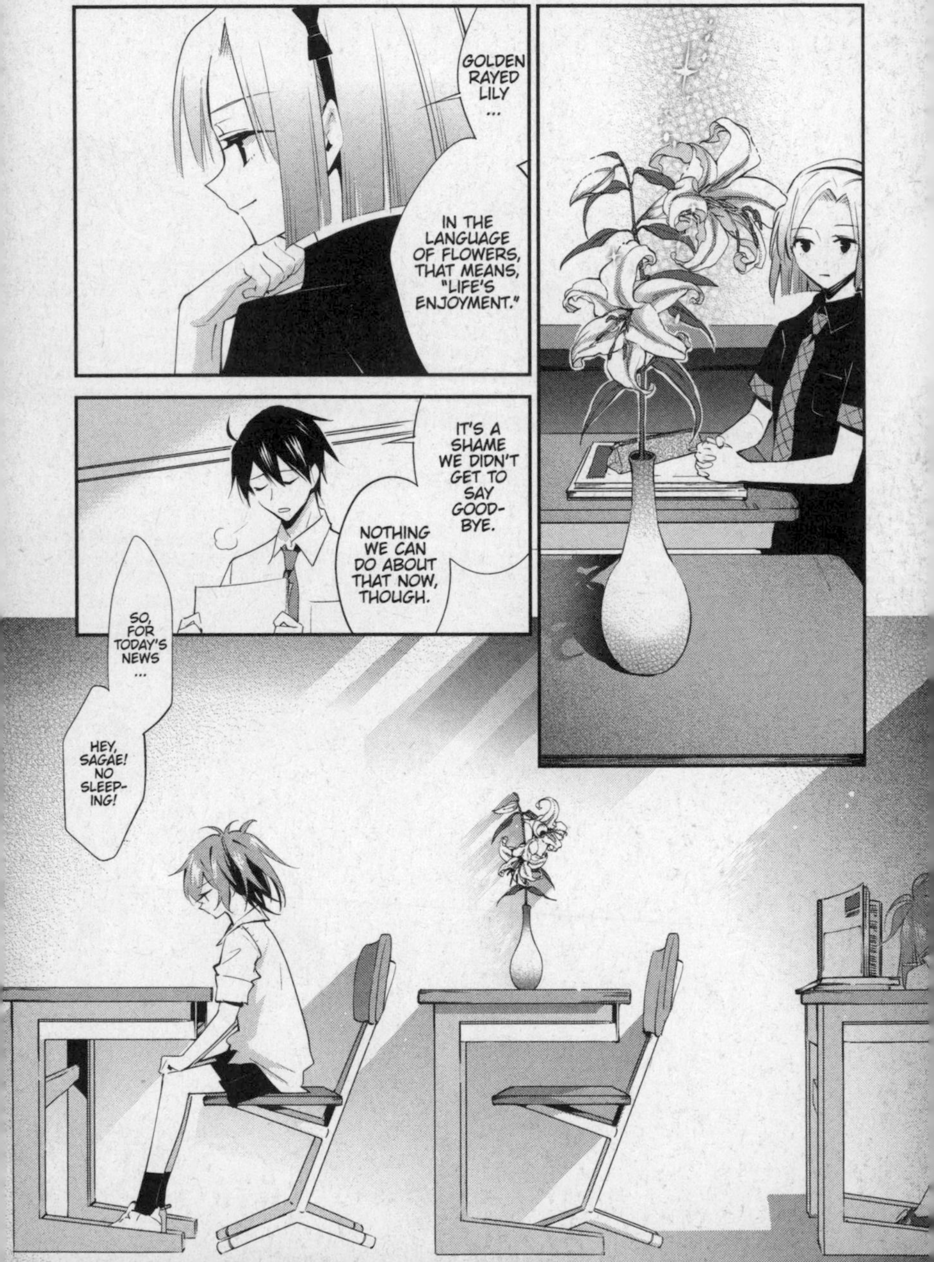
GOLDEN RAYED LILY ...
IN THE LANGUAGE OF FLOWERS, THAT MEANS, "LIFE'S ENJOYMENT."
IT'S A SHAME WE DIDN'T GET TO SAY GOOD-BYE.
NOTHING WE CAN DO ABOUT THAT NOW, THOUGH.
SO, FOR TODAY'S NEWS ...
HEY, SAGAE! NO SLEEP-ING!

riddle story of devil

Chapter 14
Can't Fail

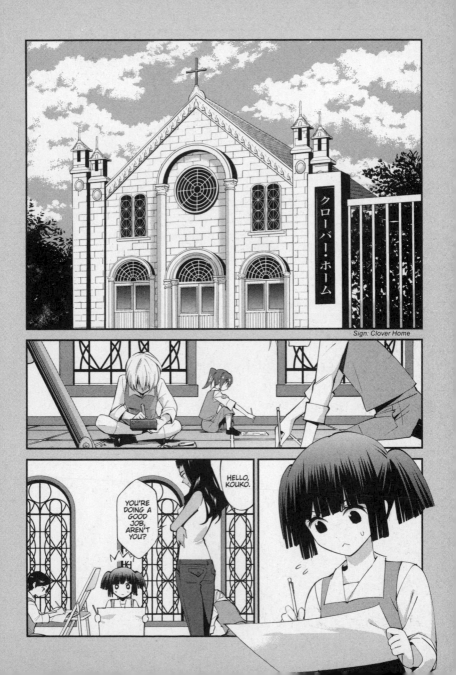

Sign: Clover Home

HELLO, KOUKO.

YOU'RE DOING A GOOD JOB, AREN'T YOU?

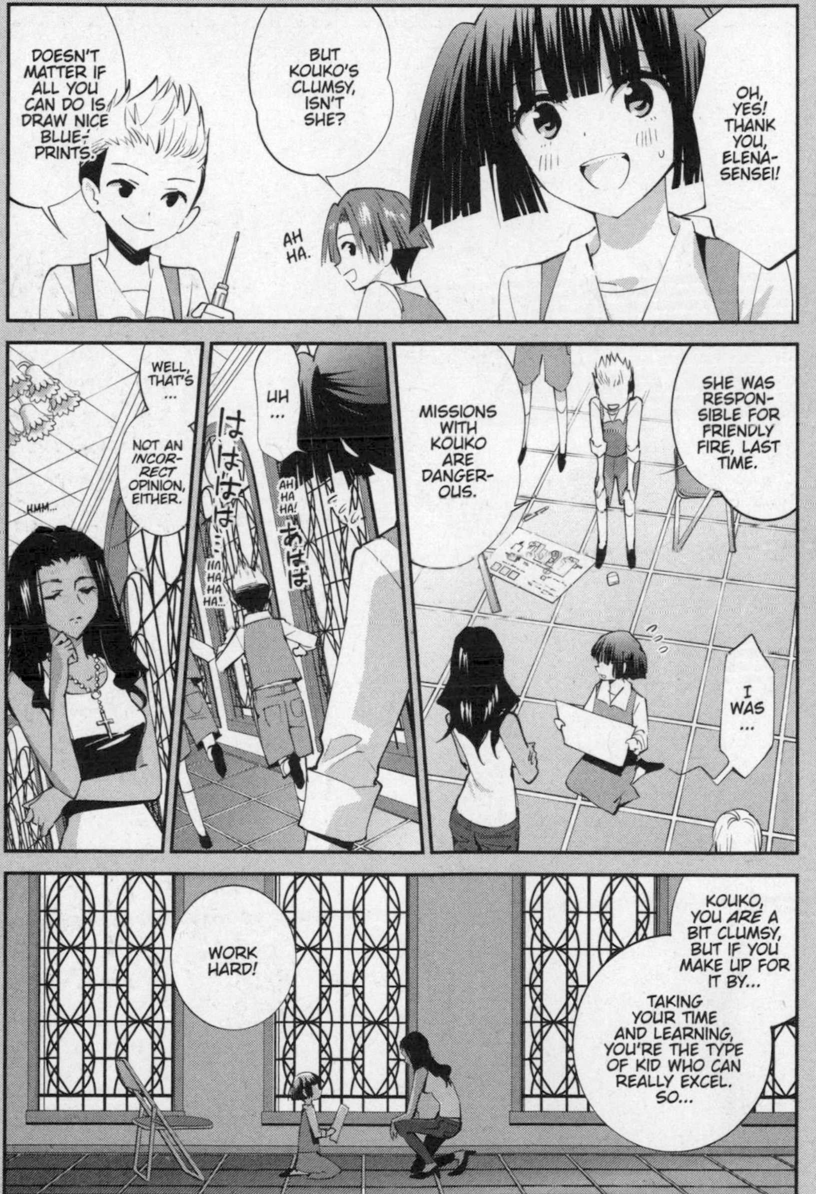

OH, YES! THANK YOU, ELENA-SENSEI!
BUT KOUKO'S CLUMSY, ISN'T SHE?
DOESN'T MATTER IF ALL YOU CAN DO IS DRAW NICE BLUE-PRINTS.
AH HA.
SHE WAS RESPONSIBLE FOR FRIENDLY FIRE, LAST TIME.
MISSIONS WITH KOUKO ARE DANGEROUS.
I WAS...
UH...
ははははは
AH HA HA!
あはは
HA HA HA HA...
WELL, THAT'S...
NOT AN *INCORRECT* OPINION, EITHER.
HMM...
KOUKO, YOU *ARE* A BIT CLUMSY, BUT IF YOU MAKE UP FOR IT BY...
TAKING YOUR TIME AND LEARNING, YOU'RE THE TYPE OF KID WHO CAN REALLY EXCEL. SO...
WORK HARD!

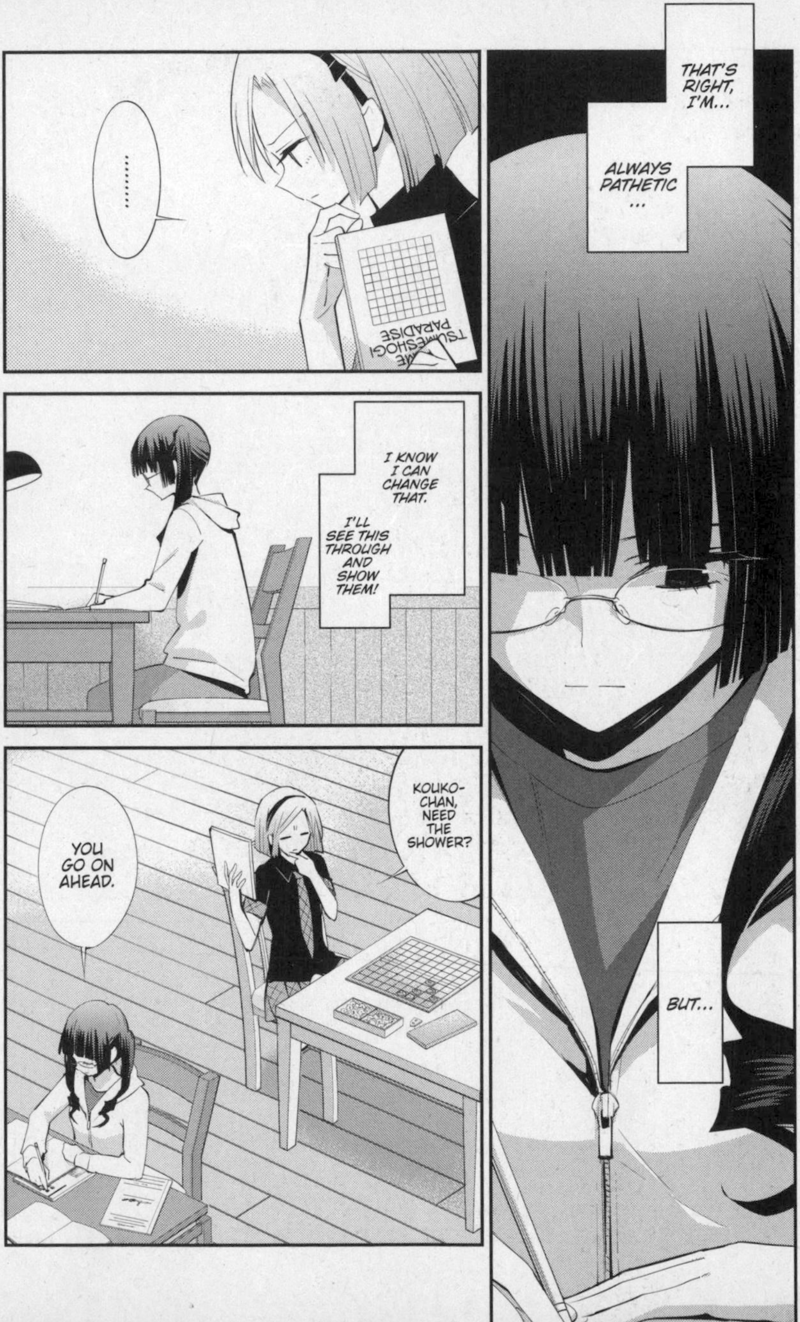
THAT'S RIGHT, I'M...
ALWAYS PATHETIC ...
BUT...
......
TSUMESHOGI PARADISE
I KNOW I CAN CHANGE THAT.
I'LL SEE THIS THROUGH AND SHOW THEM!
KOUKO-CHAN, NEED THE SHOWER?
YOU GO ON AHEAD.

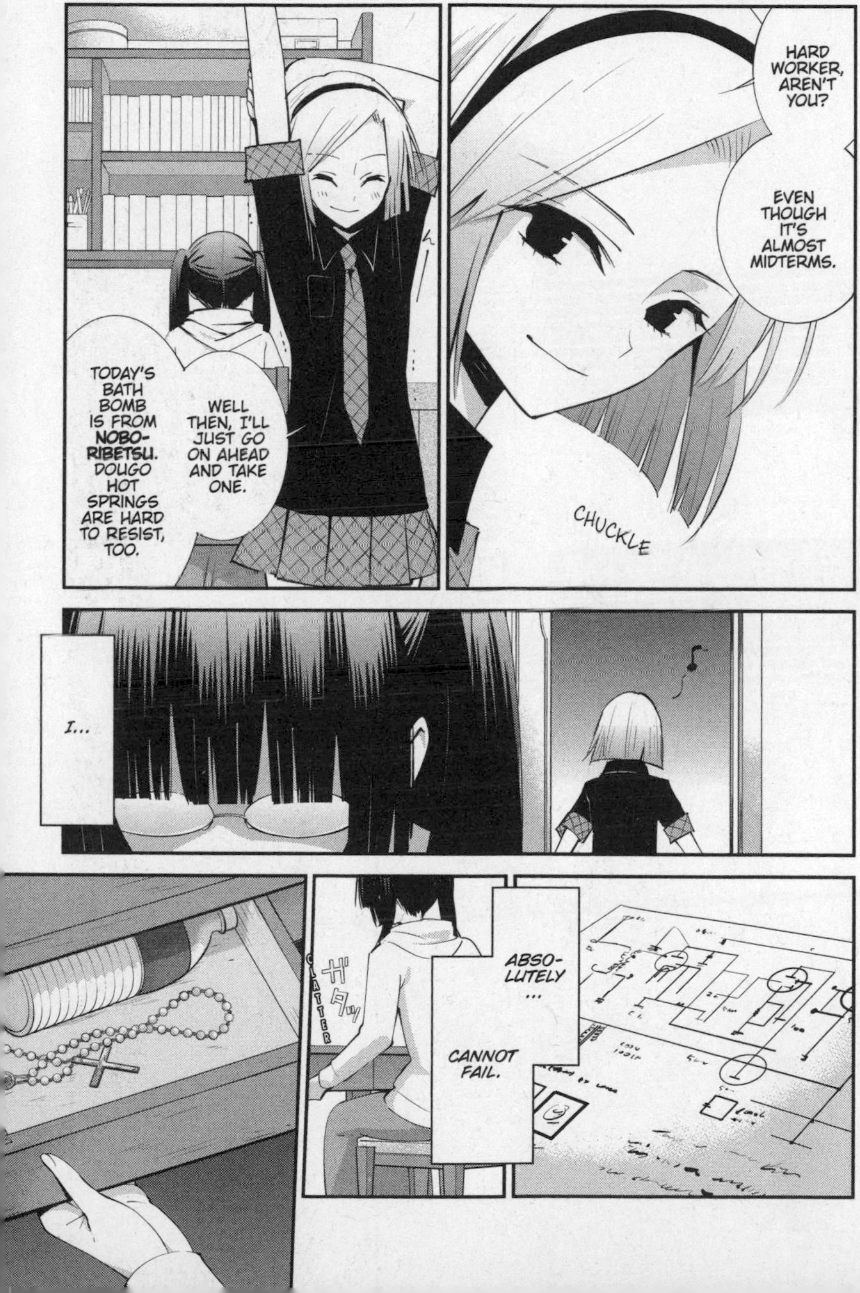
HARD WORKER, AREN'T YOU?
EVEN THOUGH IT'S ALMOST MIDTERMS.
CHUCKLE
WELL THEN, I'LL JUST GO ON AHEAD AND TAKE ONE.
TODAY'S BATH BOMB IS FROM NOBO-RIBETSU. DOUGO HOT SPRINGS ARE HARD TO RESIST, TOO.
I...
ABSO-LUTELY...
CANNOT FAIL.
ガタッ
CLATTER

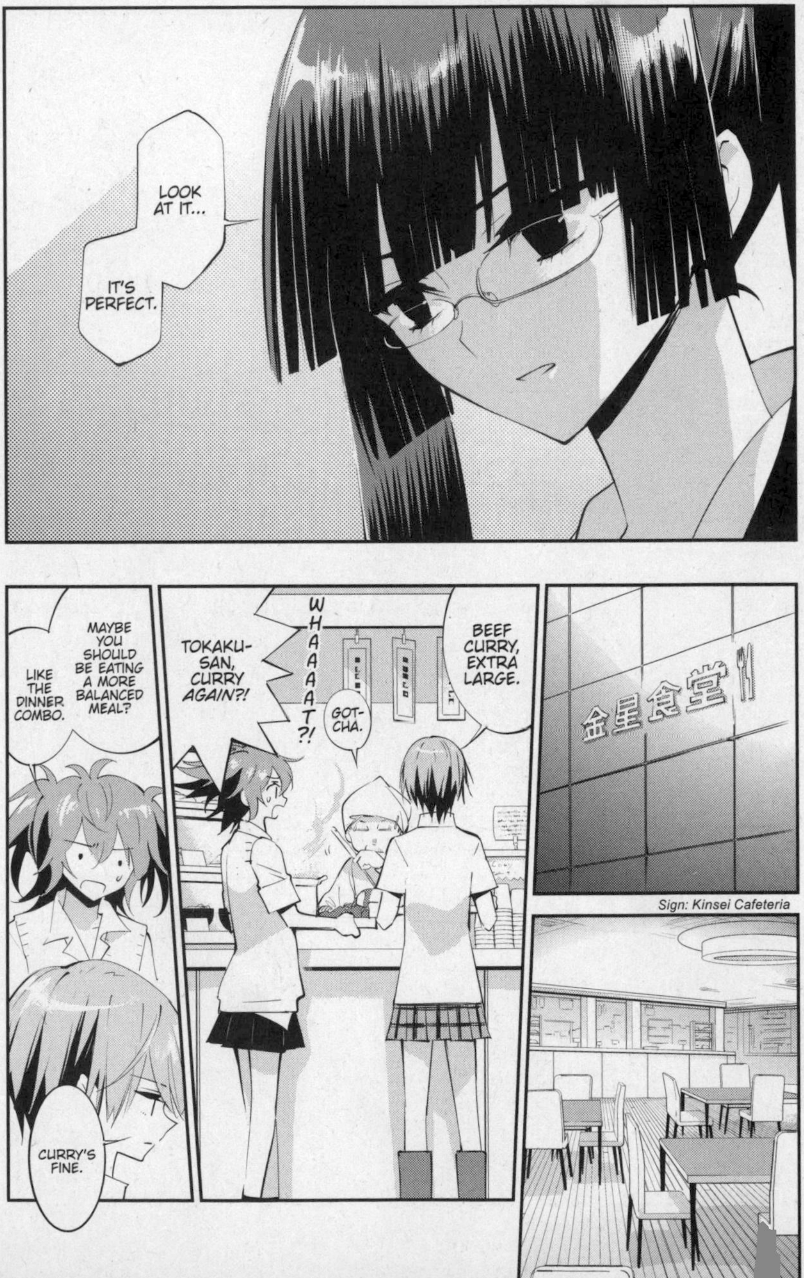
LOOK AT IT...
IT'S PERFECT.
金星食堂
Sign: Kinsei Cafeteria
BEEF CURRY, EXTRA LARGE.
GOT-CHA.
WHAAAAAT?!
TOKAKU-SAN, CURRY AGAIN?!
MAYBE YOU SHOULD BE EATING A MORE BALANCED MEAL?
LIKE THE DINNER COMBO.
CURRY'S FINE.

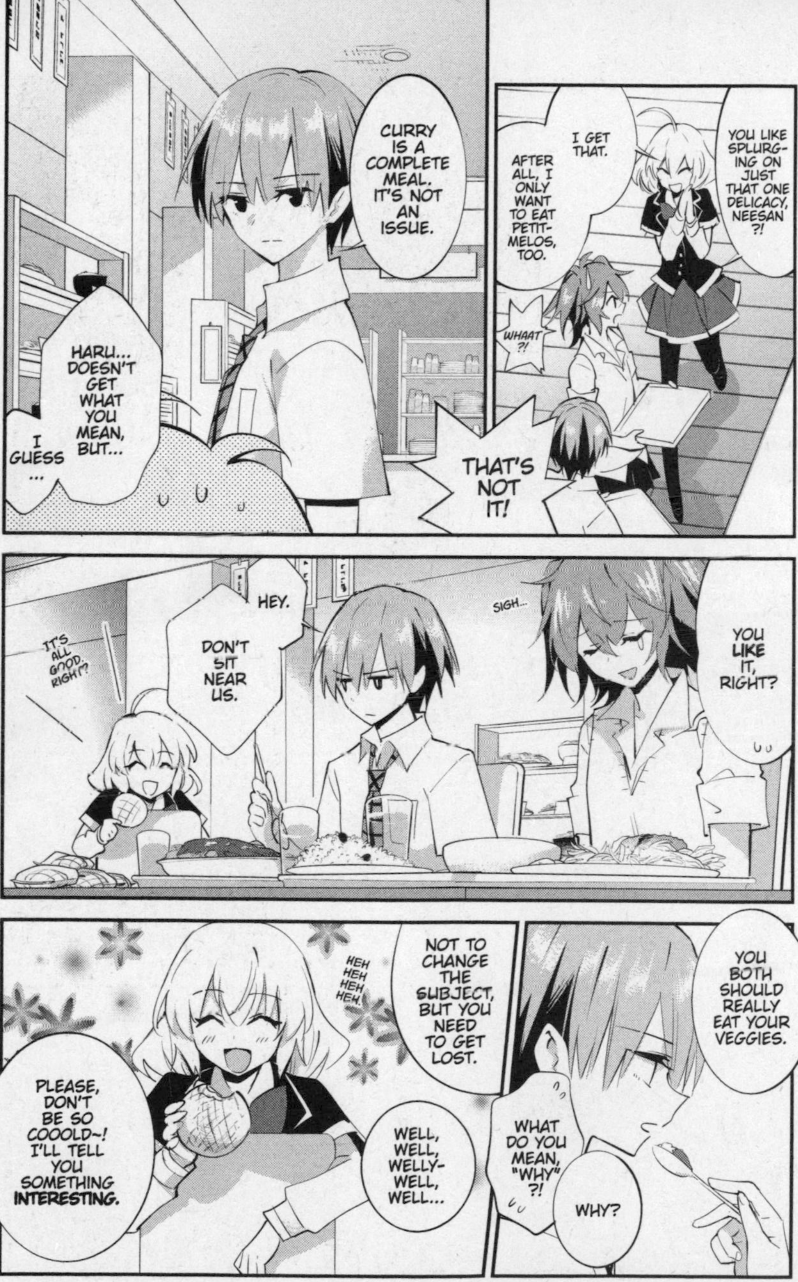
YOU LIKE SPLURGING ON JUST THAT ONE DELICACY, NEESAN?!
I GET THAT.
AFTER ALL, I ONLY WANT TO EAT PETIT-MELOS, TOO.
WHAAT?!
THAT'S NOT IT!
CURRY IS A COMPLETE MEAL. IT'S NOT AN ISSUE.
HARU... DOESN'T GET WHAT YOU MEAN, BUT...
I GUESS...
YOU LIKE IT, RIGHT?
SIGH...
HEY.
DON'T SIT NEAR US.
IT'S ALL GOOD, RIGHT?
YOU BOTH SHOULD REALLY EAT YOUR VEGGIES.
WHY?
WHAT DO YOU MEAN, "WHY"?!
NOT TO CHANGE THE SUBJECT, BUT YOU NEED TO GET LOST.
HEH HEH HEH HEH.
WELL, WELL, WELLY-WELL, WELL...
PLEASE, DON'T BE SO COOOLD~! I'LL TELL YOU SOMETHING INTERESTING.

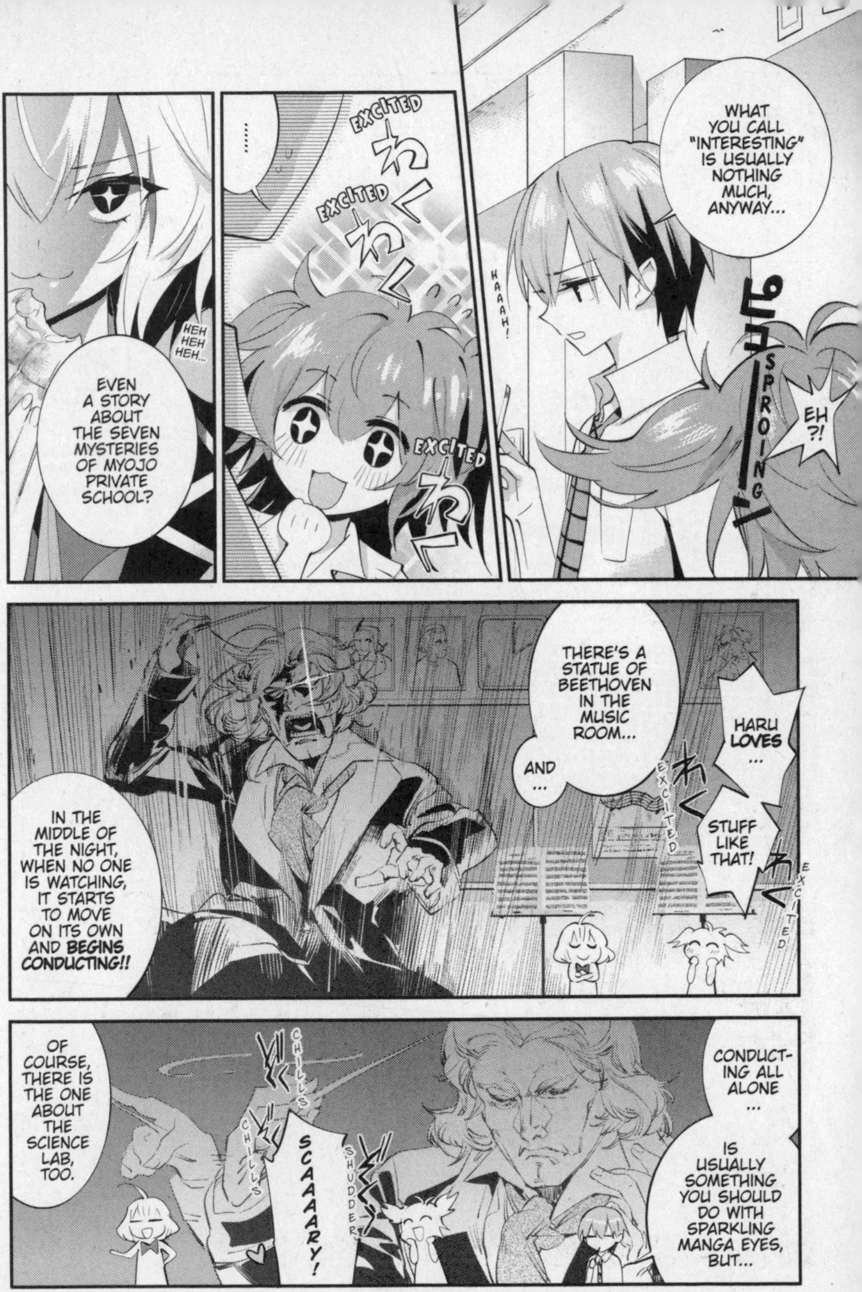
WHAT YOU CALL "INTERESTING" IS USUALLY NOTHING MUCH, ANYWAY...
EH ?!
SPROING!
HAAAAH!
EXCITED
EXCITED
EXCITED
......
HEH HEH HEH...
EVEN A STORY ABOUT THE SEVEN MYSTERIES OF MYOJO PRIVATE SCHOOL?
HARU **LOVES** ...
STUFF LIKE THAT!
EXCITED
EXCITED
THERE'S A STATUE OF BEETHOVEN IN THE MUSIC ROOM...
AND ...
IN THE MIDDLE OF THE NIGHT, WHEN NO ONE IS WATCHING, IT STARTS TO MOVE ON ITS OWN AND **BEGINS CONDUCTING!!**
CONDUCT-ING ALL ALONE ...
IS USUALLY SOMETHING YOU SHOULD DO WITH SPARKLING MANGA EYES, BUT...
SHUDDER
SCAAAARY!
CHILLS
CHILLS
OF COURSE, THERE IS THE ONE ABOUT THE SCIENCE LAB, TOO.

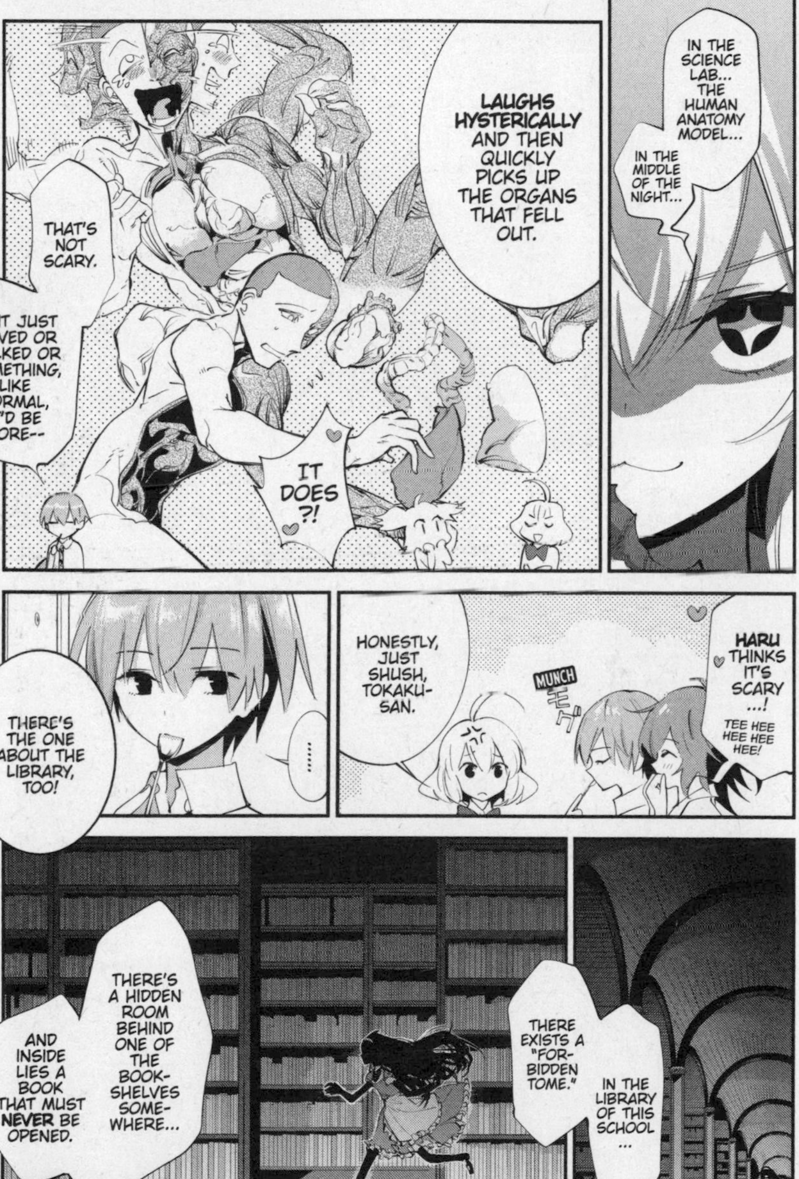
IN THE SCIENCE LAB... THE HUMAN ANATOMY MODEL...
IN THE MIDDLE OF THE NIGHT...
LAUGHS HYSTERICALLY AND THEN QUICKLY PICKS UP THE ORGANS THAT FELL OUT.
THAT'S NOT SCARY.
IF IT JUST MOVED OR WALKED OR SOMETHING, LIKE NORMAL, IT'D BE MORE--
IT DOES?!
HARU THINKS IT'S SCARY...!
TEE HEE HEE HEE HEE!
MUNCH
モグ
HONESTLY, JUST SHUSH, TOKAKU-SAN.
......
THERE'S THE ONE ABOUT THE LIBRARY, TOO!
IN THE LIBRARY OF THIS SCHOOL...
THERE EXISTS A "FORBIDDEN TOME."
THERE'S A HIDDEN ROOM BEHIND ONE OF THE BOOKSHELVES SOMEWHERE...
AND INSIDE LIES A BOOK THAT MUST NEVER BE OPENED.

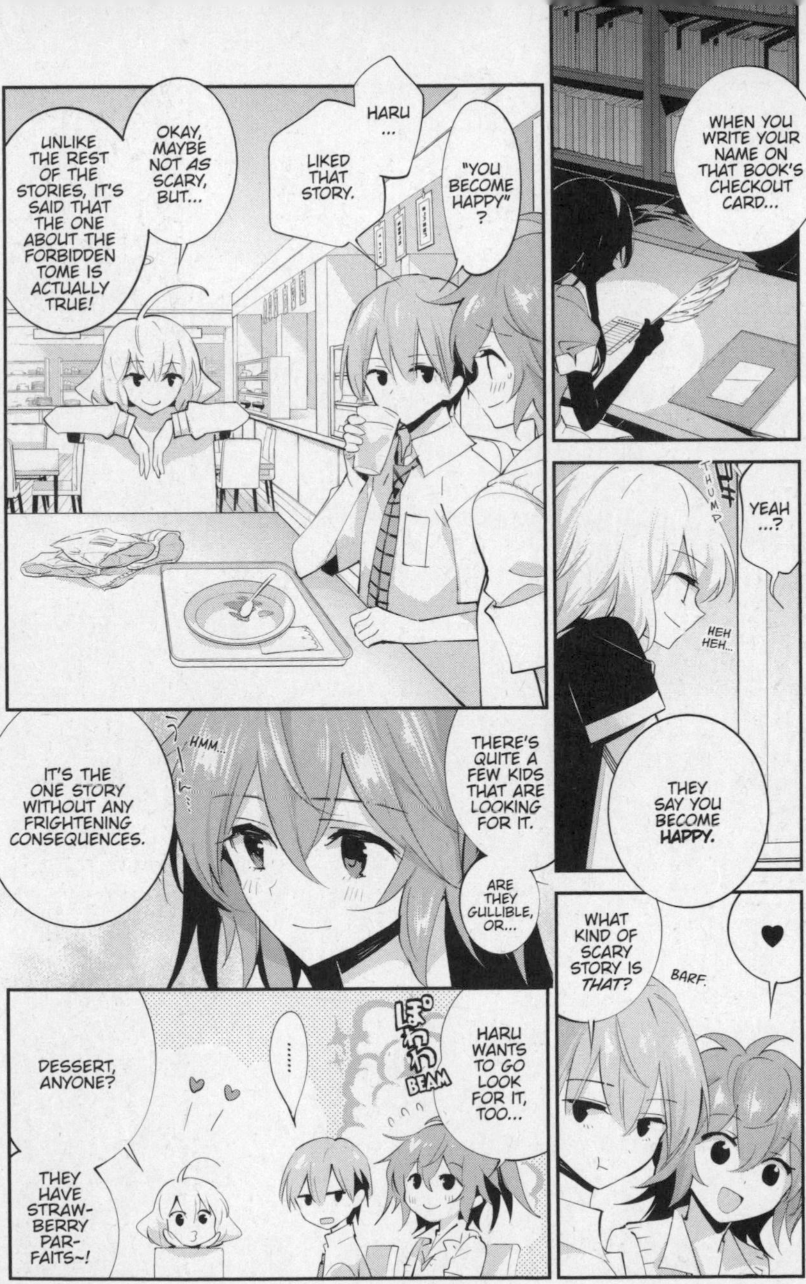
WHEN YOU WRITE YOUR NAME ON THAT BOOK'S CHECKOUT CARD...
YEAH ...?
THUMP
HEH HEH...
THEY SAY YOU BECOME **HAPPY.**
"YOU BECOME HAPPY" ?
HARU ... LIKED THAT STORY.
OKAY, MAYBE NOT AS SCARY, BUT...
UNLIKE THE REST OF THE STORIES, IT'S SAID THAT THE ONE ABOUT THE FORBIDDEN TOME IS ACTUALLY TRUE!
THERE'S QUITE A FEW KIDS THAT ARE LOOKING FOR IT.
HMM...
IT'S THE ONE STORY WITHOUT ANY FRIGHTENING CONSEQUENCES.
ARE THEY GULLIBLE, OR...
♥
BARF.
WHAT KIND OF SCARY STORY IS *THAT*?
HARU WANTS TO GO LOOK FOR IT, TOO...
BEAM
......
DESSERT, ANYONE?
THEY HAVE STRAWBERRY PARFAITS~!

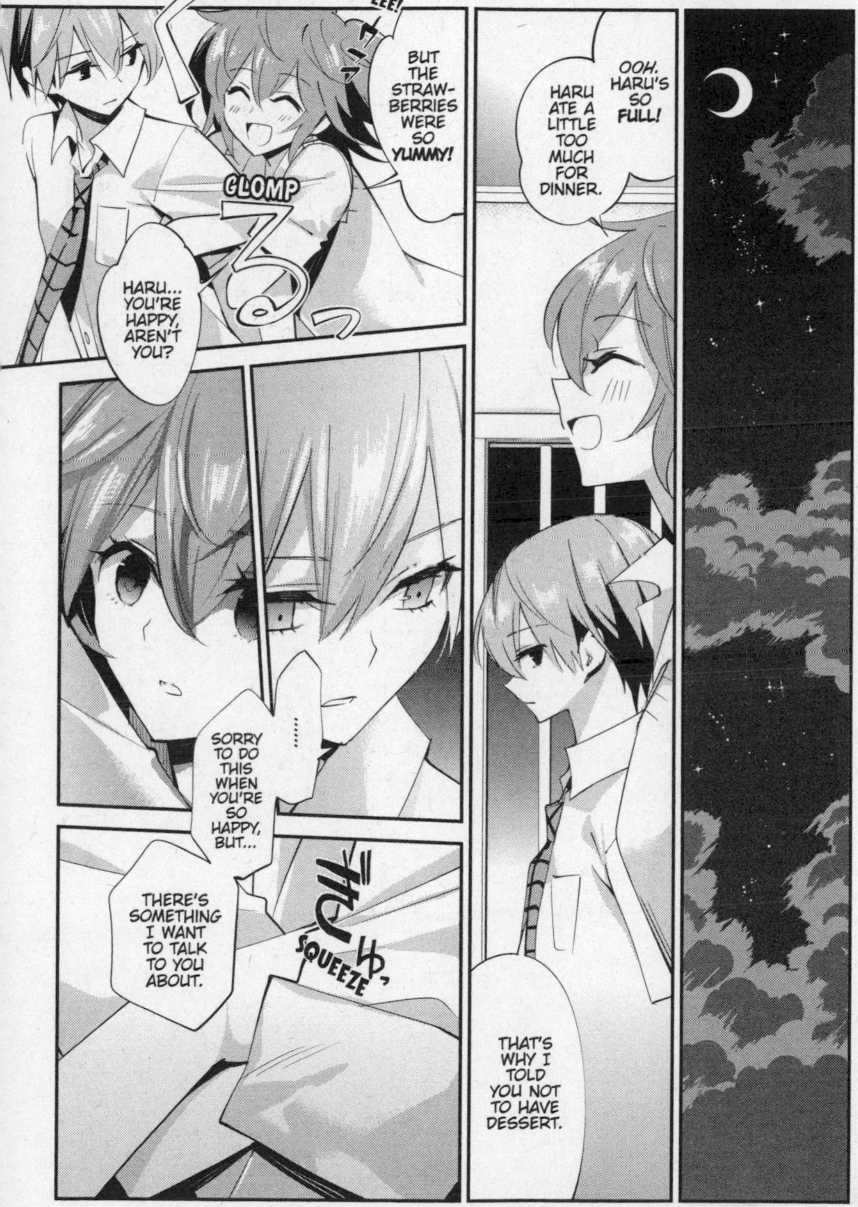
OOH. HARU'S SO FULL!
HARU ATE A LITTLE TOO MUCH FOR DINNER.
THAT'S WHY I TOLD YOU NOT TO HAVE DESSERT.
EEE!
BUT THE STRAW-BERRIES WERE SO YUMMY!
GLOMP
HARU... YOU'RE HAPPY, AREN'T YOU?
......
SORRY TO DO THIS WHEN YOU'RE SO HAPPY, BUT...
SQUEEZE
THERE'S SOMETHING I WANT TO TALK TO YOU ABOUT.

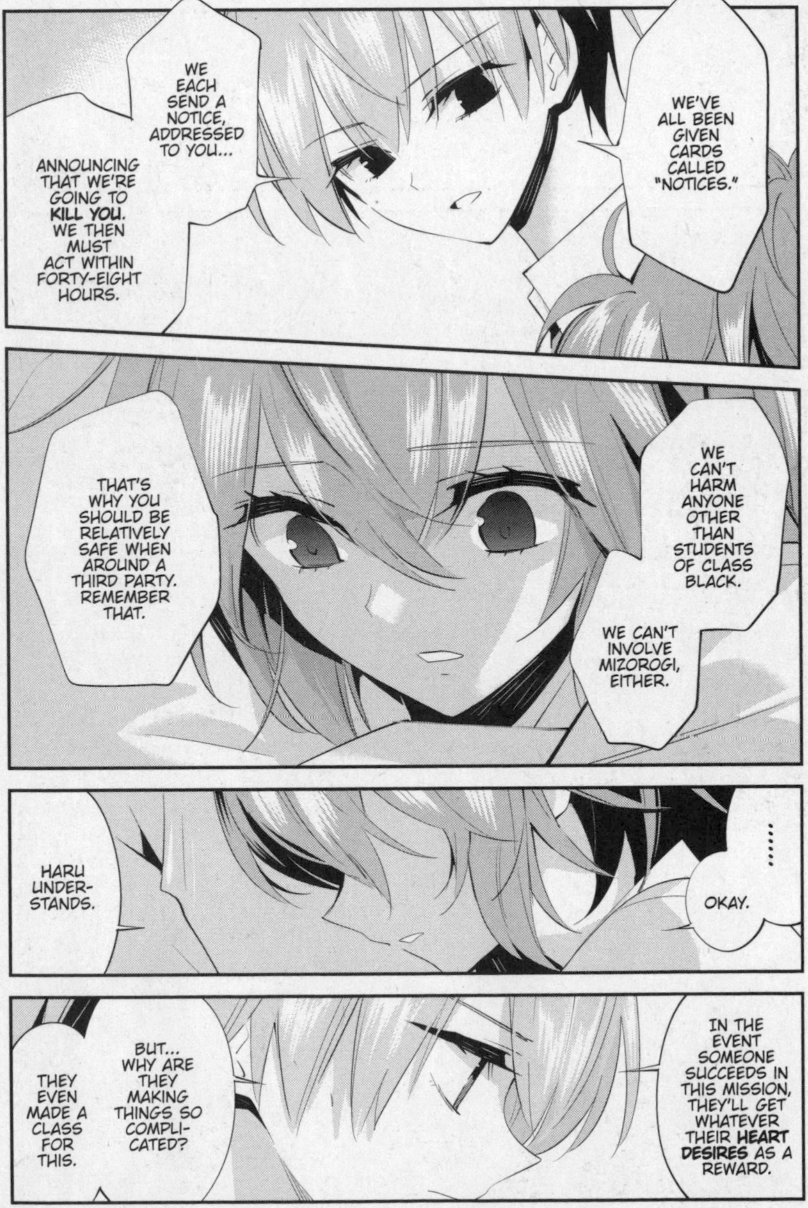
WE'VE ALL BEEN GIVEN CARDS CALLED "NOTICES."
WE EACH SEND A NOTICE, ADDRESSED TO YOU...
ANNOUNCING THAT WE'RE GOING TO **KILL YOU**. WE THEN MUST ACT WITHIN FORTY-EIGHT HOURS.
WE CAN'T HARM ANYONE OTHER THAN STUDENTS OF CLASS BLACK.
WE CAN'T INVOLVE MIZOROGI, EITHER.
THAT'S WHY YOU SHOULD BE RELATIVELY SAFE WHEN AROUND A THIRD PARTY. REMEMBER THAT.
......
OKAY.
HARU UNDER-STANDS.
IN THE EVENT SOMEONE SUCCEEDS IN THIS MISSION, THEY'LL GET WHATEVER THEIR **HEART DESIRES** AS A REWARD.
BUT... WHY ARE THEY MAKING THINGS SO COMPLI-CATED?
THEY EVEN MADE A CLASS FOR THIS.

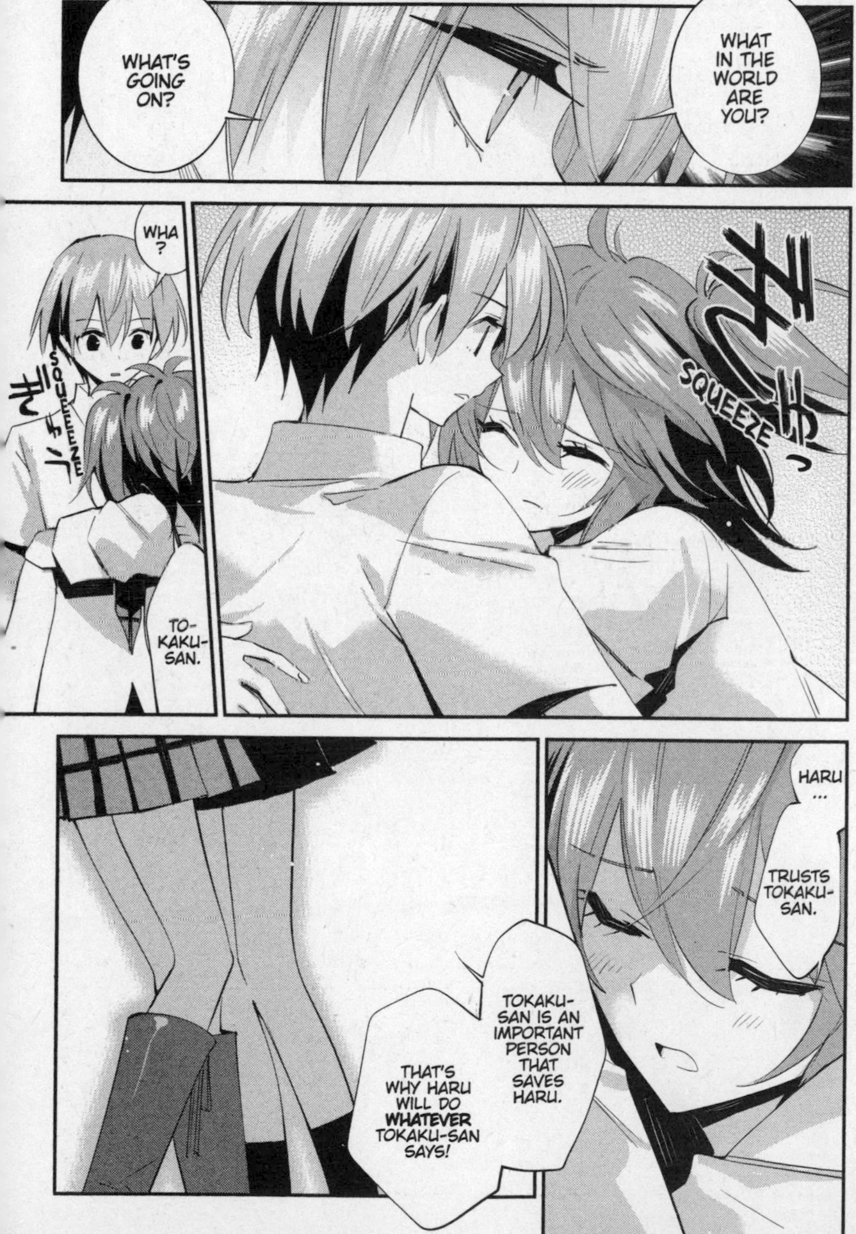
WHAT IN THE WORLD ARE YOU?
WHAT'S GOING ON?
SQUEEZE
WHA?
SQUEEEEEZE
TO-KAKU-SAN.
HARU...
TRUSTS TOKAKU-SAN.
TOKAKU-SAN IS AN IMPORTANT PERSON THAT SAVES HARU.
THAT'S WHY HARU WILL DO **WHATEVER** TOKAKU-SAN SAYS!

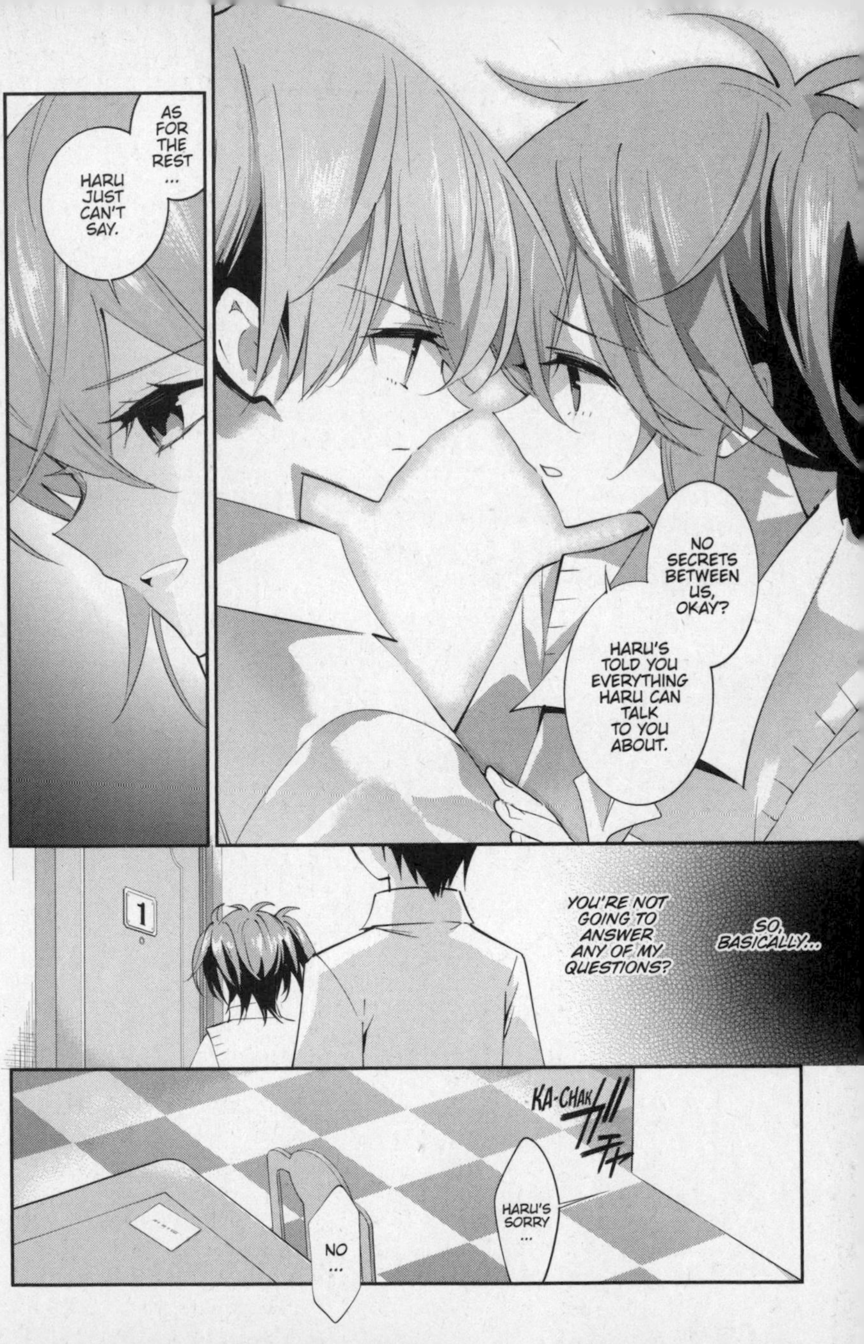
NO SECRETS BETWEEN US, OKAY?
HARU'S TOLD YOU EVERYTHING HARU CAN TALK TO YOU ABOUT.
AS FOR THE REST...
HARU JUST CAN'T SAY.
SO, BASICALLY...
YOU'RE NOT GOING TO ANSWER ANY OF MY QUESTIONS?
KA-CHAK
HARU'S SORRY...
NO...

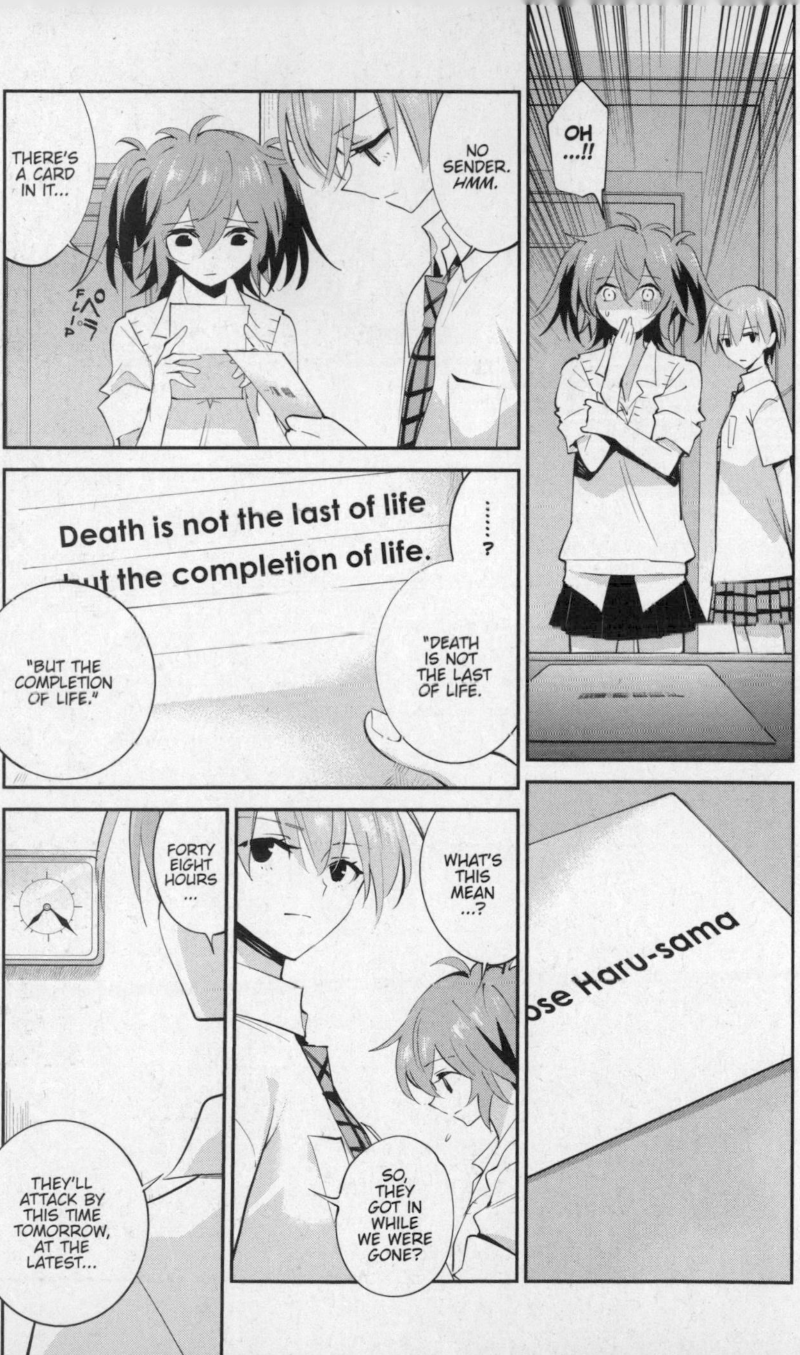
OH ...!!
NO SENDER. HMM.
THERE'S A CARD IN IT...
FLIP
......?
Death is not the last of life
ut the completion of life.
"DEATH IS NOT THE LAST OF LIFE.
"BUT THE COMPLETION OF LIFE."
ose Haru-sama
WHAT'S THIS MEAN ...?
SO, THEY GOT IN WHILE WE WERE GONE?
FORTY EIGHT HOURS ...
THEY'LL ATTACK BY THIS TIME TOMORROW, AT THE LATEST...

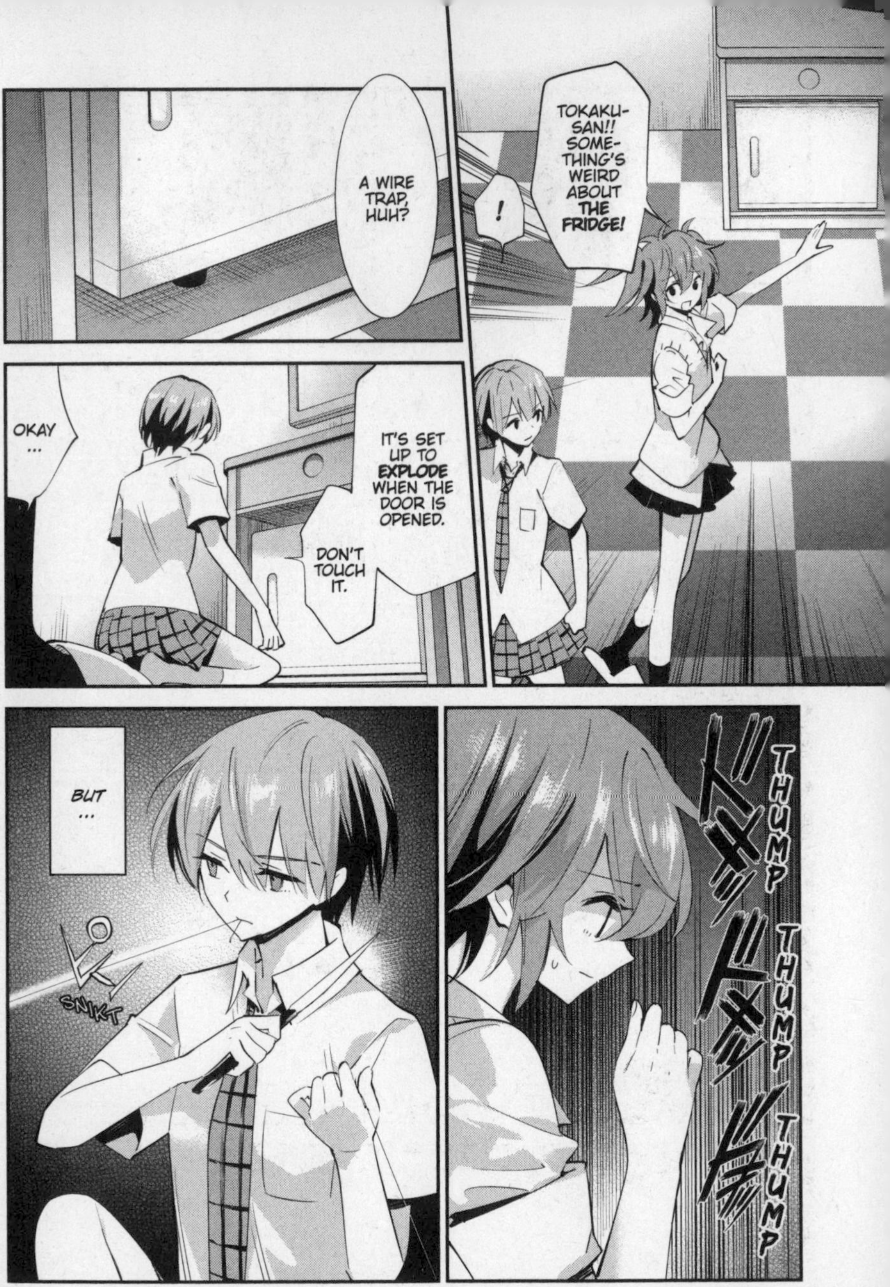
TOKAKU-SAN!! SOMETHING'S WEIRD ABOUT THE FRIDGE!
!
A WIRE TRAP, HUH?
IT'S SET UP TO EXPLODE WHEN THE DOOR IS OPENED.
DON'T TOUCH IT.
OKAY ...
THUMP THUMP THUMP THUMP
BUT ...
SNIKT

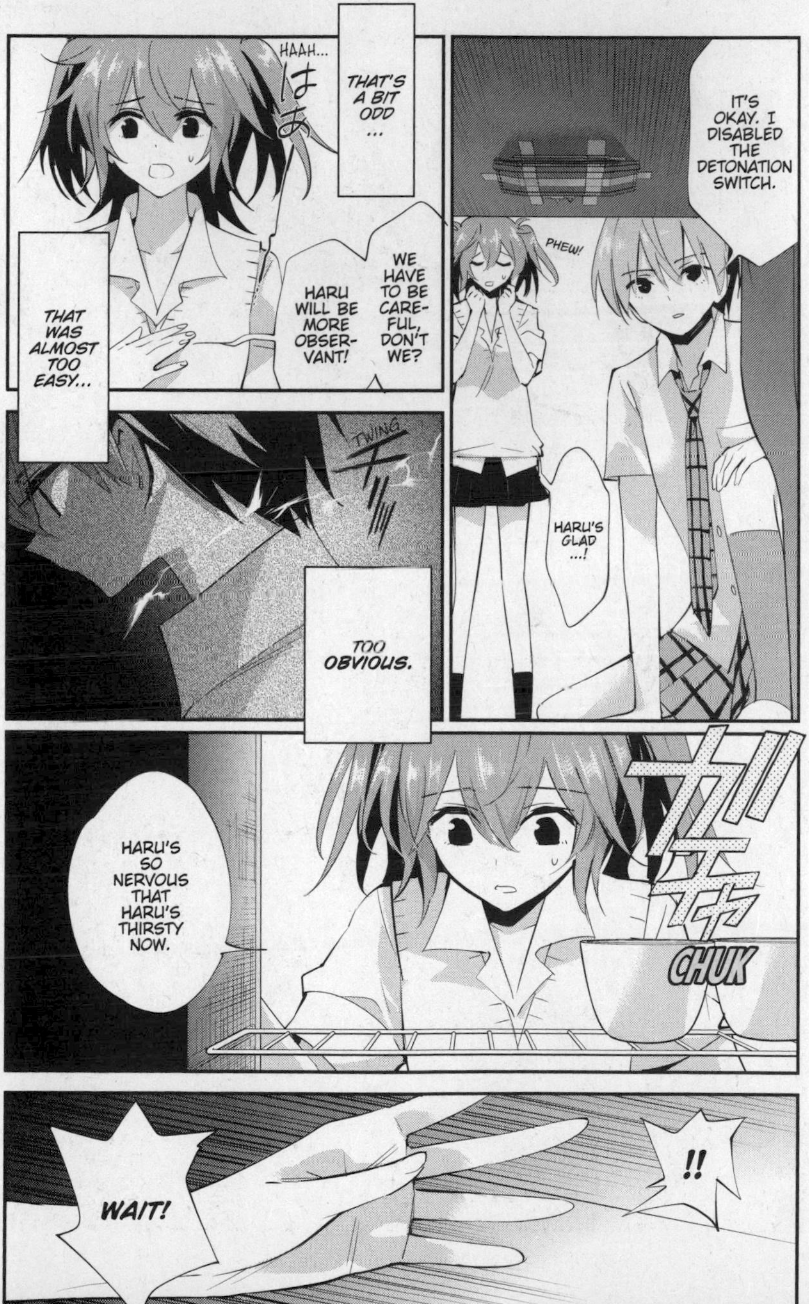
IT'S OKAY. I DISABLED THE DETONATION SWITCH.
PHEW!
HARU'S GLAD ...!
HAAH... はあ
THAT'S A BIT ODD ...
WE HAVE TO BE CARE-FUL, DON'T WE?
HARU WILL BE MORE OBSER-VANT!
THAT WAS ALMOST TOO EASY...
TWING
TOO OBVIOUS.
CHUK
HARU'S SO NERVOUS THAT HARU'S THIRSTY NOW.
!!
WAIT!

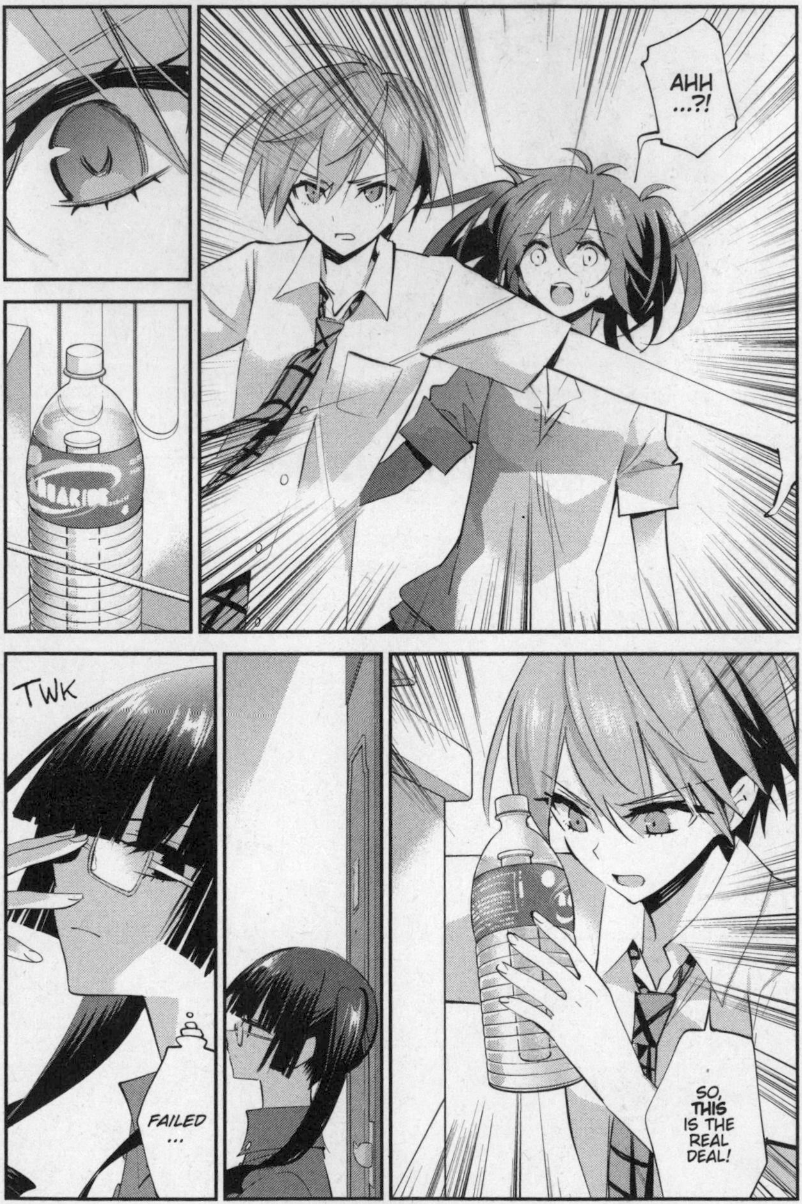
AHH ...?!
SO, **THIS** IS THE REAL DEAL!
TWK
FAILED ...

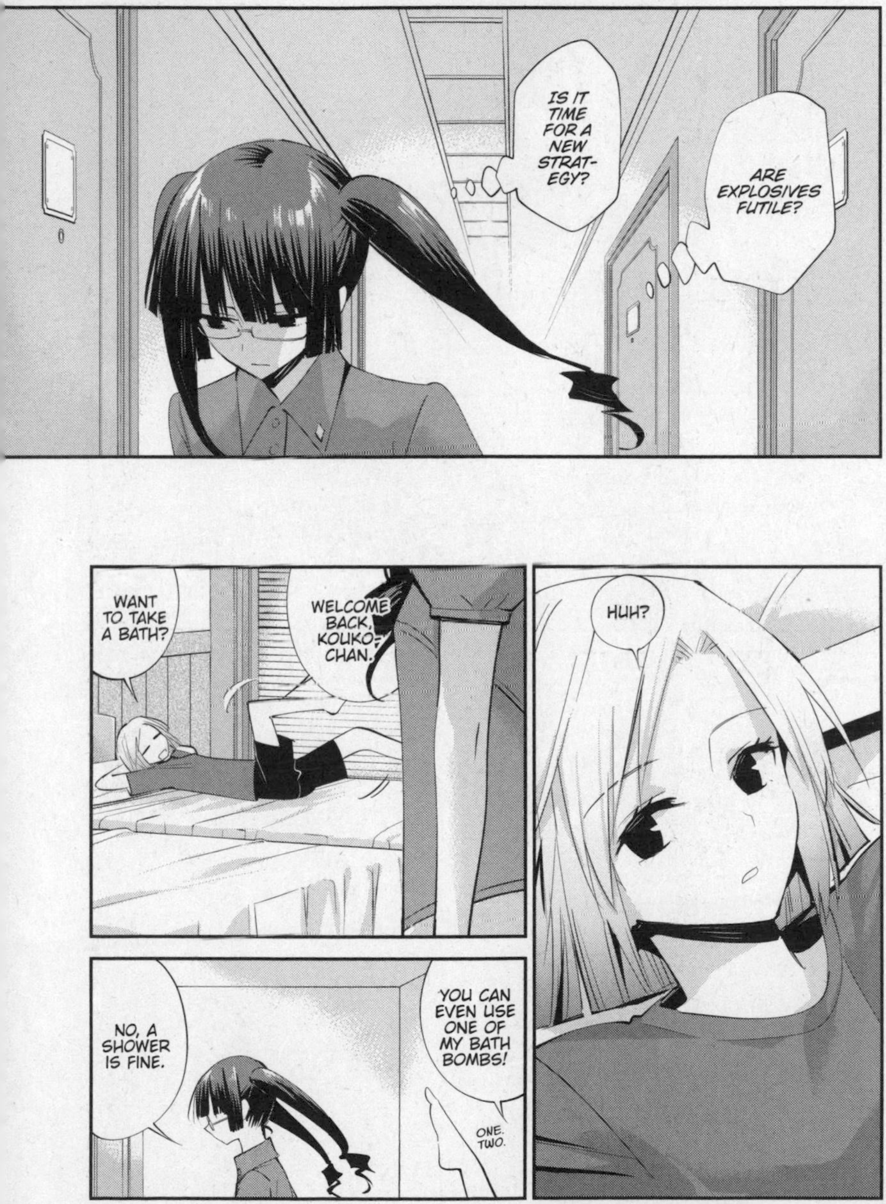
ARE EXPLOSIVES FUTILE?
IS IT TIME FOR A NEW STRATEGY?
HUH?
WELCOME BACK, KOUKO-CHAN.
WANT TO TAKE A BATH?
YOU CAN EVEN USE ONE OF MY BATH BOMBS!
ONE. TWO.
NO, A SHOWER IS FINE.

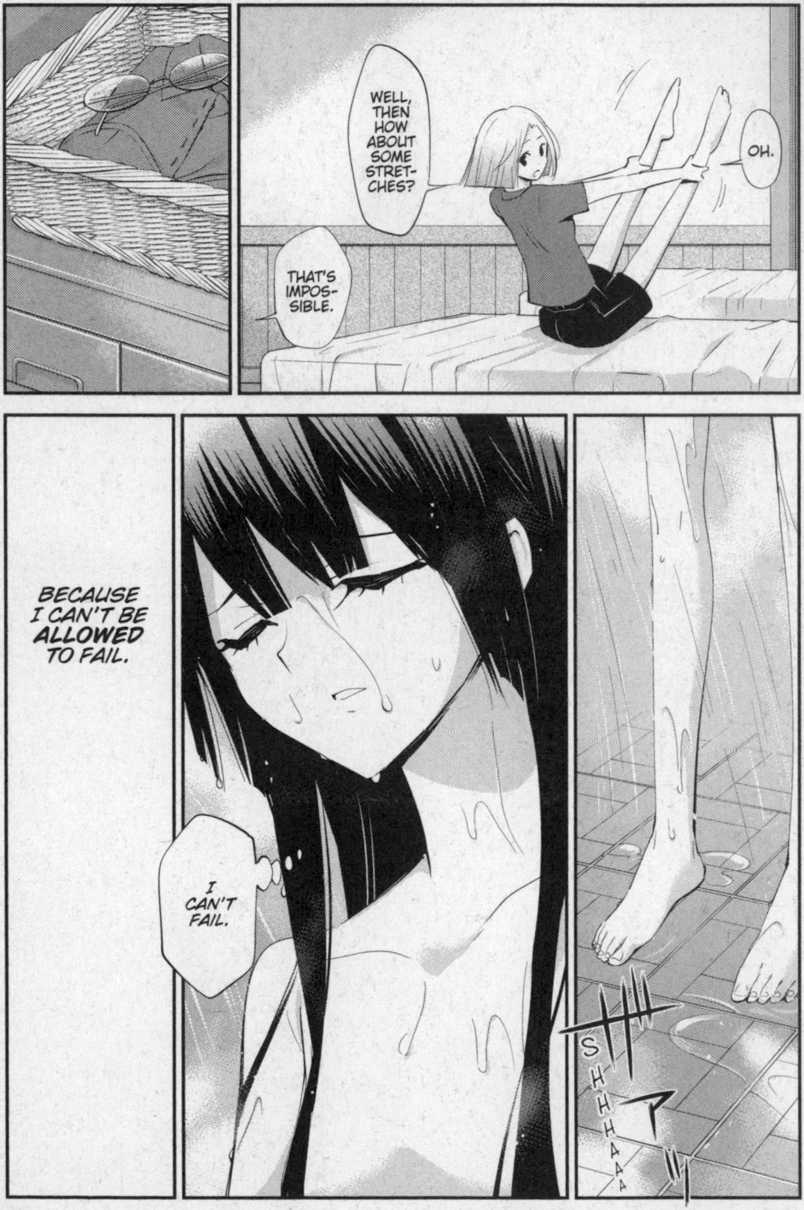
OH.
WELL, THEN HOW ABOUT SOME STRETCHES?
THAT'S IMPOSSIBLE.
SHHHAAA
I CAN'T FAIL.
BECAUSE I CAN'T BE **ALLOWED** TO FAIL.

Chapter 15
Won't Pray to God

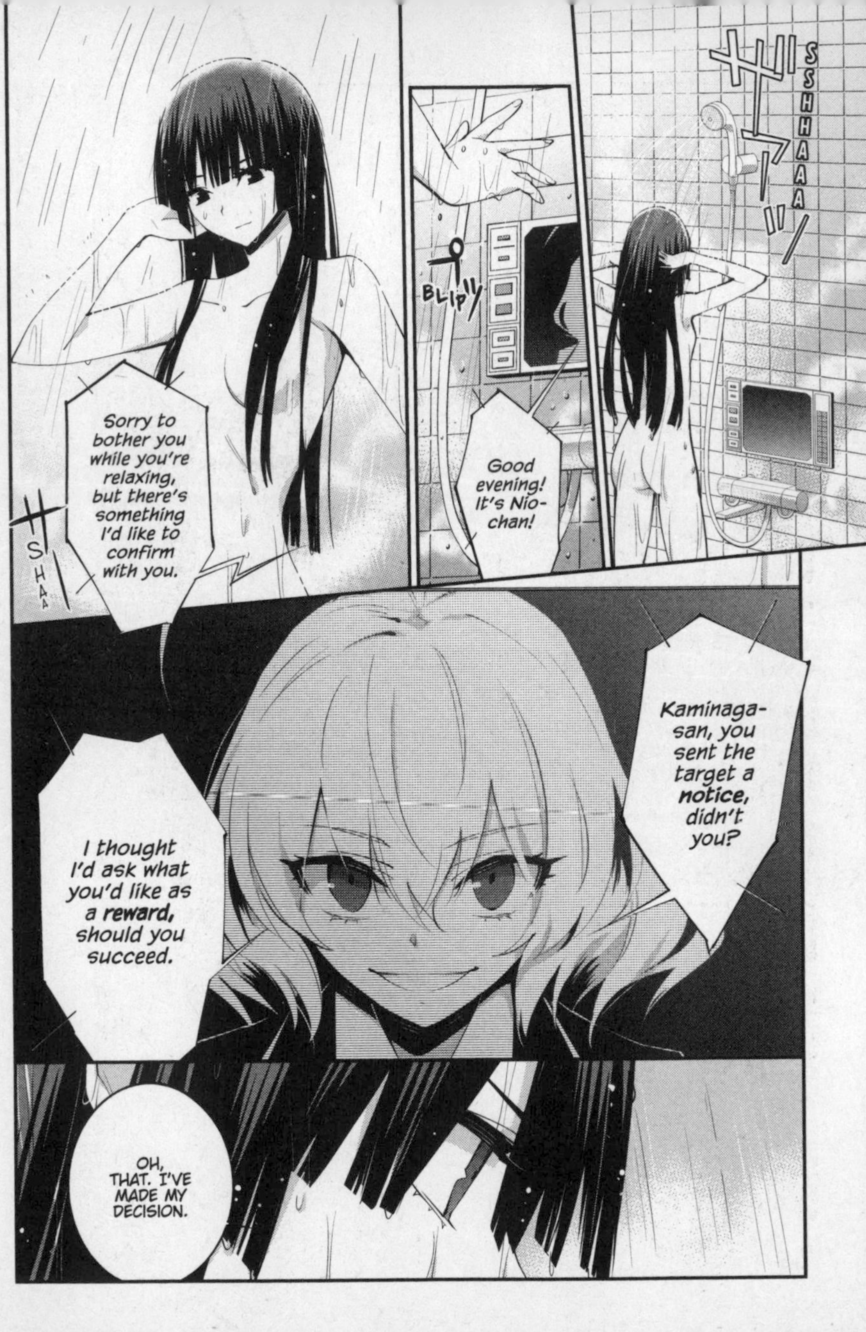
SSHHAAA
BLIP
Good evening! It's Nio-chan!
Sorry to bother you while you're relaxing, but there's something I'd like to confirm with you.
SHAA
Kaminaga-san, you sent the target a **notice,** didn't you?
I thought I'd ask what you'd like as a **reward,** should you succeed.
OH, THAT. I'VE MADE MY DECISION.

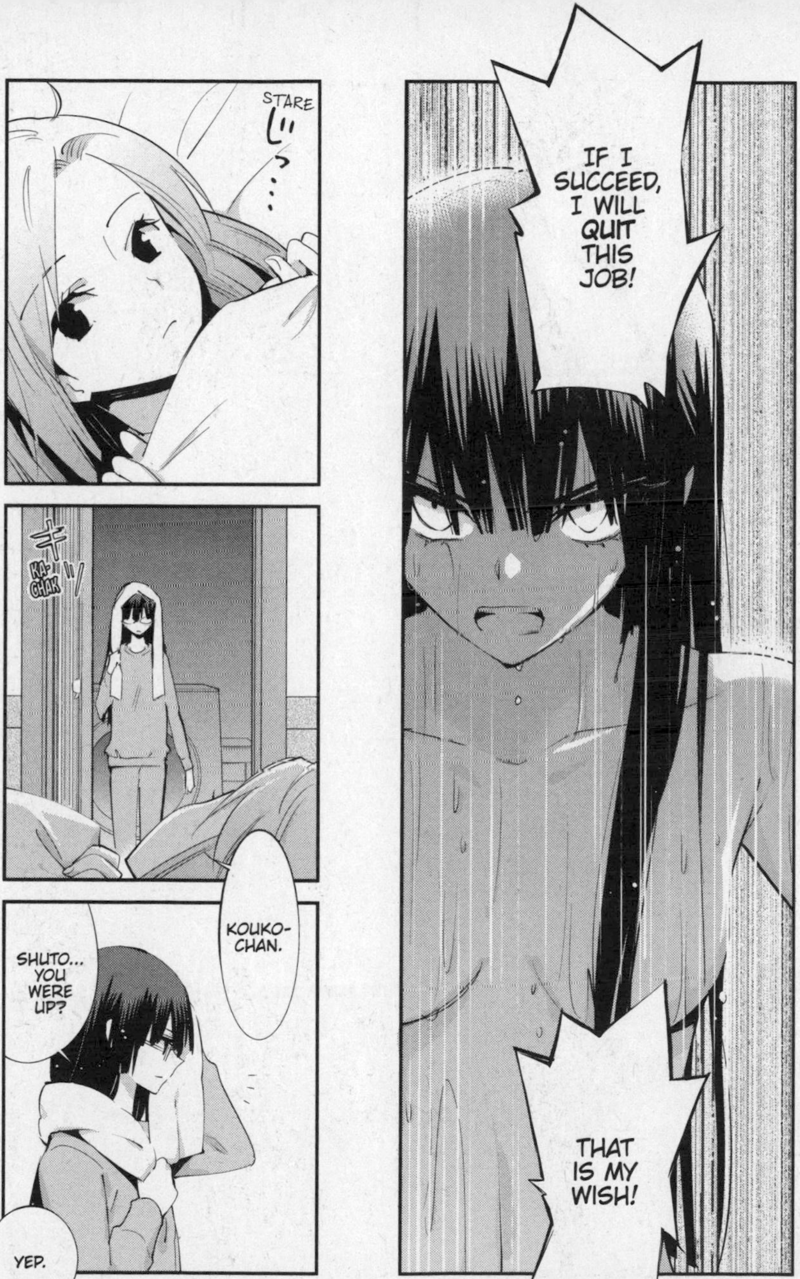
IF I SUCCEED, I WILL QUIT THIS JOB!
THAT IS MY WISH!
STARE
じっ…
KA-CHAK
KOUKO-CHAN.
SHUTO... YOU WERE UP?
YEP.

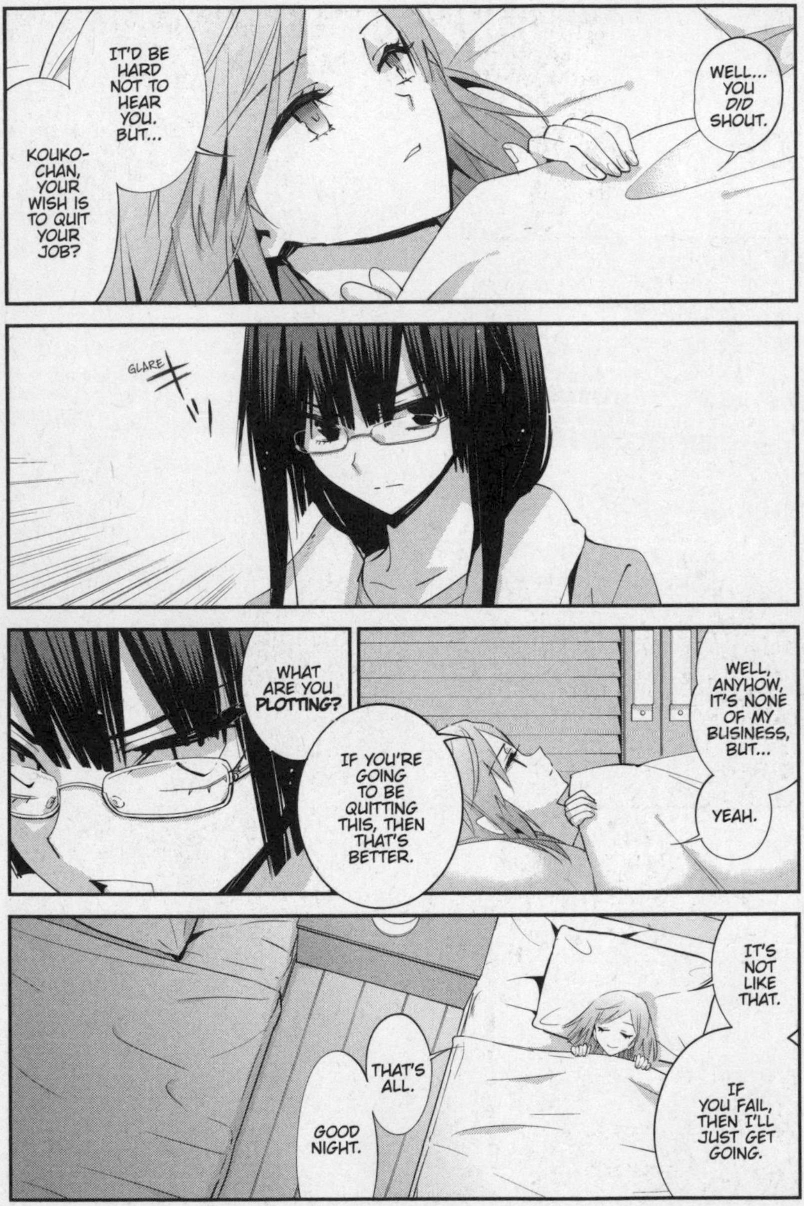
WELL... YOU DID SHOUT.
IT'D BE HARD NOT TO HEAR YOU. BUT...
KOUKO-CHAN, YOUR WISH IS TO QUIT YOUR JOB?
GLARE
WELL, ANYHOW, IT'S NONE OF MY BUSINESS, BUT...
YEAH.
IF YOU'RE GOING TO BE QUITTING THIS, THEN THAT'S BETTER.
WHAT ARE YOU PLOTTING?
IT'S NOT LIKE THAT.
IF YOU FAIL, THEN I'LL JUST GET GOING.
THAT'S ALL.
GOOD NIGHT.

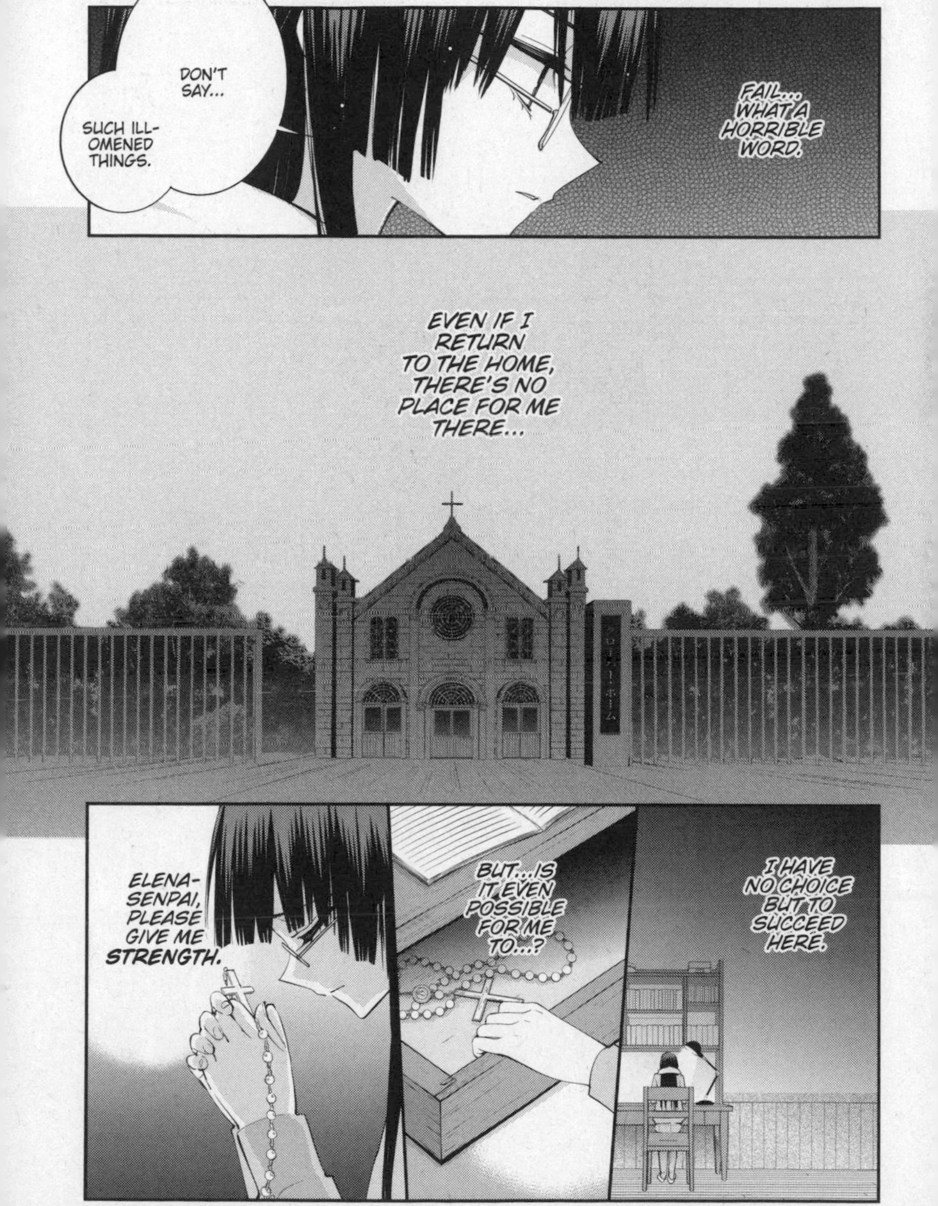
FAIL... WHAT A HORRIBLE WORD.
DON'T SAY...
SUCH ILL-OMENED THINGS.
EVEN IF I RETURN TO THE HOME, THERE'S NO PLACE FOR ME THERE...
I HAVE NO CHOICE BUT TO SUCCEED HERE.
BUT...IS IT EVEN POSSIBLE FOR ME TO...?
ELENA-SENPAI, PLEASE GIVE ME STRENGTH.

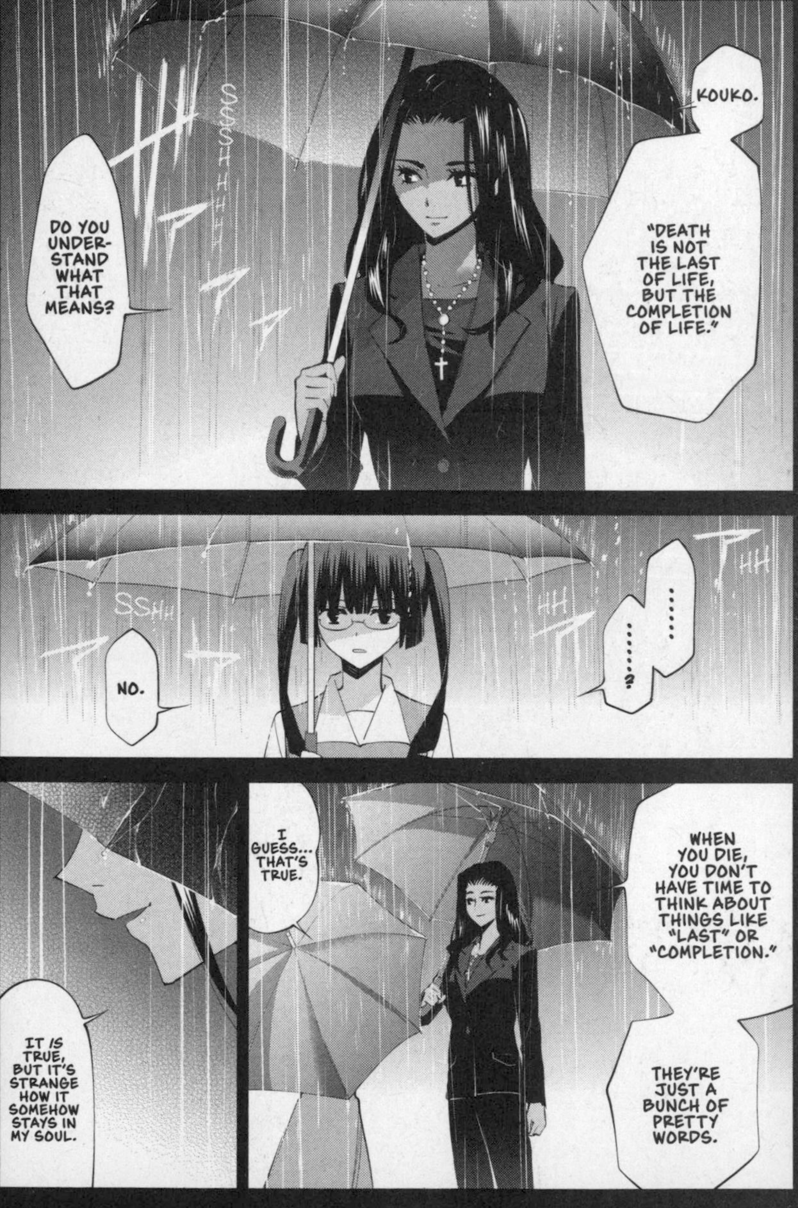
KOUKO.
"DEATH IS NOT THE LAST OF LIFE, BUT THE COMPLETION OF LIFE."
DO YOU UNDER-STAND WHAT THAT MEANS?
SSSHHHH
HH
......?
NO.
SSHH
WHEN YOU DIE, YOU DON'T HAVE TIME TO THINK ABOUT THINGS LIKE "LAST" OR "COMPLETION."
THEY'RE JUST A BUNCH OF PRETTY WORDS.
I GUESS... THAT'S TRUE.
IT IS TRUE, BUT IT'S STRANGE HOW IT SOMEHOW STAYS IN MY SOUL.

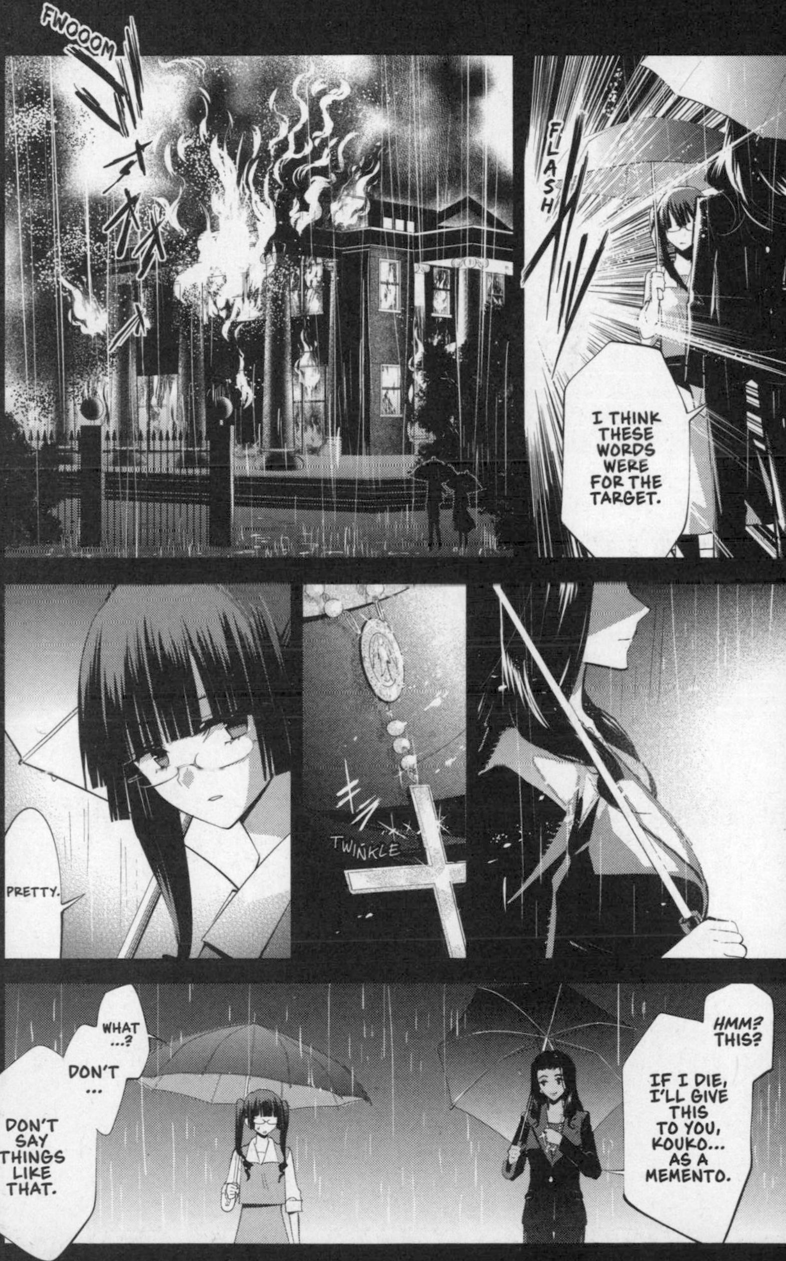
FLASH
I THINK THESE WORDS WERE FOR THE TARGET.
FWOOOM
TWINKLE
PRETTY.
HMM? THIS?
IF I DIE, I'LL GIVE THIS TO YOU, KOUKO... AS A MEMENTO.
WHAT ...?
DON'T ...
DON'T SAY THINGS LIKE THAT.

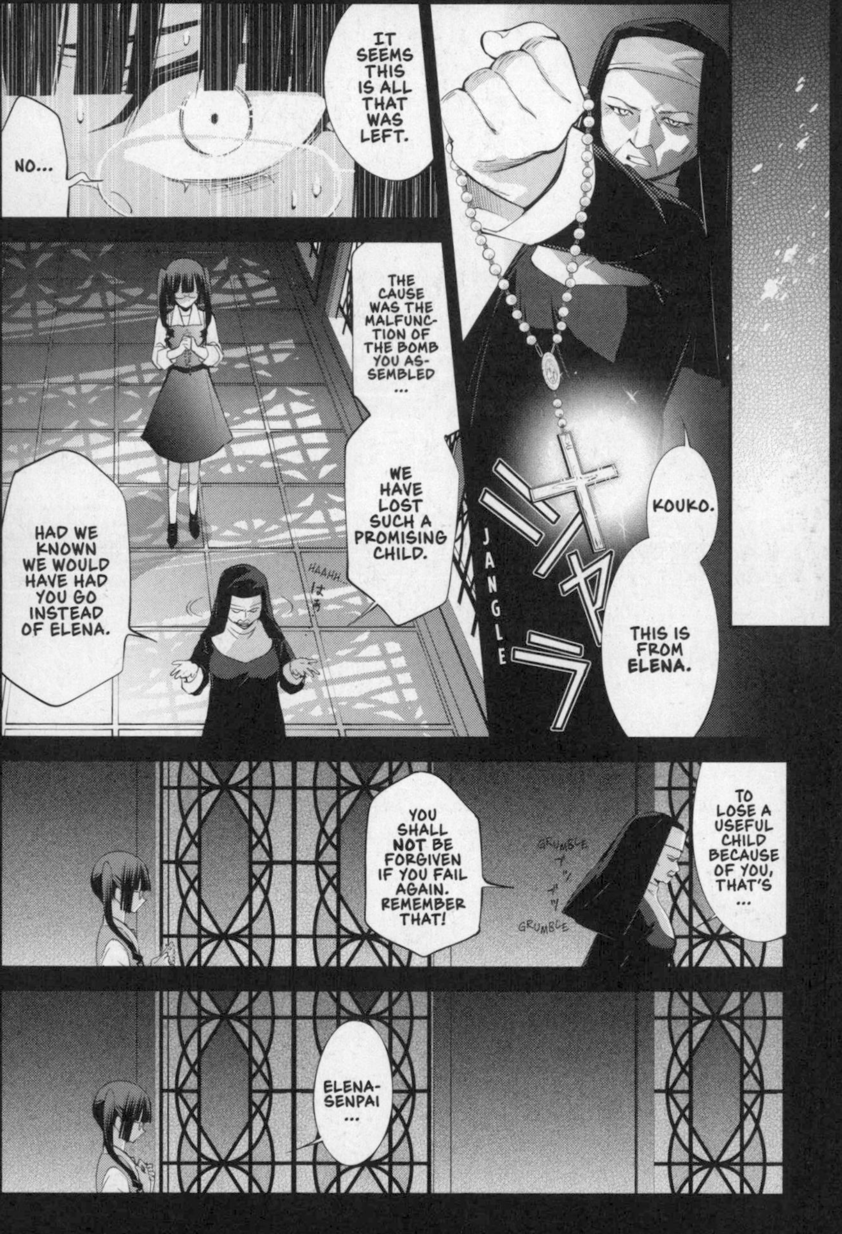
KOUKO.
THIS IS FROM ELENA.
JANGLE
IT SEEMS THIS IS ALL THAT WAS LEFT.
NO...
THE CAUSE WAS THE MALFUNCTION OF THE BOMB YOU ASSEMBLED ...
WE HAVE LOST SUCH A PROMISING CHILD.
HAAHH...
HAD WE KNOWN WE WOULD HAVE HAD YOU GO INSTEAD OF ELENA.
TO LOSE A USEFUL CHILD BECAUSE OF YOU, THAT'S ...
GRUMBLE
GRUMBLE
YOU SHALL NOT BE FORGIVEN IF YOU FAIL AGAIN. REMEMBER THAT!
ELENA-SENPAI ...

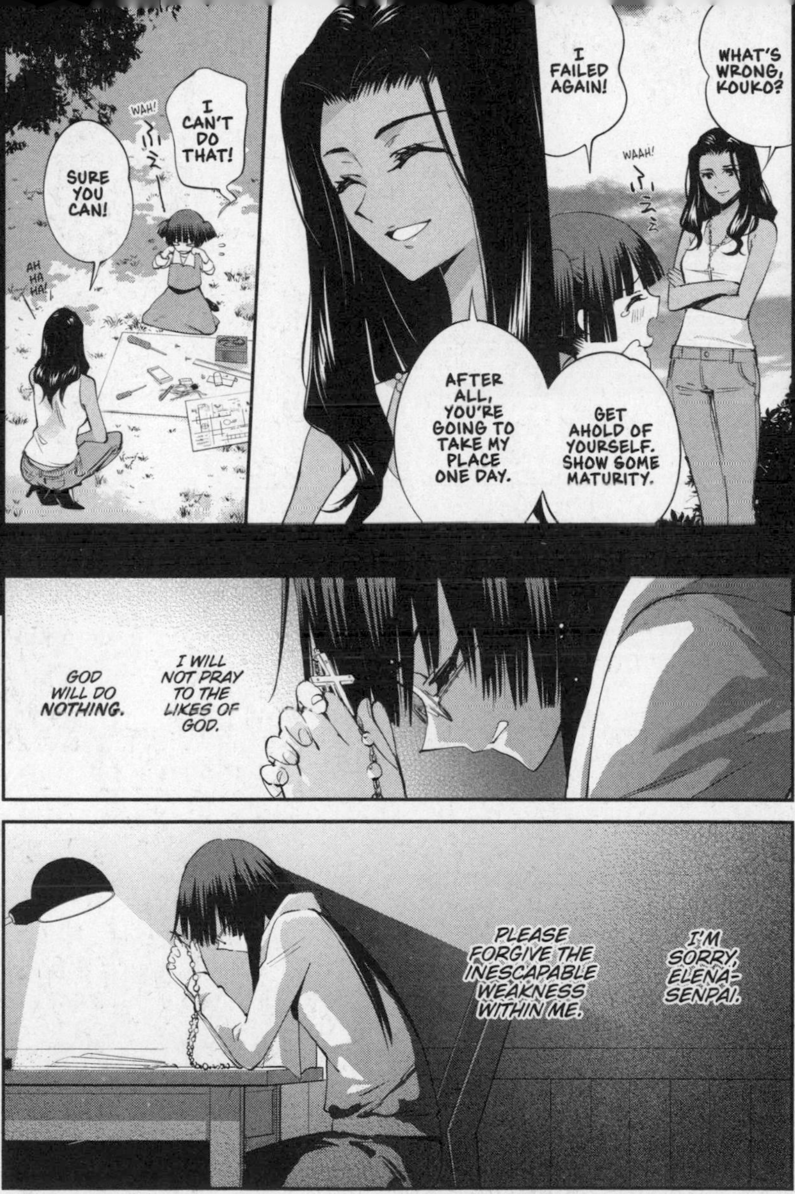
WHAT'S WRONG, KOUKO?
I FAILED AGAIN!
WAAH!
GET AHOLD OF YOURSELF. SHOW SOME MATURITY.
AFTER ALL, YOU'RE GOING TO TAKE MY PLACE ONE DAY.
I CAN'T DO THAT!
WAH!
SURE YOU CAN!
AH HA HA!
I WILL NOT PRAY TO THE LIKES OF GOD.
GOD WILL DO NOTHING.
I'M SORRY, ELENA-SENPAI.
PLEASE FORGIVE THE INESCAPABLE WEAKNESS WITHIN ME.

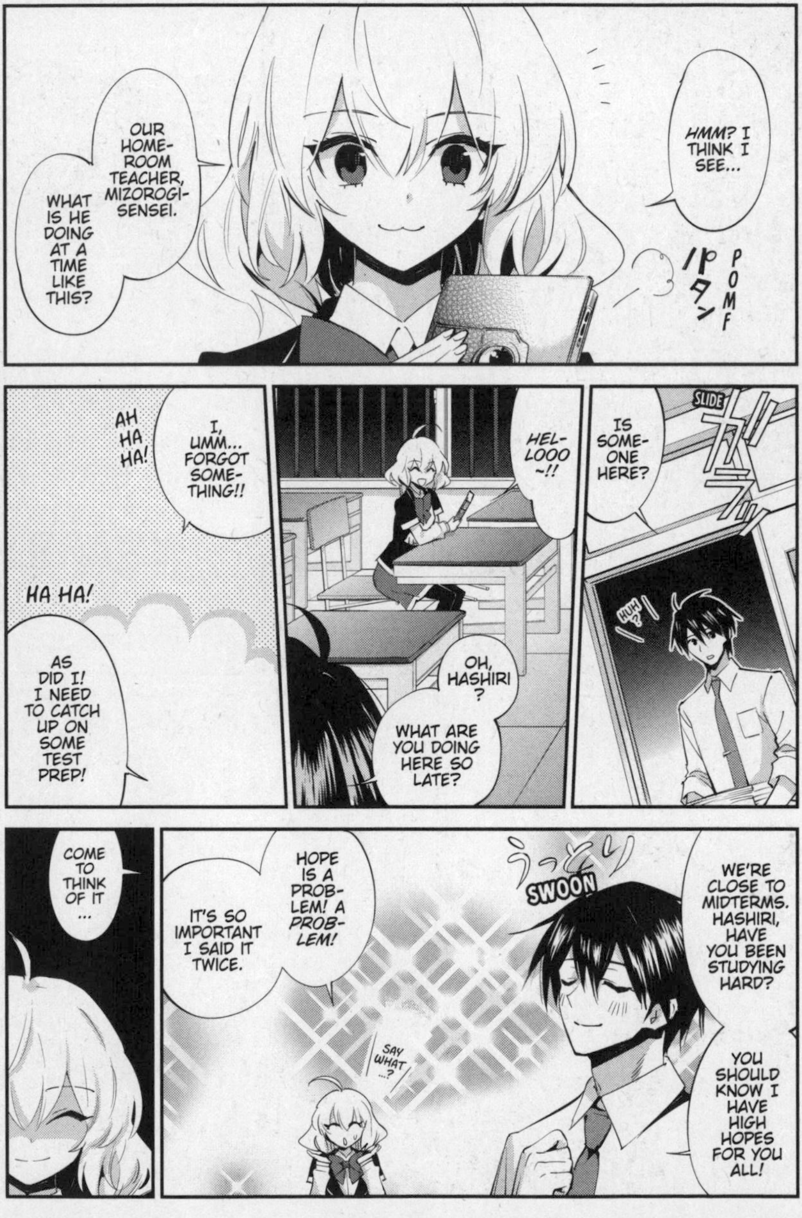
HMM? I THINK I SEE...
パタン
POMF
OUR HOME-ROOM TEACHER, MIZOROGI-SENSEI.
WHAT IS HE DOING AT A TIME LIKE THIS?
SLIDE
ガラッ
IS SOME-ONE HERE?
HUH?!
HEL-LOOO ~!!
OH, HASHIRI?
WHAT ARE YOU DOING HERE SO LATE?
I, UMM... FORGOT SOME-THING!!
AH HA HA!
HA HA!
AS DID I! I NEED TO CATCH UP ON SOME TEST PREP!
うっとり
SWOON
WE'RE CLOSE TO MIDTERMS. HASHIRI, HAVE YOU BEEN STUDYING HARD?
YOU SHOULD KNOW I HAVE HIGH HOPES FOR YOU ALL!
HOPE IS A PROB-LEM! A PROB-LEM!
IT'S SO IMPORTANT I SAID IT TWICE.
SAY WHAT ...?
COME TO THINK OF IT ...

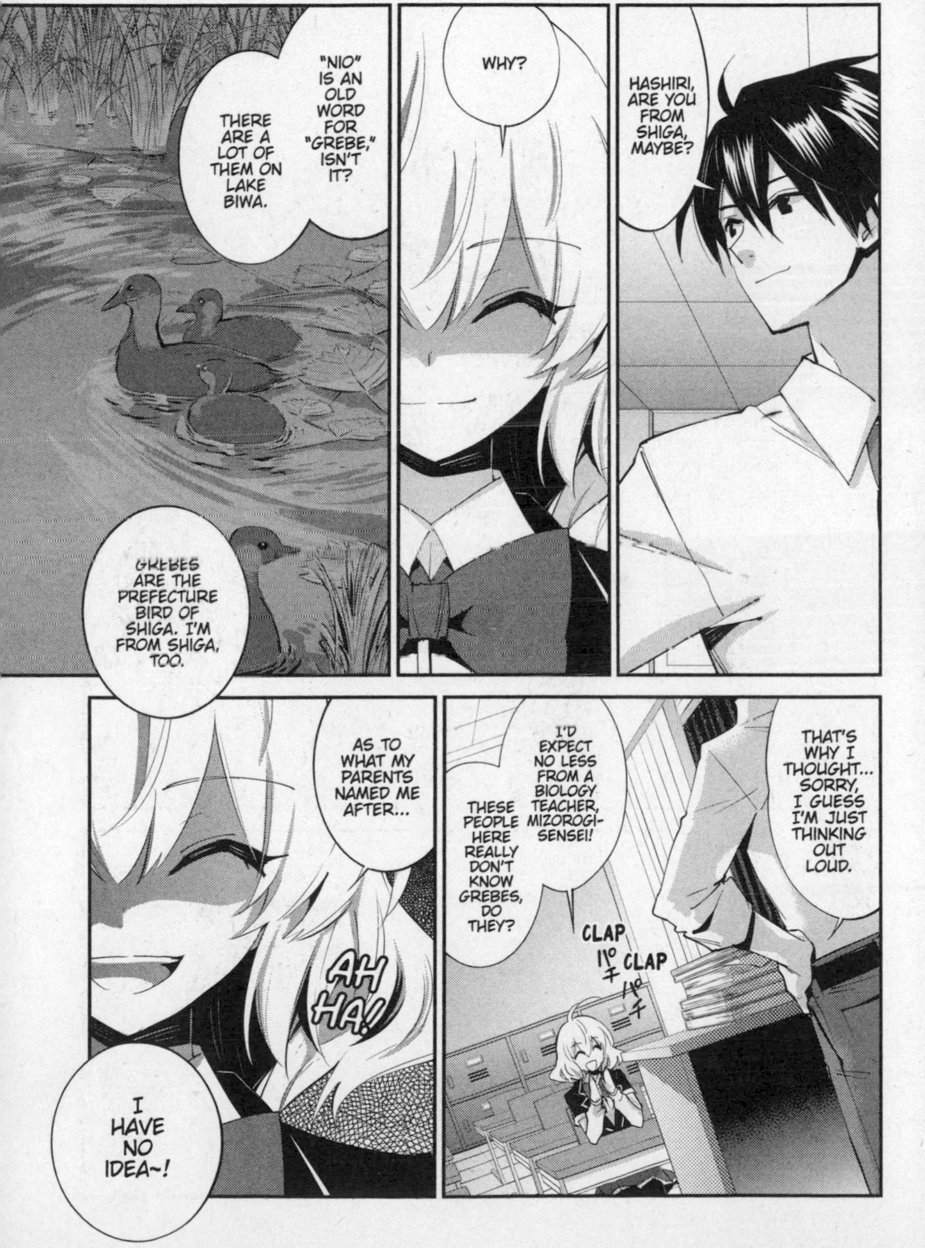
HASHIRI, ARE YOU FROM SHIGA, MAYBE?
WHY?
"NIO" IS AN OLD WORD FOR "GREBE," ISN'T IT?
THERE ARE A LOT OF THEM ON LAKE BIWA.
GREBES ARE THE PREFECTURE BIRD OF SHIGA. I'M FROM SHIGA, TOO.
THAT'S WHY I THOUGHT... SORRY, I GUESS I'M JUST THINKING OUT LOUD.
I'D EXPECT NO LESS FROM A BIOLOGY TEACHER, MIZOROGI-SENSEI!
THESE PEOPLE HERE REALLY DON'T KNOW GREBES, DO THEY?
CLAP パチ CLAP パチ
AS TO WHAT MY PARENTS NAMED ME AFTER...
AH HA!
I HAVE NO IDEA~!

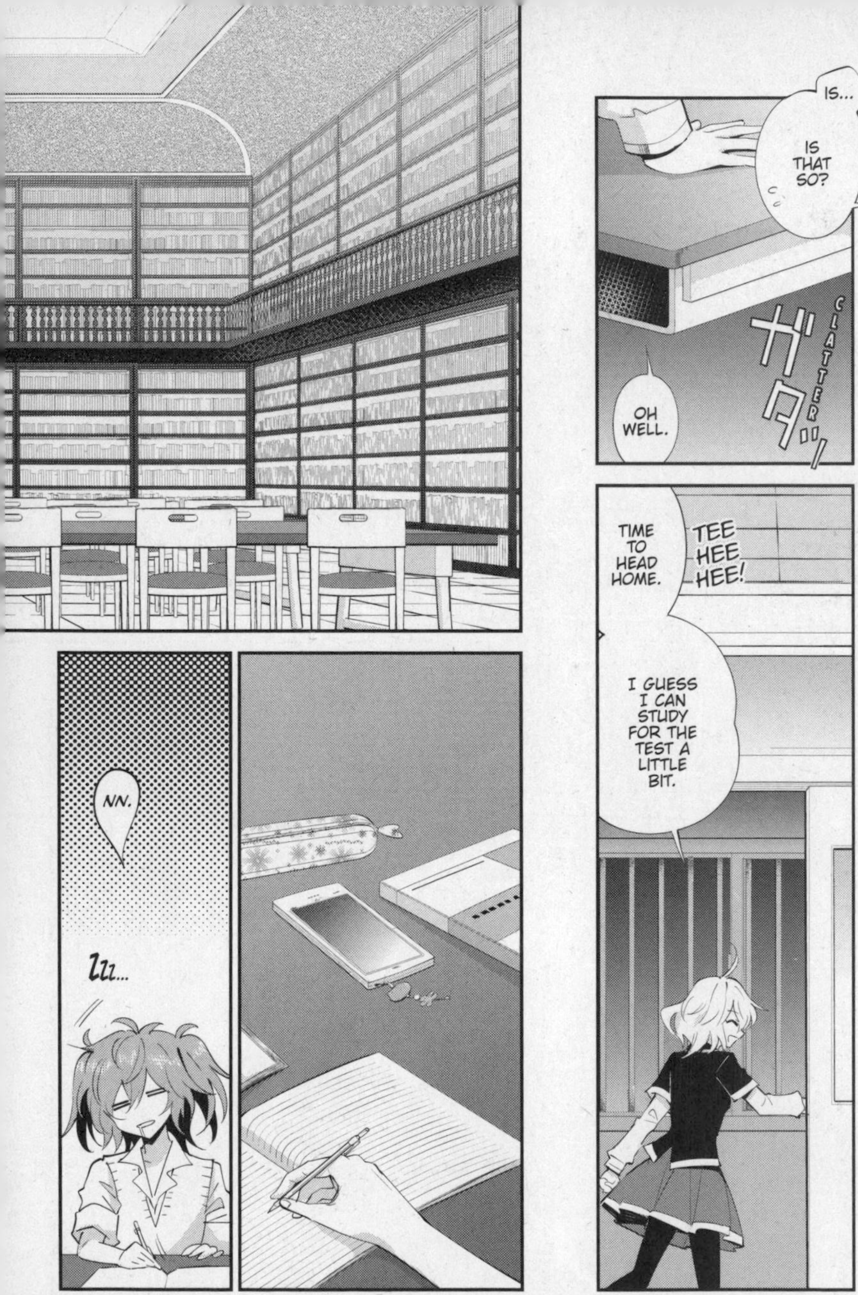
IS...
IS THAT SO?
ガタッ
CLATTER
OH WELL.
TEE HEE HEE!
TIME TO HEAD HOME.
I GUESS I CAN STUDY FOR THE TEST A LITTLE BIT.
NN.
Zzz...

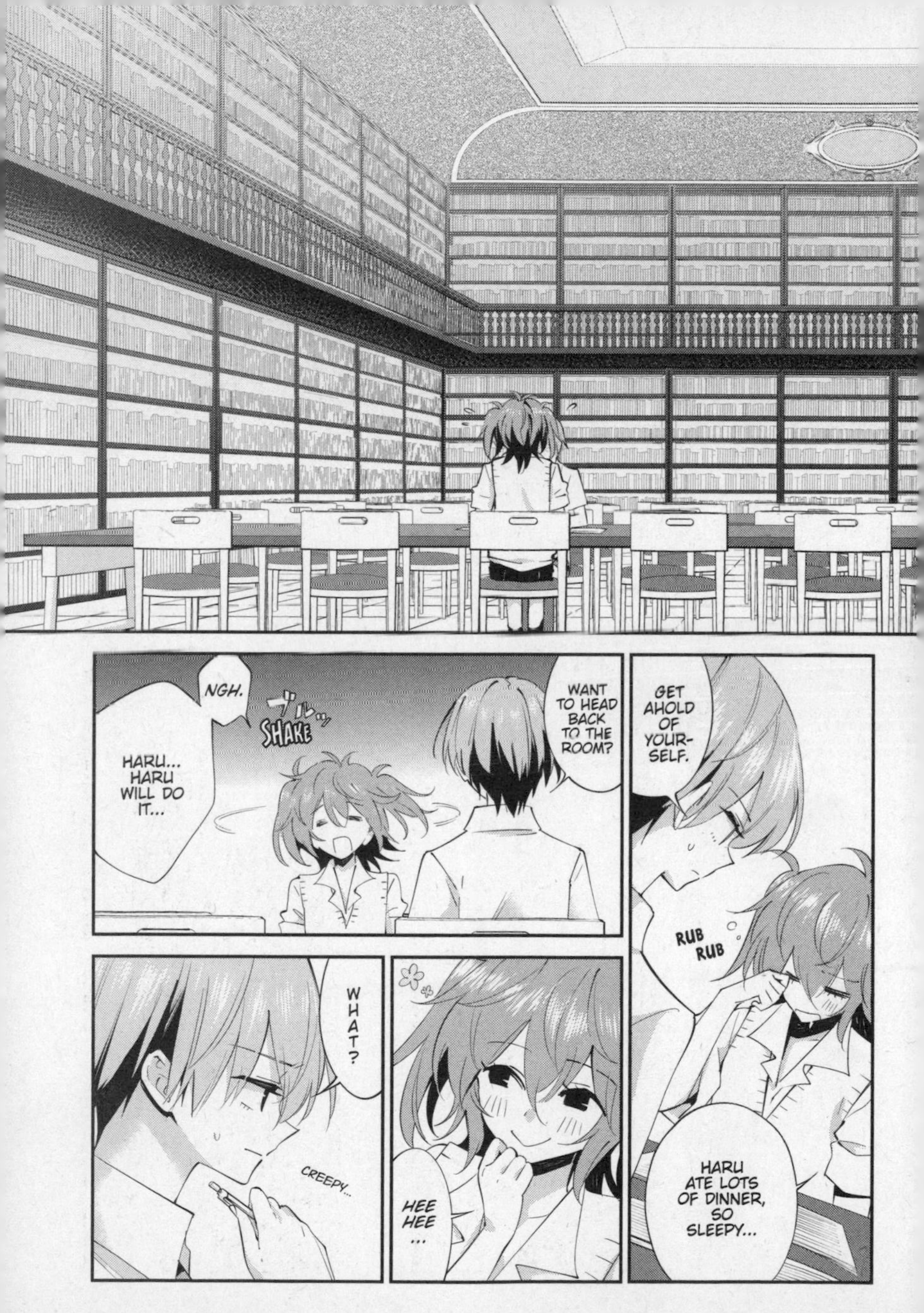
GET AHOLD OF YOUR-SELF.
RUB RUB
HARU ATE LOTS OF DINNER, SO SLEEPY...
WANT TO HEAD BACK TO THE ROOM?
SHAKE
NGH.
HARU... HARU WILL DO IT...
HEE HEE ...
WHAT?
CREEPY...

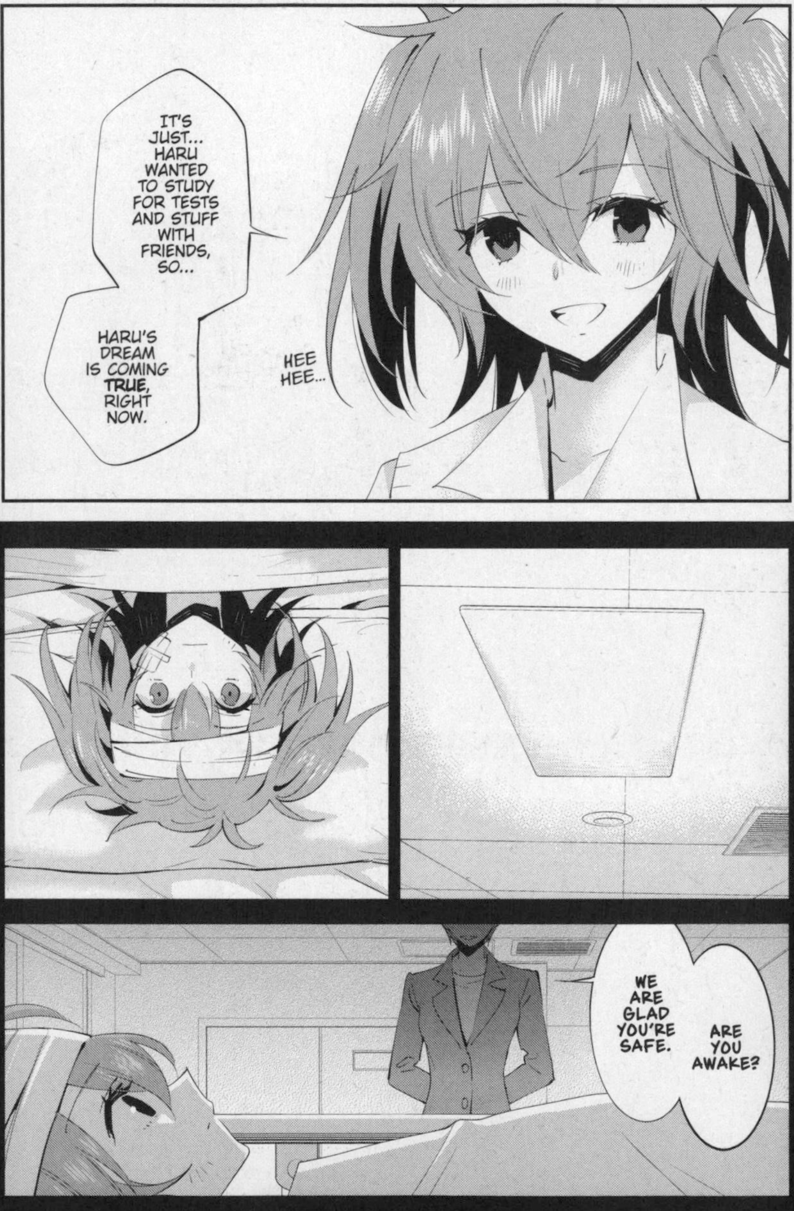
IT'S JUST... HARU WANTED TO STUDY FOR TESTS AND STUFF WITH FRIENDS, SO...
HARU'S DREAM IS COMING **TRUE**, RIGHT NOW.
HEE HEE...
ARE YOU AWAKE?
WE ARE GLAD YOU'RE SAFE.

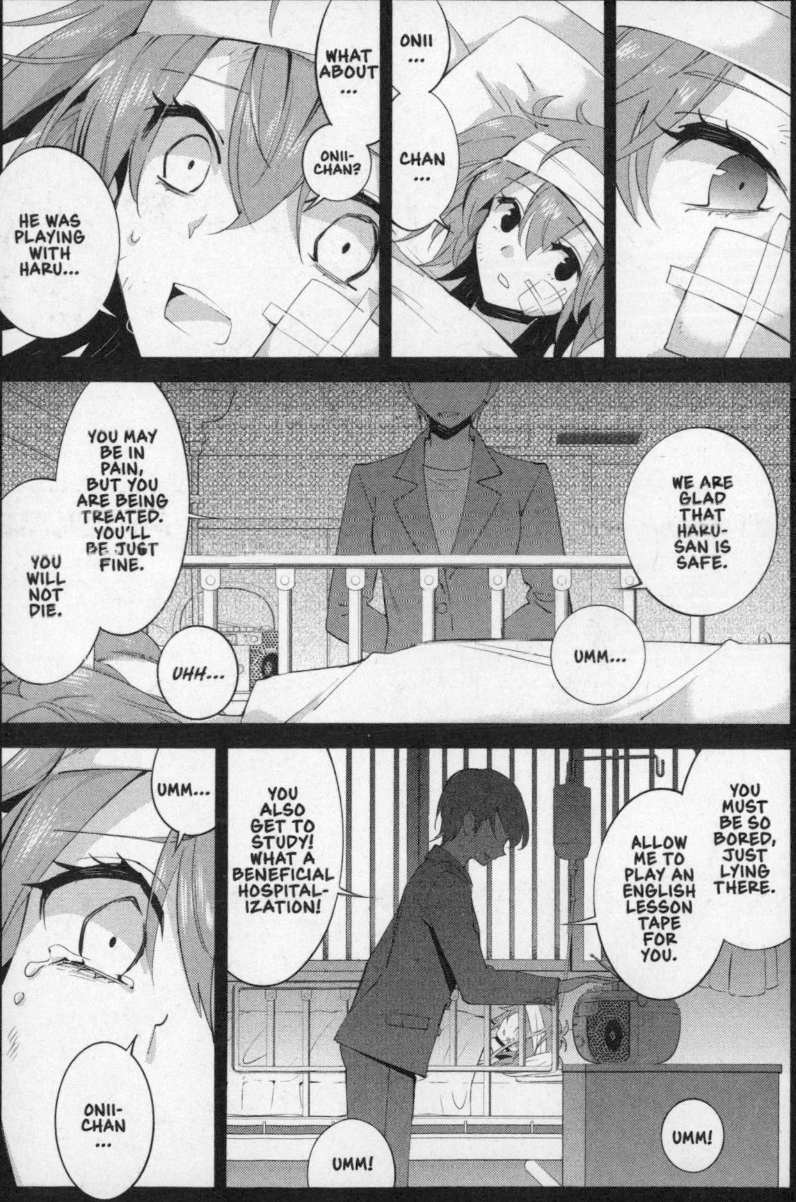
ONII ...
CHAN ...
WHAT ABOUT ...
ONII-CHAN?
HE WAS PLAYING WITH HARU...
WE ARE GLAD THAT HARU-SAN IS SAFE.
YOU MAY BE IN PAIN, BUT YOU ARE BEING TREATED. YOU'LL BE JUST FINE.
YOU WILL NOT DIE.
UMM...
UHH...
YOU MUST BE SO BORED, JUST LYING THERE.
ALLOW ME TO PLAY AN ENGLISH LESSON TAPE FOR YOU.
YOU ALSO GET TO STUDY! WHAT A BENEFICIAL HOSPITAL-IZATION!
UMM!
UMM!
UMM...
ONII-CHAN ...

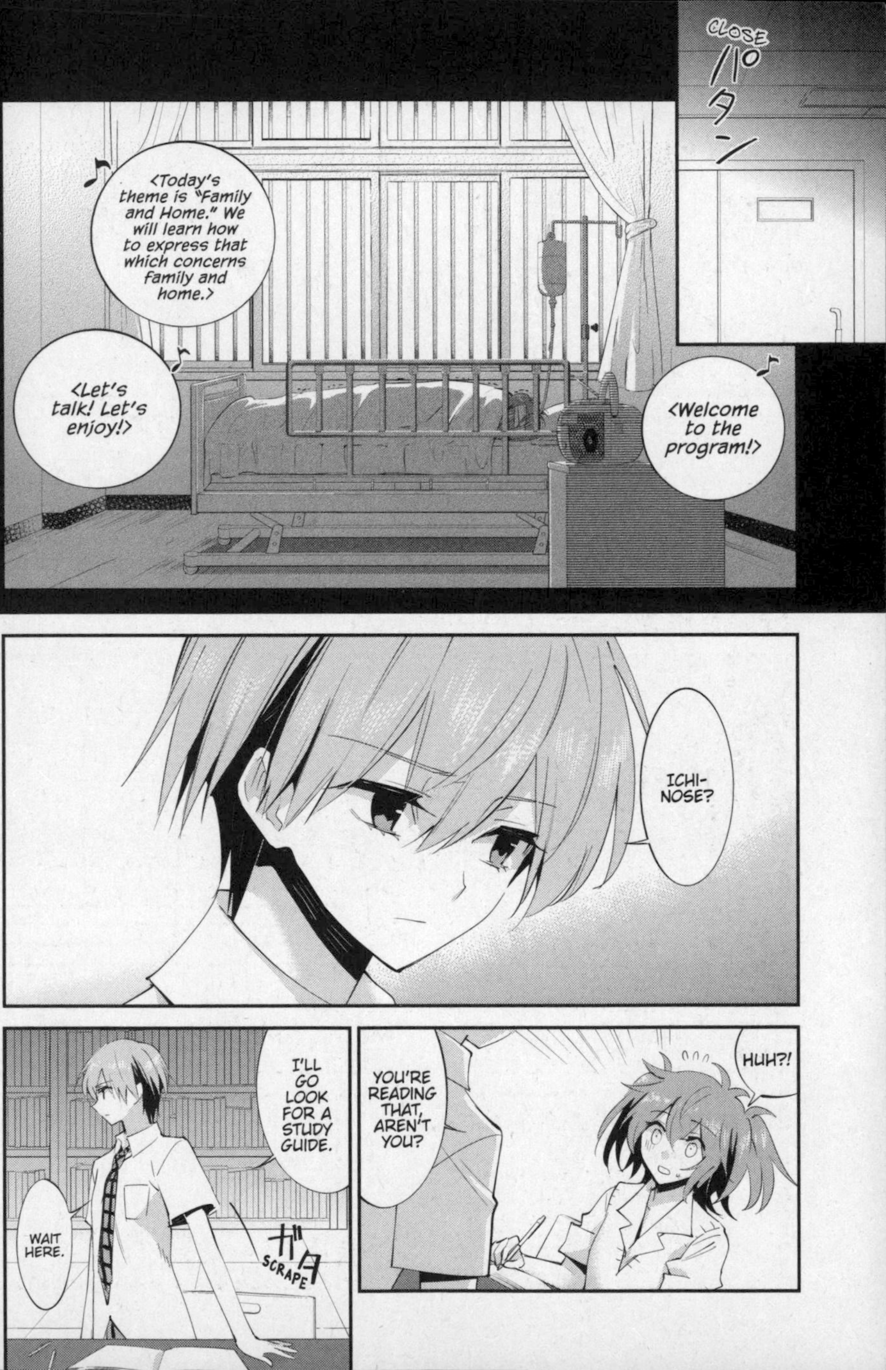
CLOSE
パタン
<Welcome to the program!>
<Let's talk! Let's enjoy!>
<Today's theme is "Family and Home." We will learn how to express that which concerns family and home.>
ICHI-NOSE?
HUH?!
YOU'RE READING THAT, AREN'T YOU?
I'LL GO LOOK FOR A STUDY GUIDE.
WAIT HERE.
ガタ
SCRAPE

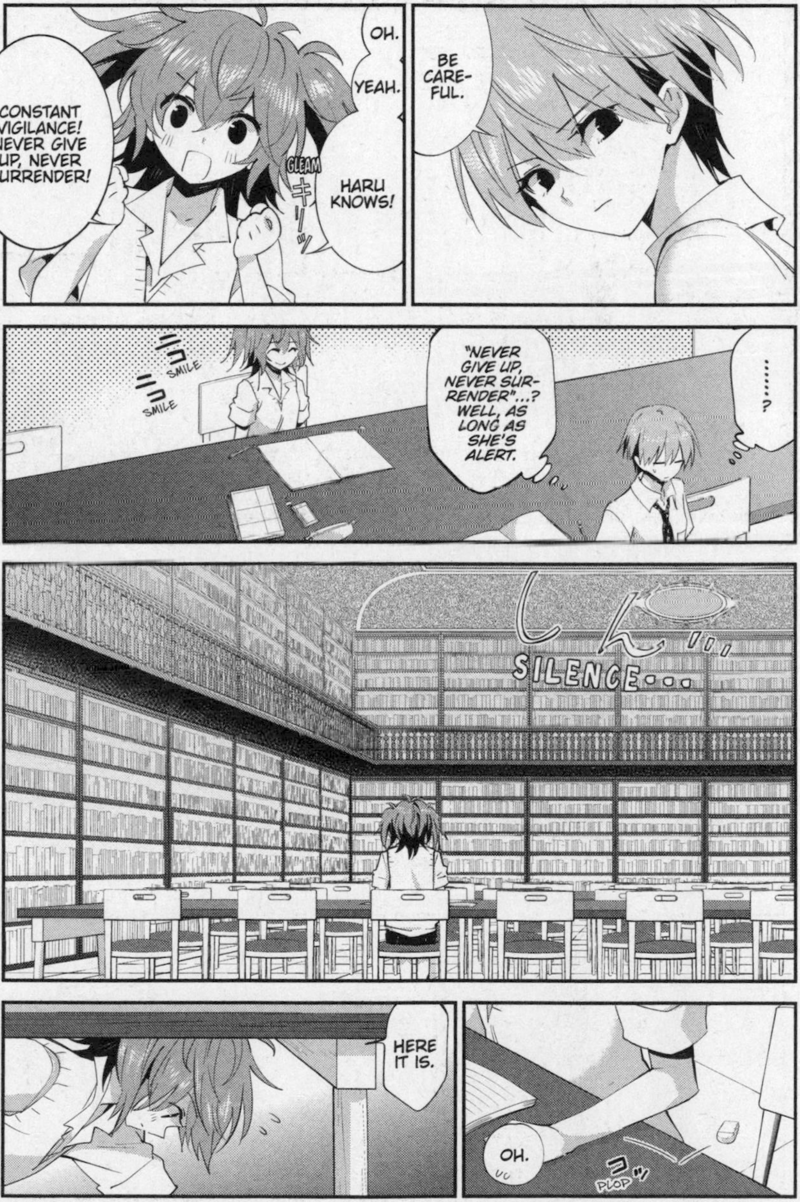
BE CARE-FUL.
OH.
YEAH.
HARU KNOWS!
GLEAM
CONSTANT VIGILANCE! NEVER GIVE UP, NEVER SURRENDER!
......?
"NEVER GIVE UP, NEVER SUR-RENDER"...? WELL, AS LONG AS SHE'S ALERT.
SMILE
SMILE
SILENCE...
OH.
PLOP
HERE IT IS.

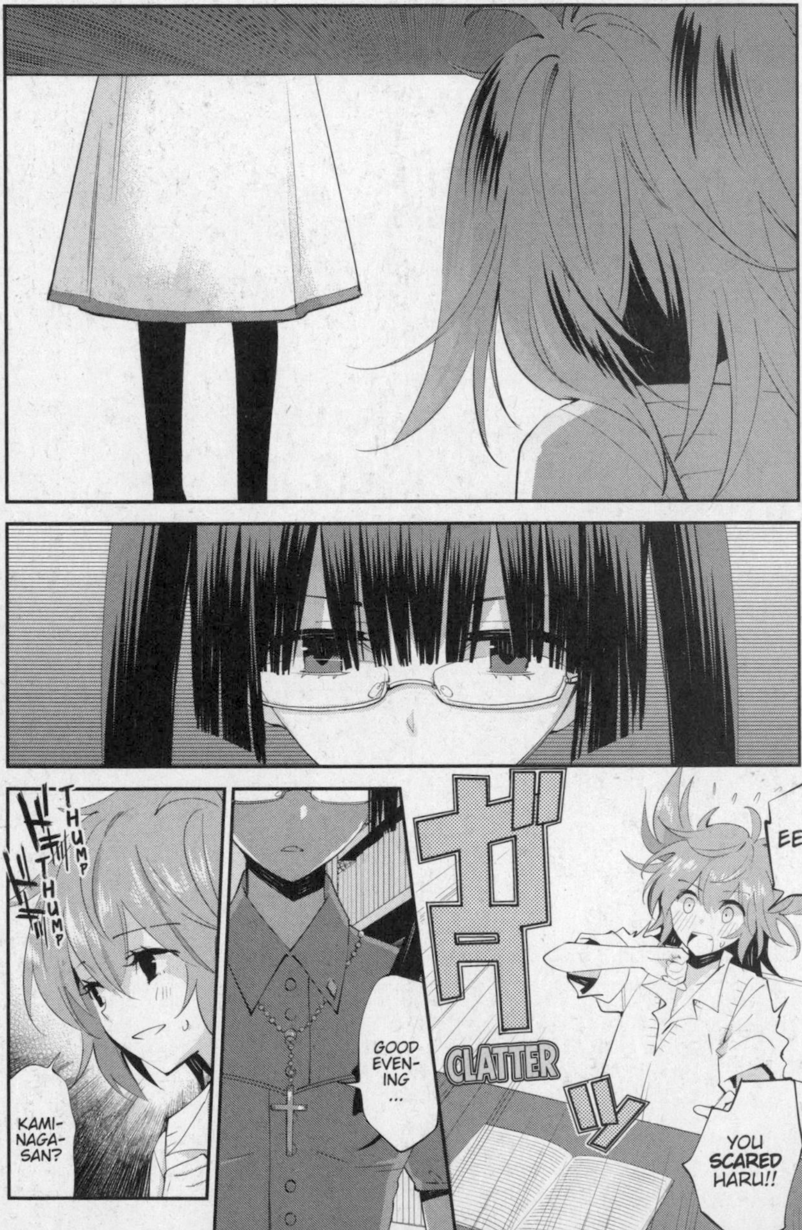
EEK!
ガッ
CLATTER
YOU SCARED HARU!!
GOOD EVENING...
THUMP THUMP
KAMINAGA-SAN?

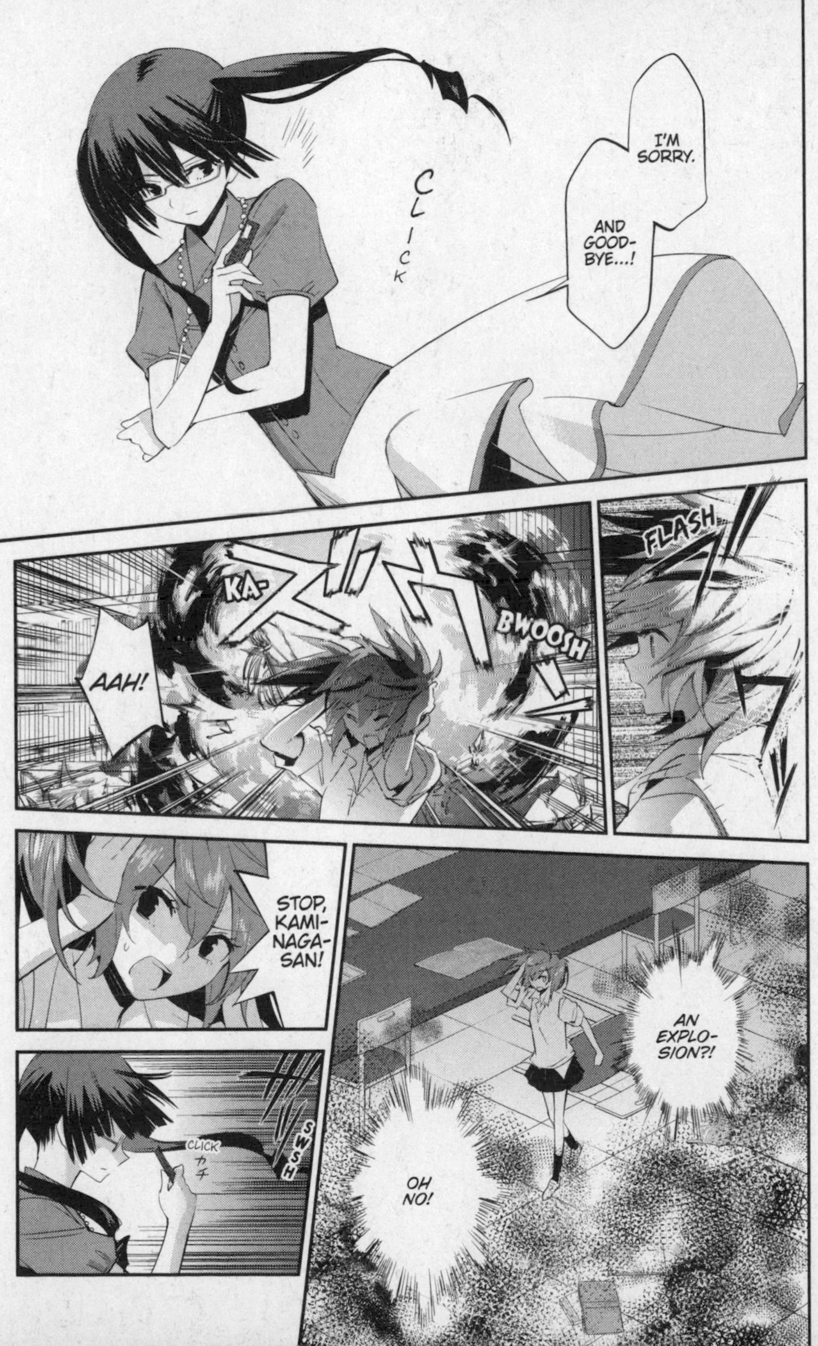

I'M SORRY.
AND GOODBYE...!
CLICK
FLASH
KA-
BWOOSH
AAH!
AN EXPLOSION?!
OH NO!
STOP, KAMINAGA-SAN!
SWSH
CLICK
カチ

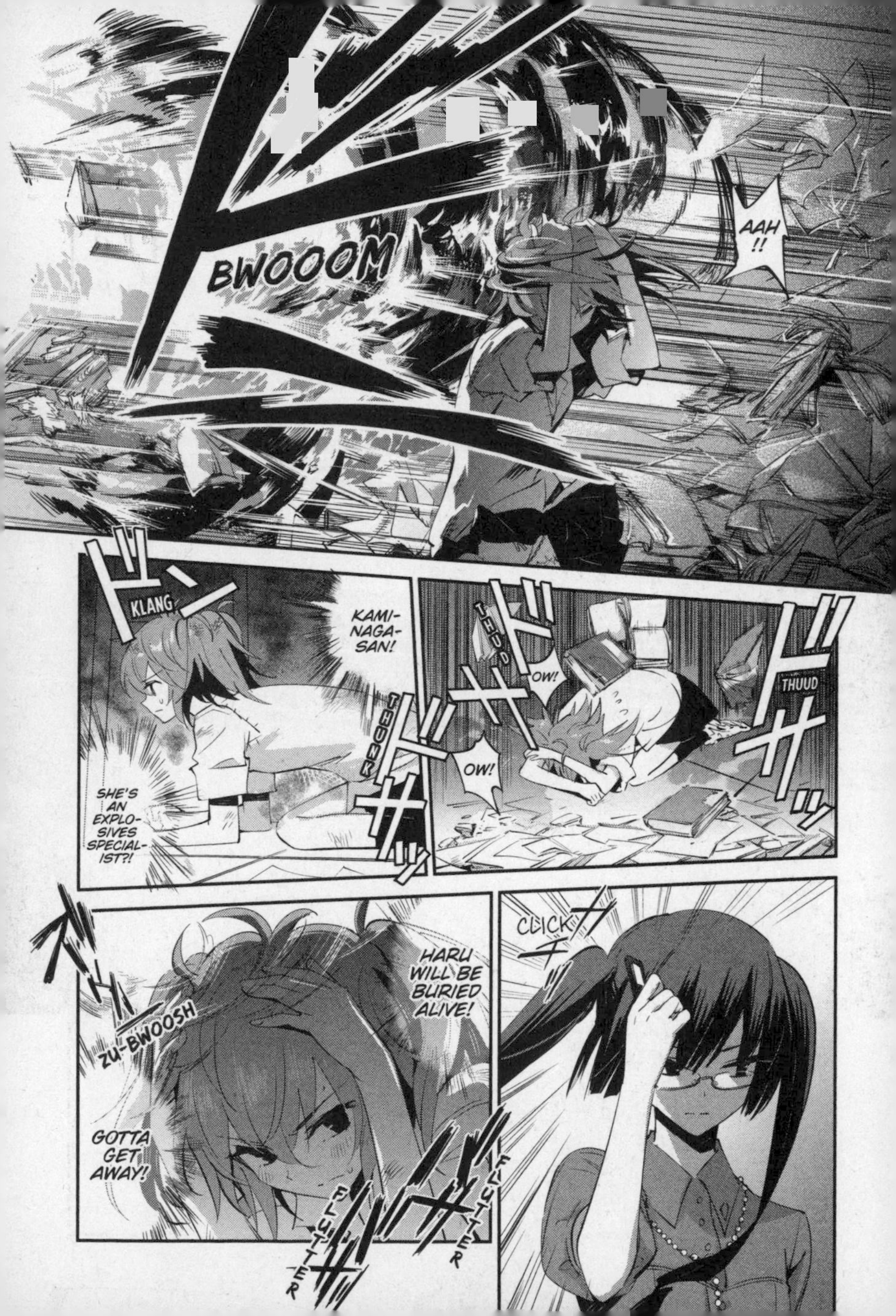
AAH!!
BWOOOM
THUD
OW!
THUUD
OW!
KLANG
KAMI-NAGA-SAN!
THUNK
SHE'S AN EXPLOSIVES SPECIALIST?!
CLICK
HARU WILL BE BURIED ALIVE!
ZU-BWOOSH
GOTTA GET AWAY!
FLUTTER
FLUTTER

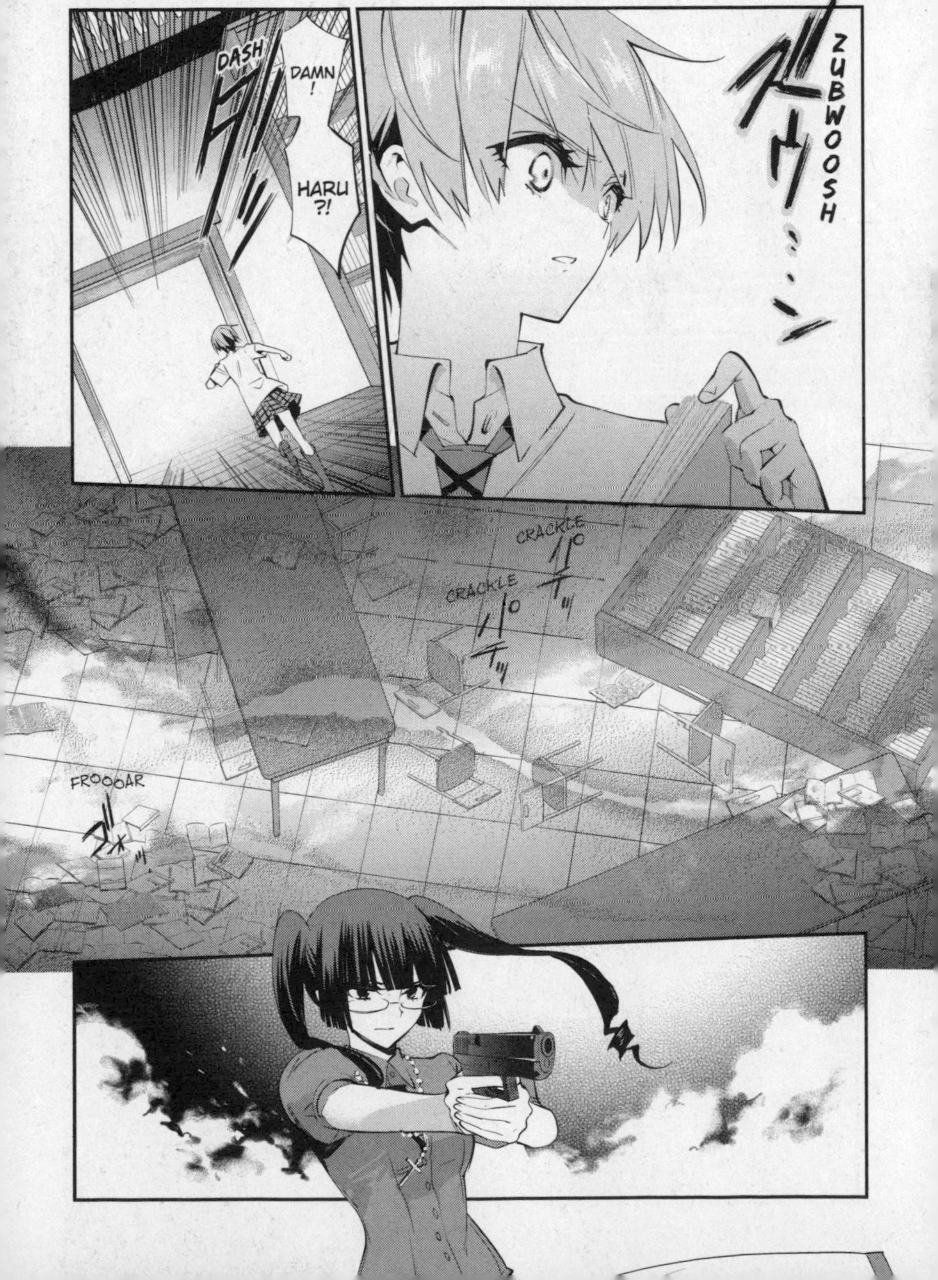
ZUBWOOSH
DASH
DAMN!
HARU?!
CRACKLE
CRACKLE
FROOOAR

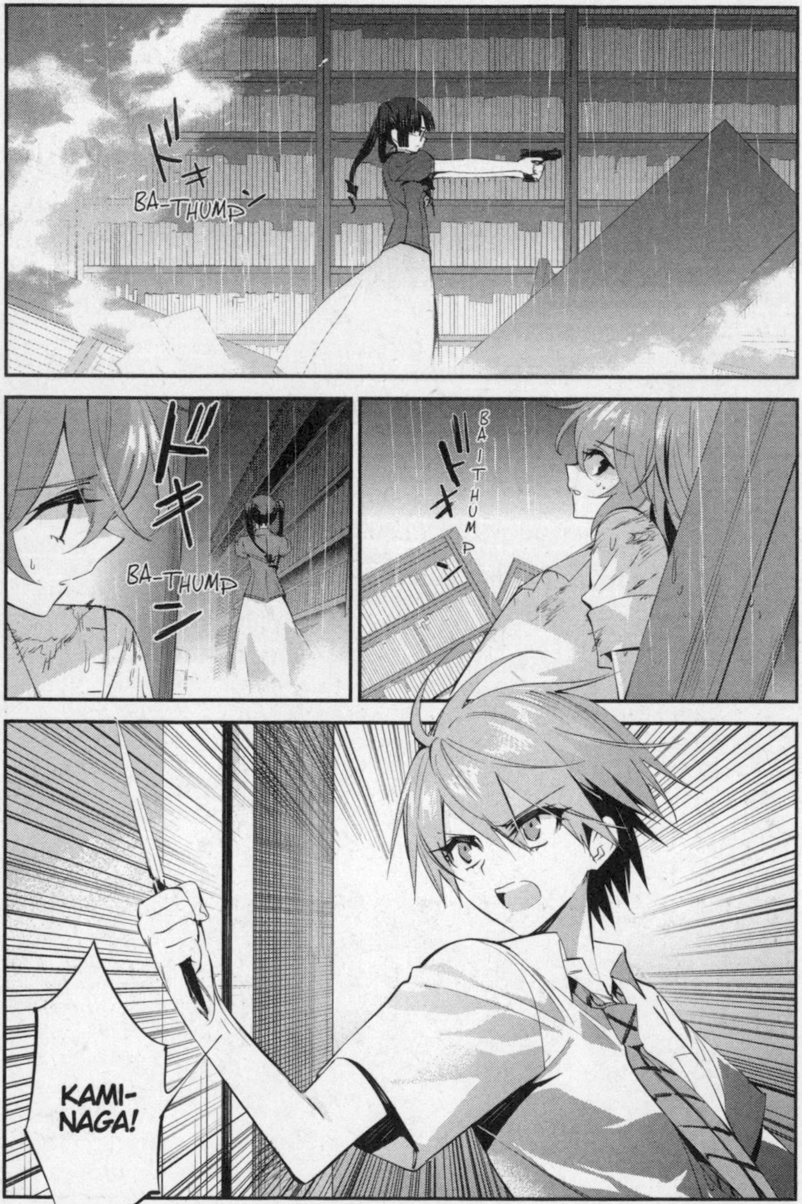
ドキ
BA-THUMP
ドキ
BA-THUMP
ドキ
BA-THUMP
KAMI-
NAGA!

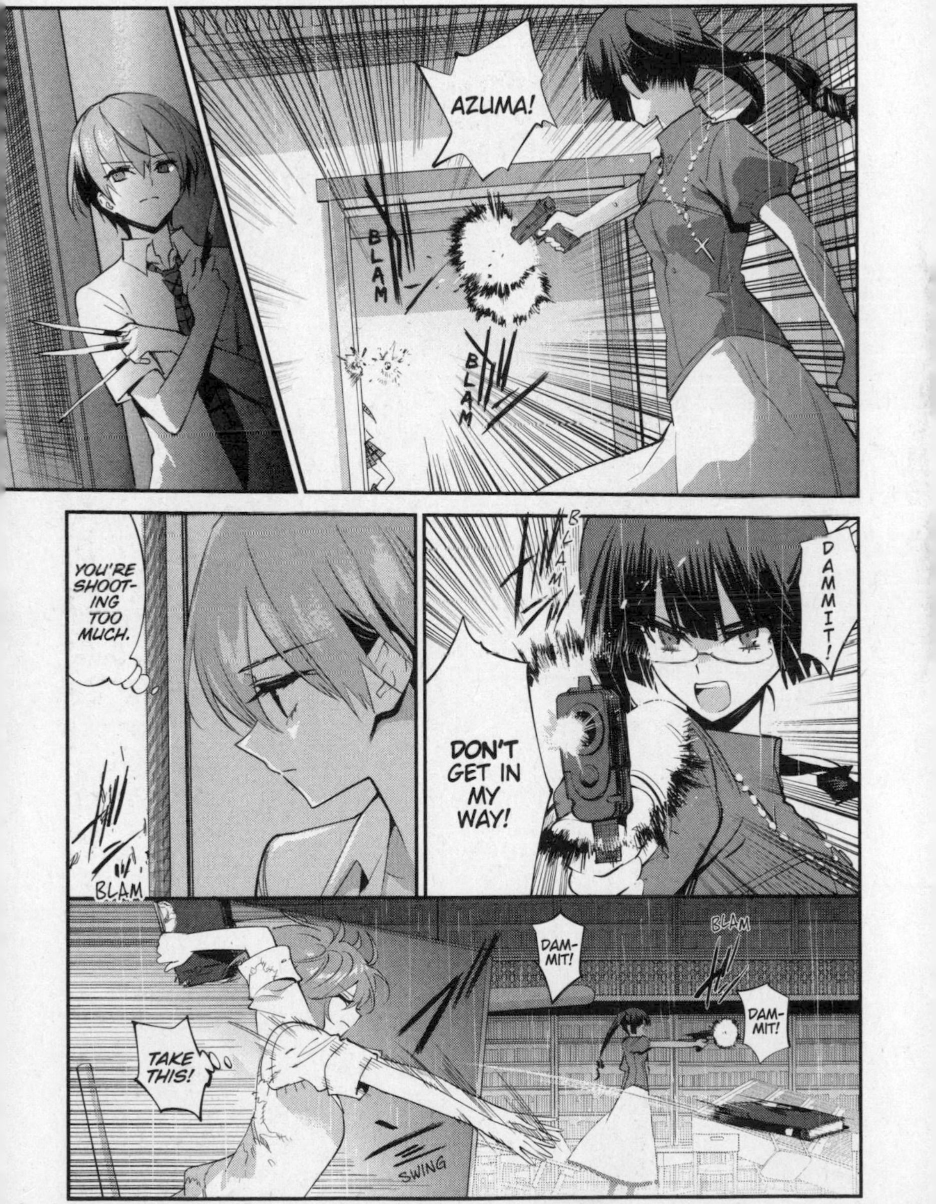
AZUMA!
BLAM
BLAM
DAMMIT!
BLAM
DON'T GET IN MY WAY!
YOU'RE SHOOTING TOO MUCH.
BLAM
BLAM
DAMMIT!
DAMMIT!
TAKE THIS!
SWING

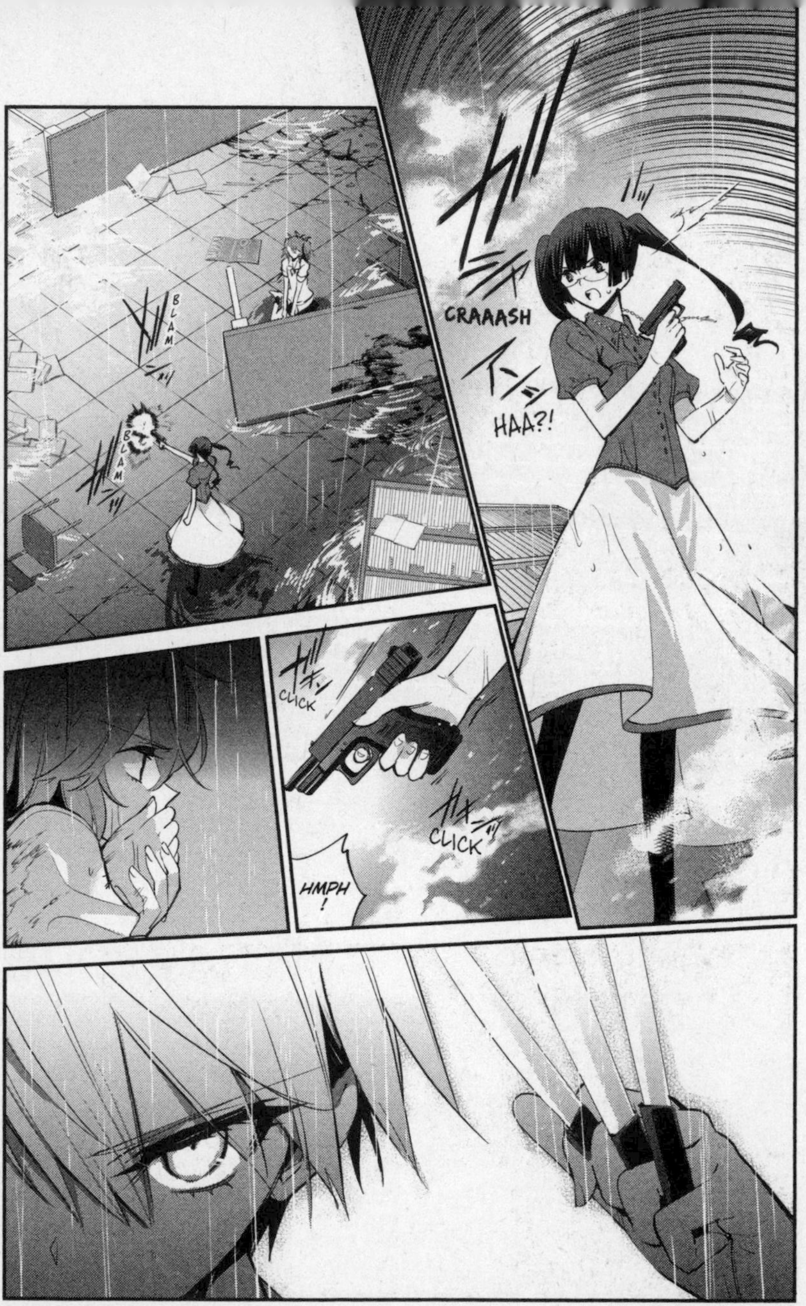
CRAAASH
HAA?!
BLAM
BLAM
CLICK
CLICK
HMPH!

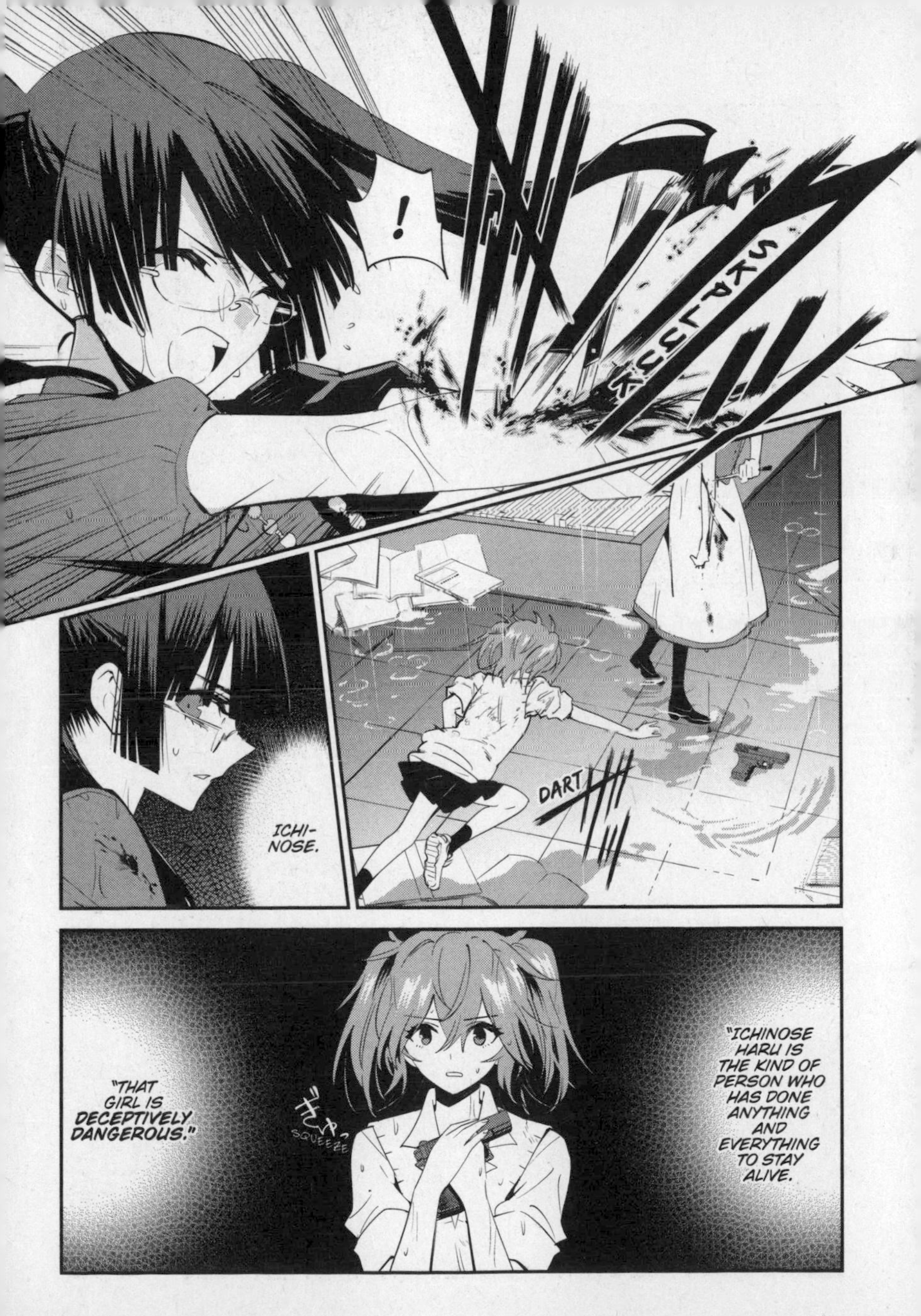
!
SKPLUCK
DART
ICHI-
NOSE.
"ICHINOSE HARU IS THE KIND OF PERSON WHO HAS DONE ANYTHING AND EVERYTHING TO STAY ALIVE.
SQUEEZE
"THAT GIRL IS DECEPTIVELY DANGEROUS."

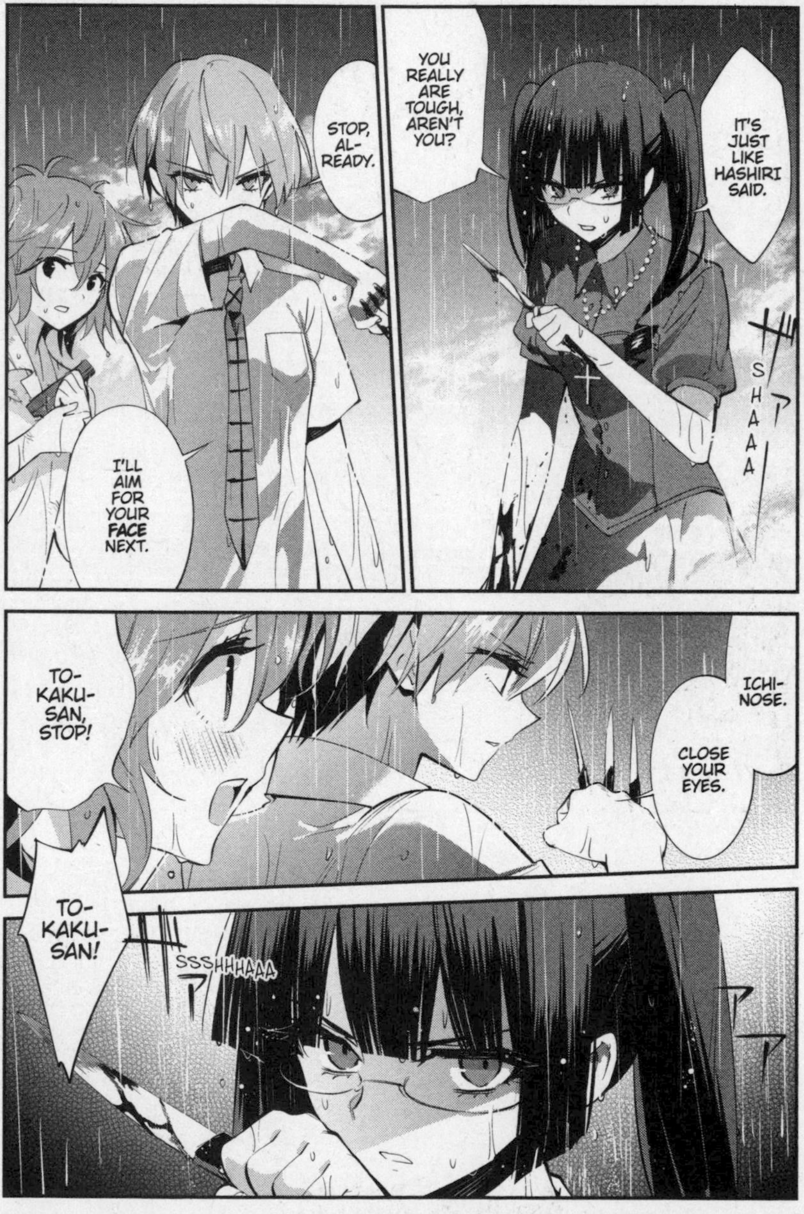
IT'S JUST LIKE HASHIRI SAID.
YOU REALLY ARE TOUGH, AREN'T YOU?
SHAAA
STOP, AL-READY.
I'LL AIM FOR YOUR FACE NEXT.
ICHI-NOSE.
CLOSE YOUR EYES.
TO-KAKU-SAN, STOP!
TO-KAKU-SAN!
SSSHHHAAA

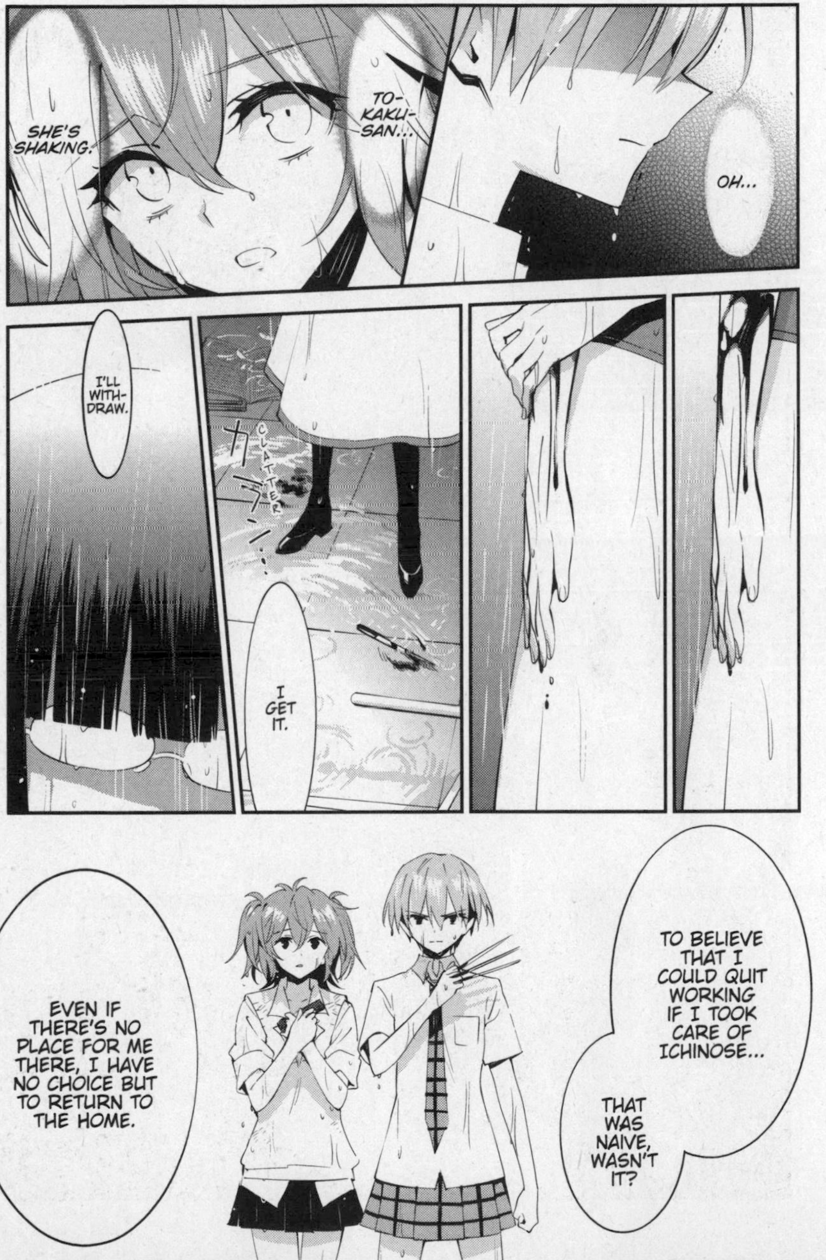
OH...
TO-KAKU-SAN...
SHE'S SHAKING.
CLATTER
I GET IT.
I'LL WITH-DRAW.
TO BELIEVE THAT I COULD QUIT WORKING IF I TOOK CARE OF ICHINOSE...
THAT WAS NAIVE, WASN'T IT?
EVEN IF THERE'S NO PLACE FOR ME THERE, I HAVE NO CHOICE BUT TO RETURN TO THE HOME.

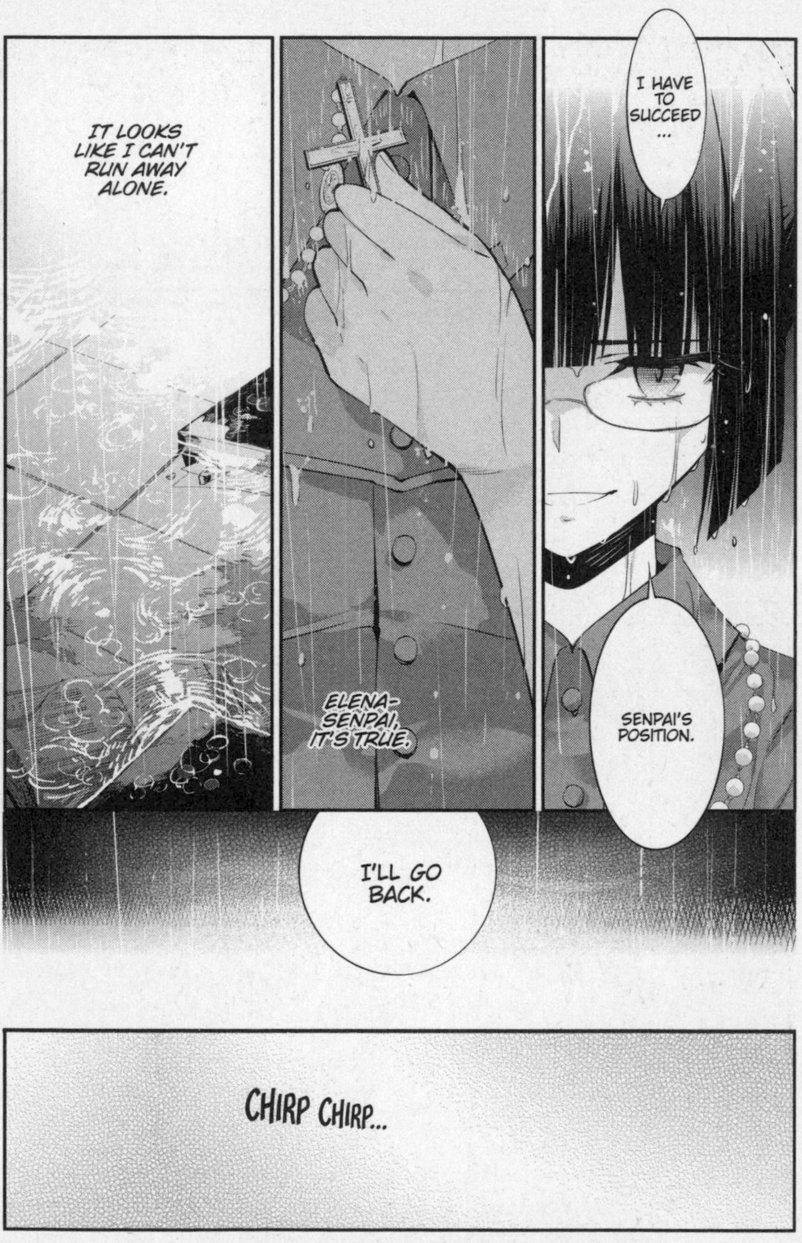
I HAVE TO SUCCEED ...
SENPAI'S POSITION.
ELENA-SENPAI, IT'S TRUE.
IT LOOKS LIKE I CAN'T RUN AWAY ALONE.
I'LL GO BACK.
CHIRP CHIRP...

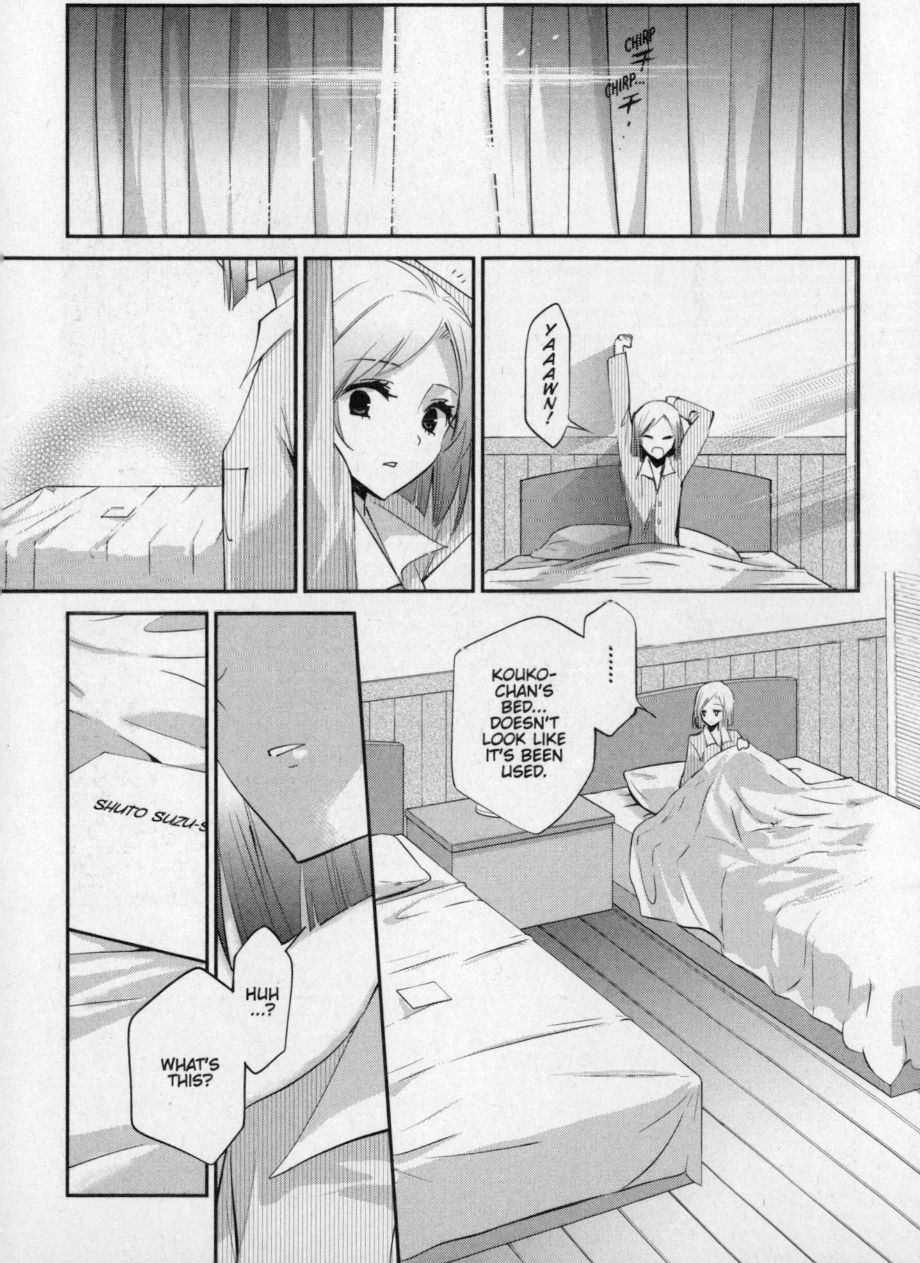
CHIRP
CHIRP...
YAAAAWN!
......
KOUKO-CHAN'S BED... DOESN'T LOOK LIKE IT'S BEEN USED.
HUH ...?
WHAT'S THIS?
SHUTO SUZU-S

SCRATCH
SCRATCH
DEAR SHUTO.
THIS LETTER,
SUCCEED MY
F PRESIDENT.
KAMINAGA KOUKO
DEAR SHUTO,
READ THIS LETTER,
LEASE SUCCEED MY
TION OF PRESIDENT.
KAMINAGA KOUK
"IF YOU READ THIS LETTER, THEN...
"PLEASE SUCCEED MY POSITION OF PRESIDENT."
KOUKO-CHAN... THIS IS...
PFFT.
SUCH A PROFESSIONAL NOTE.
YOU REALLY DID HAVE A DUTIFUL AND DIFFICULT PERSONALITY, DIDN'T YOU?

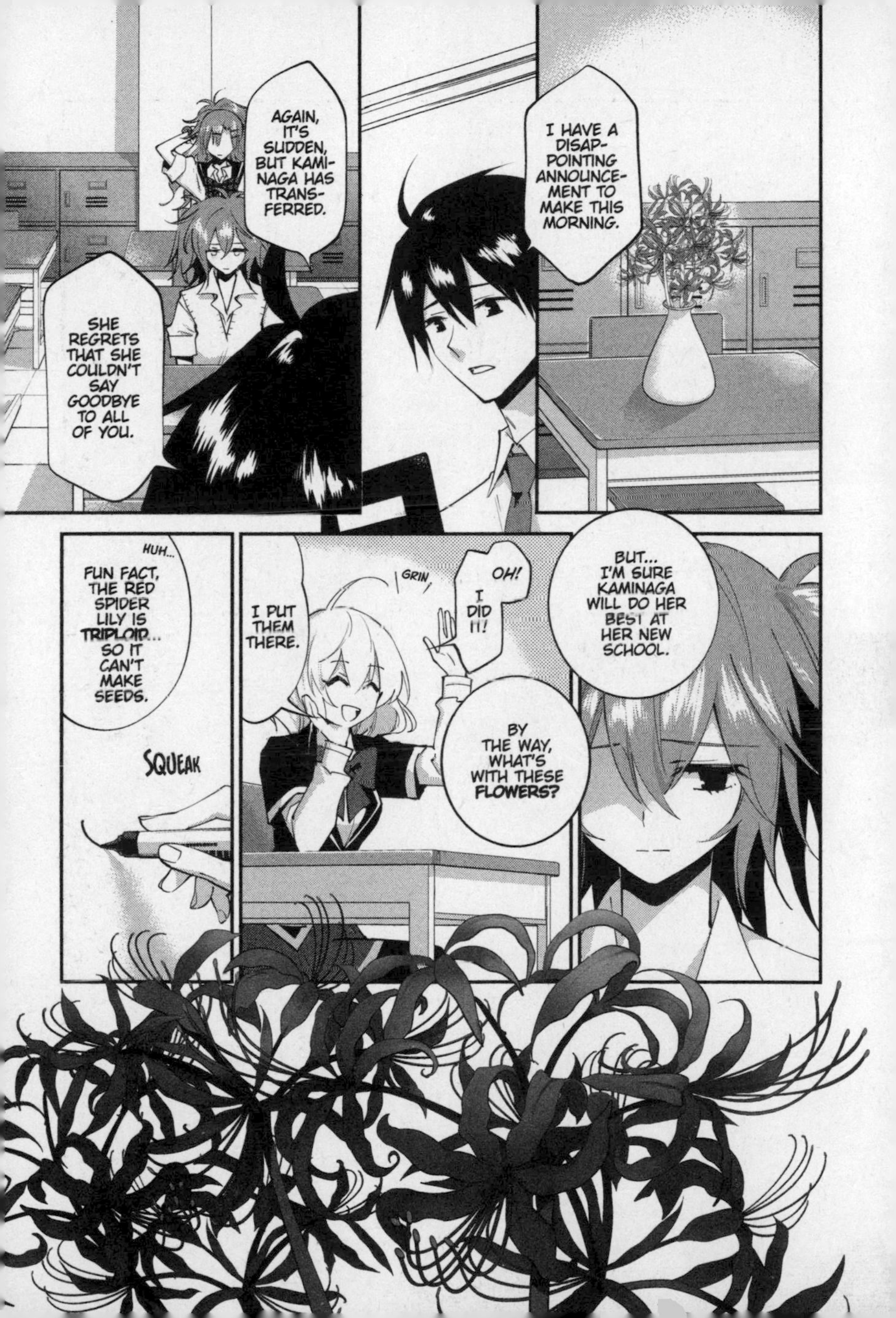
I HAVE A DISAPPOINTING ANNOUNCEMENT TO MAKE THIS MORNING.
AGAIN, IT'S SUDDEN, BUT KAMINAGA HAS TRANSFERRED.
SHE REGRETS THAT SHE COULDN'T SAY GOODBYE TO ALL OF YOU.
BUT... I'M SURE KAMINAGA WILL DO HER BEST AT HER NEW SCHOOL.
BY THE WAY, WHAT'S WITH THESE FLOWERS?
OH! I DID IT!
GRIN
I PUT THEM THERE.
HUH...
FUN FACT, THE RED SPIDER LILY IS TRIPLOID... SO IT CAN'T MAKE SEEDS.
SQUEAK

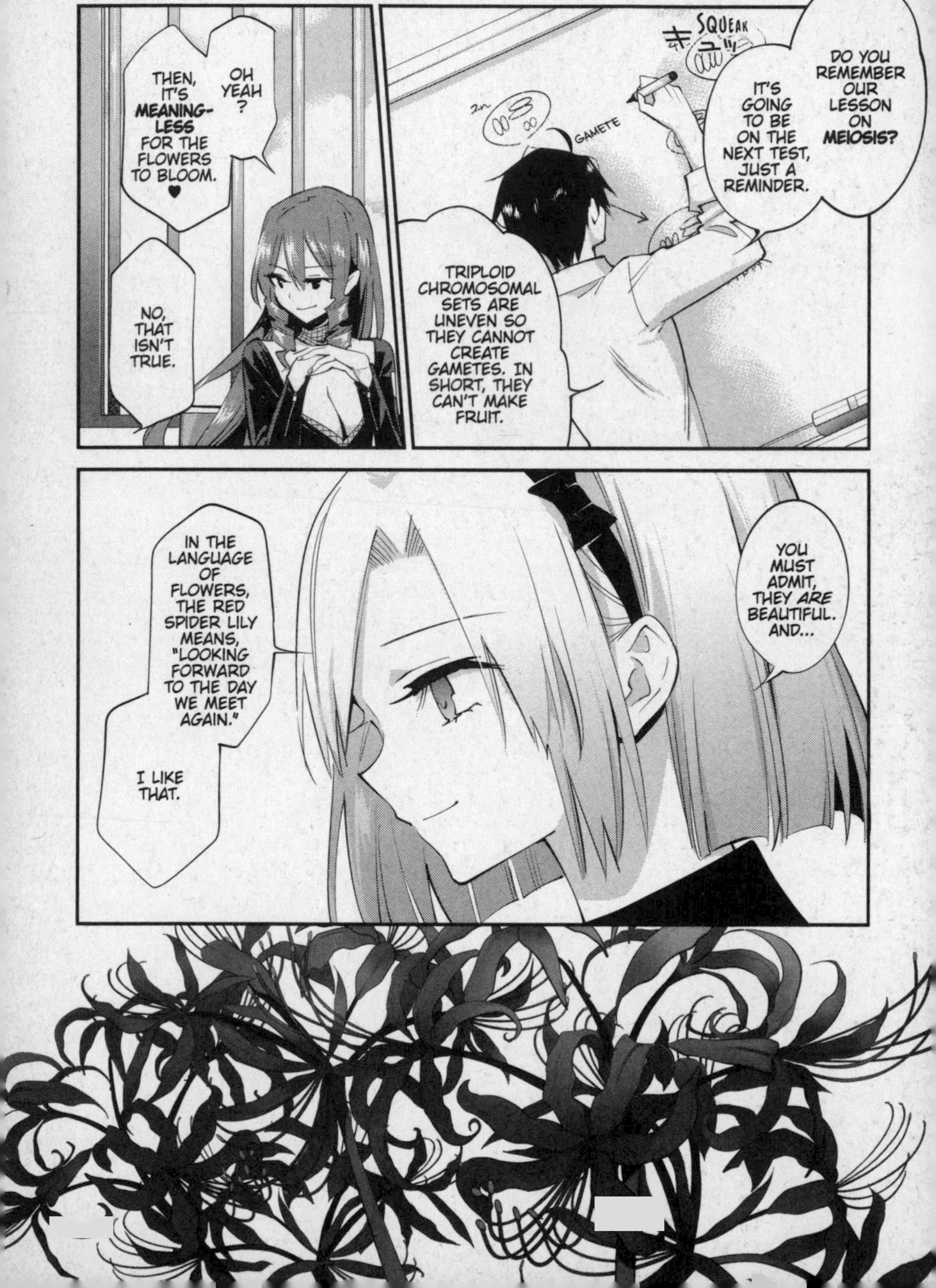
SQUEAK
DO YOU REMEMBER OUR LESSON ON **MEIOSIS?**
IT'S GOING TO BE ON THE NEXT TEST, JUST A REMINDER.
2n
GAMETE
TRIPLOID CHROMOSOMAL SETS ARE UNEVEN SO THEY CANNOT CREATE GAMETES. IN SHORT, THEY CAN'T MAKE FRUIT.
OH YEAH?
THEN, IT'S **MEANINGLESS** FOR THE FLOWERS TO BLOOM. ♥
NO, THAT ISN'T TRUE.
YOU MUST ADMIT, THEY *ARE* BEAUTIFUL. AND...
IN THE LANGUAGE OF FLOWERS, THE RED SPIDER LILY MEANS, "LOOKING FORWARD TO THE DAY WE MEET AGAIN."
I LIKE THAT.

riddle story of devil

Chapter 16
Until We Meet Again

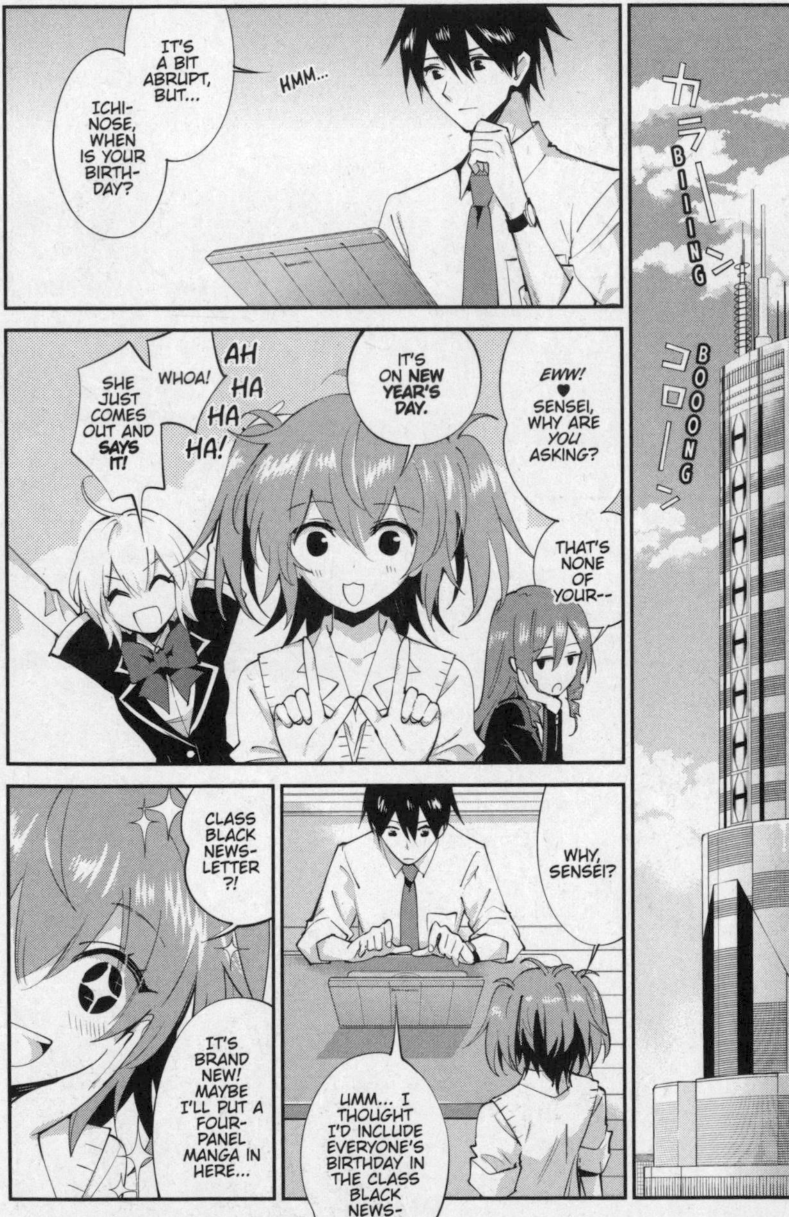
カラーン
BIIIING
コローン
BOOOONG
HMM...
IT'S A BIT ABRUPT, BUT... ICHINOSE, WHEN IS YOUR BIRTHDAY?
EWW! ♥ SENSEI, WHY ARE YOU ASKING?
THAT'S NONE OF YOUR--
IT'S ON NEW YEAR'S DAY.
AH HA HA HA!
WHOA!
SHE JUST COMES OUT AND SAYS IT!
WHY, SENSEI?
UMM... I THOUGHT I'D INCLUDE EVERYONE'S BIRTHDAY IN THE CLASS BLACK NEWSLETTER.
CLASS BLACK NEWSLETTER?!
IT'S BRAND NEW! MAYBE I'LL PUT A FOUR-PANEL MANGA IN HERE...

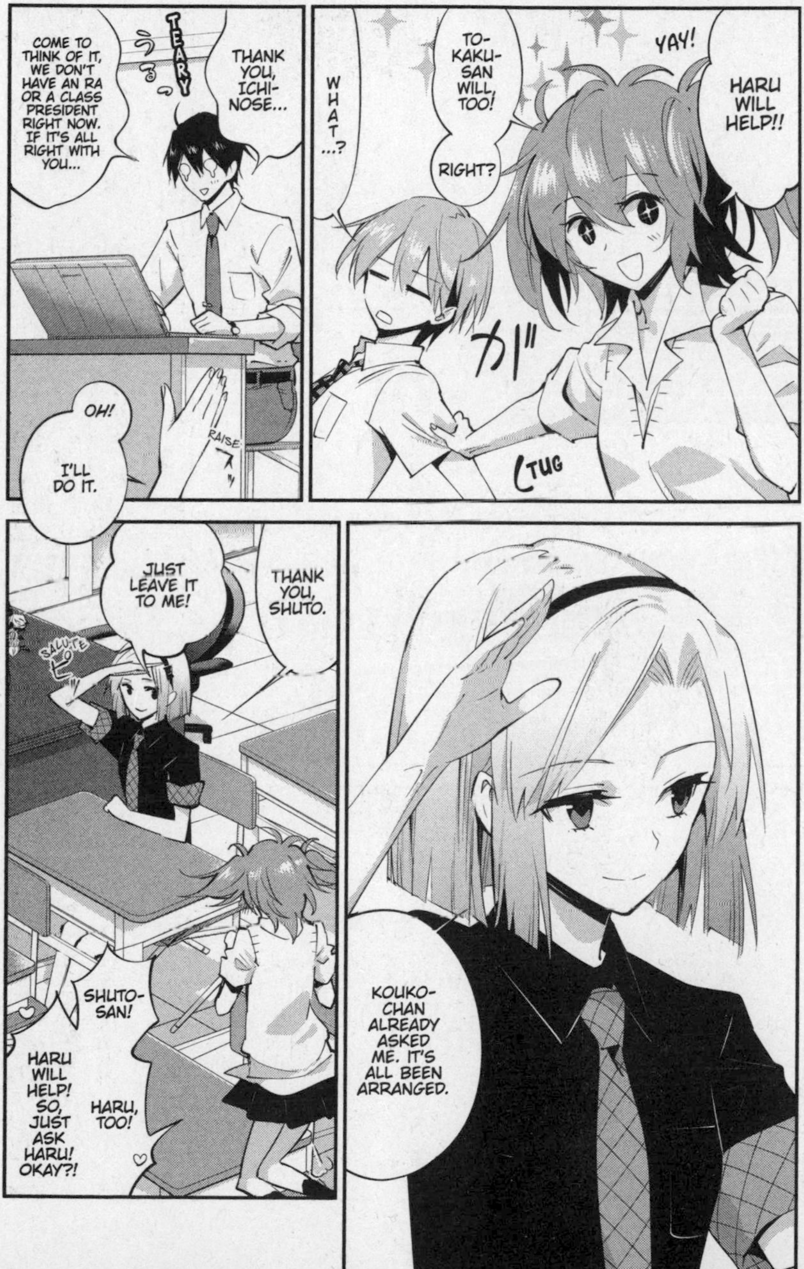
HARU WILL HELP!!
YAY!
TO-KAKU-SAN WILL, TOO!
RIGHT?
WHAT...?
TUG
THANK YOU, ICHI-NOSE...
TEARY
COME TO THINK OF IT, WE DON'T HAVE AN RA OR A CLASS PRESIDENT RIGHT NOW. IF IT'S ALL RIGHT WITH YOU...
OH!
RAISE
I'LL DO IT.
KOUKO-CHAN ALREADY ASKED ME. IT'S ALL BEEN ARRANGED.
THANK YOU, SHUTO.
JUST LEAVE IT TO ME!
SALUTE
SHUTO-SAN!
HARU, TOO!
HARU WILL HELP! SO, JUST ASK HARU! OKAY?!

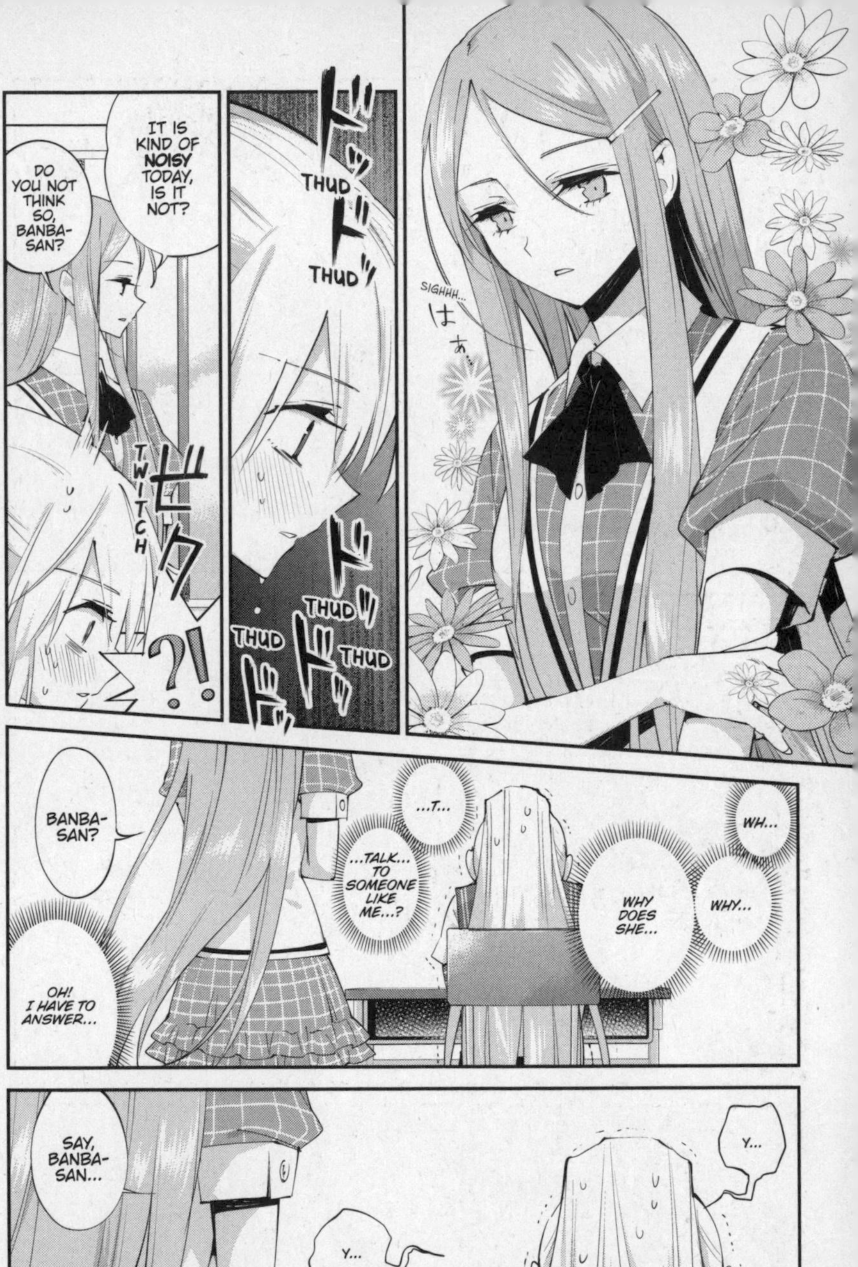
SIGHHH...
はぁ…
ドッ
THUD
ドッ
THUD
IT IS KIND OF NOISY TODAY, IS IT NOT?
DO YOU NOT THINK SO, BANBA-SAN?
ドッ
THUD
THUD
ドッ
THUD
ドッ
TWITCH
ビク
?!
WH...
WHY...
WHY DOES SHE...
...T...
...TALK... TO SOMEONE LIKE ME...?
BANBA-SAN?
OH! I HAVE TO ANSWER...
Y...
Y...
SAY, BANBA-SAN...

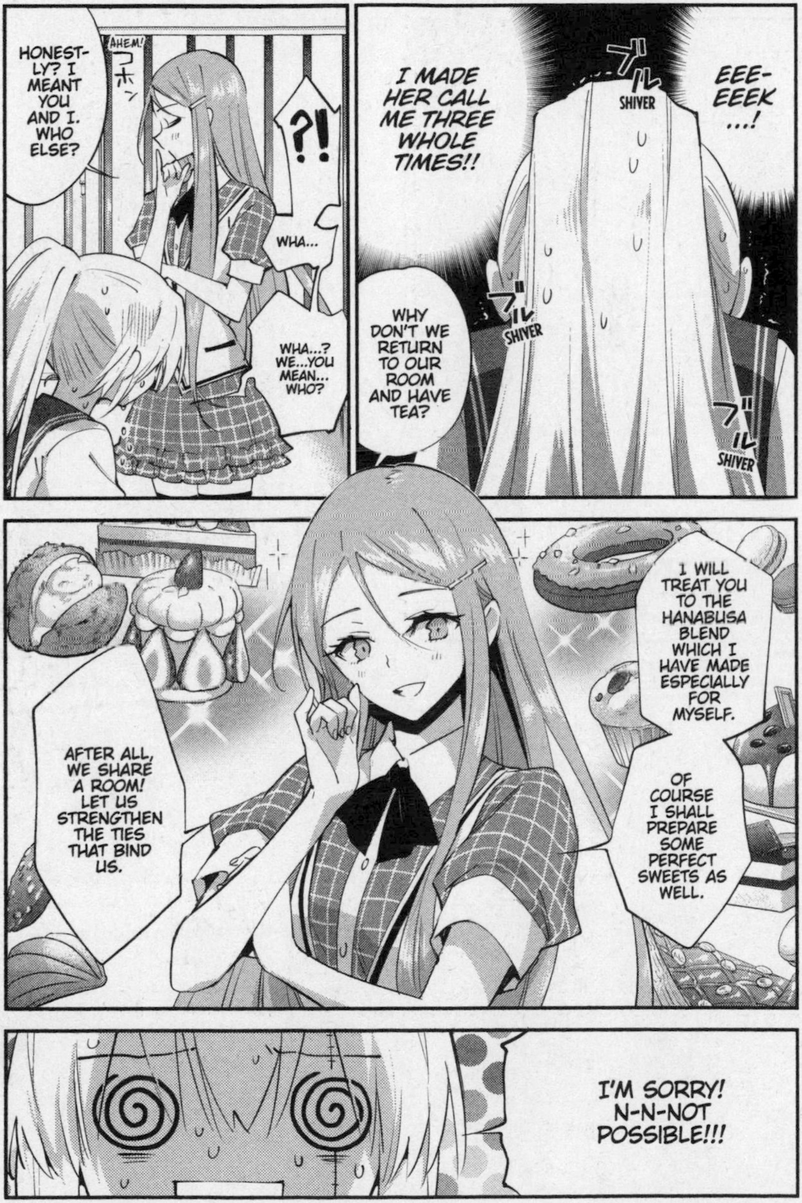
EEE-EEEK ...!
I MADE HER CALL ME THREE WHOLE TIMES!!
ブル SHIVER
ブル SHIVER
ブル SHIVER
WHY DON'T WE RETURN TO OUR ROOM AND HAVE TEA?
?!
AHEM! コホン
HONESTLY? I MEANT YOU AND I. WHO ELSE?
WHA...
WHA...? WE...YOU MEAN... WHO?
I WILL TREAT YOU TO THE HANABUSA BLEND WHICH I HAVE MADE ESPECIALLY FOR MYSELF.
OF COURSE I SHALL PREPARE SOME PERFECT SWEETS AS WELL.
AFTER ALL, WE SHARE A ROOM! LET US STRENGTHEN THE TIES THAT BIND US.
I'M SORRY! N-N-NOT POSSIBLE!!!

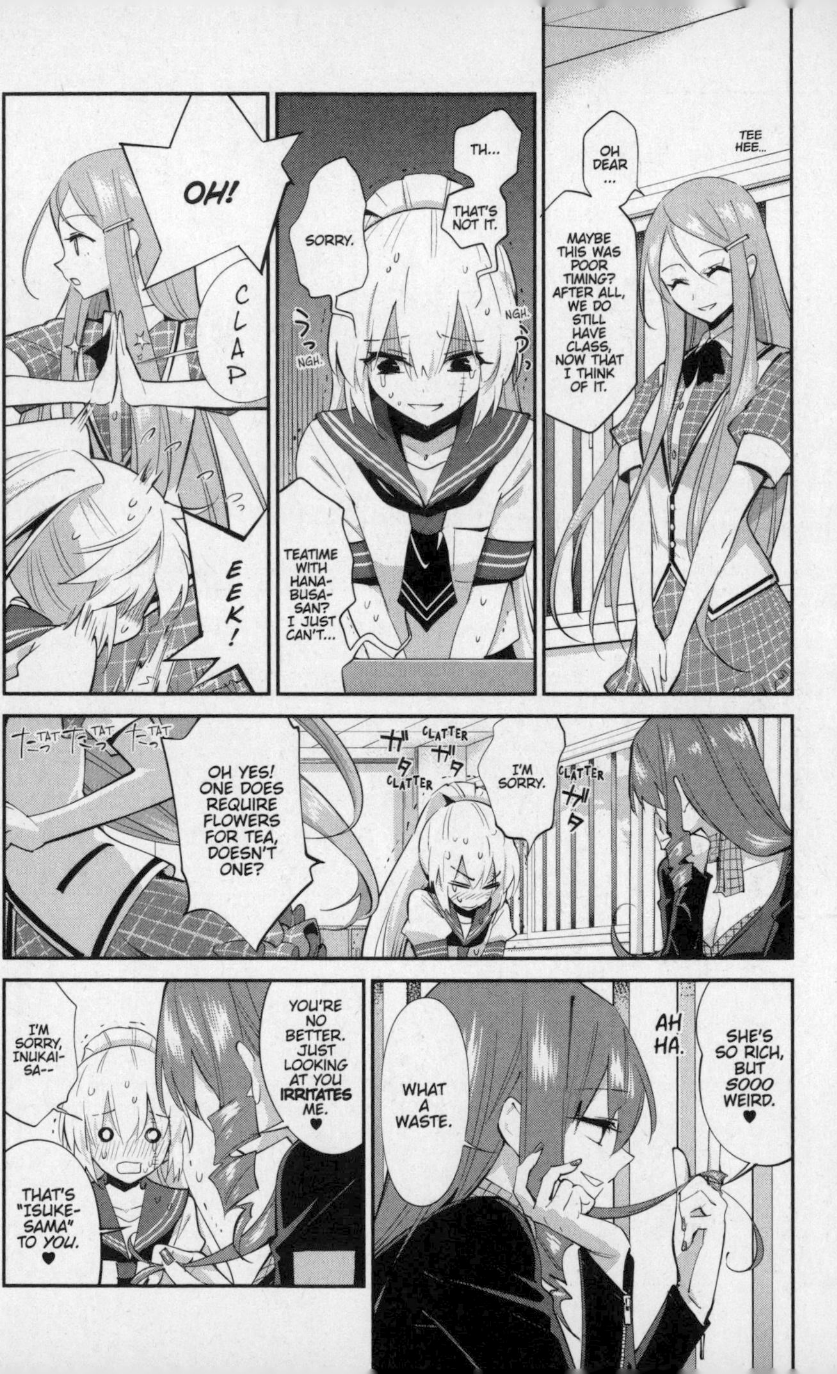
TEE HEE...
OH DEAR ...
MAYBE THIS WAS POOR TIMING? AFTER ALL, WE DO STILL HAVE CLASS, NOW THAT I THINK OF IT.
TH...
THAT'S NOT IT.
SORRY.
NGH.
NGH.
TEATIME WITH HANA-BUSA-SAN? I JUST CAN'T...
OH!
CLAP
EEK!
CLATTER
CLATTER
CLATTER
I'M SORRY.
OH YES! ONE DOES REQUIRE FLOWERS FOR TEA, DOESN'T ONE?
TAT TAT TAT
SHE'S SO RICH, BUT SOOO WEIRD. ♥
AH HA.
WHAT A WASTE.
YOU'RE NO BETTER. JUST LOOKING AT YOU **IRRITATES** ME. ♥
I'M SORRY, INUKAISA--
THAT'S "ISUKE-SAMA" TO YOU. ♥

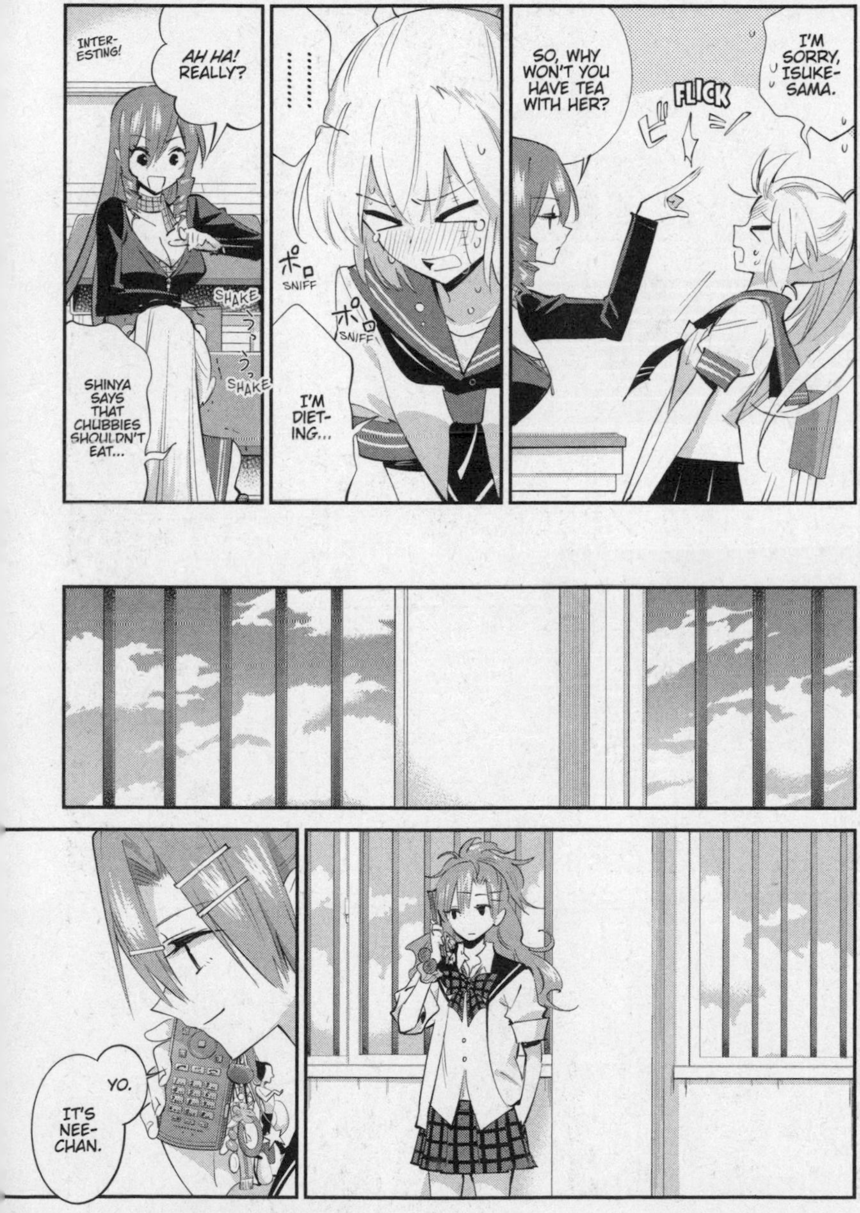
I'M SORRY, ISUKE-SAMA.
FLICK
SO, WHY WON'T YOU HAVE TEA WITH HER?
......
SNIFF
SNIFF
I'M DIETING...
AH HA! REALLY?
INTERESTING!
SHAKE
SHAKE
SHINYA SAYS THAT CHUBBIES SHOULDN'T EAT...
YO.
IT'S NEE-CHAN.

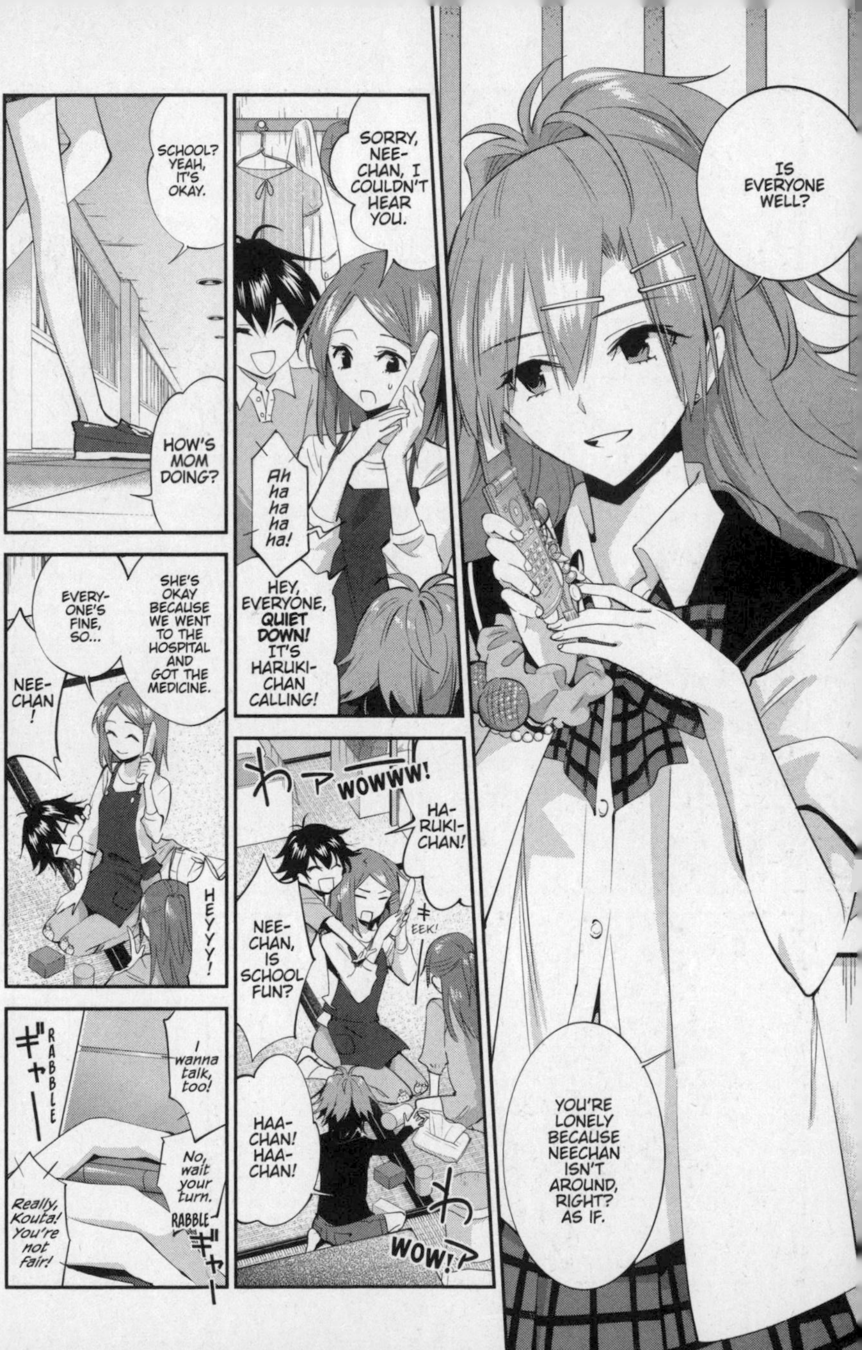
IS EVERYONE WELL?
YOU'RE LONELY BECAUSE NEECHAN ISN'T AROUND, RIGHT? AS IF.
SORRY, NEE-CHAN, I COULDN'T HEAR YOU.
Ah ha ha ha ha!
HEY, EVERYONE, **QUIET DOWN!** IT'S HARUKI-CHAN CALLING!
SCHOOL? YEAH, IT'S OKAY.
HOW'S MOM DOING?
EVERY-ONE'S FINE, SO...
SHE'S OKAY BECAUSE WE WENT TO THE HOSPITAL AND GOT THE MEDICINE.
NEE-CHAN!
HEYYY!
わァ WOWWW!
HA-RUKI-CHAN!
キ EEK!
NEE-CHAN, IS SCHOOL FUN?
HAA-CHAN! HAA-CHAN!
わ WOW!?
ギャー RABBLE
I wanna talk, too!
No, wait your turn.
Really, Kouta! You're not fair!
RABBLE ギャー

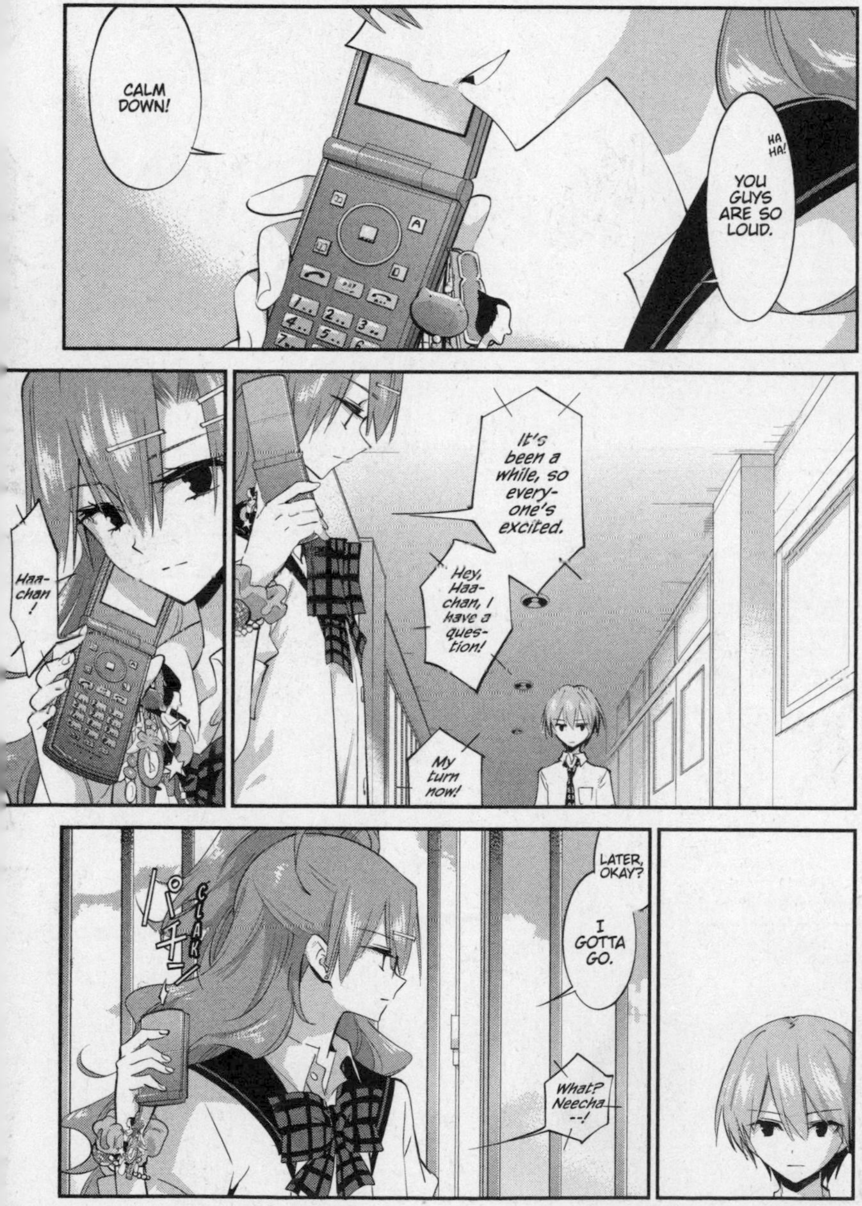
HA HA!
YOU GUYS ARE SO LOUD.
CALM DOWN!
It's been a while, so everyone's excited.
Hey, Haa-chan, I have a question!
My turn now!
Haa-chan!
LATER, OKAY?
I GOTTA GO.
CLAK
What? Neecha--!

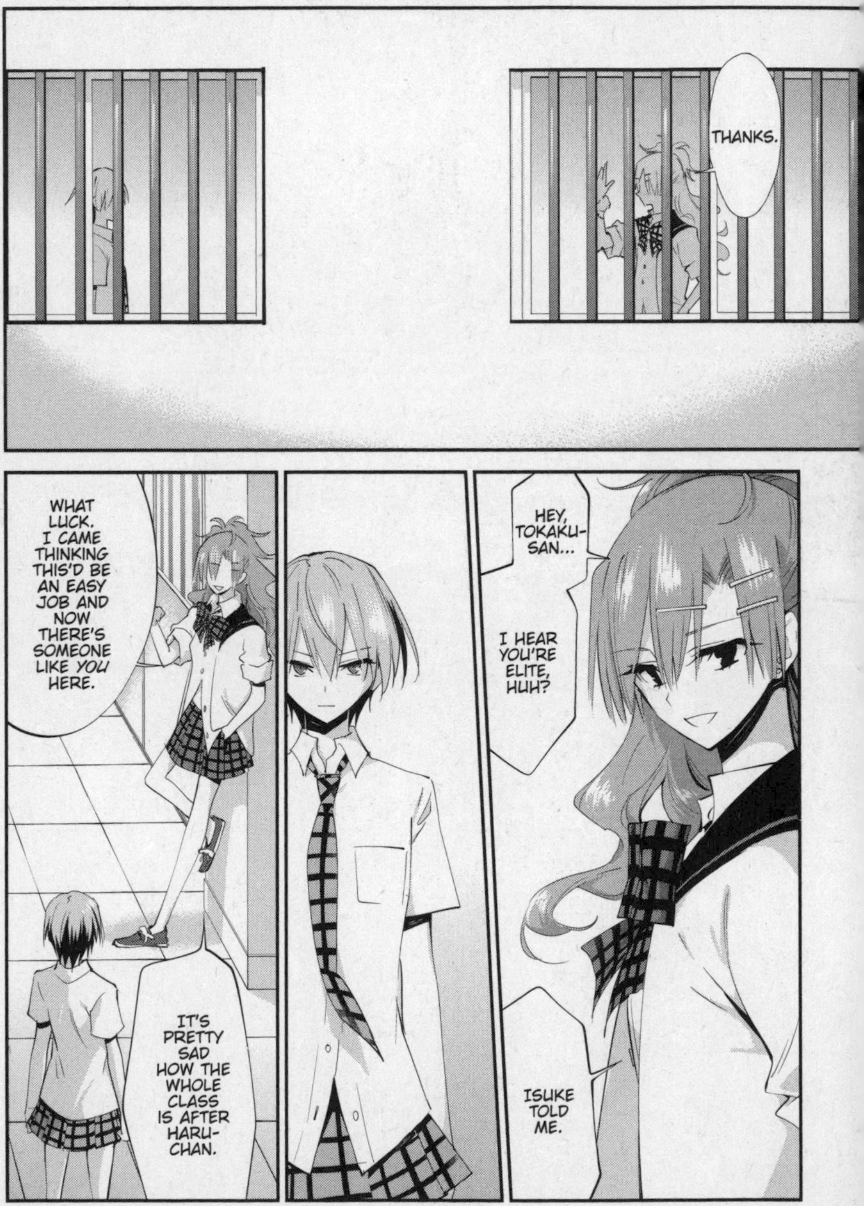
THANKS.
HEY, TOKAKU-SAN...
I HEAR YOU'RE ELITE, HUH?
ISUKE TOLD ME.
WHAT LUCK. I CAME THINKING THIS'D BE AN EASY JOB AND NOW THERE'S SOMEONE LIKE *YOU* HERE.
IT'S PRETTY SAD HOW THE WHOLE CLASS IS AFTER HARU-CHAN.

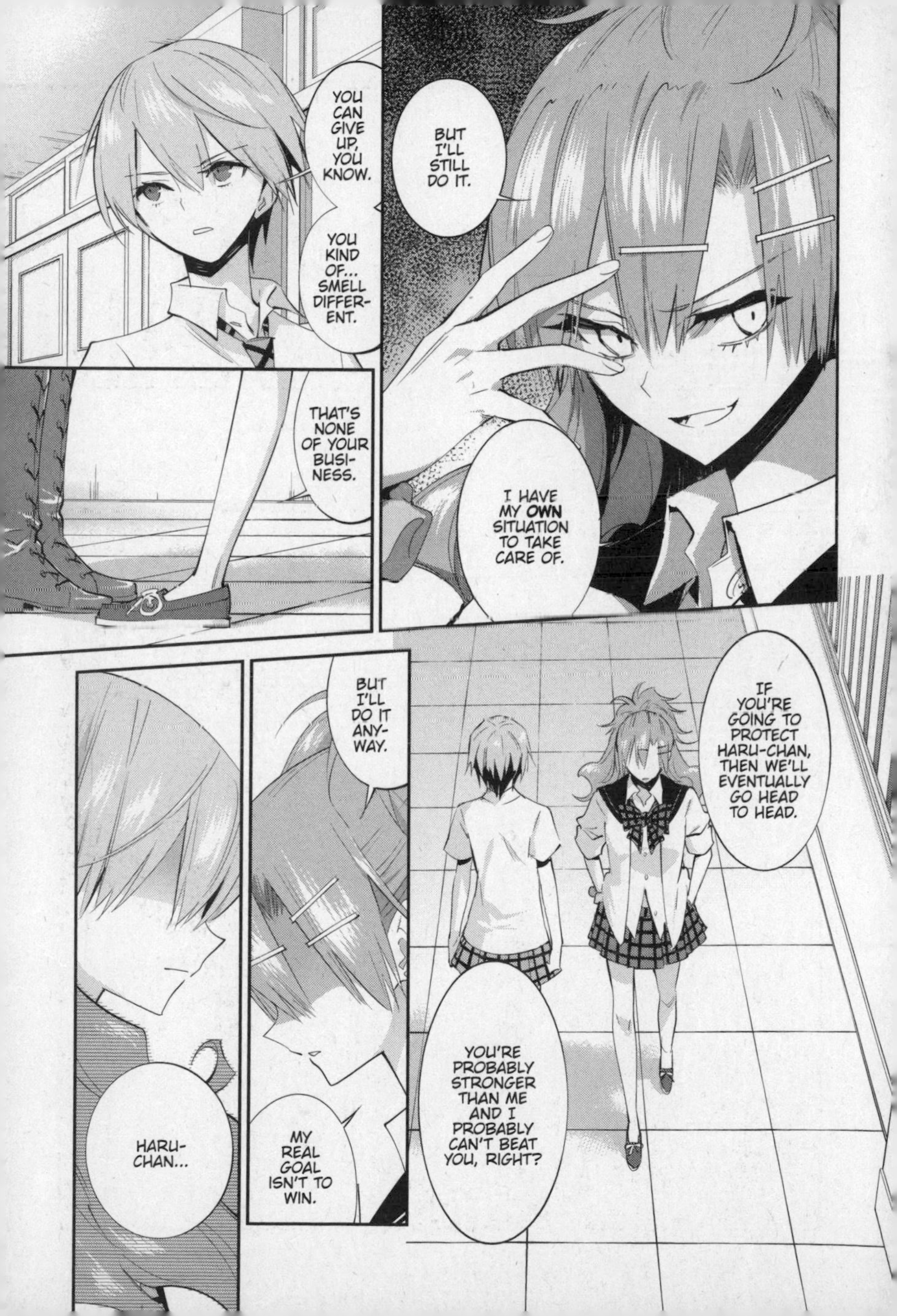
BUT I'LL STILL DO IT.
I HAVE MY **OWN** SITUATION TO TAKE CARE OF.
YOU CAN GIVE UP, YOU KNOW.
YOU KIND OF... SMELL DIFFER-ENT.
THAT'S NONE OF YOUR BUSI-NESS.
IF YOU'RE GOING TO PROTECT HARU-CHAN, THEN WE'LL EVENTUALLY GO HEAD TO HEAD.
YOU'RE PROBABLY STRONGER THAN ME AND I PROBABLY CAN'T BEAT YOU, RIGHT?
BUT I'LL DO IT ANY-WAY.
MY REAL GOAL ISN'T TO WIN.
HARU-CHAN...

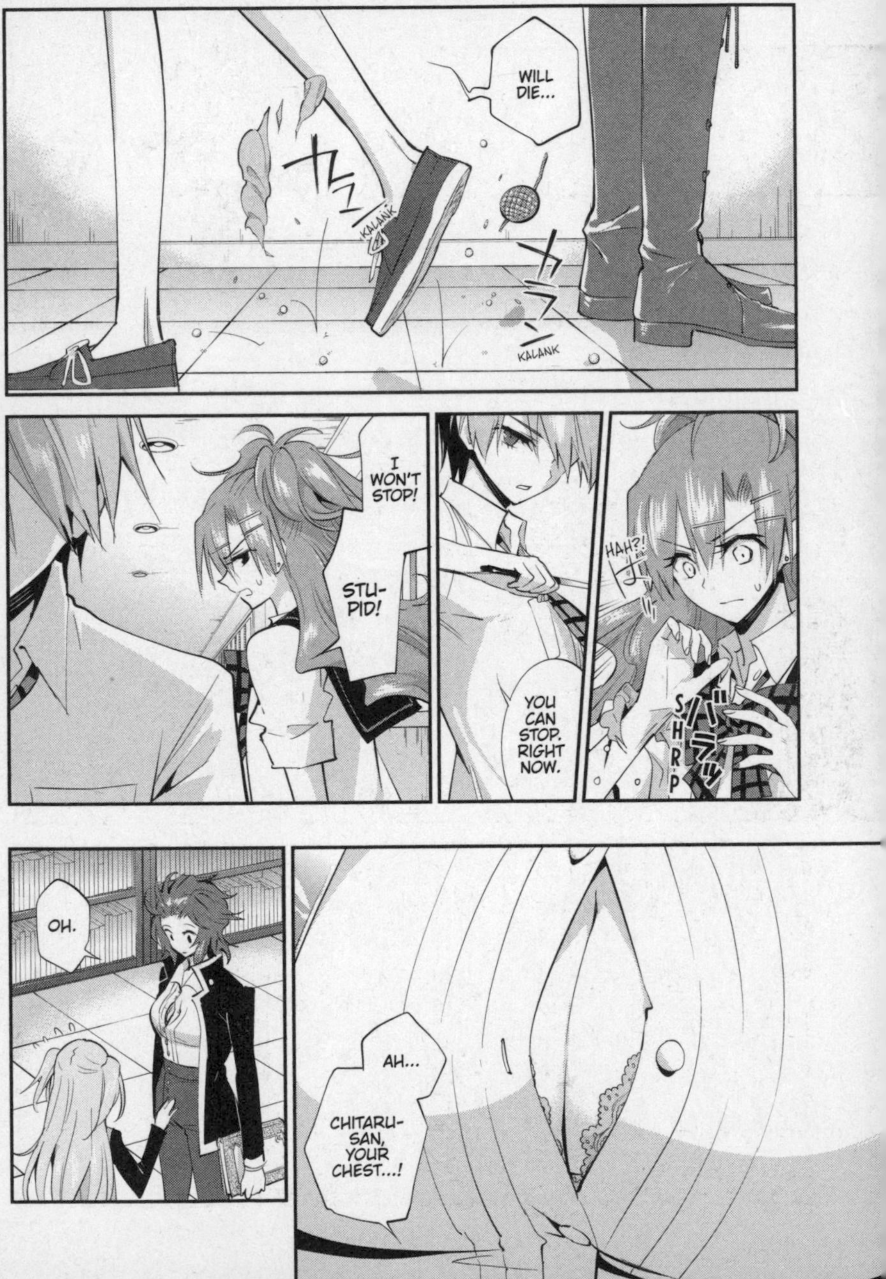
WILL DIE...
KALANK
KALANK
HAH?!
SHRP
YOU CAN STOP. RIGHT NOW.
I WON'T STOP!
STU-PID!
AH...
CHITARU-SAN, YOUR CHEST...!
OH.

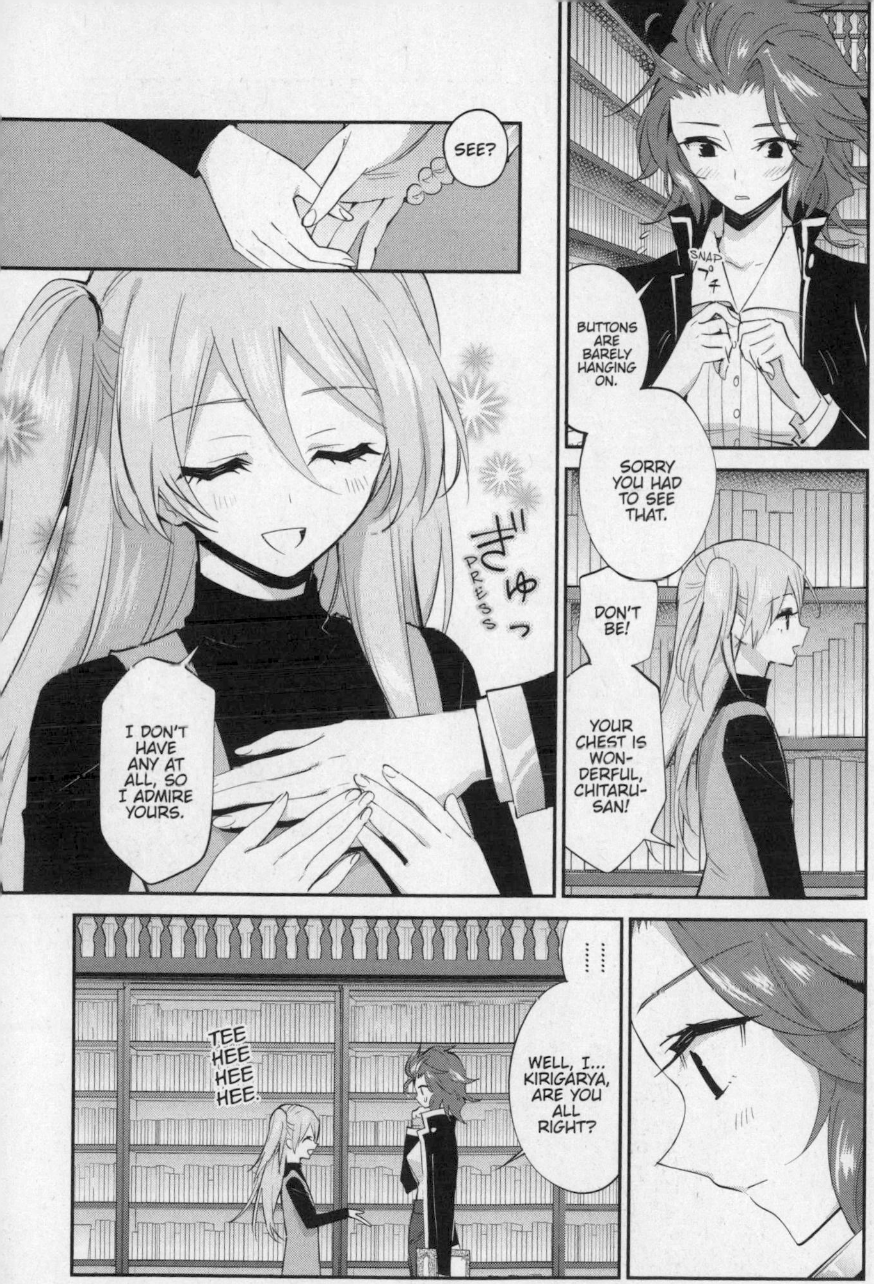
SNAP
プチ
BUTTONS ARE BARELY HANGING ON.
SEE?
SORRY YOU HAD TO SEE THAT.
DON'T BE!
YOUR CHEST IS WONDERFUL, CHITARU-SAN!
ぎゅっ
PRESS
I DON'T HAVE ANY AT ALL, SO I ADMIRE YOURS.
......!!
WELL, I... KIRIGARYA, ARE YOU ALL RIGHT?
TEE HEE HEE HEE.

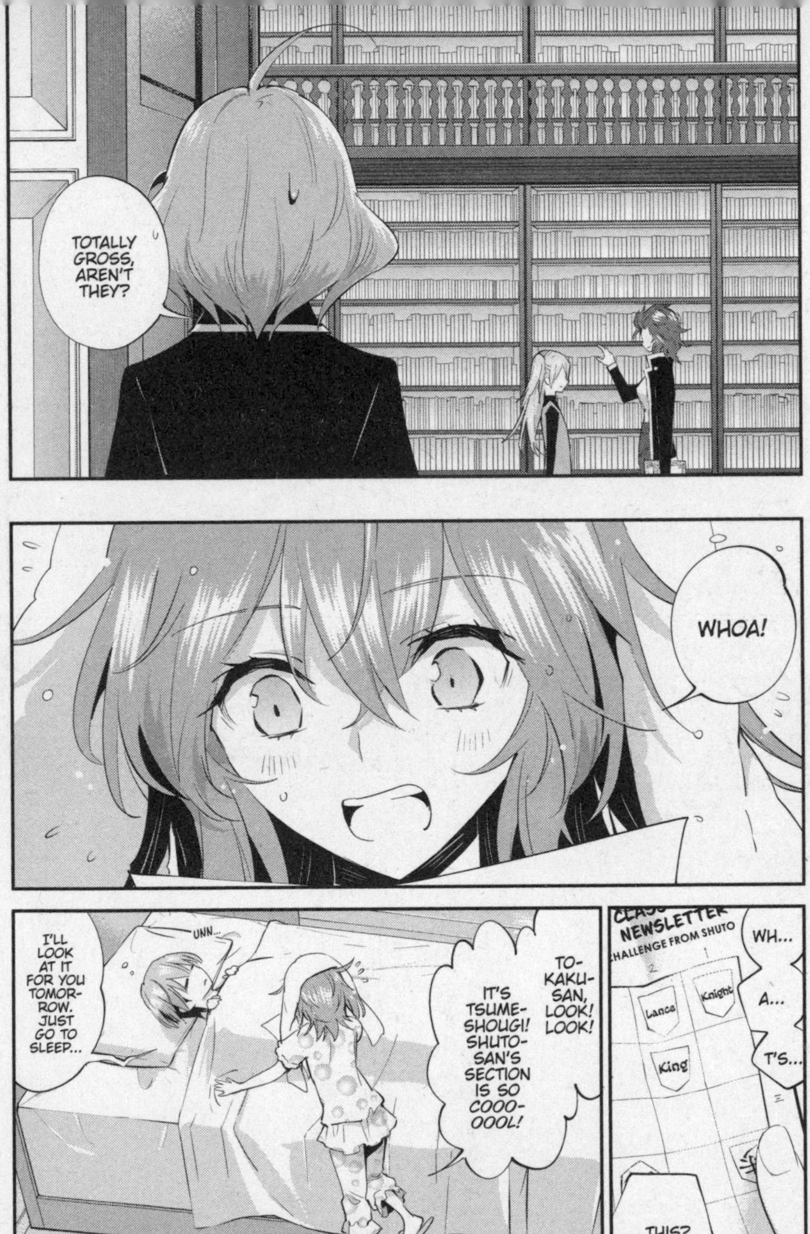
TOTALLY GROSS, AREN'T THEY?
WHOA!
WH... A... T'S...
NEWSLETTER
HALLENGE FROM SHUTO
Knight
Lance
King
...THIS?
TO-KAKU-SAN, LOOK! LOOK!
IT'S TSUME-SHOUGI! SHUTO-SAN'S SECTION IS SO COOO-OOOL!
UNN...
I'LL LOOK AT IT FOR YOU TOMOR-ROW. JUST GO TO SLEEP...

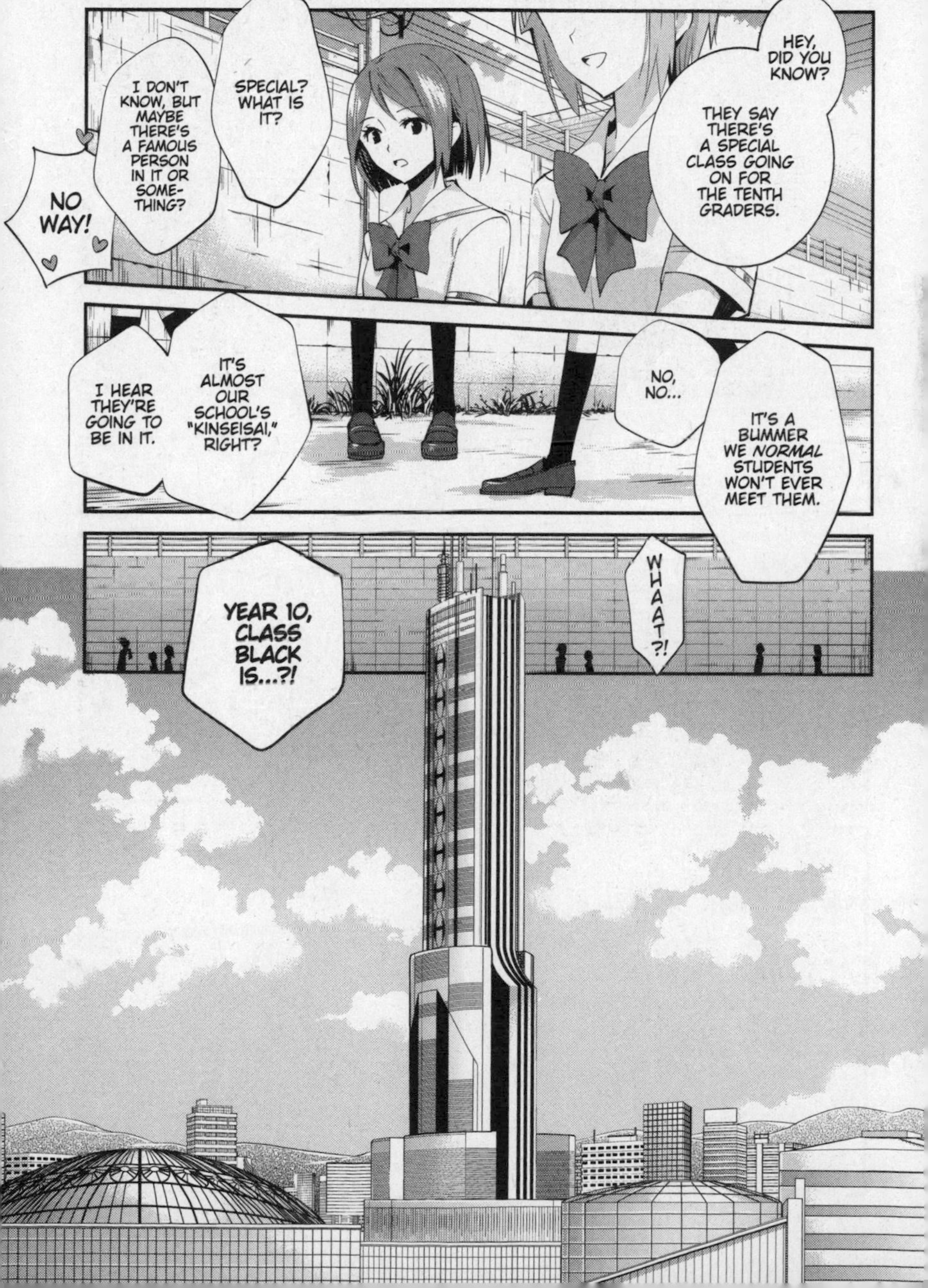
HEY, DID YOU KNOW?
THEY SAY THERE'S A SPECIAL CLASS GOING ON FOR THE TENTH GRADERS.
SPECIAL? WHAT IS IT?
I DON'T KNOW, BUT MAYBE THERE'S A FAMOUS PERSON IN IT OR SOME-THING?
NO WAY!
NO, NO...
IT'S A BUMMER WE *NORMAL* STUDENTS WON'T EVER MEET THEM.
IT'S ALMOST OUR SCHOOL'S "KINSEISAI," RIGHT?
I HEAR THEY'RE GOING TO BE IN IT.
WHAAAT?!
YEAR 10, CLASS BLACK IS...?!

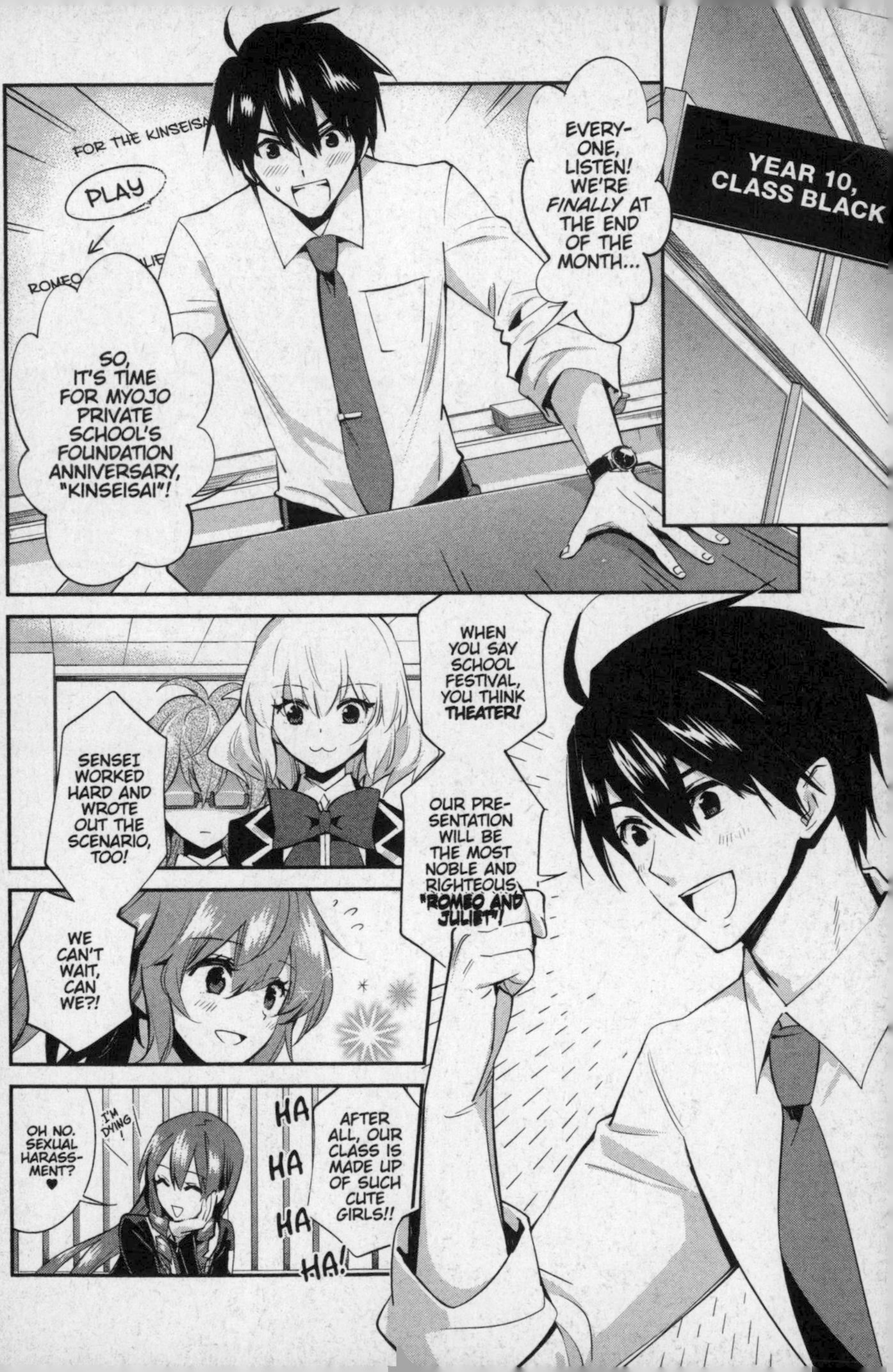

YEAR 10, CLASS BLACK
EVERYONE, LISTEN! WE'RE *FINALLY* AT THE END OF THE MONTH...
FOR THE KINSEISA
PLAY
ROMEO
SO, IT'S TIME FOR MYOJO PRIVATE SCHOOL'S FOUNDATION ANNIVERSARY, "KINSEISAI"!
WHEN YOU SAY SCHOOL FESTIVAL, YOU THINK **THEATER!**
OUR PRESENTATION WILL BE THE MOST NOBLE AND RIGHTEOUS **"ROMEO AND JULIET"!**
SENSEI WORKED HARD AND WROTE OUT THE SCENARIO, TOO!
WE CAN'T WAIT, CAN WE?!
AFTER ALL, OUR CLASS IS MADE UP OF SUCH CUTE GIRLS!!
HA HA HA HA!
I'M DYING!
OH NO. SEXUAL HARASSMENT? ♥

Chapter 17
Will Decide Myself

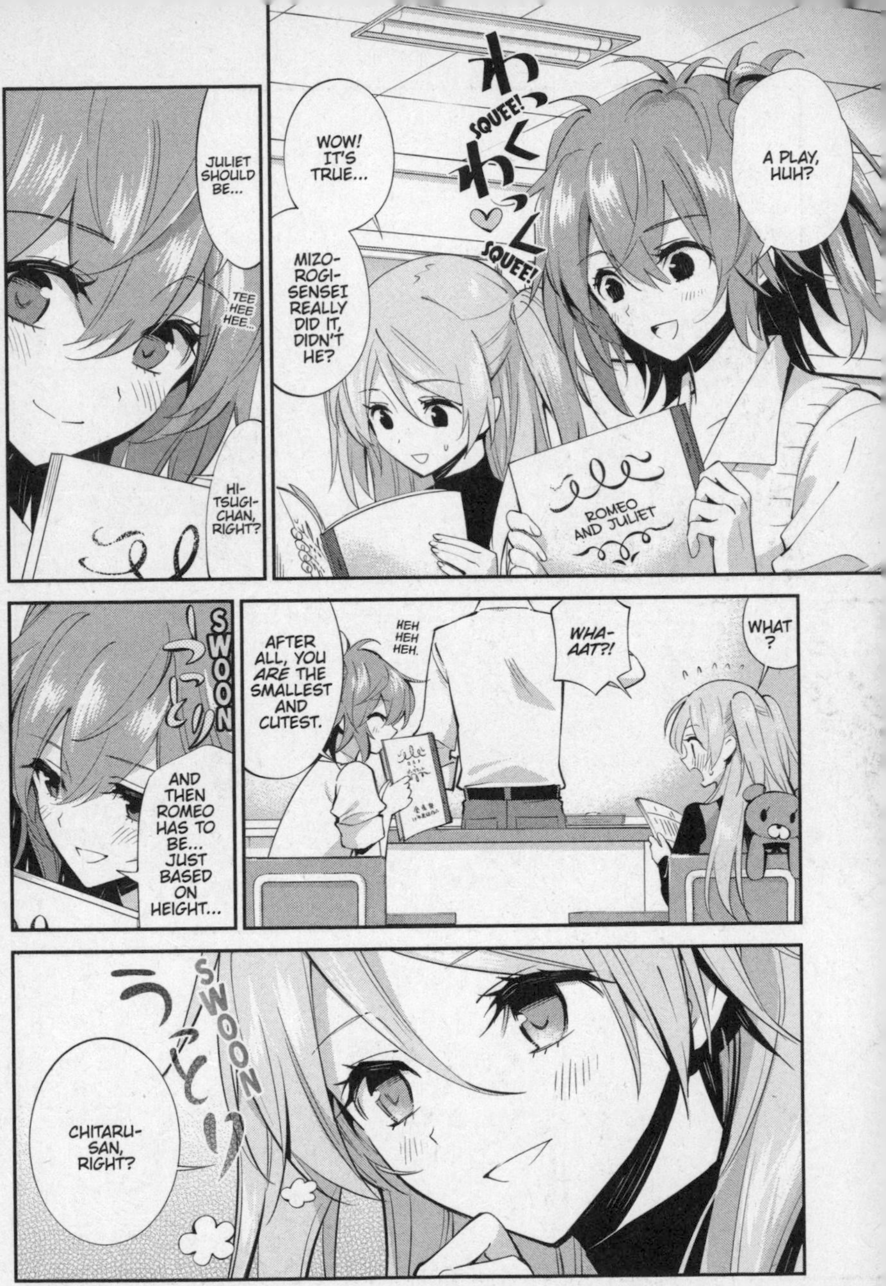
A PLAY, HUH?
SQUEE!
SQUEE!
WOW! IT'S TRUE...
MIZO-ROGI-SENSEI REALLY DID IT, DIDN'T HE?
ROMEO AND JULIET
JULIET SHOULD BE...
TEE HEE HEE...
HI-TSUGI-CHAN, RIGHT?
WHAT?
WHA-AAT?!
HEH HEH HEH.
AFTER ALL, YOU *ARE* THE SMALLEST AND CUTEST.
SWOON
AND THEN ROMEO HAS TO BE... JUST BASED ON HEIGHT...
SWOON
CHITARU-SAN, RIGHT?

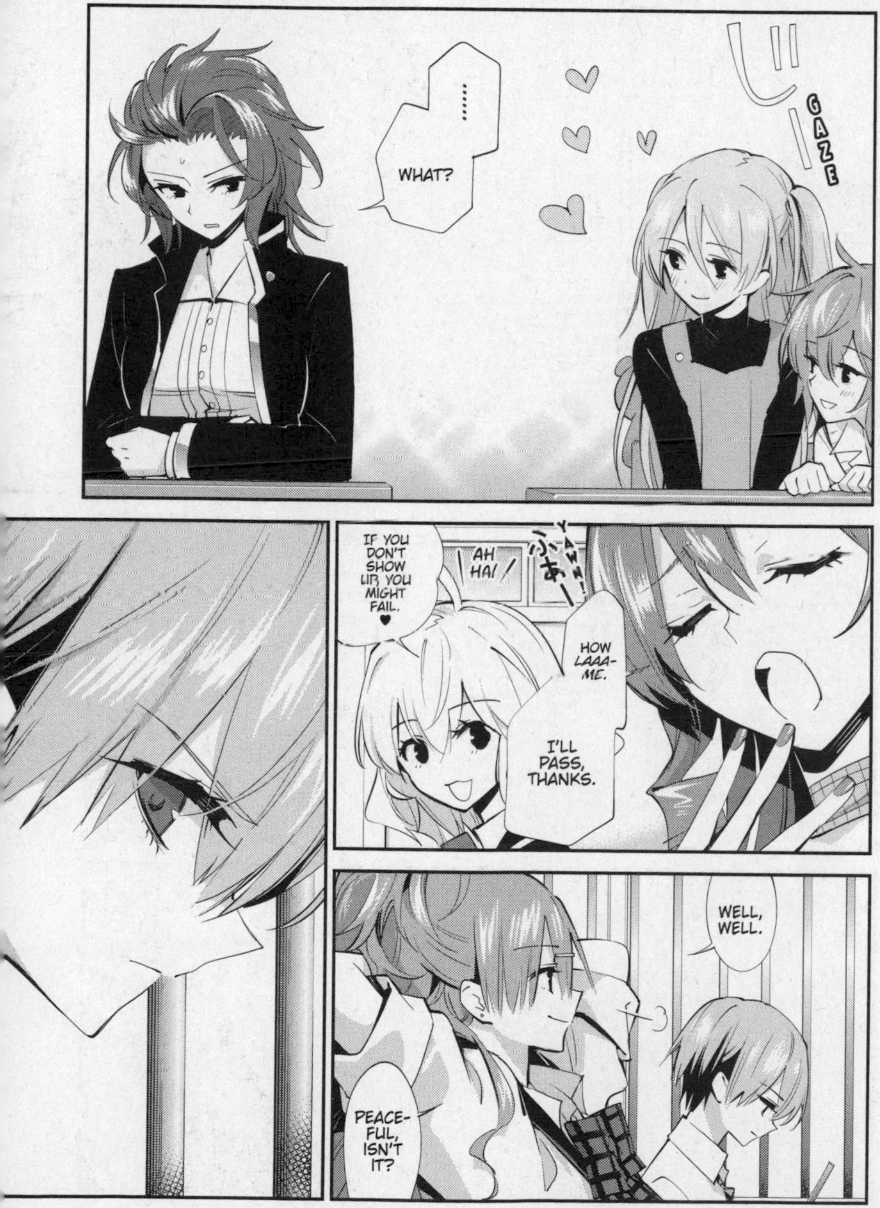

GAZE
......
WHAT?
YAWN!
AH HA!
IF YOU DON'T SHOW UP, YOU MIGHT FAIL. ♥
HOW LAAA-ME.
I'LL PASS, THANKS.
WELL, WELL.
PEACE-FUL, ISN'T IT?

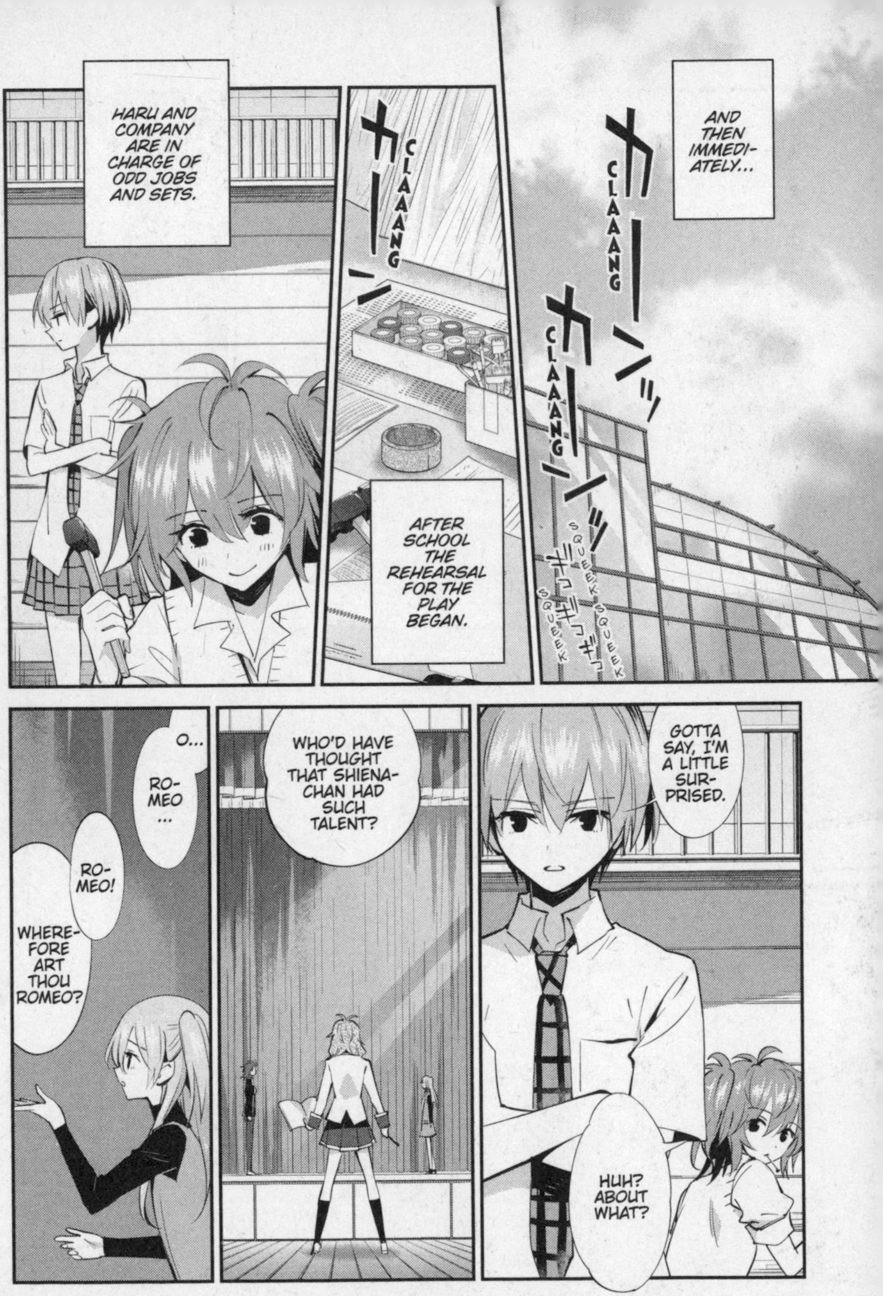
AND THEN IMMEDIATELY...
CLAAANG
CLAAANG
SQUEEK SQUEEK SQUEEK SQUEEK
CLAAANG
AFTER SCHOOL THE REHEARSAL FOR THE PLAY BEGAN.
HARU AND COMPANY ARE IN CHARGE OF ODD JOBS AND SETS.
GOTTA SAY, I'M A LITTLE SURPRISED.
HUH? ABOUT WHAT?
WHO'D HAVE THOUGHT THAT SHIENA-CHAN HAD SUCH TALENT?
O...
ROMEO...
ROMEO!
WHEREFORE ART THOU ROMEO?

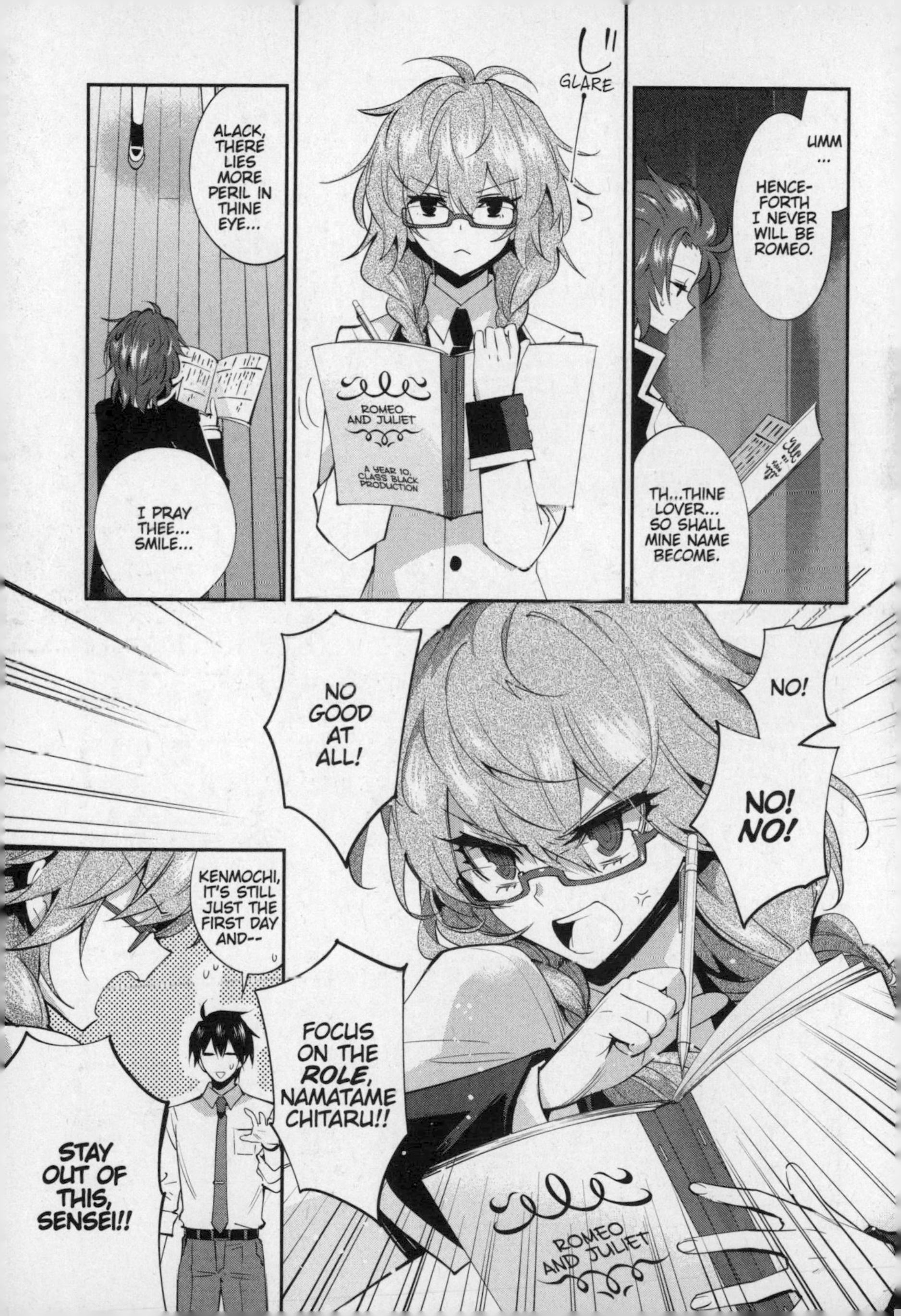
UMM ...
HENCE-FORTH I NEVER WILL BE ROMEO.
TH...THINE LOVER... SO SHALL MINE NAME BECOME.
GLARE
ROMEO AND JULIET
A YEAR 10, CLASS BLACK PRODUCTION
ALACK, THERE LIES MORE PERIL IN THINE EYE...
I PRAY THEE... SMILE...
NO!
NO! NO!
NO GOOD AT ALL!
KENMOCHI, IT'S STILL JUST THE FIRST DAY AND--
FOCUS ON THE ROLE, NAMATAME CHITARU!!
STAY OUT OF THIS, SENSEI!!
ROMEO AND JULIET

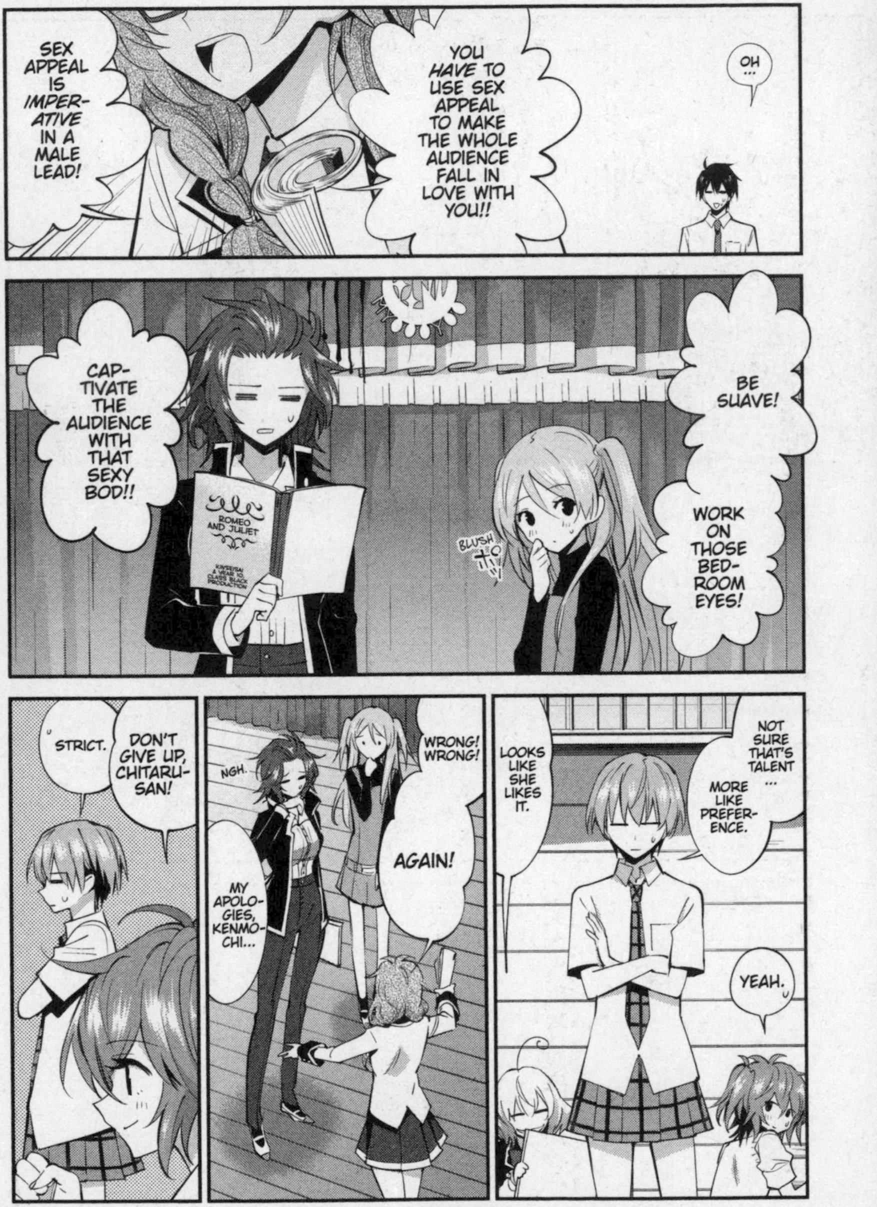

OH...
YOU HAVE TO USE SEX APPEAL TO MAKE THE WHOLE AUDIENCE FALL IN LOVE WITH YOU!!
SEX APPEAL IS IMPERATIVE IN A MALE LEAD!
BE SUAVE!
WORK ON THOSE BEDROOM EYES!
BLUSH
ROMEO AND JULIET
CAPTIVATE THE AUDIENCE WITH THAT SEXY BOD!!
NOT SURE THAT'S TALENT...
MORE LIKE PREFERENCE.
LOOKS LIKE SHE LIKES IT.
YEAH.
WRONG! WRONG!
AGAIN!
NGH.
MY APOLOGIES, KENMOCHI...
DON'T GIVE UP, CHITARU-SAN!
STRICT.

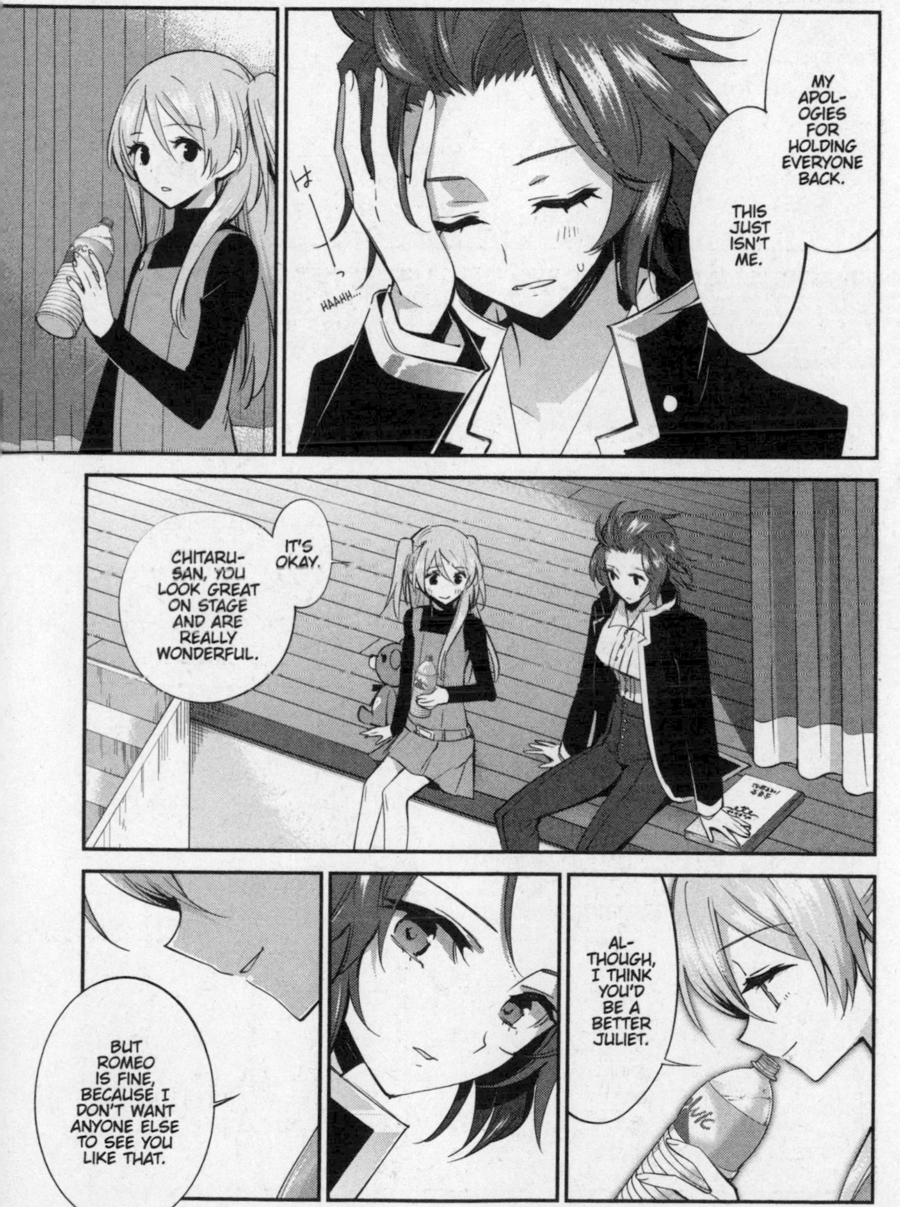
MY APOLOGIES FOR HOLDING EVERYONE BACK.
THIS JUST ISN'T ME.
は—っ
HAAHH...
IT'S OKAY.
CHITARU-SAN, YOU LOOK GREAT ON STAGE AND ARE REALLY WONDERFUL.
ALTHOUGH, I THINK YOU'D BE A BETTER JULIET.
BUT ROMEO IS FINE, BECAUSE I DON'T WANT ANYONE ELSE TO SEE YOU LIKE THAT.

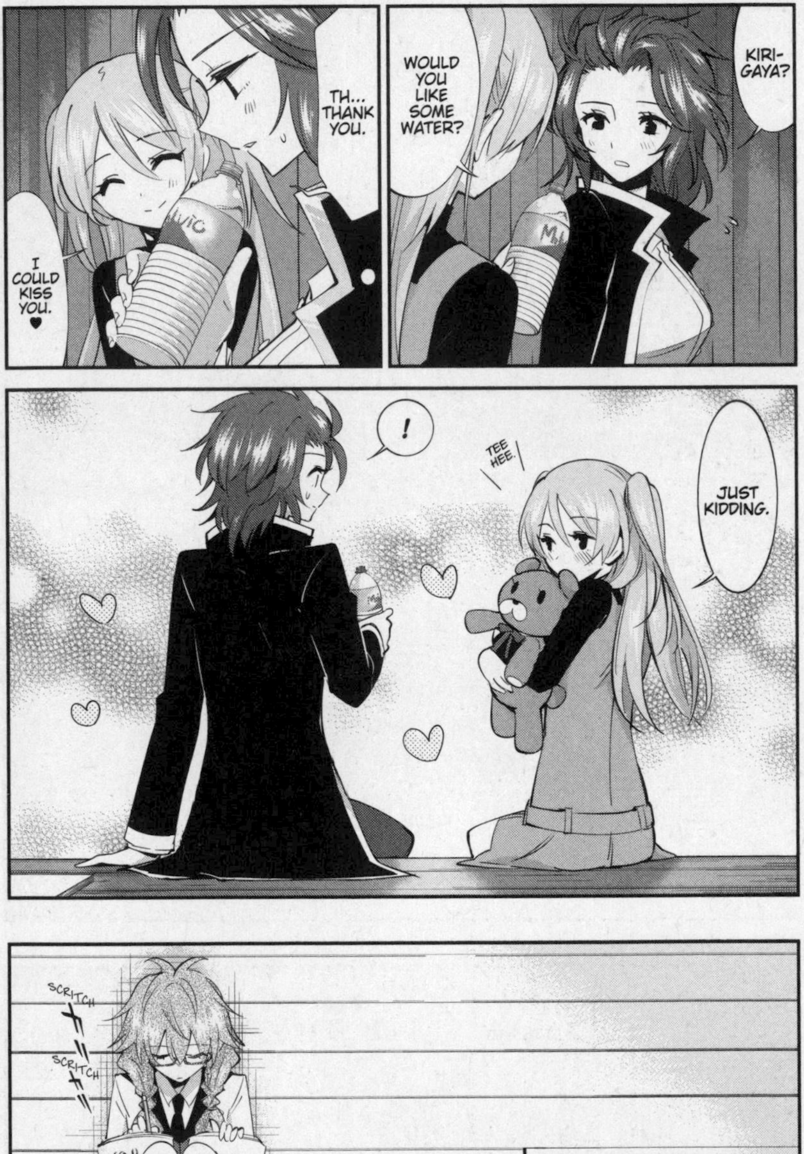
KIRI-GAYA?
WOULD YOU LIKE SOME WATER?
TH... THANK YOU.
I COULD KISS YOU. ♥
JUST KIDDING.
TEE HEE.
!
SCRITCH
SCRITCH

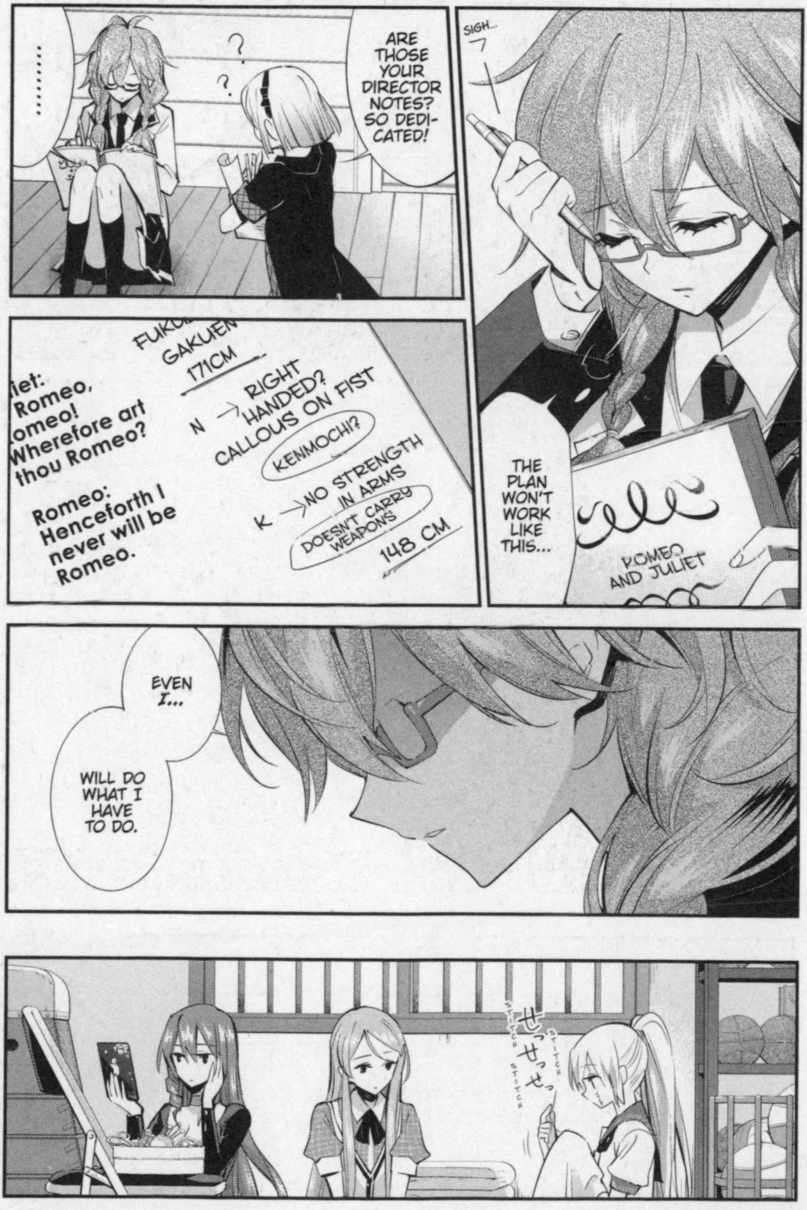
SIGH...
THE PLAN WON'T WORK LIKE THIS...
ROMEO AND JULIET
ARE THOSE YOUR DIRECTOR NOTES? SO DEDI-CATED!
?
?
......
FUKU GAKUEN
171CM
N → RIGHT HANDED? CALLOUS ON FIST
KENMOCHI?
K → NO STRENGTH IN ARMS
DOESN'T CARRY WEAPONS
148 CM
iet: Romeo, omeo! Wherefore art thou Romeo?
Romeo: Henceforth I never will be Romeo.
EVEN I...
WILL DO WHAT I HAVE TO DO.
せっせっせっ
STITCH STITCH STITCH

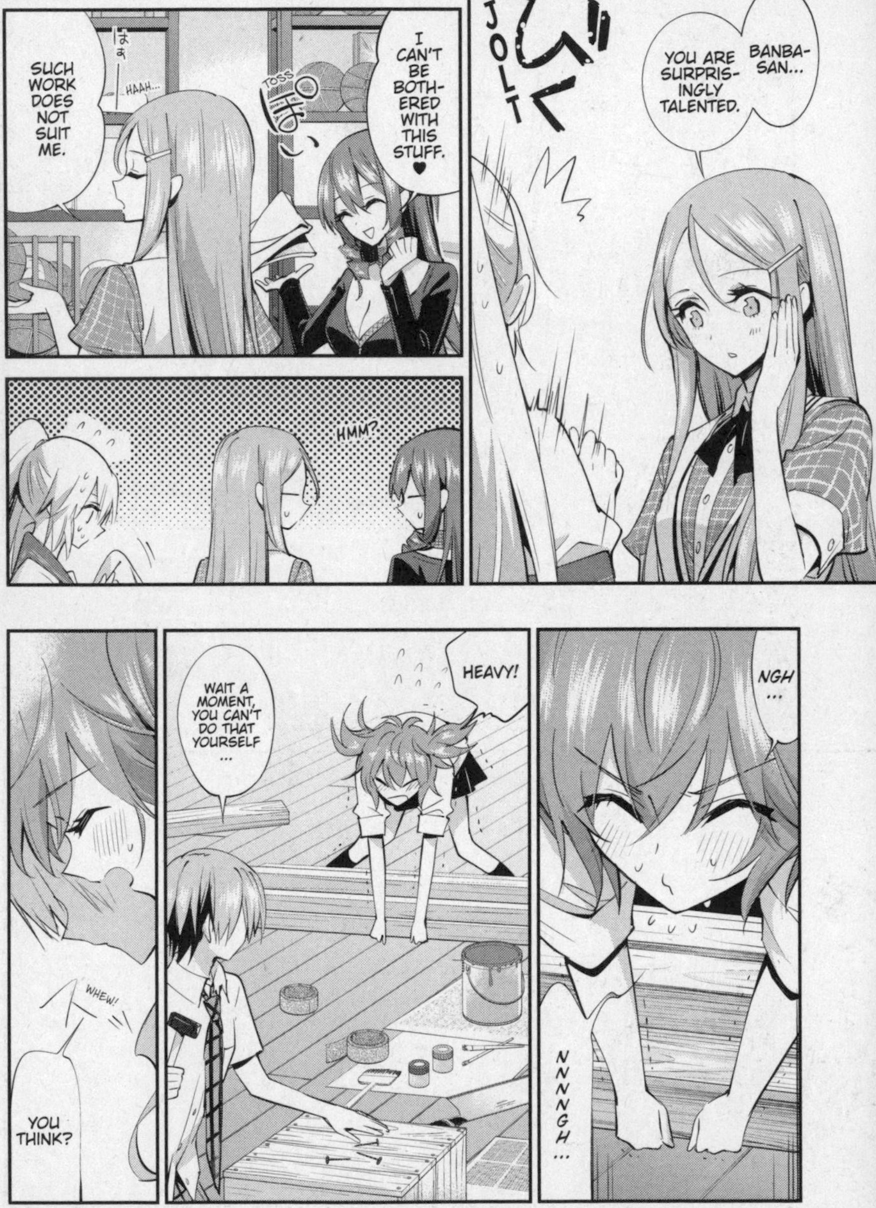
JOLT
BANBA-SAN...
YOU ARE SURPRIS-INGLY TALENTED.
I CAN'T BE BOTH-ERED WITH THIS STUFF. ♥
TOSS
HAAH...
SUCH WORK DOES NOT SUIT ME.
HMM?
NGH ...
NNNNGH ...
HEAVY!
WAIT A MOMENT, YOU CAN'T DO THAT YOURSELF ...
WHEW!
YOU THINK?

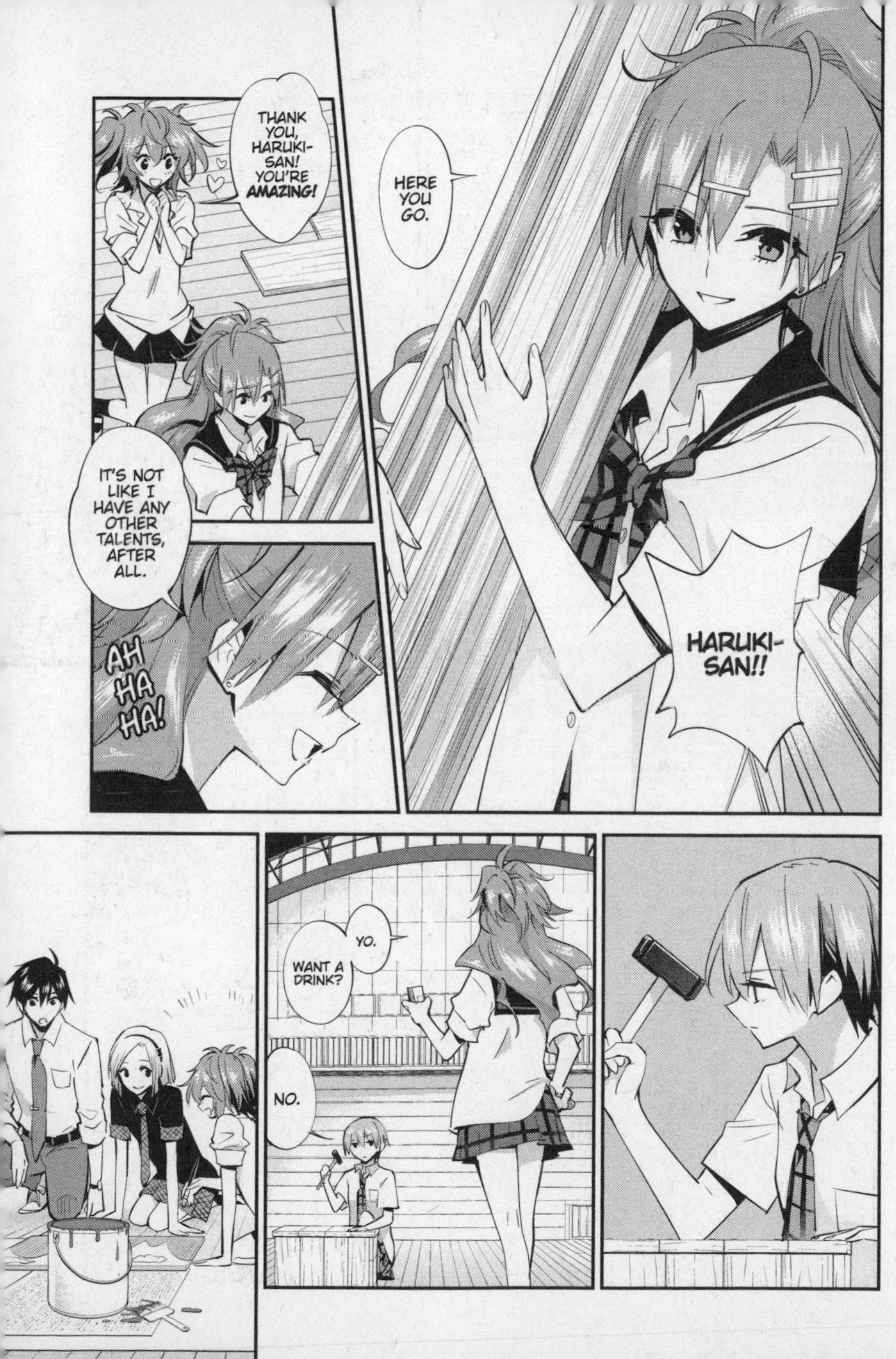
HERE YOU GO.
HARUKI-SAN!!
THANK YOU, HARUKI-SAN! YOU'RE AMAZING!
IT'S NOT LIKE I HAVE ANY OTHER TALENTS, AFTER ALL.
AH HA HA!
YO.
WANT A DRINK?
NO.

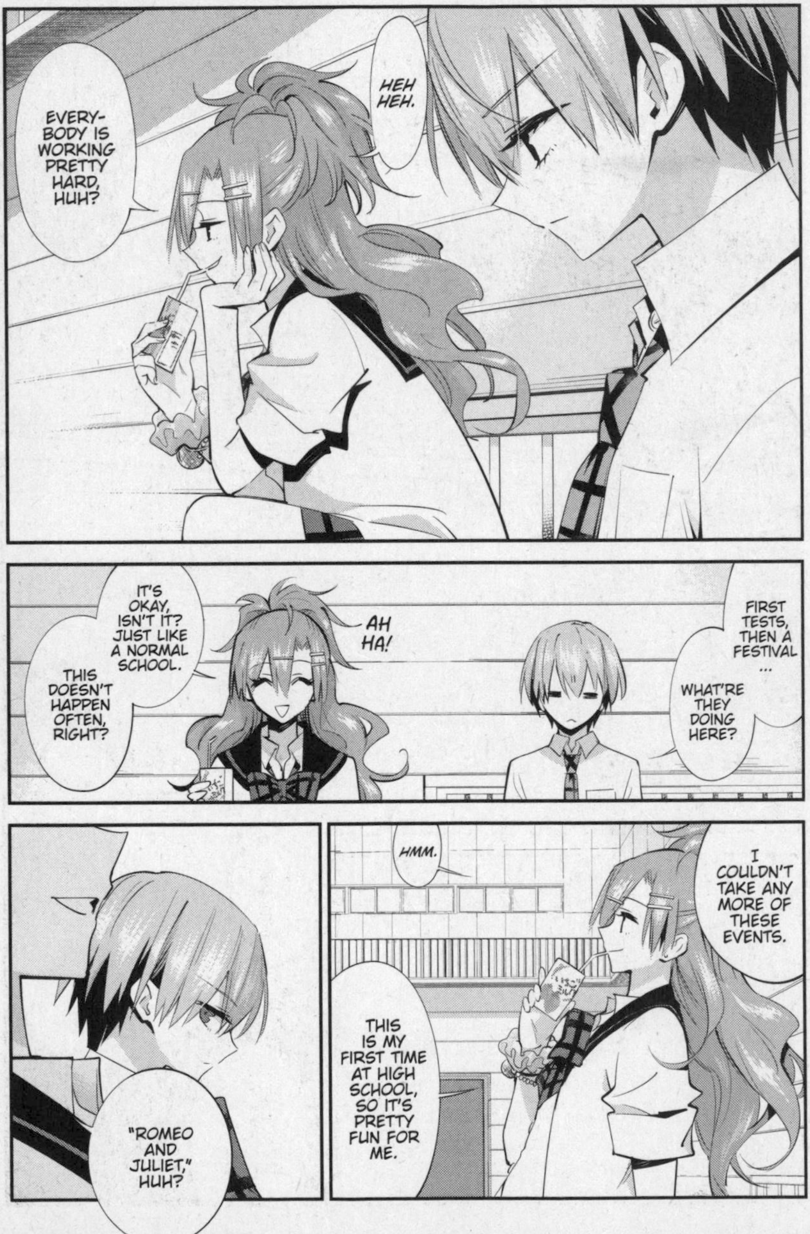
HEH HEH.
EVERY-BODY IS WORKING PRETTY HARD, HUH?
FIRST TESTS, THEN A FESTIVAL ...
WHAT'RE THEY DOING HERE?
AH HA!
IT'S OKAY, ISN'T IT? JUST LIKE A NORMAL SCHOOL.
THIS DOESN'T HAPPEN OFTEN, RIGHT?
I COULDN'T TAKE ANY MORE OF THESE EVENTS.
HMM.
THIS IS MY FIRST TIME AT HIGH SCHOOL, SO IT'S PRETTY FUN FOR ME.
"ROMEO AND JULIET," HUH?

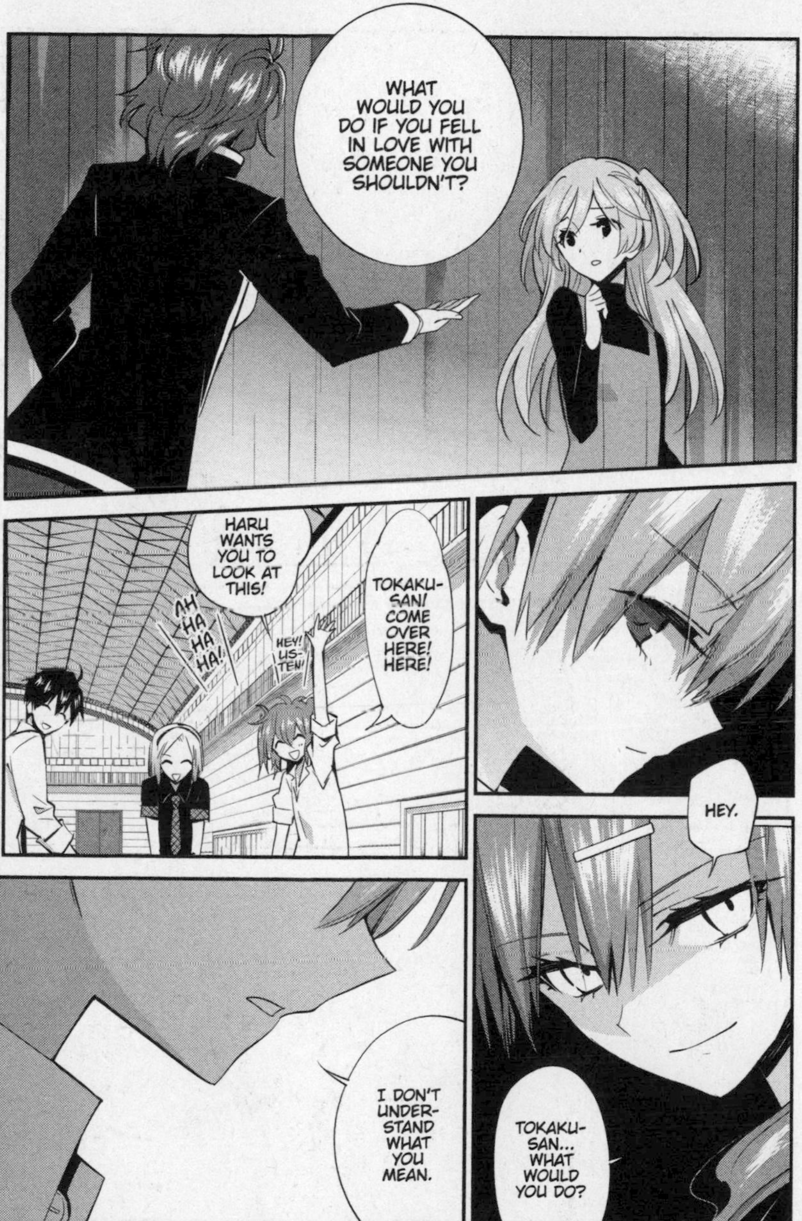
WHAT WOULD YOU DO IF YOU FELL IN LOVE WITH SOMEONE YOU SHOULDN'T?
TOKAKU-SAN! COME OVER HERE! HERE!
HARU WANTS YOU TO LOOK AT THIS!
HEY! LISTEN!
AH HA HA HA!
HEY.
TOKAKU-SAN... WHAT WOULD YOU DO?
I DON'T UNDERSTAND WHAT YOU MEAN.

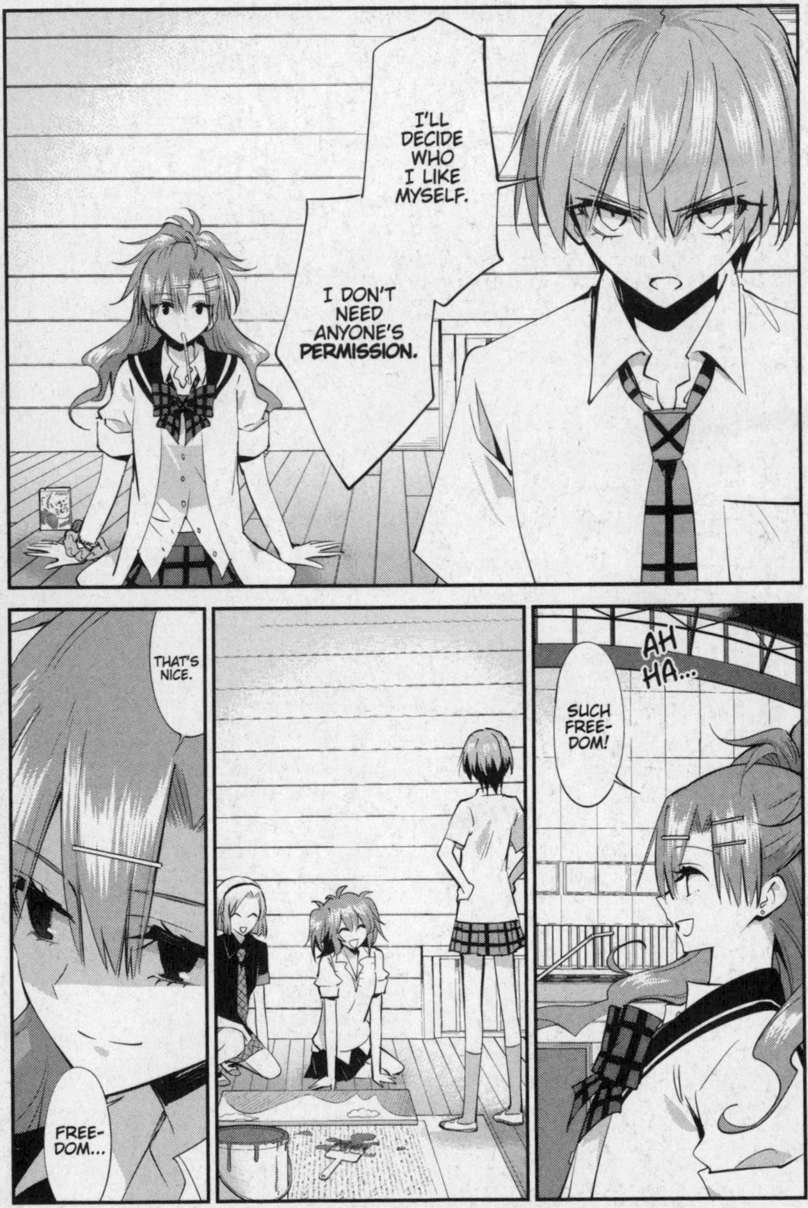
I'LL DECIDE WHO I LIKE MYSELF.
I DON'T NEED ANYONE'S PERMISSION.
AH HA...
SUCH FREE-DOM!
THAT'S NICE.
FREE-DOM...

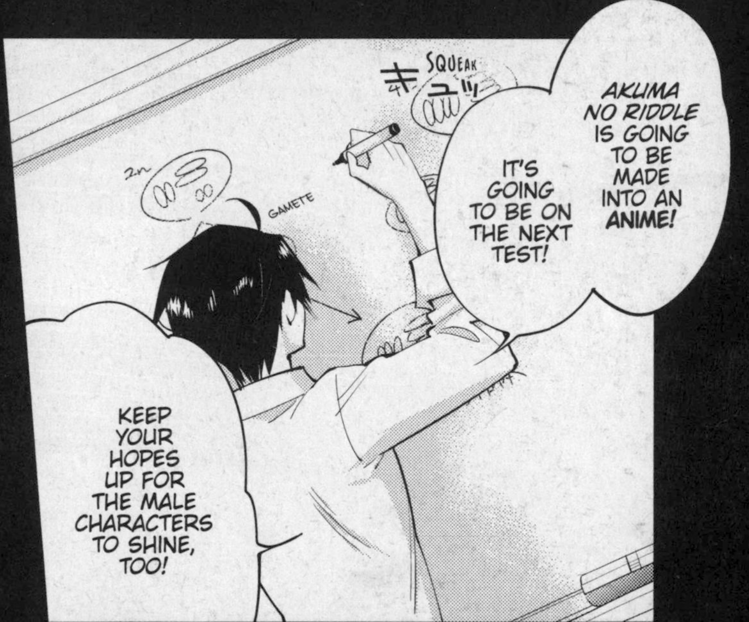
SQUEAK
AKUMA NO RIDDLE IS GOING TO BE MADE INTO AN ANIME!
IT'S GOING TO BE ON THE NEXT TEST!
GAMETE
KEEP YOUR HOPES UP FOR THE MALE CHARACTERS TO SHINE, TOO!

to be continued

SEVEN SEAS ENTERTAINMENT PRESENTS

Akuma no Riddle

riddle story of devil   volume 2

story by YUN KOUGA / art by SUNAO MINAKATA

TRANSLATION
Beni Axia Conrad

ADAPTATION
Steven Golebiewski

LETTERING AND LAYOUT
Erika Terriquez

COVER DESIGN
Nicky Lim

PROOFREADER
Shanti Whitesides

PRODUCTION MANAGER
Lissa Pattillo

EDITOR IN CHIEF
Adam Arnold

PUBLISHER
Jason DeAngelis

AKUMA NO RIDDLE: RIDDLE STORY OF DEVIL volume 2
© team ANR
© Yun KOUGA 2014
© Sunao MINAKATA 2014
Edited by KADOKAWASHOTEN.
First published in Japan in 2014 by KADOKAWA CORPORATION, Tokyo.
English translation rights arranged with KADOKAWA CORPORATION, Tokyo,
through TOHAN CORPORATION, Tokyo.

Seven Seas books may be purchased in bulk for educational, business, or
promotional use. For information on bulk purchases, please contact Macmillan
Corporate & Premium Sales Department at 1-800-221-7945 (ext 5442)
or write specialmarkets@macmillan.com.

Seven Seas and the Seven Seas logo are trademarks of
Seven Seas Entertainment, LLC. All rights reserved.

ISBN: 978-1-626922-31-0
Printed in Canada
First Printing: January 2016
10 9 8 7 6 5 4 3 2 1

FOLLOW US ONLINE: *www.gomanga.com*

READING DIRECTIONS

This book reads from *right to left*, Japanese style. If
this is your first time reading manga, you start
reading from the top right panel on each page and
take it from there. If you get lost, just follow the
numbered diagram here. It may seem backwards at
first, but you'll get the hang of it! Have fun!!

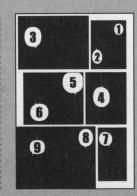